Security Frameworks in Contemporary Electronic Government

Ryma Abassi
Carthage University, Tunisia

Aida Ben Chehida Douss
Carthage University, Tunisia

A volume in the Advances in
Electronic Government, Digital
Divide, and Regional Development
(AEGDDRD) Book Series

Published in the United States of America by
    IGI Global
    Information Science Reference (an imprint of IGI Global)
    701 E. Chocolate Avenue
    Hershey PA, USA 17033
    Tel: 717-533-8845
    Fax: 717-533-8661
    E-mail: cust@igi-global.com
    Web site: http://www.igi-global.com

Library of Congress Cataloging-in-Publication Data

Names: Abassi, Ryma, 1980- editor. | Ben Chehida Douss, Aida, 1986- editor.
Title: Security frameworks in contemporary electronic government / Ryma
  Abassi and Aida Ben Chehida Douss, editors.
Description: Hershey, PA : Information Science Reference, [2018]
Identifiers: LCCN 2017061521| ISBN 9781522559849 (hardcover) | ISBN
  9781522559856 (ebook)
Subjects: LCSH: Internet in public administration. | Computer security.
Classification: LCC JF1525.A8 S44 2018 | DDC 352.3/8028558--dc23 LC record available at
https://lccn.loc.gov/2017061521

This book is published in the IGI Global book series Advances in Electronic Government, Digital Divide, and Regional Development (AEGDDRD) (ISSN: 2326-9103; eISSN: 2326-9111)

British Cataloguing in Publication Data
A Cataloguing in Publication record for this book is available from the British Library.

All work contributed to this book is new, previously-unpublished material.
The views expressed in this book are those of the authors, but not necessarily of the publisher.

For electronic access to this publication, please contact: eresources@igi-global.com.

Advances in Electronic Government, Digital Divide, and Regional Development (AEGDDRD) Book Series

ISSN:2326-9103
EISSN:2326-9111

Editor-in-Chief: Zaigham Mahmood, University of Derby, UK & North West University, South Africa

MISSION

The successful use of digital technologies (including social media and mobile technologies) to provide public services and foster economic development has become an objective for governments around the world. The development towards electronic government (or e-government) not only affects the efficiency and effectiveness of public services, but also has the potential to transform the nature of government interactions with its citizens. Current research and practice on the adoption of electronic/ digital government and the implementation in organizations around the world aims to emphasize the extensiveness of this growing field.

The Advances in Electronic Government, Digital Divide & Regional Development (AEGDDRD) book series aims to publish authored, edited and case books encompassing the current and innovative research and practice discussing all aspects of electronic government development, implementation and adoption as well the effective use of the emerging technologies (including social media and mobile technologies) for a more effective electronic governance (or e-governance).

COVERAGE

- Emerging Technologies within the Public Sector
- Case Studies and Practical Approaches to E-Government and E-Governance
- Public Information Management, Regional Planning, Rural Development
- ICT within Government and Public Sectors
- E-Governance and Use of Technology for Effective Government
- Frameworks and Methodologies for E-Government Development
- Social Media, Web 2.0, and Mobile Technologies in E-Government
- Current Research and Emerging Trends in E-Government Development
- Electronic Government, Digital Democracy, Digital Government
- Issues and Challenges in E-Government Adoption

IGI Global is currently accepting manuscripts for publication within this series. To submit a proposal for a volume in this series, please contact our Acquisition Editors at Acquisitions@igi-global.com or visit: http://www.igi-global.com/publish/.

Titles in this Series

For a list of additional titles in this series, please visit:
https://www.igi-global.com/book-series/advances-electronic-government-digital-divide/37153

Media Diplomacy and Its Evolving Role in the Current Geopolitical Climate
Swati Jaywant Rao Bute (Jagran Lakecity University, India)
Information Science Reference • ©2018 • 211pp • H/C (ISBN: 9781522538592) • US $195.00

Global Leadership Initiatives for Conflict Resolution and Peacebuilding
Andrew H. Campbell (International Peace and Leadership Institute, USA)
Information Science Reference • ©2018 • 331pp • H/C (ISBN: 9781522549932) • US $225.00

Financial Sustainability and Intergenerational Equity in Local Governments
Manuel Pedro Rodríguez Bolívar (University of Granada, Spain) and María Deseada López
Subires (University of Granada, Spain)
Information Science Reference • ©2018 • 343pp • H/C (ISBN: 9781522537137) • US $205.00

Handbook of Research on Modernization and Accountability in Public Sector Management
Graça Maria do Carmo Azevedo (University of Aveiro, Portugal) Jonas da Silva Oliveira
(ISCTE – Instituto Universitário de Lisboa, Portugal) Rui Pedro Figueiredo Marques
(University of Aveiro, Portugal) and Augusta da Conceição Santos Ferreira (University of
Aveiro, Portugal)
Information Science Reference • ©2018 • 539pp • H/C (ISBN: 9781522537311) • US $285.00

Knowledge-Based Urban Development in the Middle East
Ali A. Alraouf (Qatar Urban Planning, Qatar)
Information Science Reference • ©2018 • 310pp • H/C (ISBN: 9781522537342) • US $185.00

Nationalism, Social Movements, and Activism in Contemporary Society Emerging...
Emily Stacey (Swansea University, UK)
Information Science Reference • ©2018 • 135pp • H/C (ISBN: 9781522554332) • US $155.00

For an entire list of titles in this series, please visit:
https://www.igi-global.com/book-series/advances-electronic-government-digital-divide/37153

701 East Chocolate Avenue, Hershey, PA 17033, USA
Tel: 717-533-8845 x100 • Fax: 717-533-8661
E-Mail: cust@igi-global.com • www.igi-global.com

Table of Contents

Detailed Table of Contents

Chapter 1

Vannie Naidoo, University of KwaZulu-Natal, South Africa
Thokozani Ian Nzimakwe, University of KwaZulu-Natal, South Africa

Technology has taken over every aspect of society. It is only fitting that governments embrace technological changes in society and develop m-government for the technologically savvy people of today's society. A global change that is transforming the government sector is the use of ICTs to improve service delivery. In this chapter, the following themes will be investigated and discussed: e-government, defining mobile government, different perspectives on mobile government, mobile government in developed countries, mobile government in developing countries, benefits and limitations of mobile government, way forward in implementing mobile government, and future research in areas of mobile government.

Chapter 2

Ayda Saidane, Independent Researcher, Canada
Saleh Al-Sharieh, University of Groningen, The Netherlands

Regulatory compliance is a top priority for organizations in highly regulated ecosystems. As most operations are automated, the compliance efforts focus on the information systems supporting the business processes of the organizations and, to a lesser extent, on the humans using, managing, and maintaining them. Yet, the human factor is an unpredictable and challenging component of a secure system development and should be considered throughout the development process as both a legitimate user and a threat. In this chapter, the authors propose COMPARCH as a compliance-driven system engineering framework for privacy and security in socio-technical systems. It consists of (1) a risk-based requirement management process, (2) a test-driven security and privacy modeling framework, and (3) a simulation-based validation approach. The satisfaction of the regulatory requirements is evaluated through the simulation traces analysis. The authors use as a running example an E-CITY system providing municipality services to local communities.

Chapter 3

    Balkis Hamdane, Carthage University, Tunisia & University of Tunis –
      El Manar, Tunisia
    Sihem Guemara El Fatmi, Carthage University, Tunisia

The internet was initially proposed to interconnect a few trusted hosts. However, its continued success has caused many security problems. New internet services, such as e-government, must address these security issues. A host-centric security model tied to information location and based on various partial corrections has been proposed. However, this model hasn't brought radical solutions and has largely contributed to architecture ossification. In this context, the idea of a clean slate approach, satisfying the new requirements and without any compatibility obligation, has emerged. The information-centric networking approach represents one of these architectures. Its main idea is to consider the named information as the central element rather than the IP addresses. To ensure security requirements, it adopts an information-centric security. This chapter is a survey on security in the ICN, satisfying the internet security requirements in general and particularly e-government services.

Chapter 4

    Ines Mezghani Daoud, Carthage University, Tunisia
    Marwa Meddeb, Carthage University, Tunisia

Non-communicable diseases (NCDs) such as obesity, diabetes, cardiovascular diseases, and cancers have become a major health concern for most countries around the world. Different elements such as social, biological, and environmental cause the NCDs. But the only way that one can intentionally modify to avoid these diseases is the desire to reduce risk factors for physical activity, tobacco, and diet. Several prevention strategies have been launched worldwide thorough governmental programs by implementing policies/laws. However, these programs don't integrate active communicate participation and support with the social community. This chapter aims to bring out the priority of enhancing the level of public awareness of NCDs. To ensure public responsiveness, the focus of this research is to create an effective solution to prevent risky behavior. The authors focus on the construction of "Sahtek," a social media solution developed on the fundamentals of social marketing, to better coach and promote awareness of NCDs prevention.

This chapter uses a historical perspective to examine the development trajectory of e-government in Singapore, the trends and patterns of cybercrimes and cyber-attacks, and the measures taken by the government to combat cybercrimes and cyber-attacks. It shows that the government has adopted a proactive, holistic, and cooperative approach to cybersecurity in order to tackle the ever-increasing cybersecurity challenges. It has regularly reviewed and improved cybersecurity measures to ensure their effectiveness and strengthened its defense capabilities over time through coordinating national efforts with public and private sectors and cooperating with regional and international counterparts. The chase for a perfect cybersecurity system or strategy is both impossible and unnecessary. However, it is important and necessary to establish a cybersecurity system or formulate a cybersecurity strategy that can monitor, detect, respond to, recover from, and prevent cyber-attacks in a timely manner, and make the nation stronger, safer, and more secure.

Chapter 6

E-governance is a technological innovation that brings governance to the fore of integrity and accountability. It requires high technological commitment so as to bring the government closer to the people. Corruption on the other hand is a bane to growth and development in any country. E-governance is a corrective measure to corruption which prevents government officials from shady activities due to its transparency nature. The connection between e-governance and corruption is analyzed in this chapter, and Nigeria is selected as a case study in developing countries. The chapter concludes on the premise that e-governance reduces the strength of corruption in any country and more investment is needed to enhance this development.

Chapter 7

The growing menace of cyber-related crimes in Nigeria is giving the government and other stakeholders in the information and communication technology sector a cause to worry. Apart from taking a toll on the nation's economic sphere, it has also affected the image of the country negatively especially when viewed against the backdrop of the recent ranking of Nigeria as third in global internet crimes behind United Kingdom and the United States. This scenario, no doubt, requires urgent attention. This chapter, therefore, proffer solutions and recommend ways to make the country's cyberspace free from incessant criminal attacks.

Different systems require different levels of security according to the services they provide to their users. Cyberspace is the alliance of various networks together connected through internet service providers (ISPs). However, the alliance of these networks often faces security issues. Some use the internet as a path for illegal activities such as breaching of others computer or networks, damaging and stealing information, and blocking or denying legitimate users from services they subscribe. So, the purpose of this chapter is to review the responsibilities of ISPs in securing their customers' network, and find out whether there are legal provisions, or liabilities that are bindings on the ISPs to provide security for their customers. What protections are envisaged under the umbrella of safe harbors? Are ISPs responsible for end users' network security? The Swedish Court recently found The Pirate Bay (TPB) guilty of making copyright works available. Finally, this chapter will analyze the issues raised in the TPB along with ISPs liability.

Chapter 9

The trend of e-governance and m-governance in governance is increasing rapidly and the instrument of governance is getting closer to the citizens. This chapter considers the trust and reputation of the digital environment of e-governance and m-governance in the world from the existing legal and judicial inkling. How sufficient are the international policies and benchmarks on the use of information communication technology (ICT) for e-governance and m-governance within and among nations to be trusted and judged to be of good repute among the users and has it been able to promote the use of e-governance and m-governance among the nations of the world? The theoretical framework that this chapter hinges on is the actor network theory (ANT). It emerged from a line of research broadly referred to as the social shaping of technology. The methodology adopted focuses on the United Nation survey data on e-governance from 2005-2016. The data collected is analyzed based on regional and economic groupings for e-government development index (EGDI) of Africa, Americas, Asia, Europe, and Oceania.

Chapter 10

Muhammad Imran Khan, Insight Centre for Data Analytics, Ireland
Simon N. Foley, IMT Atlantique, France
Barry O'Sullivan, University College Cork, Ireland

Insiders are legitimate users of a system; however, they pose a threat because of their granted access privileges. Anomaly-based intrusion detection approaches have been shown to be effective in the detection of insiders' malicious behavior. Database management systems (DBMS) are the core of any contemporary organization enabling them to store and manage their data. Yet insiders may misuse their privileges to access stored data via a DBMS with malicious intentions. In this chapter, a taxonomy of anomalous DBMS access detection systems is presented. Secondly, an anomaly-based mechanism that detects insider attacks within a DBMS framework is proposed whereby a model of normative behavior of insiders n-grams are used to capture normal query patterns in a log of SQL queries generated from a synthetic banking application system. It is demonstrated that n-grams do capture the short-term correlations inherent in the application. This chapter also outlines challenges pertaining to the design of more effective anomaly-based intrusion detection systems to detect insider attacks.

Preface

The recent rise of emerging networking technologies such as social networks, content centric networks, IoT networks, etc. have attracted lots of attention from academia as well as industry.

Such technologies should help facilitate the socio-economic development in the countries as well as an effective operational management within central government. Making use of emerging technologies in systems of governance for a wide range participation and an intense involvement of citizens, institutions and civil society groups in the decision making process of governance is called e-Governance.

The United Nations defines e-Government as the use of Information and Communications Technologies (ICT) and its application by the government for the provision of information and public services to the people. E-Governance and m-Governance is also described by Agrawal, Sethi and Mittal (2015) and Meijer (2015) as a process of reform in the way government works, shares information, engages citizens and delivers services to external and internal clients for the benefit of both government and the clients that they serve.

Paradoxically, the use of such technologies in e-government/ m-government services raise issues relating to Security, Privacy and Data Protection.

In fact, in order to fully exploit the benefits of e-government, there is a number of special security requirements which are dictated by the sensitive nature of the data transmitted during e-government transactions. These data may include personal data, such as identity and contact details, government data, such as record / registration numbers and certificates, as well as financial data, such as credit card and bank account numbers. Furthermore, these security requirements have become even more crucial with the advent of m-government. Security and privacy are specific concerns in wireless communication because of the case of connecting to the wireless link anonymously. The citizens want that the government agencies should safeguard their key data from moving into the hands of unauthorized agencies or hackers, thus preventing its misuse (Mengistu et al. 2009).

This book discusses and addresses the difficulties and security related challenges faced in implementing e-government/m-government technologies and applications.

ORGANIZATION OF THE BOOK

The book is organized into 10 chapters. A brief description of each of the chapters follows:

Chapter 1 presents m-Government and its applications on public service delivery. In this chapter, authors investigate and discuss various themes namely E-Government, Mobile Government, different perspectives on Mobile Government, Mobile Government in developed countries, benefits and limitations of Mobile Government, way forward in implementing Mobile Government and future research in areas of Mobile Government.

Chapter 2 proposes COMPARCH as a compliance-driven system engineering framework for privacy and security in socio-technical systems. It consists of: (1) a risk-based requirement management process, (2) a test-driven security and privacy modeling framework and (3) a simulation-based validation approach. The satisfaction of the regulatory requirements is evaluated through the simulation traces analysis. Authors use as a running example an E-CITY system providing municipality services to local communities.

Chapter 3 presents the different aspects of the Information Centric Networking (ICN) and analyses its security services. Based on a case study, the authors of this chapter demonstrate that the ICN meets the security requirements in e-government services.

Chapter 4 aims to bring out, the priority of enhancing the level of public awareness of Non-Communicable Diseases (NCDs). To ensure public responsiveness, this research focuses on creating an effective solution to prevent risky behavior. The authors construct "Sahtek", a social media solution developed on the fundamentals of Social Marketing, to better coach and promote awareness of NCDs prevention.

Chapter 5 deals with strengthening Cybersecurity in Singapore. The author uses a historical and policy perspectives to examine the development trajectory of e-government in Singapore, the trends and patterns of cybercrimes and cyber attacks, and the measures taken by the government to combat cybercrimes and cyber attacks.

Chapter 6 analyses the connection between e-Governance and corruption in Nigeria. The focus in this chapter is that the more entrenched e-Governance is adopted in contemporary governance the lower the corruption tendency in government service delivery. The authors conclude on the premise that e-governance reduces the strength of corruption in any country and more investments are needed to enhance this development.

Chapter 7 examines cybercrime and the challenges of securing Nigeria's cyberspace against criminal attacks. Author proffers solutions and recommends ways to make the country's cyberspace free from incessant criminal attacks.

Chapter 8 reviews the responsibilities of Internet Service Providers (ISPs) in securing their customers' network. The author finds out also whether there are legal provisions, or liabilities that are bindings on the ISPs to provide security for their customers.

Chapter 9 considers the trust and reputation of the digital environment of e-governance and m-governance in the world from the existing legal and judicial inkling. The author discusses how sufficient is the international policies and benchmarks on the use of ICT for e-Governance and m-Governance within and among nations to be trusted and judged to be of good repute among the users. The theoretical framework that this chapter hinges on is the Actor Network theory (ANT).

Chapter 10 presents a taxonomy of anomalous DBMS-access detection systems. Along with the taxonomy, a mechanism to detect insider threats is also proposed to construct a model for normative behavior for insiders which is extracted from logs of DBMS queries. In this book chapter, authors demonstrate that n-grams do capture the short-term correlations inherent in the application and outlines challenges pertaining to the design of more effective anomaly-based intrusion detection systems to detect insider attack.

Ryma Abassi
Carthage University, Tunisia

Aida Ben Chehida Douss
Carthage University, Tunisia

REFERENCES

Agrawal, S., Sethi, P., & Mittal, M. (2015). E-Governance: An Analysis of Citizens' Perception. *IUP Journal of Information Technology*, *11*(3), 34.

Meijer, A. (2015). E-governance innovation: Barriers and strategies. *Government Information Quarterly*, *32*(2), 198–206. doi:10.1016/j.giq.2015.01.001

Mengistu, Zo, & Rho. (2009). *M-government: Opportunities and Challenges to Deliver Mobile Government Services in Developing Countries*. Academic Press.

Chapter 1

M–Government and Its Application on Public Service Delivery

Vannie Naidoo
University of KwaZulu-Natal, South Africa

Thokozani Ian Nzimakwe
University of KwaZulu-Natal, South Africa

ABSTRACT

Technology has taken over every aspect of society. It is only fitting that governments embrace technological changes in society and develop m-government for the technologically savvy people of today's society. A global change that is transforming the government sector is the use of ICTs to improve service delivery. In this chapter, the following themes will be investigated and discussed: e-government, defining mobile government, different perspectives on mobile government, mobile government in developed countries, mobile government in developing countries, benefits and limitations of mobile government, way forward in implementing mobile government, and future research in areas of mobile government.

INTRODUCTION

ICTs have permeated every area of society it has only been a matter of time that government has caught on and embarked on m-Government and e-Government. Government had to keep abreast of the changes in society and they therefore utilize technology and ICT's to improve service quality. In the developed world countries m

DOI: 10.4018/978-1-5225-5984-9.ch001

Government has been easy to implement. In developing countries m-Government is still slow to catch on. There are many different views put forward in this chapter on m-Government and e-Government and what is the future for technology in government. The idea of m-Government is highly relevant in this day and age when wireless technology surrounds many of societies in the world. The developing world countries also have a lot to benefit from m Government despite the challenges faced. The belief is that although initial infrastructure, mobile and computer access, administration and labor and training costs may be very large at first, for the implementation of m-Government, the long term benefits are still very appealing

E-GOVERNMENT

E-Government has been a major breakthrough that has added value to government services and citizens in a country.

E-Government' refers to the use by government agencies of information technologies (such as Wide Area Networks, the Internet, and mobile computing) that have the ability to transform relations with citizens, businesses, and other arms of government. These technologies can serve a variety of different ends: better delivery of government services to citizens, improved interactions with business and industry, citizen empowerment through access to information, or more efficient government management. The resulting benefits can be less corruption, increased transparency greater convenience, revenue growth, and/or cost reductions (The World Bank Group, 2011).

Brown (2005) argues that Electronic government encompasses all government roles and activities, shaped by information and communications technologies (ICTs). Going well beyond analogies to e-commerce, it encompasses the four domains of governance and public administration: the state's economic and social programs; its relationships with the citizen and the rule of law (e-democracy), its internal operations and its relationship with the international environment. E-government builds on three evolving forces: technology, management concepts and government itself. It has given rise to several phenomena that are redefining the public sector environment, including the International Institute of Administrative Sciences. Four aspects of e-government have lasting impacts on public administration: citizen-centered service, information as a public resource, new skills and working relationships, and accountability and management models.

E-government, in its broad sense, is the use of information technology to enable or enhance government processes, of which the use of the Internet is only one part

(Grant, Hackney, & Edgar, 2010). State of Texas E-government Task Force (2003) indicates that Government activities that take place by digital processes over a computer network, usually the Internet, between the government and members of the public and entities in the private sector, especially regulated entities. These activities generally involve the electronic exchange of information to acquire or provide products or services, to place or receive orders, to provide or obtain information, or to complete financial transactions.

According to the E-government handbook published by Infodev (2002), "e-government is not simply a matter of giving government officials computers or automating old practices. Neither the use of computers nor the automation of complex procedures can bring about greater effectiveness in government or promote civic participation... Understood correctly, e-government utilizes technology to accomplish reform by fostering transparency, eliminating distance and other divides, and empowering people to participate in the political processes that affect their lives."

Another comment made by Advic et al (2014) is that e-government uses information technology such as WAN, Internet, and mobile computing in order to put public sector jobs at the service of citizens. On the other hand, m-Government uses mobile and wireless technologies such as mobile phones, PDA devices with Internet connection for improving government services and its accessibility to people anywhere and anytime.

DEFINING MOBILE GOVERNMENT

Since Mobile government (m-Government) is a fairly new concept it is important to view how different organizations and theorists unpack the definition.

Kushchu and Kuscu (2003) define m-Government as a "strategy and its implementation involving the utilization of all kinds of wireless and mobile technology, services, applications and devices for improving benefits to the parties involved in e-Government including citizens, businesses and all government units". M-Government is defined as "the provision of government services through the use of information and communication technologies" (El Kiki, Lawrence & Steele, 2005).

GBDe (2001) define m-Government as follows: "Electronic government ... refers to a situation in which administrative, legislative and judicial agencies (including both central and local governments) digitize their internal and external operations and utilize networked systems efficiently to realize better quality in the provision of public services."

Mobile government (m-Government) refers to the use of ICTs by government institutions with the help of mobile technologies to deliver electronic services to the public. This definition is derived from the definition of electronic government because m-Government is its subset of electronic government (Ntaliani, Costopoulou & Karetsos, 2007)

In the discussion below different perspectives on Mobile government is reflected on.

DIFFERENT PERSPECTIVES ON M- GOVERNMENT

M-Government is a new order of doing business by government. The services provided by m-Government are especially useful and beneficial for those techno savvy individuals especially the millennials. The perceptions of different theories from around the world are put forward and discussed below.

Albesher and Stone (2016) posit that research on m-government has started in the last decade. The use of m-government has been rapidly increasing due to the high penetration of mobile devices in the general population. Kushchu and Kuscu (2003) argue that citizens' demands increase for better public services, mobile technologies are paving the way for governments to deliver better, quick and on time information as well as transactional services to the citizens. M-government helps governments to provide anytime and anywhere services for citizens.

The statement "M-Government is inevitable" by Kushchu (2007), who was one of the first scholars starting the academic discussion about this topic, is more and more a reality than a future vision. After a time when short-message-services in the event of a disaster were the only mobile communication means used by the government, nowadays m-government is defined as mobile services offered by the government and used by the citizens in terms of mobile Internet services, particularly with special applications (apps), developed for their sole usage on mobile devices by means of mobile Internet.

Mobile technologies are considered one of the most important government's service sectors in various countries. It is predicted that by the end of 2011, nearly 80 percent of world's population will join to the cell phone users (Rannu et al., 2010). For the public sector therefore, m-Government appears to be an attractive alternative, as well as adjunct, to e-Government, in particular for the developing world, where internet access rates are very low, but mobile phone penetration is growing rapidly (Kumar and Sinha, 2007). Digital technologies allow governments to develop strategies for improving their performance management by using information systems (Heeks, 1999). Advocates of direct democracy hope that by facilitating new forms of interaction between citizens and governments, ICTs can channel citizens' voices and priorities into the policymaking process (Norris, 2003). Belanger and Jannie (2006) comment that in this day and age, most of developed countries and some of developing countries (such as Iran) are implementing e-government projects toward development and improvement of electronic services provision by governments. Ndou (2004) has determined the advantages of m-Government in providing electronic services, which include reduction of organizational bureaucracy, faster access to information, created opportunities for interactions of G2B and G2C and promoting the quality of public services.

In contrast to e-Government, m-Government uses contexts that are not known and the physical constraints of interacting with mobile devices limit both the amount and type of information that can be located and accessed. Moreover, accessing a government service within a mobile environment is frequently one of several other activities that are undertaken simultaneously (Carroll, 2006).

One of the major arguments of m-Government being slow to adapt in developing countries is that it costs too much. Zmijewska, Elaine and Seele (2004) argue that developing countries are able to bypass building heavy infrastructure required for regular internet access by adopting the wireless internet technologies that save them cost and time. Bagui, Sigwejo and Bytheway (2011) argue that while the potential of mobile to transform government interaction with citizens is widely acknowledged, the use of existing mobile government services is not widespread. Zejnullahu and Baholli (2017) add another downside to m-Government by saying that in the context of m-government, despite the opportunities created by m-Government in improving access to public information and government services, one should not ignore the fact that these services may not be accepted by targeted users. Such a huge global acceptance of mobile technologies is not a guarantee for governments that these technologies, in addition to daily activities, will be used by citizens to consume public services and that the investment in adopting mobile technologies in government services will be profitable and safe.

Other views on m government are put forward by Al-Thunibat, Zin and Sahari (2011) who comment that with the increasing number of m-Government services offered, the use of m-Government has also increased annually. It has been difficult for citizens to find an appropriate service according to their needs and interests. They prefer services that are easy to use, can be accessed anytime and at anywhere, and more personalized. Recent work by Wu et al. (2009) pinpoints as one fundamental challenge for the successful deployment of m-Government how the technology can be accessible in two particular populations, the physically challenged and the aging. Ease of access to m-Government information will be crucial in order to improve citizen participation and promote citizen-oriented services.

In the discussion that follows key themes on M-Government in developed and developing countries are expanded on and discussed.

M-GOVERNMENT IN DEVELOPED COUNTRIES

This section reviews international e-government experience and the role for m-government services. Japan and the United States of America will be highlighted and discussed.

For *Japan*, while mobile phones are abundant, the question is whether advanced mobile devices (i.e. smartphones) increase the potential demand for m-government services. Important Japanese e-government services include Juki cards and e-tax payment system. Acceptance, or otherwise, of these services should influence potential demand for m-government services. The empirical analysis allows consideration of whether Juki cards and the e-tax payment system are useful tools to promote m-government adoption (Maddena, Bohlinb, Onikic and Tran, 2013).

The cell phone is the most heavily adopted technology in the world, and it is currently owned by approximately 91% of the adult population in the *United States*. Growth in the field of m-government can be directly related to the global proliferation of mobile devices (Joseph, 2017). M-government is the use of mobile applications and devices for the delivery of government products and services. Through the use of wireless networks governments are able to communicate with citizens about current events and other relevant issues (Trimi & Shen, 2008). As citizens use mobile devices for many aspects of their personal and professional lives, there is also an inherent expectation that they can communicate with governments in a similar manner. Today's landscape of mobile devices includes cellular phones, smart phones, personal digital assistants, iPods, iPads, tablets, and others. With these different devices many users are able to connect via a wireless access point and perform tasks such as web browsing, e-mail retrieval, social media interaction, text messaging, location dependent activities and other mobile app functions (Joseph, 2017).

According to Joseph (2017), both SMS and mobile apps provide an opportunity for governments to engage directly with citizens. However, the user of mobile devices in the government domain is not void of challenges. One primary challenge pertains directly to the mobile devices themselves, since they can be restrictive to some users due to their small sizes and smaller screens.

M-GOVERNMENT IN DEVELOPING COUNTRIES

Under this theme three countries namely Pakistan, Serbia and The United Arab Emirates will be discussed.

Pakistan

M-governance holds great promise for public service provision in Pakistan due to the large growth of the telecommunications sector in the country in recent years, which has placed Pakistan among emerging East Asian economies like Malaysia and Singapore.

Pakistan has been one of the fastest growing markets among the emerging telecommunications markets, with its cellular mobile penetration surpassing that of its South Asian counterparts (PTA, 2008). Total subscribers crossed 108 million at the end of 2011 (ITU, 2012) and the number of subscribers has increased threefold since 2005. In 2009, Pakistan's cellular mobile penetration was 55.3 per cent, 10.8 per cent higher than that of its neighbor India and 18.7 per cent higher than Bangladesh. All of this compared to only 3.7 million internet subscribers, making the internet penetration rate 2.2 per cent by 2009 (ITU, 2012). These figures indicate that m-governance is a more viable option for successfully providing public services to citizens as compared to e-governance (Awan, 2015).

Serbia

M-Government is particularly suitable for countries those are in transition, where rates of Internet access are low, but the use of mobile phones is growing rapidly in urban and rural areas. Globally, the number of mobile phones has surpassed the number of fixed phone, as it is the case in Republic of Serbia.

The Strategy for e-Government Development in Serbia is contained in the Strategy for Development of Information Society in the Republic of Serbia to the 2020th year, in the National Strategy for Sustainable Development and the Strategy for e-Government Development in the Republic of Serbia for the period since 2009th to the 2013th year (Avdic et al, 2014). Strategy of Information Society of the Republic of Serbia to the 2020th that provides reform and modernization of public administration based on the widespread use of information and communication technologies is one of the key elements of the overall transition of the Republic of Serbia in the modern information society. According to the National Strategy for Sustainable Development in the Republic of Serbia is necessary to support increasing the level of digital literacy among citizens and introducing a quality education in terms of information and communication technology is at the elementary school level. It should provide conditions for further increase in the number of Internet users and the accessibility of ICT to all, both physical and legal entities (Avdic et al, 2014).

Avdic et al (2014) argue that laws of the Republic of Serbia, which were passed in recent years and which are consistent with the European Union, specifically refers to the Law on Business Registration Law on Access to Information of Public

Importance and the Law on Electronic Signatures and the relevant by-laws, comprise the essential elements concept of e-Government, such as the introduction of electronic signatures and digital certificates, the possibility of fi ling of the application of natural and legal persons (beneficiaries) electronically providing customer service via the Internet, the communication of users and authorities by e-mail, sanctioning negligent and malicious acts.

United Arab Emirates

It is to be noted that technology is advancing very fast, and governments around the globe, particularly in the United Arab Emirates (UAE), are managing to utilize the latest devices and technologies to provide their services to the public. For example, since smartphone penetration is high, it is critical to know which factors will encourage the public to use m-government services via smartphones (Almuraqab & Jasimuddin, 2017). The UAE government is making efforts and spending resources in order to implement m-government services successfully. Against this background, it is very important to study the factors in the adoption of the latest technologies to avoid failure in smart government implementation.

The next theme will discuss key benefits and limitations of M – Government.

BENEFITS AND LIMITATIONS OF M-GOVERNMENT

Mobile phones can reach remote areas where the infrastructure essential for internet or wired phone services is difficult to set up. Also relevant to such areas, mobile phones are usually inexpensive and fairly easy to use, much more so than computers and internet connections. Since operating mobile phones requires only basic literacy, barriers to entry are much lower than with other modern ICTs. The mobile platform has the capability to provide location specific information, for instance with regard to emergency services, locating a nearby bank or ATM and accessing information regarding traffic and weather conditions in a locality (Vijayakumar, Sabarish and Krishnan, 2010).

Therefore, mobile technologies are starting to have a permanent impact on human development, improving democratic governance and other development areas such as health, education, agriculture, employment, crisis prevention and the environment (UNDP, 2012). Other benefits include increased telecom-based tax revenues, improved employment opportunities and overall increased productivity, with the addition of a flourishing telecommunications industry that attracts foreign direct investment (UNDP, 2012).

Police can use mobile phones to capture pictures and videos of crimes as they witness them, which can then make it easier for them to process the case and make informed decisions. A successful example of mobile usage in this particular way is that of Kerala, India, where an exclusive solution has been developed for the police to efficiently deal with crimes, accidents and traffic issues, called MCARP (Mobile Crime and Accident Reporting Platform). Police use mobile phone cameras to capture images, which are uploaded instantly to the central server via MMS/GPRS (Vijayakumar, Sabarish and Krishnan, 2010). All of this goes to show what a significant role mobile technology can play in the provision and improvement of public service delivery and enhancement of development objectives.

Though m-Government is mentioned in terms of improving the functionalities of e-Government, despite numerous advantages, it carries certain restrictions.

According to Avdic et al (2014), *the advantages* include the following:

- **Overcoming Spatial and Temporal Restrictions:** The main advantage of m-Government is ability to overcome the limitations of e-Governance, as it is available anywhere and anytime;
- **Increasing the Productivity of Personnel in Public Institutions:** m-Government reduces necessary time for the actions of employees, because important information are carried with them and they don't have to spend time on activities such as recording data on paper, then going to the database and entering the data, but the operations can be performed in real time;
- **Improving of Information and Services Availability:** A consequence of the first advantages is the fact that the use of m-Government information may be submitted to the citizen no matter where he is; and
- **Reducing the Cost of Communication:** This involves informing citizens using mobile communications, and e-Voting.

The limitations/Disadvantages of m-government include the following:

- Unavailability to the poorer part of population
- **The Anonymity of Users and the Use of Cells for Entertainment:** Mobile phones are usually unregistered, which can lead to the data abusing, and since cells are used so far more for entertainment purposes, it is difficult to convince people that cells can be used for doing serious work related to the public sector;
- **(In) Security of e-Payments:** The ability to intercept transactions;
- **Information Overloads:** The existence of users who are always involved;

- **A Wide Range of Mobile Platforms:** It is necessary to design a variety of clients in order to cover a lot of platforms, which produces additional development costs.

WAYFORWARD IN IMPLEMENTING OF M-GOVERNMENT

Globally, more people now have more access to a mobile device. Because of this, m-government enables cost effective, timely delivery of information necessary for citizens to make informed, educated decisions – an important but often difficult responsibility of any government to discharge. M-governance is seen as a way of promoting democracy, accountability and transparency (Ghyasi and Kushchu, 2004), particularly in developing countries, not only through improvements in government to citizen (G2C) and citizen to government (C2G) communication, and efficiency gains among government agencies, but also through civil society use.

M-Government is an integral part of the e-Governance, which expands the range of its capabilities. E-Government represents the usage of information and communication technologies in order to improve the activities of public sector organisations, and m-Government is used to make public information and management services available "anytime, anywhere" to citizens and employees in the public sector. One of the reasons of the m-government existence is the fact that mobile services are cheaper and more accessible. According to Avdic et al (2014) m-Government is particularly suitable for countries those are in transition, where rates of Internet access are low, but the use of mobile phones is growing rapidly in urban and rural areas. Globally, the number of mobile phones has surpassed the number of fixed phone, as it is the case in Republic of Serbia. A goal of m-Government is not to replace e-Government; it is used to complement e-Government functionalities

In the discussion below Future research areas on Mobile Government will be explored.

FUTURE RESEARCH

Mobile applications cannot lead to any of the aforementioned advantages by themselves. Rather, they are catalysts that improve and expand development programming when used strategically. They require a sound set of policies to help fully realise their potential. They are the gateway to communication between the poor and the government, thus allowing the poor to freely access public services, have a platform for their voices to be heard and have new opportunities of engaging in larger governance processes (UNDP, 2012).

To reach both the developed and under-developed parts of most states, however, policies need to be designed and implemented in a way that fully exploits and utilises the potential of mobile technologies. It is essential that these policies support widespread access to information and service distribution so that it becomes possible to provide mobile services to the majority of citizens in all states. It is also important to pay heed to infrastructure limitations as well as to the countries' literacy challenges when developing these policies, in order to diminish the digital divide.

The penetration, usability, affordability and mobility of mobile phones present significant opportunities to reach and tailor services to citizens in most countries. However, further research is required to determine the relative opportunities and weaknesses of e-government and m-government in developing nations in terms of improving government efficiency and service delivery, increasing transparency and strengthening accountability.

The m-governance system needs to be enhanced with careful deliberation and long-term planning by members of the government and ICT experts, and building a citizen-centric roadmap for m-governance in developing states should be the first step. It is important for these planners and experts to understand the ways in which ICTs can help improve development programming, with particular focus on connecting to the poor, marginalised, vulnerable and underserved through citizen-centric services.

CONCLUSION

In the concluding remarks it is only fair to say that in all honesty like any new system, m-Government will have challenges for both the government sector that is implementing it and also for the users that is connecting to it. There is no easy or quick or fast solution. As time goes by the system supporting m-Government will become less difficult to implement as more training is given to staff within government sectors that interact with these systems. For the user, government should role out some form of training to the disabled, elderly, illiterate or semi-literate members of society or anyone who wants to learn how m Government systems work. This training can be in collaboration with NGOs so that the training costs accrued will be lesser on the pocket of government. The future is m-Government. The next step we take as citizens in any country in the world is to get on board with m Government. It is here to stay and as citizens we need to take the opportunity that m Government can bring to our lives.

REFERENCES

Al-Thunibat A, Zin N, Sahari N. (2011). Identifying User Requirements of Mobile Government Services in Malaysia Using Focus Group Methodology. *Journal of E-Government Studies and Best Practice*, 1–14.

Albesher, A. S., & Stone, R. T. (2016). Current state of m-government research: Identifying future research opportunities. *International Journal of Electronic Governance*, 8(2), 1–10. doi:10.1504/IJEG.2016.078118

Almuraqab, N. A. S., & Jasimuddin, S. J. (2017). Factors that Influence End-Users' Adoption of Smart Government Services in the UAE: A Conceptual Framework. *Electronic Journal of Information Systems Evaluation*, 20(1), 11–23.

Avdic, D., Avdic, A., Spalević, Z., Marovac, U., & Crnisanin, A. (2014). M-government Application Intended to Search Documents Written in Serbian Language. *Journal of Applied Sciences (Faisalabad)*, 902–906.

Awan, O. (2015). Bringing citizens closer to government: Is there a role for m-governance in Pakistan? *Commonwealth Governance Handbook, 2013*(14), 87–90.

Bagui, L., Sigwejo, A., & Bytheway, A. (2011). Public participation in government: assessing m-Participation in South Africa and Tanzania. In A. Koch, & P. A. van Brakel (Ed.), *Proceedings of the 13th Annual Conference on World Wide Web Applications* (pp. 5-26). Johannesburg: Cape Peninsula University of Technology.

Belanger, F., & Jannie, S. H. (2006). A framework for e-government: Privacy implications. *Business Process Management Journal*, 12(1), 48–60. doi:10.1108/14637150610643751

Brown, D. (2005). Electronic government and public administration. *International Review of Administrative Sciences, 71*(2), 241–254. doi:10.1177/0020852305053883

Carroll, J. (2006). 'What's in It for Me?': Taking M-Government to the People. Paper presented at the 19th Bled eConference eValue, Bled, Slovenia.

El-Kiki, T., Lawrence, E., & Steele, R. (2005). *A management framework for mobile government services*. CollECTeR. Retrieved from http://spa.hust.edu.cn/ 2008/uploadfile/2009-4/20090427230800732.pdf

GBDe. (2001). *e-Government*. GBDe. Retrieved December 13, 2012, from http://www.gbd-e.org/ig/egov/eGov_Recommendation_Sep01.pdf

Ghyasi, F., & Kushchu, I. (2004). M-Government: Cases of Developing Countries. *Proceedings from the fourth European conference on e-government*, 887–898.

Grant, K., Hackney, R., & Edgar, D. (2010). *Strategic Information Systems Management*. Andover: Cengage Learning.

Heeks, R. (1999). *Information and communication technologies, poverty and development*. Development informatics working paper no. 5. IDPM, University of Manchester.

Infodev. (2002). *The e-government handbook for developing countries*. Retrieved May 15, 2006, from the Center for Democracy and Technology Website: http://www.cdt.org/egov/handbook/part1.shtml

Joseph, R. C. (2017). There's an App for That? Perspectives from the Public Sector. *Proceedings for the Northeast Region Decision Sciences Institute (NEDSI)*.

Kumar, M., & Sinha, O. P. (2007). M-Government – Mobile Technology for eGovernment. In *Towards Next Generation E-government, iceg'07*. Retrieved from http://www.iceg.net/2007/books/2/32_343_2.pdf

Kushchu, I. (2007). *Mobile government: An emerging direction in e-government*. Hershey, PA: IGI. doi:10.4018/978-1-59140-884-0

Kushchu, I., & Kuscu, H. (2003). From E-government to M-government: Facing the Inevitable. Paper Presented at the *European Conference on E-Government (ECEG 2003)*, Dublin, Ireland.

Maddena, G., Bohlinb, E., Onikic, H., & Tran, T. (2013). Potential Demand for M-government Services in Japan. *Applied Economics Letters*, *20*(8), 732–736. doi:10.1080/13504851.2012.736939

Ndou, V. (2004). *E-Government for developing countries: Opportunities and challenges*. Retrieved from http://unpan1.un.org/intradoc/groups/public/documents/UNTC/UNPAN018634.pdf

Norris, P. (2003). *Deepening democracy via e-governance*. Report for the UN World Public Sector Report. Retrieved May 15, 2006: http://ksghome.harvard.edu/~pnorris/ACROBAT/e-governance.pdf

Ntaliani, M., Costopoulou, C., & Karetsos, S. (2008). Mobile government: A challenge for agriculture. *Government Information Quarterly*, *25*(4), 699–716. doi:10.1016/j.giq.2007.04.010

Rannu, R., Saksing, S., & Mahlakõiv, M. (2010). *MobileGovernment: 2010 and beyond*. Mobil Solutions Ltd. Retrieved Dec. 17, from: http://www.mobisolutions.com

State of Texas E-government Task Force. (2003). Retrieved from www.dir.state.tx.us/taskforce/Surveys/State_Survey/app_b.htm

The World Bank Group. (2011). *Definition of E-Government.* World Bank. Retrieved December 13, 2012, from http://go.worldbank.org/M1JHE0Z280

Trimi, S., & Shen, H. (2008). Emerging Trends in M-Government. *Communications of the ACM, 51*(5), 53–58. doi:10.1145/1342327.1342338

United Nations Development Programme (UNDP). (2012). *Mobile Technologies and Empowerment: Enhancing human development through participation and innovation.* Democratic Governance Division, United Nations Development Programme.

Vijayakumar, S., Sabarish, K., & Krishnan, G. (2010). *Innovation and M-Governance: The Kerala Mobile Governance Experience and Road-Map for a Comprehensive M-Governance Strategy.* Retrieved from: http://www.ipeglobal.com/newsletter/May_2011/Kerala%20Mgovernance%20Strategy.pdf

Wu, H., Ozok, A. A., Gurses, A. P., & Wei, J. (2009). User aspects of electronic and mobile government: Results from a review of current research. *Electronic Government: An International Journal, 6*(3), 233–251. doi:10.1504/EG.2009.024942

Zejnullahu, F., & Baholli, I. (2017). Overview of researches on the influential factors of m-government's adoption. *European Journal of Management and Marketing Studies, 2*(2), 1-19. Available at: https://oapub.org/soc/index.php/EJMMS/article/view/166/488

Zmijewska, A., Elaine, L., & Seele, R. (2004). Towards understanding of factors influencing user acceptance of mobile payment systems. *Proceedings of IADIS International Conference.*

Chapter 2
A Compliance-Driven Framework for Privacy and Security in Highly Regulated Socio-Technical Environments:
An E-Government Case Study

Ayda Saidane
Independent Researcher, Canada

Saleh Al-Sharieh
University of Groningen, The Netherlands

ABSTRACT

Regulatory compliance is a top priority for organizations in highly regulated ecosystems. As most operations are automated, the compliance efforts focus on the information systems supporting the business processes of the organizations and, to a lesser extent, on the humans using, managing, and maintaining them. Yet, the human factor is an unpredictable and challenging component of a secure system development and should be considered throughout the development process as both a legitimate user and a threat. In this chapter, the authors propose COMPARCH as a compliance-driven system engineering framework for privacy and security in socio-technical systems. It consists of (1) a risk-based requirement management process, (2) a test-driven security and privacy modeling framework, and (3) a simulation-based validation approach. The satisfaction of the regulatory requirements is evaluated through the simulation traces analysis. The authors use as a running example an E-CITY system providing municipality services to local communities.

DOI: 10.4018/978-1-5225-5984-9.ch002

INTRODUCTION

Computer systems are too complex to be error-free. They are often dependent on off-the-shelf components, delegations to external service providers or non-documented legacy systems. These challenges make it difficult for organizations to both develop systems satisfying regulatory compliance and, the more so, diagnose failures and correct vulnerabilities. Meanwhile, hackers have become faster and faster in exploiting vulnerabilities and developing successful and widely spread attacks. Notably, there are no universal attacks; every attack targets specific vulnerabilities in specific software applications, hardware platforms or operation systems. Therefore, it is necessary to consider the threats and hazards that may violate the regulatory requirements of each computer system. Moreover, for security-critical and highly regulated ecosystems, it is crucial to ensure that the failure modes of the system-to-be fall always within fail-secure states.

Developing secure and compliant socio-technical systems is a complex and multi-dimensional issue that requires considering both the security functional aspects and the insider and outsider threat model for all the parties of the ecosystem. There are different proposals addressing individual steps of the development process, such as requirement engineering (e.g. secure Tropos, ACSP-RSL), security modeling (e.g. UMLsec, secureUML) or testing (e.g. Mouelhi et al. 2008, Bertolino et al. 2001). However, there are a few comprehensive end-to-end development frameworks that cover all the development process in a manner that addresses and enforces the security and compliance concerns at every step. In this chapter, the authors propose a comprehensive and complete development framework for highly regulated socio-technical systems. The authors address the regulatory compliance challenges using the Model Driven Engineering (MDE) methodology. The MDE development processes are automated using model transformations that are less error-prone than classical methodologies. In order to meet our own objectives of automated and documented validation activities, the authors enrich the MDE development process with compliance and security artifacts at every step.

As the quality of software systems depends on their architecture, the authors adopt this abstraction level for our framework. The early architecture model validation facilitates the detection and correction of design errors and reduces the costs of compliance management. In this research, the authors are interested in the privacy and security critical systems that require a reliable validation process. The authors propose a compliance management framework integrating 3 important views on the software ecosystem: 1) a risk-based requirements management process, 2) a modeling framework capable of integrating the security and privacy requirements, and 3) a simulation-based validation approach.

The chapter has 6 sections: following this introduction, section 2 provides a critical overview of the literature on security modeling and model driven security testing. Section 3 describes the e-government case study. Section 4 presents the regulatory requirements. Section 5 describes the COMPARCH framework. And, section 6 provides conclusions.

BACKGROUND

AADL: SAE Architecture Analysis and Design Language[1]

AADL is a standardized architecture description language released in 2006 by the SAE. It is proposed for specifying a multi-aspect model suitable for analyzing both functional and non-functional requirements. In addition, it offers textual and graphic notation with precise semantics for modelling both software and hardware layers. For interoperability purposes, a UML profile representing AADL was proposed.

The main concepts of the AADL modelling framework can be split into 3 categories related to the software system design: (1) Software components such as Thread, Data and Subprogram; (2) the runtime platform such as Execution Platform components: Processor, Bus, and Device; and (3) composite components: system. AADL allows the definition of component types and their implementation where the type defines the interface and their implementation in/as an internal structure including subcomponents and their interconnections. In addition to these elements, AADL supports an annex extension mechanism to customize the description capabilities of the language by introducing a dedicated sub-language.

AADL has been enriched by the definition of 2 standardized annexes: the first is a framework for supporting fault/reliability modelling and hazard analysis through the error model annex; and the second is a framework for specifying the dynamics of the system and simulation-based validation through behavioral annex.

In Saidane et al. 2012, the authors have analyzed the AADL modeling framework and identified different artefacts for modeling security related aspects of information systems.

Security and Privacy Modeling

Modeling security and privacy concerns at the architecture level has been an active research field in which there are sophisticated proposals essentially based on architecture description languages' extensions. Nevertheless, there are a few proposals that use such a modeling language for security testing and none of them allow the generation of both security functional test cases and malicious test cases.

Table 1. AADL main concepts and their graphical notations

Description and Textual Notation	Graphical Notation
System: it represents a composite of software, execution platform, or system components. **system** name **system implementation** name.basic **end** name; **end** name.baisc;	SystemType1
Process: represents a protected address space where protection is provided from other components accessing anything inside the process. **process** name **process implementation** name.basic **end** name; **end** name.baisc;	ProcessType1
Data: it represents static data (e.g., numerical data or source text) and data types within a system. **data** name **data implementation** name.basic **end** name; **end** name.baisc;	DataType1
Subprogram: it represents a callable component with or without parameters that operates on data or provides server functions to components that call it. **subprogram** name **subprogram implementation** name.basic **end** name; **end** name.baisc;	SubprogramType1
Event data port: interfaces for message transmission with queuing port_name : **event data port** [data classifier]; **Data access:** there are 2 types: provide and require. It indicates that a component provides (requires) access to a data. port_name : **data access** [data classifier];	DataPort1 EventPort1 DataAccess
Data connections (event, event data): a connection instance represents the actual flow of data and control between components of a system instance model. **Connections:** connection_label: **event[data|event data]** port1 -> port2;	DataPort2 <<Data>> DataPort1 EventPort2 <<Event>> EventPort1 DataAccess2 <<DataAccess>> DataAccess1
Flows: AADL flows specification capabilities enable the detailed description and analysis of an abstract information path through a system **source**: a feature of a component label: **flow source** port; **sink**: a feature of a component label: **flow sink** port; **flow path**: a flow through a component from one feature to another label: **path flow** port|flow_label ->... port|flow_label	No graphical notation
Property set: A property has a name, type, and an associated value. Properties can be assigned values through property association declarations. They provide descriptive information about: components, subcomponents, features, connections, flows, modes and subprogram calls.	
Behavioral model: it can be associated to any component and it is described textually. annex behavior_specification {** <state_variables>?::= state variables (<identifier>: <data_classifier> ;)+ <initialization> ? <states>? <transitions>::= transitions((<label>:)? <state_identifier> -[<guard>?]-> state_identifier> [{ <action>* }];)+ <connections>? <composite_declaration>***} Where actions represent subprogram call, receipt/sending data or event on port, state variables update, etc.**};	

UMLSec is a UML extension (Jurjens 2008) to express security requirements like data secrecy and integrity, information flows restrictions and role-based access control. SecureUML (Lodderstedt et al. 2002) is a modeling language and security analysis approach for specifying secure distributed systems. SecureUML focuses on role-based access control policies enriched with authorization constraints. Secure i* (Elahi et al. 2007) is a goal-oriented approach suitable for modeling security concerns as competing goals of multiple actors. The framework allows qualitative and quantitative security assessments.

MoDELO (Arzapalo et al. 2013) is a Model-Driven security policy approach that extends UMLSec with OrBAC elements in order to allow early validation of authorization policies. SysML-Sec (Apvrille et al. 2014) is a SysML based MDE environment inspired by KAOS. SysML-Sec process includes three stages: system analysis (identification of security requirements and threats by system's partitioning), system design (implementation of software security mechanisms) and system validation (formal verification, simulation and test of the models). Secure xADL (Ren 2006) proposes a modeling framework for a unified access control model that integrates the classic, role-based, and trust management models. These security modeling constructs are identified: subject, principal, resource, privilege, safeguard and policy.

The following table provides an overview of the main differences between the different proposals with regards to:

- **The Modeling Capabilities:** (1) scope of the language; (2) threats and vulnerabilities; (3) safeguards; and
- The availability of security assessment methodology.

Model Based Security Testing

Security testing is an important activity within secure software systems lifecycle. It is the most popular validation technique in industry by opposition to formal verification. It is mainly used to ensure the compliance of the final product with the system specification. The adoption of the model driven engineering paradigm for test generation resulted in Model-Based Security Testing (MBTS). The approach has received a lot of interest since it offers automation possibilities for test cases generation and execution tasks by model transformations. This section provides an overview of the state of the art in model-based security testing according to the classification depicted in Figure 1.

Table 2. Main security and privacy modeling languages and their evaluations

Modeling Language	Generic vs. Specific	Threats	Safeguards	Security Assessment Methodology
UMLsec	*Generic*	X	X	X
secureUML	*Access control*	-	-	-
Secure i*	*Generic*	X	X	X
MoDELO	*Generic*	X	X	X
SysML-Sec	*Generic*	X	X	X
Secure xADL	*Generic*	-	X	X

Figure 1. Classification of model-based security testing approaches

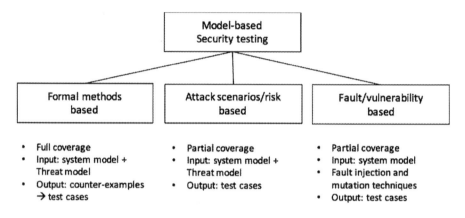

Formal Methods Based MBST Approaches

Theorem proving has been used for model-based testing (Castanet et al 2002; Subramaniam et al 2009) since late 1990's. However, there are only a few attempts in model-based security. An interesting contribution in the field is based on the UMLsec language (Jurjens 2005), which is an UML extension adding standard concepts from formal methods for security engineering to UML (i.e. security requirements: secrecy, integrity; security mechanisms: access control, encryption; or threat scenarios: adversary type, threats). The security test cases (Jurjens 2008) are generated automatically from the SUT UMLsec specification using a theorem proofer and an attacker model generator.

Model checking has been widely used for test generation (Koo et al. 2009). In fact, the counter-examples, which are generated automatically, represent test cases violating the target properties. Armando et al (2010) presented their model checking-based security testing approach for vulnerability detection and illustrated it by an analysis of a real commercial system analysis. They were able to generate an attack scenario against the authentication mechanism deployed by google web-based applications.

The main weakness of these approaches concerns the state explosion, which makes them not suitable for validating large systems.

Attack Scenarios and Risk Based MBST Approaches

Penetration testing is a widely used method for validating secure software systems. However, it is not done systematically, and it requires an in-depth knowledge of security. Public databases of known vulnerabilities and attacks are used to drive penetration testing, but testers need to understand them and interpret them into executable test cases. In a MBST context, this activity is fully automated (Moutartidis et al. 2007; Xiong et al. 2009; Zulkernine et al. 2009; Zech 2011). It proposes a risk-based test generation approach targeting cloud environments where the security requirement analysis is complemented by the definition of negative requirements derived from risk analysis.

These approaches should be associated with other MBST approaches that take into account the SUT architecture in order to generate SUT specific attack scenarios if applicable.

Fault and Vulnerability Based MBST Approaches

Fault injection-based MBST is mostly carried out by mutation techniques. Research is rich in this field (e.g. Marquis et al. 2005; Pretschner et al. 2008; Mouelhi et al. 2008). The purpose of these approaches is the functional testing of security mechanisms such as Policy Decision Point in access control systems. Pretschner et al. (2013) proposed a generic fault model and showed how it could be instantiated to different context specific fault models and used to derive test cases. Bertolino et al. (2001) proposed a fault model-based approach targeting authorization systems and focusing on the Policy decision point. This approach is popular for compliance testing, but it is not suitable for identifying complex multi-step attacks. Moreover, the evaluation of the test generation coverage is generally disconnected from the targeted security properties to be satisfied.

Analysis and Evaluation

As shown in Figure 2, failures and degradations in security critical systems can be caused by 2 different interaction faults either executed by a legitimate user or a malicious attacker. The authors associate different categories to the test cases describing these scenarios:

Figure 2. Relationships between attacks, vulnerabilities and test observations[2]

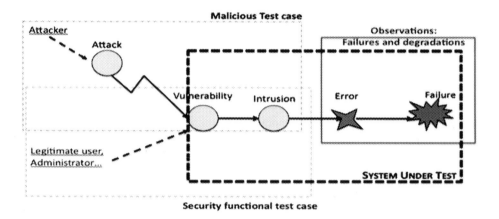

- *Malicious Test Cases* aim at validating the system against attack attempts. This category requires an appropriate specification of potential attackers' capabilities in terms of knowledge and interaction with the system. Consequently, an attacker model should be included in the test model.
- *Security Functional Test cases* aim at validating the system against its functional security requirements. This category can be generated from the system functional specifications.

Therefore, testing the security of a system should encompass testing both legal and illegal means for interacting with the system-to-be and accessing protected resources. The legal means should be derived from the system functional model while the illegal means are derived from the threat model. When analyzing the state of the art in model-based security testing, the authors notice that most proposals exclusively focus on one aspect.

The following table provides an overview of the main differences between the different proposals with regards to:

- The modeling framework used for the test generation
- **The Categories of the Generated Test Case:** (1) malicious test cases and (2) security functional test cases as shown in Figure 2.

THE E-CITY CASE STUDY

Description

"X" is the municipality of the capital city of a Member State of the European Union (EU). Its policies must comply with applicable EU law, including the privacy and personal data protection framework. The municipality intends to implement a new electronic system, called E-CITY, which makes many of the municipality services available and accessible online. Specifically, the organization has decided to start by the following online services:

- **Registration:** Residents wishing to use E-CITY must go through an online registration process to create their personal accounts. For this purpose, they must provide information such as: 1) full name; 2) place and date of birth; 3) gender; 4) nationality; 5) marital status; and 6) address. Upon the completion

Table 3. Some model-based security testing approaches, their classes and their evaluations

Model-Based Security Testing Approach		Modeling Framework	Malicious Test Cases	Security Functional Test Cases
Formal methods based	*Castanet et al, 2002*	*High Order Logic/ Timed automata*	-	*X*
	Subramaniam et al. 2009	*Extended finite state machine*	-	*X*
	Jurjens 2008	*UMLsec*	*X*	*X*
	Armando et al 2010	*SAT Logic*	*X*	-
	Koo et al. 2009	ADL^3 + logic of graphs	-	*X*
Attack scenario and risk based	*Mouratidis et al. 2007*	*Secure TROPOS*	*X*	-
	Xiong et al., 2009	*TTCN-3*	*X*	-
	Zulkernine et al. 2009	*Extended abstract finite state machine*	*X*	-
	Zech 2017	*Prolog*	*X*	-
Fault and vulnerability based	Marquis et al. 2005	*SCL*	-	*X*
	Moelhi et al. 2008	*Own domain specific language (DSL)*	-	*X*
	Pretschner et al. 2013	*Metamodeling- generic fault model*	-	*X*
	Bertolino et al. 2001	*Labeled Transition System*	-	*X*

of the registration process, E-CITY verifies the authenticity of the information provided. Once the account is approved, the user can access a set of online municipal services.

- **Parking Permit Request:** This service allows the resident to buy a parking pass for certain zones in the city. For this purpose, the resident needs to provide the information about the car, his/her own information and the selected zone. The pass is then generated and can be printed and attached to the car.

- **Public Library Pass Request:** The residents can subscribe to the public libraries of the city through this service. The subscription requires the identity of the resident and additional information about his employment and studies status. The subscription can be on a monthly or yearly basis.

- **Non-EU Family Members Invitation:** This service allows the resident to create an application for inviting his/her non-European family members to visit. For this purpose, the resident should provide information about his/her (1) identity, (2) address, (3) income, (4) citizenship status and (5) relationship with the invitee. Moreover, the resident is required to upload documents supporting the information included in the application. Once the application is processed, a formal document will be sent to his address. This document is required for the family member's visa application.

Modeling the Security Aspects With AADL

There are two important categories of security concepts that need to be integrated into the architecture model: security requirements and security mechanisms. The security properties expressed in the requirements must be explicitly specified because they represent the evaluation target. The security mechanisms are components or features in charge of providing some security functions like encryption, access control or authentication. It is important to differentiate this type of components from the other components of the system-to-be, because all security functional test cases will be related to testing that these security mechanisms behave normally in all contexts.

AADL proposes the notion of properties as a declarative mean for specifying non-functional properties over components, connections or features. The expressiveness of the AADL properties is reduced to the definition of some attributes to which a type is associated. The standard does not define any standard properties; however, SEI defines a set of interesting properties provided as a default set in the OSATE tool[4]. Thus, the system engineer decides the definition and usage of this artifact in an ad-hoc and project specific manner.

Figure 3 shows the E-City case study's properties as defined in AADL while Figure 4 presents the AADL graphical model for the E-CITY ecosystem including the following actors: (1) E-city system (blue), (2) its external environments including

Figure 3. E-City's properties set

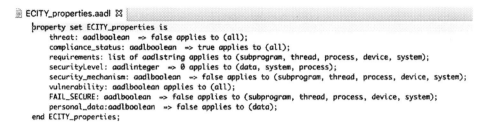

```
ECITY_properties.aadl
    property set ECITY_properties is
        threat: aadlboolean => false applies to (all);
        compliance_status: aadlboolean => true applies to (all);
        requirements: list of aadlstring applies to (subprogram, thread, process, device, system);
        securityLevel: aadlinteger => 0 applies to (data, system, process);
        security_mechanism: aadlboolean => false applies to (subprogram, thread, process, device, system);
        vulnerability: aadlboolean applies to (all);
        FAIL_SECURE: aadlboolean => false applies to (subprogram, thread, process, device, system);
        personal_data:aadlboolean => false applies to (data);
    end ECITY_properties;
```

Figure 4. AADL graphical models for the E-CITY ecosystem

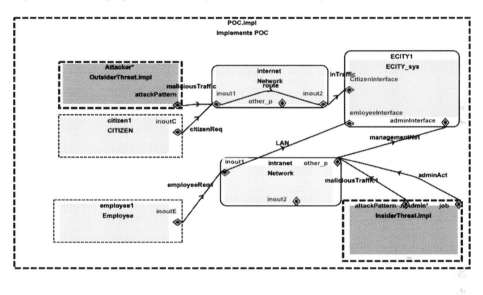

3 actors: the internet network (grey), the honest citizen (green) and an instance of the outsider threat model (red) and (3) its environment inside the municipality infrastructure including 3 actors: the administrator, the intranet network and the honest employee. Each of these actors has its specific detailed model and behavior model. For example, it this chapter the authors provide the detailed model for the outsider threat model in Figure 5. Moreover, these diagrams along with the complete set of models representing the different actors of the E-CITY are produced at the step 3 of the COMPARCH framework presented in Figure 7.

In Figure 4, the authors can see all the actors involved in the E-City ecosystem as black boxes where only the external interfaces are visible. Particularly, it presents an overview of the system-to-be and its environment (both internal within the municipality infrastructure and external on the internet), the authors might notice that the authors show the components of the threat model and their interactions with

Figure 5. AADL graphical models for the outsider threat model of the case study

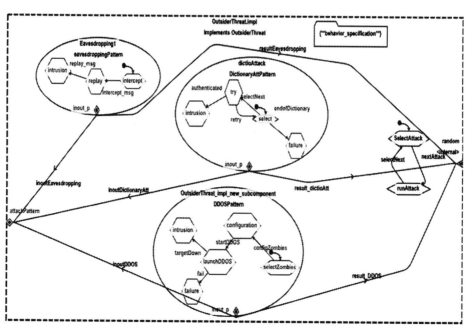

the system-to-be, although they do not belong to the system development. This is done in the perspective of the test generation step that requires a complete view on the system's environment. Moreover, the malicious components are tagged as none part of the system-to-be using the "threat" property (Figure 3) that allows the different contributors to the system development to share this information.

Threat and Risk Model

The threat model for our case study is composed of:

- **The Insider Threat:** This part of the threat model covers both (1) malicious administrator and (2) unaware client service agent.
- **The Outsider Threat:** This part of the threat model covers hackers from all over the Internet. For our proof of concept, the authors consider the following attack patterns: eavesdropping/identity theft, dictionary attack and BF attack.

In Table 4, the authors represent some potential hazards and risks for E-CITY. This sample of risks serves only as a running example for the chapter.

For testability purposes, the authors identify potential hazards in terms of vulnerabilities (i.e. shared memory, unchecked user input, etc.) and attacker's profiles

Table 4. Sample of business security risks for the case study

#RISK	DESCRIPTION
R1	**Identity theft** caused by a weak identification process when creating a user account and/or a weak authentication solution when accessing the user account.
R2	**Non-authorized record alteration** caused by a weak access control solution and/or an accidental error while manipulating the information resulting in an authenticity loss of the record data.
R3	**Citizen safety threatened** by the disclosure of its identity.
R4	**Unlawful disclosure of personal or confidential information** caused by an authorized X's employee unreliability or a hacker that succeeds in penetrating the stored data including citizens' personal information or intercepting citizen's messages.
R5	**Reputation compromised** by the medialization of some successful attacks on the E-CITY system disclosing personal information of the citizens.

(i.e. insider/outsider, administrator, etc.) whose interactions with the system-to-be components comply with attacks patterns (i.e. Buffer overflow, Covert channel, etc.). These threats should be modeled explicitly for generating malicious attack test cases.

Malicious components represent the insider and the outsider threat. They are the non-system-to-be components that are added to the architecture model for testing purposes. They should not be considered during the detailed design phases of the system-to-be development lifecycle. The identified risk scenarios are modeled through the interactions between the malicious components and the system-to-be components. More specifically, they are defined in the behavior model.

In the AADL language, the threat model can be represented by one or more malicious components of the ecosystem. In order to simplify the analysis, the authors use two systems: one to represent the insider threat model and another to represent the outsider threat model as shown by Figure 4. The outsider threat model instance that is marked in red in Figure 4 is represented in Figure 5 as a white box where all the sub-components, their dynamics and logics are represented.

REGULATORY REQUIREMENTS

Legal Framework

The General Data Protection Regulation (GDPR)[5] is a legal instrument that protects the human right of natural persons to the protection of their personal data in the EU Member States.[6] The GDPR defines "personal data" as "any information relating to an identified or identifiable natural person ('data subject')"[7] and defines "processing" as "any operation or set of operations which is performed on personal data or on sets of personal data, whether or not by automated means."[8] The GDPR establishes, *inter alia*, the legal requirements for the protection of personal data and provides data subjects with specific rights.

Personal Data Protection Principles (Legal Requirements)

Under the GDPR, there are generally10 principles, legal requirements (LR), for the protection of personal data, which Municipality X must comply with when processing personal data by the E-CITY:

- **LR1: Lawful Processing of Personal Data:**[9] The processing of personal data is lawful when the data subject has provided his/her informed and unambiguous consent to the processing of the data or when the processing of the personal data is necessary for: 1) the performance of a contract to which the data subject is a party (or for the preparations requested by him/her prior contracting); 2) the compliance with a legal obligation; 3) the protection of the vital interests of the data subject; 4) the protection of the public interest or the exercise of public authority; or 5) the protection of the legitimate interests of the data controller, or a third party, unless such interests are overridden by the human rights of the data subject.[10] E-CITY should have a mechanism that collects users' informed and unambiguous consent to the processing of their personal data for the specific services provided by E-CITY. This is to avoid any difficulties in proving the lawful processing of the personal data, especially since all the other lawfulness bases involve a necessity test that may limit their applications.[11]

- **LR2: Purpose Limitation:** The GDPR requires that the processing of personal data be only for "specified, explicit and legitimate purposes" and after clearly and precisely disclosing to the data subject the specific purpose(s), scope and nature of the data processing.[12] It is illegal to further process the personal data for purposes incompatible with the disclosed purposes, unless another legal ground exists for this further processing.[13] E-CITY may comply with this requirement by: 1) presenting its users with a clear, precise and accessible "privacy statement" explaining the specific purposes of the processing, its nature, and scope; 2) limiting the processing of the personal data to the specific purposes of which the data subject has been informed; and 3) applying measures to discourage further processing that is incompatible with the disclosed purposes.

- **LR3: Data Minimization:** The GDPR requires that only the minimum, and relevant, personal information necessary for the specific, explicit and legitimate purposes be processed.[14] E-CITY therefore must process the minimum and relevant personal information necessary to achieve the specific purposes disclosed to the data subject and to which he/she has consented.

- **LR4: Storage Limitation:** The personal data must be stored only for the minimum amount of time necessary for the specific, explicit and legitimate purposes of the data processing.[15] This principle is inherently connected with the purpose limitation and data minimization principles.[16] For example, if E-CITY collects cars' plate numbers from users wising to obtain a parking permit, the system needs to have a mechanism that deletes these data upon the expiry of those permits or reasonably soon after.

- **LR5: Data Accuracy:** The data controller must ensure that the personal data are kept accurate and, where necessary, up to date.[17] Personal data that are no longer accurate in light of the specific purpose(s) of the processing must be erased or corrected.[18] For this purpose, for example, E-CITY needs to have a mechanism that enables its users to update and correct their personal data.

- **LR6: Data Security:** The data controllers must apply appropriate technical and organizational measures to protect the integrity and confidentiality of the personal data they process.[19] They must secure the personal data against, for example, any unauthorized or unlawful access, disclosure, processing, accidental loss, destruction, alteration, or damage.[20] The applied technical and organizational measures must provide a level of security that mitigates the risks associated with the processing of the personal data.[21] A number of factors determine whether the security measures applied are appropriate or not: the nature of the risks associated with the processing, the nature of the personal data, the scope of the processing, the state of the art in security measures, and the cost of such measures.[22] The GDPR refers to several examples of technical and organizational measures for securing the integrity of personal data,[23] which E-CITY may apply to secure the personal data it processes, such as pseudonymisation, encryption, regular testing and evaluation, and other measure necessary to ensure the availability, resilience, availability and accessibility of the system processing the data.[24] In addition to providing data security, the data controller must keep the personal data confidential. Processing or accessing the data is done by the controller, or upon the controller's instructions, or is required by law.[25]

- **LR7: Transparency:** The data controller must communicate to the data subjects in an accessible language and format the basic information about the processing of their personal data, including the identity of the data controller, the purpose(s) of the processing, the legal basis of the processing, and the recipient(s) of the personal data.[26] The data controller has also a duty to provide the data subjects with further information such as the information on their rights to access and rectify the data.[27] Transparency is necessary for satisfying the requirement of the informed consent as a basis for the lawful processing of the personal data. It is "a condition of being in control and for rendering the consent valid."[28] E-CITY may comply with this requirement by making available to the data subjects, both during the registration process and afterwards, a clear and accessible document, such as a privacy policy, that includes both the basic and the additional information required by the GDPR.

- **LR8: Enablement:** Under the GDPR data subjects have a set of rights such as the right to access, rectify, erase and block personal data; the right to object to the processing of personal data; the right to be notified in the case of a data breach violating their human rights; and the right to withdraw consent.[29] E-CITY muse enable users to exercise these rights by, for example, making available a mechanism for this purpose.

- **LR9: Accountability**: Data controllers must take all the appropriate measures to implement, and demonstrate the compliance with, the data protection principles.[30] An important channel for this is performing a data protection impact assessment that explains the details of the processing of the personal data, its purposes, the necessity of the processing and its proportionality with the specific purposes of the processing, the risks associated with the processing, and the appropriate technical and organizational measures applied to mitigate the risks.[31] The data controller must consult with the country's data protection supervising authority before processing the data when the data protection impact assessment revels risks to the rights and freedoms of the data subject but fails to identify mitigating measures.[32] In

Figure 6. Legal requirements on security and privacy in the European Union

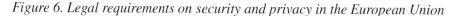

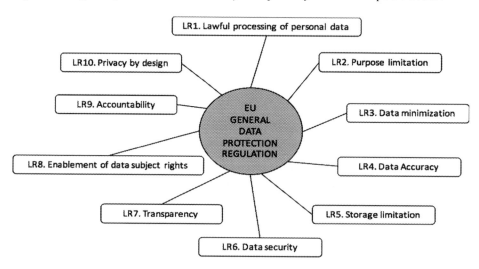

return, the authority may provide advice, issue a warning or disapprove the processing.[33] It is worth noting that, in specific situations, the GDPR requires the designation of a data protection officer, such as when the data controller's main activity is to process sensitive data.[34] Prior to processing personal data, Municipality X needs to subject E-CITY to a data protection impact assessment, given the nature, context and scope of the data processing that will occur in the system.

- **LR10. Privacy by Design:** Data controllers must apply appropriate technical and organizational measures to implement the data protection principles and protect the data subject rights provided in the GDPR "both at the time of the determination of the means for processing and at the time of the processing itself."[35] This means that Municipality X must consider and target the compliance with the principles of the personal data protection of the GDPR at both the design stage of E-CITY and throughout its personal data processing operations.[36]

COMPARCH: COMPLIANCE DRIVEN SECURITY AND PRIVACY DEVELOPMENT FRAMEWORK

COMPARCH Framework Overview

The COMPARCH framework (Figure 7) is based on a stepwise approach designed to continuously assess the compliance status of the system-to-be before moving forward to the next step. It is an extension of any typical model engineering process and relies on the following artifacts:

- **A Risk-Based Requirement Management Process:** The regulatory compliance is guaranteed through a risk-based management process where an acceptable low risk-level of requirements' violation has to be reached before considering that the development phase is satisfactory and that the authors can move to the next step. The compliance is assessed in both the design and implementation phases.
- **A Security Modeling Language:** Secure-ADL extends the AADL language with the required concepts allowing a proper security and privacy modeling and analysis.
- **A Simulation-Based Validation Framework:** The simulation framework aims at: (1) identifying any non-desirable emerging behavior that reflects unknown vulnerabilities in the E-CITY system's architecture through emergent behaviors' scenarios that need to be addressed at the design level

Figure 7. COMPARCH: A compliance driven security and privacy development framework

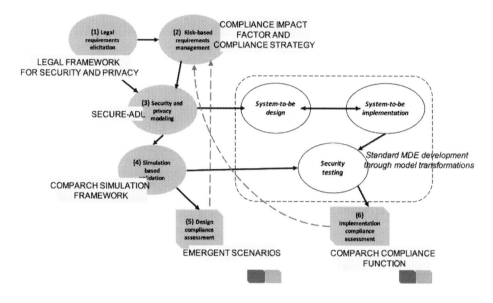

and (2) generating the test cases required for evaluating the compliance of the implementation.

In the following sections, the authors detail the different artifacts of the framework.

A Risk-Based Requirement Management Process

Regulatory compliance is an important issue to be considered all along the lifecycle of any information system. It is important to identify the applicable legal requirements early in order to select the appropriate organisational and technical solutions and ensure an accurate traceability between the requirements and the decision made on how to address them.

Figure 8 presents a regulatory compliance process to be considered for the E-CITY system. It is driven by a risk assessment and composed of the following activities:

- **Legal Requirements Elicitation**: The business and functional requirements for the system-to-be are analyzed in order to identify the applicable laws and regulations and derive system specific law requirements. In the context of the E-CITY system, the authors focus on the privacy and security.

Figure 8. A risk-based requirement management process

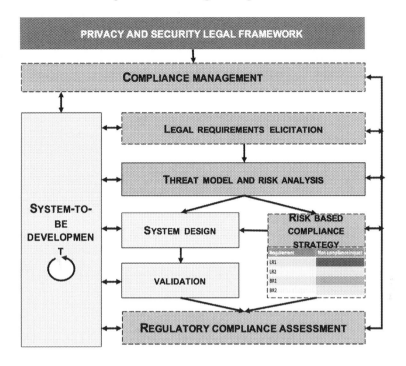

- **Compliance Impact Factor (CIF):** It is assigned to each requirement according to the impact of its violation on the E-CITY system and the municipality.

Example 1: Consider the two requirements LR1 and LR5 and suppose that the privacy policy of the E-CITY system waves any limitation on the duration of the personal data storage. Therefore, the impact of the non-compliance with LR5 is smaller than the impact of non-compliance with LR1.

→ the authors attribute the impact factors according to the previous example $CIF_1=10$ and $CIF_5=0$

- **Risk-Based Compliance Strategy:** The requirements are classified according to their CIF in 3 categories that reflect a priority level associated with the requirements. In our context, this means that in cases of incompatibility or conflict, the preference is given to the satisfaction of the requirement with the higher level of priority. In the case of conflicting requirements from the same priority level, the legal requirements are given priority over other kinds of requirements.

The security engineer defines the strategy of how to address them and to assess the implementation of the defined strategy. This information is added to the requirements' management registry.

Example 2: Consider the following examples for managing the E-CITY system's compliance with some data protection requirements.

Ultimately, the classification and the strategy should be approved by the assets' owners or the CISO (Chief Information Security Officer).

- **Regulatory Compliance Assessment:** The compliance assessment is carried out at the end of the validation phase through:

    ◦ Emergent behaviors of the system that are defined as test cases exposing behaviors that were not defined in the analysis and architecture phases. They are analyzed in order to assess any vulnerability in the architecture designed and correct it as required. A secure system is a predictable system by design that guarantees that failures' modes end up into FAIL_ SECURE states. Moreover, what the authors might discover as emergent behaviors might be caused by a design error, incomplete specification or a maliciously added behavior to the system-to-be model.

    ◦ The generated test cases are executed in the validation phase of the implemented system and the results of the executions are analyzed through the compliance satisfaction function against the initially defined risk appetite of the organization. The security engineer should define a strategy for evaluating the compliance with the 10 legal requirements for security and privacy.

        ▪ **The Compliance Satisfaction Function (CSF):** $\dfrac{\sum_{i=1}^{n} CIFi * Ci}{\sum_{i=1}^{n} CIFi}$

        x 100 where C_i is a Boolean that expresses the compliance status for the requirement i and CFI_i represents the compliance impact factor of i.

        ▪ The organization also defines the compliance threshold (CT) as the minimum level of compliance acceptable for it. CT reflects a minimal level of assurance and a risk appetite from the organization.

Table 5. An example of privacy strategy elements for the case study.

Legal Requirements	How to Comply?	How to Assess the Implementation?
LR1	In order to ensure the lawful processing requirement, some components should be in charge of satisfying it (e.g. collecting the consent before the data). The concerned components will have: ECITY_properties::requirements=LR1	When all the functional test cases covering the concerned components are successful and all the malicious test cases involving them are unsuccessful then the authors consider the E-CITY compliant.
LR6	In order to ensure data security, the authors need to ensure availability, integrity and confidentiality of the personal data in all situations. This requirement is associated with any test case involving personal data. All the data components modeling personal data will have ECITY_properties::requirements=LR6	When all the functional test cases covering the personal data components are successful and all the malicious test cases involving them are unsuccessful then the authors consider the E-CITY compliant. A perfectly secure system is an impossible goal to achieve; therefore, the compliance is evaluated within the scope of the threat model and functional requirements of the system.
LR9	In order to ensure accountability, all the access to the data should be logged and: (1) there is no way to circumvent or disable the logging solution and (2) there is no way to compromise the logs. A logging component should be added and all the information flow from and to the data should go through the logging component. Both the component and the data will be associated with this requirement.	The E-CITY is considered compliant with this requirement when (1) all the test cases involving the data involve also the logging function and (2) all the functional test cases including the logging component are successful and all the malicious test cases involving the logging function are unsuccessful.
LR 10	In order to ensure compliance with the privacy by design requirement: (1) the personal data should be identified from the beginning of the development process and should be identifiable all along the development process through a property ECITY_properties::personal_data of type Boolean; (2) in the implementation of the data model a specific meta-data should distinguish the personal data from the other in order to apply the specific rules related, for example, to the principle "need to know" that supports the requirement LR1 on purpose limitation; (3) wherever the personal data is used (business processes), it should be protected from any illegitimate access. From a legal perspective there are two constraints that regulate the legitimate access of this data: (1) the role of the access requester in a given business process whose scope is included in the purpose for which the data has been collected. For example: client service agents providing support to the residents are generally allowed to access resident's data but only when they are processing a certain client request. (2) For this reason, the second constraint is about the need to know: an agent who is processing a request of a resident's R is only allowed to access the data of R related to the request and not all R's data nor other residents' data at a given moment in time. A systemic actor accessing the data is evaluated against the same principles. The security policy will include rules specific to the personal data and they will be enforcing LR10.	The E-CITY system is considered as compliant with this requirement when all the functional test cases covering the rules related to LR10 are successful and all the malicious test cases involving them are unsuccessful.

Since a perfectly secure system is impossible to achieve, the organization has to show due diligence in dealing with the security and privacy requirements.

Moreover, the regulatory compliance should be maintained throughout the system lifecycle. Accordingly, a monitoring process should be established to ensure that changes occurring in the system and its environment, including the legal framework, do not negatively impact the compliance. Otherwise, appropriate measures have to be taken in order to restore the regulatory compliance status.

SECURE-ADL: A Test-Driven Security Architecture Description Language

The authors have proposed a first version of secure-ADL in (saidane et al. 2013) as an extension to the AADL language, which allows the specification of the security relevant information needed for generating both security functional test cases and malicious test cases (Figure 2). The extension is based on concepts coming from the XACML language and from compliance and security concepts of the COMPARCH framework.

More specifically, the SECURE-ADL annex (Figure 9) integrates the specification of:

- The security policy at the architecture level and
- The traceability dependencies between requirement - threats - countermeasures.

As for the specification of security policies at the architecture level, XACML rules' structure is well suited for this purpose. In fact, a security policy consists of a set of rules determining who are legitimate subjects to access protected resources

Figure 9. Secure-ADL annex metamodel

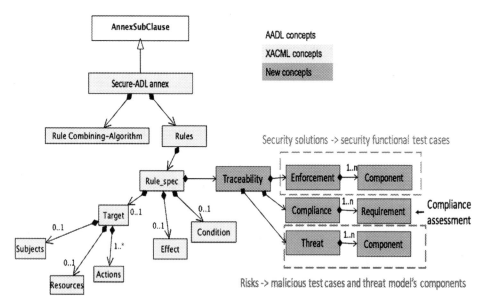

and what actions they can execute. This facilitates the specification of confidentiality, integrity and availability requirements.

Syntactically, the SECURE-ADL annex is described textually in an AADL-annex-like style, where the authors redefine the XACML concept to fit the ADDL model:

- **Attributes:** They are used to characterize subjects, resources, actions or environments. In our context, the attributes must be AADL properties derived from the system model.
- **Subjects:** A subject is an actor who makes a request to access certain protected resources. In our context, a subject could be a system, process, thread or subprogram. Therefore, the subject type refers to the component type.
- **Resources:** A resource is a data, system component or service (AADL server subprogram). This definition remains unchanged.
- **Actions:** An action is an operation executed on a resource such as access (read/write) or execution (service call). The action should be compliant with the AADL system model.
- **Rules:** A rule is a representation of a micro-security requirement. In fact, the high-level regulatory requirements such as LR_x are redefined in more specific requirements, which compose the security policy of the system to-be. It is a tuple = (target, effect, condition, traceability where target=(subjects, resources, actions), effect=allow/deny, traceability=(compliance, enforcement, threat).
  - Compliance represents the list of the high-level requirements fulfilled by the rule.
  - Enforcement represents the list of security solutions enforcing the rule.
  - Threat represents the list of the malicious components attempting to violate the rule.

The authors highlight here that the secure-ADL policy integrates information related to the requirements, the risks and enforcement mechanisms. This information is used for the compliance assessment, the test selection and system validation. In fact, the authors specify for each rule the components that enforce it and the components that might violate it. The security-functional test cases to be derived for the rule must involve all the components enforcing it. Similarly, the malicious test cases to be derived for the rule must involve all the components threatening it.

Example 3: Consider the following requirements: LR4 (Data accuracy) and LR6 (Data security).

The security policy of the E-CITY system will include many rules in order to cover these requirements in different scenarios. The following rule is a basic and fundamental one:

Confidential data can be accessed only by authorized users

This requirement can be specified in SECURE-ADL as shown in Figure 9. It is modeled as one SECURE-ADL rule whose target consists of the two kinds of subjects defined either explicitly through their credentials or with a condition over their credentials: "credentials belong to the list of authorized users". All the attributes used to define the subjects must be defined in the AADL architecture model as AADL-properties associated to the components' types referenced as subjects.

As explained earlier, validating a secure system requires the validation of its behavior against both trusted and hostile environments. According to the SECURE-ADL model, the authors consider that a security requirement has been covered by the test selection if the authors find in the final test suite one or more test cases involving all subjects, enforcement mechanisms, threats and actions referenced in the rule representing the requirement. Specifically, the authors need at least two test cases validating a normal access to the protected resources and validating the robustness of the system against the threats. Furthermore, gathering all the components in the same test case might not be feasible. In that case the authors need several test cases to cover the requirement. For example, the security requirement R_1 (Figure 10)

Figure 10. An example of a secure-ADL rule corresponding to the example 3

```
Rule ECITY_R1
      effect allow
      target
            subjects
                  S1 component_type in (client, outsider_threat)
                  Credentials: in ECITY.authorizedUsers
            end subjects
            resources
                  confdentialData1   component_type in
                  (ECITY.confidentialData)
            end resources
            actions read, write
      end target
      Traceability
            enforcement
                  ECITY.authentication, ECITY.authorization, ECITY.log
            End enforcement
            Compliance
                  LR4, LR6
            end compliance
            threat
                  outsider_threat
            end threat

      end traceability
  End ECITY_R1
```

is covered by the generation of at least 3 test cases involving the E-CITY system with: (1) the client and/or (2) the outsider threat and/or (3) the insider threat. The definition of the nonfunctional aspects of security and privacy and their compliance management is carried out at the step 3 of the COMPARCH framework represented in Figure 3.

A Simulation-Based Validation Approach

Simulation Framework for COMPARCH

At the architecture level, the system is seen as a set of interacting components globally providing a set of functional and non-functional properties. AADL allows the modelling of both the structural and the behavioral aspects of the system. The AADL behavior model[37] is defined as a Timed state-transition system that can be interpreted in terms of Timed input/output transition systems (Timed IOTS). The authors consider Timed IOTS because, from a testing perspective, the authors need to differentiate inputs and outputs between the system-to-be and the environment and, particularly, they are the only observable events in the context of black box testing.

In AADL, the differentiation between input and output events is not explicit. However, the authors can distinguish them as follows:

- **AADL Input Events:** Receiving data/events on ports (port_name?), or receiving a server subprogram call (subprogram_name ?)
- **AADL Output Events:** Sending data/events on ports (port_name!), or sending a server subprogram call (subprogram_name !)

Considering the detailed models of the components allows studying the internal mechanisms enabling and generating the observable interactions. Also, it ensures more precision in evaluating the generated traces in terms of some coverage criteria that might be structural, behavioural or security related. Therefore, the authors transform the different components' behaviour model into i network of Timed IOTS that are composed in parallel. From our architecture model-based security testing perspective, this representation is more interesting because it allows the specification of the ecosystem including trusted-parties and hostile-parties as independent autonomous systems that are interacting in the context of a closed system. .

The COMPARCH simulation framework as shown in Figure 11 is based on the UPPAAL model checker. In the following sections, the authors present the different artifacts of the simulation framework. As discussed earlier, the first step for using the COMPARCH simulation framework consists in transforming all the behavior models

Figure 11. Simulation framework for COMPARCH

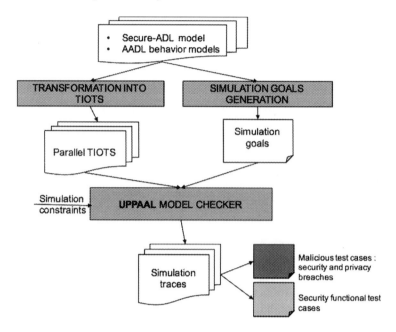

of the different actors of the system-to-be and its environment in Timed IOTSs as discussed in Saidane et al (2013). Figure 12 shows the timed IOTS corresponding to the outsider threat model of the E-CITY system presented in Figure 5.

Simulation's Goals Identification

The simulation goals have to cover at least all the threat model's states and transitions and all the enforcement mechanisms allowing their mitigation. An enforcement mechanism goal is refined in terms of states and transitions coverage-arrays or coverage rates if the authors are not targeting the coverage of specific states or transitions.

According to the structure of secure-ADL rules, the authors refine the coverage of a security requirement (i.e. a *secureAADL* rule) into coverage of the components appearing in the rule. The authors will derive 3 kinds of coverage criteria for each rule:

- **Security Functional Goals:** For every security requirement SR_i, the authors define security functional coverage goals in terms of a pair (*SR_i-Func-E-CITY* transitions-coverage-array, *SR_i-Func-citizen* transitions-coverage-array).
  - For the security requirements, the coverage goals satisfaction is evaluated against single test cases, not against the whole test suite. A single test case covers partially the security functional criteria of a

Figure 12. Timed IO automaton for the outsider threat model of E-CITY system (figure 5)

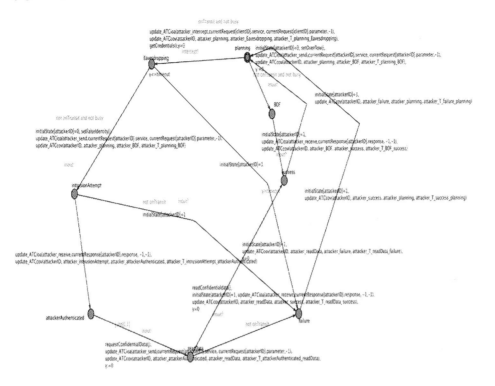

security requirement if it covers partially and simultaneously SR_i-*Func-E-CITY* transitions-coverage-array and SR_i-*Func-citizen* transitions-coverage-array. Similarly, a test case covers partially and simultaneously SR_i-*Threat-E-CITY* transitions-coverage-array a SR_i-*Threat-attacker* transitions-coverage-array.

- **Threats Coverage Goals:** For every security requirement SR_i, the authors define threats coverage goals in terms of a pair (SR_i-*Threat-E-CITY* transitions-coverage-array, SR_i-*Threat-attacker* transitions-coverage-array). Optionally, the authors might add client-coverage-array in the threats coverage goals when some attack scenarios elicited during the threat analysis phase involve both attacker and client.
  - The threat coverage is defined as a structural coverage goals of the malicious components. The structural coverage goal is evaluated against the whole test suite. The authors use transitions and states coverage arrays to specify such coverage goals. For structural coverage, the authors might define the coverage goal in terms of a coverage rate (i.e.

41

state-coverage(SUT)=90%). All coverage arrays and rates are given as input for the selection algorithm.

- **FAIL_SECURE States:** For every security requirement, the authors define a set of FAIL_SECURE states that identify acceptable degradations states that are certified compliant either because no legal requirement is violated or because the sequence of transitions leading to the states show due diligence with regards to the legal requirements.

Test Cases Generation

Exhaustive testing is unfeasible in most real cases. Consequently, selection criteria are used to limit the search domain. In our study, the authors target socio-technical systems, behavioral models which might generate infinite traces. Thus, selection criteria, such as final states and maximum test case's length, must be defined to avoid endless execution sequences during test generation and selection steps. Ultimately, the test suite will be evaluated using a coverage model. Coverage is a measure of the quality of a test suite that is based on some statistical measurements on the test suite and the test model.

In coverage-driven validation process, there are 2 activities: 1) coverage metric definition and 2) test generation (Lettnin et al. 2007, Chen et al. 2008, Cichos et al. 2011). Our test selection proposal complies with this approach. A test case generated through such process activates some test targets and reduces considerably the number of tests compared to a random generation.

The authors implement our test selection algorithm with UPAAL using the coverage criteria defined in the previous section. By construction, the test suite generated by our selection algorithm: (1) satisfies all the coverage goals (structural and security) and (2) eliminates any redundant test cases. In addition, it tries to minimize the test suite size through the acceptance condition requiring that any new test case must provide additional coverage in order to be added to the test suite. However, different selection strategies can be implemented by varying the acceptance conditions. Therefore, the evaluation of the selection algorithm will focus on metrics measuring the size of the generated test suite, computation time and scalability:

- **Test Suite Size:** The size of a test suite is defined by the number of the generated test cases. In the best case, the authors could generate the minimal test suite satisfying all the goals.
- **Computation Time:** It characterizes the cost of the test selection and generation. UPPAAL provides the computation time after each run. This metric influences the scalability capabilities of the testing system.

However, in some cases the authors might reach the maximal length of the test suites without satisfying all the goal coverage. In this case, the authors need to evaluate the generated test suite in order to decide whether to accept it as-is or to increase the maximal size. The Figure 13 shows an example of a malicious abstract test case for an eavesdropping and identity theft attack that triggers transitions from the outsider threat model represented in Figure 12.

Compliance Assessment

The generated test cases can be classified into 2 classes: (1) security functional test cases and (2) malicious test cases. Accordingly, the compliance assessment takes into account both the type of the test case and the requirements associated with the test case.

The execution of the test case can result in 3 possible outcomes: (1) pass, (2) fail or (3) interrupted.

Once all the tests have been executed, the compliance satisfaction function can be computed taking into account that any requirement that is violated in one test case is considered not satisfied.

Figure 13. An example of an abstract malicious test case by our selection algorithm

```
selectedTestCases[1].n = 3
selectedTestCases[1].IOa[0]'= client.clp!
selectedTestCases[1].IOa[1] = attacker.intercept!
selectedTestCases[1].IOa[2] = attacker.inout!
selectedTestCases[1].param[0][0] = Authentication_req
selectedTestCases[1].param[0][1] = invalid_credentials
selectedTestCases[1].param[1][0] = Authentication_req
selectedTestCases[1].param[1][1] = invalid_credentials
selectedTestCases[1].param[2][0] = Authentication_req
selectedTestCases[1].param[2][1] = invalid_credentials
```

Table 6. Test results and compliance assessment

Class of the Test Case	PASS	FAIL	Interrupted
Security functional	System satisfies requirements	System does not satisfy requirements	Emergent behavior to be analyzed manually
Malicious	System does not satisfy requirements	System satisfies requirements	

CONCLUSION

In this chapter, the authors present the COMPARCH framework as a compliance and security extension for model driven engineering development processes. The purpose is to guarantee a continuous assessment of the regulatory compliance of the system-to-be at the stage of both the design and the implementation. It consists of: (1) a risk-based requirement management process, (2) a test-driven security and privacy modeling framework and (3) a simulation-based validation approach. The satisfaction of the regulatory compliance is evaluated through the analysis of the simulation traces. For this research, the authors use the E-City system as a case study to show the suitability of the approach for highly regulated software systems with an important need to ensure regulatory compliance and due diligence when dealing with citizen's personal data. Moreover, the chapter provides an overview of the EU legal framework and requirements for privacy and security as a starting point for the compliance driven development process.

REFERENCES

Apvrille, L., & Roudier, Y. (2014). Towards the model-driven engineering of secure yet safe embedded systems. *1st International Workshop on Graphical Models for Security*. 10.4204/EPTCS.148.2

Armando, A., Carbone, R., Compagna, L., Li, K., & Pellegrino, G. (2010). Model-Checking Driven Security Testing of Web-Based Applications. In *Proceedings of the 2010 Third International Conference on Software Testing, Verification, and Validation Workshops, ICSTW'10*. IEEE Computer Society Press. 10.1109/ICSTW.2010.54

Arzapalo, D., Gallon, L., & Aniorte, P. (2013). *MoDELO: a MOdel-Driven sEcurity poLicy approach based on Orbac. In 8ème conférence sur la Sécurité des Architectures Réseaux et des Systèmes d'Information*. Mont de Marsan.

Bertolino, A., Inverardi, P., & Muccini, H. (2001). An Explorative Journey from Architectural Tests Definition down to Code Tests Execution. In *Software Engineering, 23rd International Conference on Software Engineering (ICSE'01)*. IEEE Computer Society Press.

Brun, M., Delatour, J., & Trinquet, Y. (2008). Code Generation from AADL to a Real-Time Operating System: An Experimentation Feedback on the Use of Model Transformation. In *Proceedings of the 13th IEEE International Conference on on Engineering of Complex Computer Systems (ICECCS '08)*. IEEE Computer Society.

Bucchiarone, Muccini, & Pelliccione. (2007). Architecting Fault-tolerant Component-based Systems: From requirements to testing. In *Electronic Notes in Theoretical Computer Science*. Elsevier.

Castanet, R., & Rouillard, R. (2002). Generate Certified Test Cases by Combining Theorem Proving and Reachability Analysis. *Proceedings of the IFIP 14th International Conference on Testing Communicating Systems*. 10.1007/978-0-387-35497-2_19

Chen, M., Mishra, P., & Kalita, D. (2008). Coverage-driven automatic test generation for uml activity diagrams. In *Proceedings of the 18th ACM Great Lakes symposium on VLSI (GLSVLSI '08)*. ACM 10.1145/1366110.1366145

Cichos, O., Lochau, & Schürr. (2011). Model-based coverage-driven test suite generation for software product lines. *Proceedings of the 14th international conference on Model driven engineering languages and systems (MODELS'11)*.

Elahi, G., & Yu, E. (2007). *A goal-oriented approach for modeling and analyzing security trade-offs*. International Conference on Conceptual Modeling, Auckland, New Zealand. 10.1007/978-3-540-75563-0_26

Franca, R. B., Bodeveix, J., Filali, M., Rolland, J., Chemouil, D., & Thomas, D. (2007). The AADL behaviour annex -- experiments and roadmap. In *Proceedings of the 12th IEEE international Conference on Engineering Complex Computer Systems*. IEEE Computer Society.

Górski, J., Rydzak, F., Breistrand, L., Sveen, F., Qian, Y., & Gonzalez, J. (2006). *Exploring Resilience Towards Risks in eOperations in the Oil and Gas Industry*. Computer Safety, Reliability, and Security. LNCS.

Hessel, L., & Mikucionis, N. Pettersson, & Skou. (2008). Testing real-time systems using UPPAAL. In Lecture Notes In Computer Science: Vol. 4949. Springer-Verlag.

Jin, Z. (2000). *A Software Architecture-based Testing Technique* (PhD thesis). George Mason University.

Jin, Z., & Offutt, J. (2001). Deriving Tests From Software Architectures. In *Proceedings of the 12th International Symposium on Software Reliability Engineering (ISSRE '01)*. IEEE Computer Society.

Jurjens, J. (2005). *Secure Systems Development with UML*. Springer-Verlag.

Jurjens, J. (2008). *Model-based Security Testing Using UMLsec. Electronic Notes in Theoretical Computer Science*. Springer.

Kaynar, D. K., Lynch, N., Segala, R., & Vaandrager, F. (2003). Timed I/O Automata: A Mathematical Framework for Modeling and Analyzing Real-Time Systems. In *Proceedings of the 24th IEEE International Real-Time Systems Symposium (RTSS '03)*. IEEE Computer Society. 10.1109/REAL.2003.1253264

Koo & Mishra. (2009). Functional test generation using design and property decomposition techniques. *ACM Trans. Embed. Comput. Syst.*

Lettnin, W., Braun, G., & Ruf, K., & Rosenstiel. (2007). Coverage Driven Verification applied to Embedded Software. In *Proceedings of the IEEE Computer Society Annual Symposium on VLSI (ISVLSI '07)*. IEEE Computer Society.

Lim, K., Lynch, & Mitra. (2005). Translating timed i/o automata specifications for theorem proving in PVS. *Proceedings of the Third international conference on Formal Modeling and Analysis of Timed Systems (FORMATS'05)*.

Lodderstedt, T., Basin, D., & Doser, J. (2002). SecureUML: A UML Based Modeling Language for Model-Driven Security. *International Conference Unified Modeling Language, Model Engineering, Languages Concepts and Tools*. 10.1007/3-540-45800-X_33

Lynch, N., & Tuttle, M. R. (1989). An Introduction to Input/Output Automata. C. W. I. Quarterly, 2(3).

MAFTIA Consortium. (2003). Conceptual Model and Architecture of MAFTIA (Malicious- and Accidental-Fault Tolerance for Internet Applications), Public Deliverable, EU MAFTIA Project. Retrieved from http://spiderman-2.laas.fr/TSF/cabernet/maftia/deliverables/D21.pdf

Marquis, S., Dean, T. R., & Knight, S. (2005). SCL: a language for security testing of network applications. *Proceedings of the 2005 conference of the Centre for Advanced Studies on Collaborative research (CASCON '05)*.

Mouelhi, T., Fleurey, F., Baudry, B., & Traon, Y. (2008). A Model-Based Framework for Security Policy Specification, Deployment and Testing. *Proceedings of the 11th international conference on Model Driven Engineering Languages and Systems (MoDELS '08)*. 10.1007/978-3-540-87875-9_38

Mouratidis & Giorgini. (2007). *Security Attack Testing (SAT)-testing the security of information systems at design time. Information Systems Journal*.

Muccini, H. (2002). *Software Architecture for Testing, Coordination and Views Model Checking* (PhD Thesis). University La Sapienza, Rome, Italy.

Petrenko, Y., & Huo. (2003). Testing transition systems with input and output testers. In *Proceedings of the 15th IFIP international conference on Testing of communicating systems (TestCom'03)*. Springer-Verlag.

Pretschner, A., Holling, D., Eschbach, R., & Gemmar, M. (2013). A Generic Fault Model for Quality Assurance. In A. Moreira, B. Schätz, J. Gray, A. Vallecillo, & P. Clarke (Eds.), Lecture Notes in Computer Science: Vol. 8107. *Model-Driven Engineering Languages and Systems. MODELS 2013*. Berlin: Springer. doi:10.1007/978-3-642-41533-3_6

Pretschner, A., Mouelhi, T., & Le Traon, Y. (2008), Model-Based Tests for Access Control Policies. In *Proceedings of the 2008 International Conference on Software Testing, Verification, and Validation (ICST '08)*. IEEE Computer Society Press 10.1109/ICST.2008.44

Raihan & Uddin. (2009). Towards Model-Based Automatic Testing of Attack Scenarios. *Proceedings of the 28th International Conference on Computer Safety, Reliability, and Security (SAFECOMP '09)*.

Ren, J. (2006). *A Connector-Centric Approach to Architectural Access Control* (PhD thesis). University of California, Irvine, CA.

Richardson, D. J., & Wolf, A. L. (1996). Software testing at the architectural level. *Joint proceedings of the second international software architecture workshop (ISAW-2) and international workshop on multiple perspectives in software development (Viewpoints '96) on SIGSOFT '96 workshops (ISAW '96)*. 10.1145/243327.243605

Ries, B. (2009). *SESAME - A Model-driven Process for the Test Selection of Small-size Safety-related Embedded Software* (PhD thesis). Laboratory for Advanced Software Systems, University of Luxembourg.

Robson. (2004). *TIOA and UPPAAL* (Master's thesis). MIT. Retrieved from http://dspace.mit.edu/bitstream/handle/1721.1/17979/57188153.pdf?sequence=1

Saidane & Guelfi. (2011). Towards improving security testability of AADL architecture models. In *Proceedings of the International Conference on Network and System Security*. IEEE.

Saidane & Guelfi. (2012). SETER: towards architecture model-based security engineering. International Journal of Secure Software Engineering.

Saidane & Guelfi. (2013). Towards test-driven and architecture model-based security and resilience engineering. In Designing, Engineering, and Analyzing Reliable and Efficient Software. IGI Global.

Schulz, S., Honkola, J., & Huima, A. (2007). Towards Model-Based Testing with Architecture Models. *Proceedings of the 14th Annual IEEE International Conference and Workshops on the Engineering of Computer-Based Systems (ECBS '07).* 10.1109/ECBS.2007.73

Subramaniam, M., Xiao, L., Guo, B., & Pap, Z. (2009). An Approach for Test Selection for EFSMs Using a Theorem Prover. *Proceedings of the 21st IFIP WG 6.1 International Conference on Testing of Software and Communication Systems and 9th International FATES Workshop (TESTCOM '09/FATES '09).* 10.1007/978-3-642-05031-2_10

von Oheimb & Lotz. (2002). Formal Security Analysis with Interacting State Machines. In *Proceedings of the 7th European Symposium on Research in Computer Security (ESORICS '02).* Springer-Verlag.

Wang, W., & Ji. (2009). An Automatic Generation Method of Executable Test Case Using Model-Driven Architecture. In *Proceedings of the 2009 Fourth International Conference on Innovative Computing, Information and Control (ICICIC '09).* IEEE Computer Society.

Xiong, P., Stepien, B., & Peyton, L. (2009). *Model-Based Penetration Test Framework for Web Applications Using TTCN-3. E-Technologies: Innovation in an Open World.* Springer.

Yang, J., Wang, & Xia. (2009). A Task-Deployment Model for the Simulation of Computer Network Attack and Defense Exercises. In *Proceedings of the 2009 First IEEE International Conference on Information Science and Engineering (ICISE '09).* IEEE Computer Society.

Zhou, C., & Kumar, R. (2009). Modeling Simulink Diagrams Using Input/Output Extended Finite Automata. In *Proceedings of the 2009 33rd Annual IEEE International Computer Software and Applications Conference* (vol. 2). IEEE. 10.1109/COMPSAC.2009.176

ENDNOTES

[1]   AADL: Architecture Analysis and Description language www.aadl.info

[2]   Derived from the fault model proposed by MAFTIA project: http://research.cs.ncl.ac.uk/cabernet/www.laas.research.ec.org/maftia/

[3]   ADL: Architecture Description Language.

[4]   Error! Hyperlink reference not valid.

[5]   Regulation (EU) 2016/679 of the European Parliament and of the Council of 27 April 2016 on the protection of natural persons with regard to the processing of personal data and on the free movement of such data, and repealing Directive 95/46/EC (General Data Protection Regulation), L 119/1, 4.5.2016 (GDPR).

[6]   GDPR, art. 1(2).

[7]   GDPR, art. 4(1).

[8]   GDPR, art. 4(2).

[9]   GDPR, art. 5(1)(a).

[10]   GDPR, art. 6(1).

[11]   Article 29 Data Protection Working Party, Opinion 15/2011 on the Definition of Consent, Doc. 01197/11/EN, WP187 (13 July 2011) at 7.

[12]   GDRP, art. 5(1)(b). See also Article 29 Data Protection Working Party, Opinion 03/2013 on Purpose Limitation, Doc. 00569/13/EN, WP 203 (2 April 2013) at 39.

[13]   GDRP, art. 5(1)(b).

[14]   GDRP, arts. 5(1)(c) & 25. See also Article 29 Data Protection Working Party, Opinion 01/2014 on the Application of Necessity and Proportionality Concepts and Data Protection within the Law Enforcement Sector, Doc. 536/14/EN, WP 211 (27 February 2014) at 16.

[15]   GDRP, arts. 5(1)(e) &25.

[16]   Article 29 Data Protection Working Party, Opinion 01/2014 on the Application of Necessity and Proportionality Concepts and Data Protection within the Law Enforcement Sector, Doc. 536/14/EN, WP 211 (27 February 2014) at 16.

[17]   GDPR, art. 5(1)(d).

[18]   GDPR, art. 5(1)(d).

[19]   GDPR, art. 5(1)(f).

[20]   GDPR, art. 5(1)(f).

[21]   GDPR, art. 32(1)

[22]   GDPR, art. 32(1)

[23]   GDPR, art. 32(1).

[24]   GDPR, art. 32(1).

[25]   GDPR, art. 32(4).

[26]   GDPR, art. 12; GDPR, arts. 12 & 13(1). See also "Berlin Privacy Notices Memorandum" in The Centre for Information Policy Leadership, Multi-Layered Notices Explained: A White Paper, a submission by the United States, First Data Privacy Subgroup Meeting: Asia-Pacific Economic Cooperation APEC (Seoul, Korea 23-24 February 2005), Appendix B.

[27]   GDPR, art. GDPR, arts. 12 &13(2).

[28]   Opinion 15/2011 on the Definition of Consent, supra note 54 at 9.

[29]   See, e.g. GDPR, arts. 7(3), 15-18, 21, & 31.

[30]   GDPR, art. 5(2). See also Article 29 Data Protection Working Party, Opinion 3/2010 on the Principle of Accountability, Doc. 00062/10/EN (13 July 2010) at 5&9; Article 29 Data Protection Working Party, The Future of Privacy: Joint Contribution to the Consultation of the European Commission on the Legal Framework for the Fundamental right to Protection of Personal Data, Doc. 02356/09/EN, WP 168 (1 December 2009) at 20.

[31]   GDPR, art. 35.

[32]   GDPR, art. 36.

[33]   GDPR, art 58.

[34]   GDPR, art. 39.

[35]   GDPR, art. 25(1).

[36]   For a discussion of the privacy sby design approach and its benefits, see Inga Kroener and David Wright, "A Strategy for Operationalizing Privacy by Design" (2014) 30 The Information Society 355; Peter Schaar, "Privacy by Design" (2010) 3 Identity in the Information Society 267; Ann Cavoukian, "Privacy by Design: The Definitive Workshop: A foreword" (2010) 3 Identity in the Information Society 247;Dirk van Rooy & Jacques Bus, "Trust and Privacy in the Future Internet—a Research Perspective" (2010) 3 Identity in the Information Society 397 at 398; Ann Cavoukian, Scott Taylor & Martin E. Abrams, "Privacy by Design: Essential for Organizational Accountability and Strong Business Practices" (2010) 33 Identity in the Information Society 405.

[37]   For more information please see: Error! Hyperlink reference not valid.

Chapter 3
Information-Centric Networking, E-Government, and Security

Balkis Hamdane
Carthage University, Tunisia & University of Tunis – El Manar, Tunisia

Sihem Guemara El Fatmi
Carthage University, Tunisia

ABSTRACT

The internet was initially proposed to interconnect a few trusted hosts. However, its continued success has caused many security problems. New internet services, such as e-government, must address these security issues. A host-centric security model tied to information location and based on various partial corrections has been proposed. However, this model hasn't brought radical solutions and has largely contributed to architecture ossification. In this context, the idea of a clean slate approach, satisfying the new requirements and without any compatibility obligation, has emerged. The information-centric networking approach represents one of these architectures. Its main idea is to consider the named information as the central element rather than the IP addresses. To ensure security requirements, it adopts an information-centric security. This chapter is a survey on security in the ICN, satisfying the internet security requirements in general and particularly e-government services.

DOI: 10.4018/978-1-5225-5984-9.ch003

INTRODUCTION

The e-government concept refers to the use of Information and Communications Technologies (ICT) to implement public services. It aims to facilitate access to government information and services to citizens, businesses and government agencies. When it is set up correctly, it contributes greatly in improving the quality of service. However, it must ensure several challenges. Security represents one of the most important challenges (Sulaiman, Othman, Othman, Rahim, & Pee, 2015; Gorantla, Gangishetti, & Saxena, 2005). This is due to the use of the Internet as a medium of providing e-government services. Indeed, at its design, the Internet focused on the interconnection of a few trusted remote hosts. However, its continued success has caused many security issues and more sophisticated attacks (Lagutin, 2010). Several security protocols have emerged (Dierks, 2008; Frankel & Krishnan, 2011; Weiler & Blacka, 2013). However, in addition to the generated performance problems, each protocol aims to secure a particular protocol and their composition doesn't necessarily guarantee a secure system (Lagutin, 2010). On the other hand, the security model links the security of content to (1) the security of the host storing it and (2) the security of the communication channel used to retrieve it (Yaqub, 2016) (Peltier and Simon, 2012). But a communication channel is not permanent. A user who stores content, previously retrieved from the original source, can't be sure that this content hasn't been modified (by malicious software for example). In addition, a second user interested in the same content can't get it from the first one, although he is geographically closer. He must recover it from the original source, by establishing a secure channel.

In this context, the idea of a revolutionary and a clean slate approach, proposing an alternative architecture for the Internet, was born (Lagutin, 2010). The Information Centric Networking (ICN) approach (Lagutin, 2010; Bari, Rahman Chowdhury, Ahmed, Boutaba, & Mathieu 2012; Weiler & Blacka, 2013; Yaqub, 2016), represents one of the most emerging architecture. This approach considers the named content as the central element rather than the IP addresses, which identify the hosts in the current networks. It also replaces the traditional security model by a content-oriented one. This model is based on the integration of security mechanisms in the content itself as well as the use of an adequate naming system. Thus, citizens can ensure the security of retrieved content, regardless of its source and at any time (Smetters & Jacobson, 2009).

This chapter aims first to present the basic concepts of the ICN approach in general and more particularly those related the security aspect. It also aims to explain how the ICN meets the security requirements in e-government services (Piro et al., 2014). That's why, a use case for an e-government service over ICN is provided. It details the management of a start-up event of a new business in a foreign country and it proves the important role of the use of NDN as a main medium, on security.

The remainder of this chapter is structured as follows: section II introduces the basic concepts of ICN. It then presents the architectures the most emerging and the most representative of the ICN aspects. These architectures are NDN and NetInf. They share the basic concepts of the ICN approach but differ mainly in the adopted naming aspect, having a significant, but different impact on other aspects. Section III analyzes security in ICN. Indeed, the security services are defined. The security in NDN and NetInf are then analyzed to illustrate the impact of the naming system adopted by each architecture on security. The requirements of the ICN naming system are concluded and a naming system adaptation for both architectures, satisfying the deducted requirements is presented. Section IV analyzes the security in e-government over NDN, by presenting a use case. Finally, section V concludes the chapter.

THE INFORMATION CENTRIC NETWORKING APPROACH

The Internet was initially designed more than forty years ago. Its purpose was to interconnect a few remote and trusted hosts, each characterized by an IP address. However, with its rapid growth, its main use has radically changed. This new context has motivated the development of the Information Centric Networking (ICN) approach, with the aim of natively supporting the new use of the Internet. This approach has no compatibility obligations with the current Internet architecture. Its main idea is to consider the named content as the central element rather than the IP addresses.

To retrieve content in ICN, a requester expresses interest in this content by specifying its name. The network is responsible for routing the request to the best source storing a copy and then for returning this content to the requester through the reverse path.

Terminology and Basic Concepts in the ICN Approach

The Information Centric Networking approach introduces a radical change in the Internet's communication model. It is based on new concepts, defined according to a specific terminology.

Terminology in the ICN Approach

The architecture and operations in ICN networks are described using a number of terms. This paragraph is dedicated to the definition of these terms that will be used throughout this chapter (Vasilakos et al., 2015).

- **Content:** This is the addressable data unit in an ICN network. It is composed of a name identifying it, data and security information called metadata. Content is independent of its location and can be of any type such as web applications, static or dynamic content, real-time applications or interactive multimedia communications. It can correspond to a part (a segment) of data of large size.
- **An Entity:** It refers to any element of the network, including users, user groups and routers.
- **A Requester:** This is an entity that sends a request for content.
- **A Producer:** This is the entity responsible for informing the network of its possession of content by publishing its name on the network, so that a request for that content can be forwarded to it. The producer is mostly the creator or the owner of the content, but in some cases it may be any other entity that stores permanently the content.
- **A Network Node:** This is any router or host that can make routing and caching decisions.
- **A Content Source:** This is a network node storing the content.

Basic Concepts in the ICN Approach

The ICN approach is based on a common set of concepts that can be categorized as follows: the naming, the name resolution and the routing, the caching, the communication model and the security.

The Naming

Content names play an essential role in the ICN approach. They are used to identify unambiguously the associated content. They are also used in all network operations such as the announcement, the request and the distribution of content.

There are mainly two naming approaches ((Bari et al., 2012; Ghodsi, Koponen, Rajahalme, Sarolahti, & Shenker, 2011a). The first one proposes hierarchical and human-readable names (Burke et al., 2012). These names consist of several components arranged in a hierarchical manner. Each component may reflect information related to the nature of the content itself.

The second naming approach proposes self-certifying and flat names (Dannewitz, 2013). In this approach, cryptographic mechanisms are included in the names and ensure data integrity without using a trusted third party.

The Caching

Caching allows content temporary storage in a particular location for later use. In the ICN approach, it is natively supported by the network nodes. This caching property improves network performance by retrieving content from a node that is geographically closer to the requester and that holds a copy.

There are two approaches to caching: on-path and off-path. On-path caching allows content retrieval from only the nodes on the transmission path. However, off-path caching allows this retrieval from of any node storing a copy of the content (Weiler & Blacka, 2013; Abdullahi, Arif, & Hassan 2015).

The Name Resolution and the Routing

Name-based routing is an important concept in the ICN approach. It is based on the name initially indicated by the requester and it consists of two phases: (1) the request routing to a node storing a copy and (2) the routing of the content to its requestor.

There are mainly two routing approaches. The first one uses a Name Resolution System (NRS) that stores the links between the names and the associated content locators (Bari et al. (2012). This approach consists of three phases: the first one corresponds to the routing of the content request to the responsible NRS that makes the necessary resolution. The second phase is related to the routing of the content request to the specified node locator. The third phase corresponds the routing of the requested content from the source to the requester. All of these phases can use different routing algorithms (Kutscher et al., 2016).

The second approach uses name-based routing (Wang, Hoque, Yi, Alyyan, & Zhang, 2012; Burke et al., 2012). No name resolution is performed and the request is routed directly from the requestor to one or more content sources based on the name. Once the source receives the request, the desired content is routed to the requester, which is equivalent to the third phase in the first approach (Bari et al., 2012).

The Communication Model

The communication model in the ICN approach is based on the request and the distribution of content (Ghodsi et al., 2011b). In this model, as illustrated in Figure 1, a producer announces to the network the availability of named content, without any prior knowledge of the potential requesters (step 1 in Figure 1). A requester can then declare his interest in this content by specifying its name, without the knowledge of the corresponding producer (step 2). To satisfy this request, the network uses the specified name of content to search for it. It finally launches a distribution path to the requester (step 3). On-path network nodes store a copy in their caches to respond

Figure 1. Communication model in the ICN approach

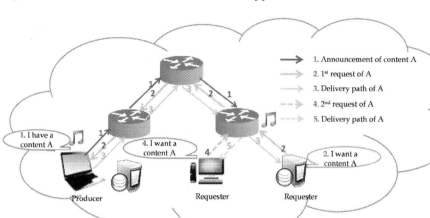

to future requests. A second request for the same content A (step 4) can then be satisfied from the nearest node having a copy of the content in its cache (step 5).

Table 1 summarizes the basic concepts of the ICN previously presented and compares them to those of the current Internet (AbdAllah et al., 2015).

Network of Information: NetInf

Network of Information (NetInf) represents an European ICN architecture (Dannewitz et al., 2013). It was proposed in 2008 as part of 4WARD which is one of the Seventh projects Framework Program (FP7) of the Internet of the future. From 2010 to 2013, NetInf evolved as part of another FP7 project called Scalable & Adaptive Internet Solutions (SAIL) and produced an open source prototype called OpenNetInf.

Table 1. Comparison between the ICN and the current Internet

Concept	*Current Internet*	ICN
Naming	Related to the host location	Content-related, independent of location
Caching	In specific servers	In any network node
Routing	Between hosts using IP addresses	Between a requester and any network node holding a content copy, based on its content name

The Naming

In NetInf, contents are called Named Data Objects (NDO) (Dannewitz et al., 2013). As illustrated in Figure 2, each NDO is composed by a unique name *ID*, data, and metadata. These metadata contain attributes describing the contents as well as information necessary for the security functions.

The name is flat without any hierarchical structure (Dannewitz et al., 2013). It consists of two parts: *P* and *L*. *P* represents the hash of a public key belonging to the content producer. *L* is a label that identifies the NDO and it is chosen by that producer. It is equal to the hash of the data when they are static (Bari et al., 2012).

The Name Resolution and the Routing

The communication model in NetInf is essentially based on three pairs of messages: *GET / GET-RESP, PUBLISH / PUBLISH-RESP and SEARCH / REARCH-RESP* (Kauffmann et al., 2013; Kutscher et al., 2012). The *GET* message represents a request for content, identified by a unique name ID. A *GET-RESP* message is sent as a response to this request by a Network Node (NN), if the latter has in its cache the requested content, characterized by the same ID. The *PUBLISH* message primarily allows a producer to announce the availability of an NDO to routers or to the Name Resolution System (NRS). It can also contain the corresponding NDO, which permits the storage a copy of this NDO and associated metadata in the network. The *PUBLISH-RESP* message is sent as a response to the *PUBLISH* message to acknowledge its reception (Dannewitz, 2013). The *SEARCH* message allows a requester to send a search query for content containing search keywords. This requester receives as a response, a *SEARCH-RESP* message. This message contains a list of names of NDOs that can match his request as well as metadata associated with each name, facilitating the choice of a name among those received (Sunde, 2013).

Figure 2. NDO structure in NetInf

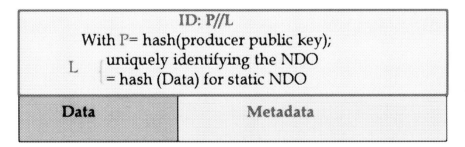

To retrieve content, NetInf supports 3 approaches. The first one is based on names' resolution. The second one uses a name-based routing. The third one is hybrid and combines both approaches (Dannewitz et al., 2013).

The Caching

NetInf supports on-path and off-path caching. For on-path caching, a network node can store previously requested content (the node corresponds to a user) or transmitted (the node corresponds to a router). This node can in turn respond to future requests for this content (Dannewitz et al., 2013).

For off-path caching, an additional step to store copies of the content in the NRS is required. Thus, when the NRS receives a request for content stored in an off-path cache, it returns the cache locator that will be used to route this request.

Named Data Networking: NDN

Content Centric Networking (CCN) (Jacobson et al., 2009) is one of the first ICN architectures. It was originally proposed in 2006 at the Xerox Palo Alto PARC Research Center, by Van Jacobson. Since then, it has grown and produced an open source prototype called CCNx. In September 2010, CCN was selected from the four projects of the National Science Foundation for Future Internet Architecture. In this new context, CCN is officially known as Named Data Networking (NDN).

The Naming

The names in NDN have a hierarchical structure. They are mainly formed by three parties. Each one has one or more legible component, delimited by the character '/'. The first part of the name provides global routing information. The second part contains organizational routing information and the last part gives information about the version and the segment number. Segmentation is used when the data are large; it allows splitting these data in several parts. Each of these parts is identified by a segment number and can be retrieved individually. The notion of version permits the modification of a previously published content and its publication under a new name. Indeed, once published, the content can't be modified and re-published with the same name since it can already be dispersed in several caches (Yu et al., 2014).

The Name Resolution and the Routing

NDN is based on 2 packet types: Interest and Data (Zhang et al., 2014). The Interest packet represents a request for content and the Data packet represents the response to the first one (see Figure 3).

To declare his interest in content, a requester broadcasts the associated Interest packet on all available interfaces. As shown in Figure 3, this packet consists mainly of the desired content name and selectors. This last field contains information on the content to be recovered, such as the producer public key hash. The Interest packet also contains a nonce value, preventing the loop formation, as well as information called Guiders, such as the packet lifetime.

The Data packet consists of a name and metadata. These metadata include information about the content (*MetaInfo*), such as its type that can be *ENC* when the content is encrypted or *key* when the content packet matches a public key. This packet also contains the data (*Content*) as well as a signature of all the packet fields. In addition, it includes information about this signature, such as the type of the signature or the locator of the public key (*KeyLocator*), necessary for its verification.

A Data packet satisfies an Interest if the names of these two packets are equal. This Data packet can be sent by any network node that has intercepted the Interest packet and stores the requested data.

All Interest packets are forwarded hop by hop in routers. Each router maintains three main data structures: the Forwarding Information Base (FIB), the Content Store (CS) buffer, and the Pending Interest Table (PIT) (Jacobson et al., 2009). The FIB is used to transmit Interest packets to the producers of the requested content. It contains the prefixes of the content names and the next interfaces to the destination. The Content Store is similar to the buffer of an IP router, but it also allows to cache

Figure 3. Interest and Data packets in NDN

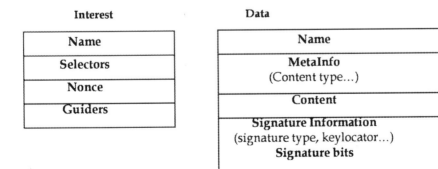

data for as long as possible for later reuse. The PIT keeps track of the Interests transmitted upstream to the source of the content. Each of their lines contains the name of a requested content and the list of interfaces that sent the corresponding Interest packet.

As shown in Figure 4, when an Interest packet arrives at a router (step 1), the search for the longest match between its name and the entries of these three data structures is made (step 2). If the Content Store stores a Data packet with the same name as the Interest packet, this Data packet will be sent through the interface that received the Interest. The latter will then be eliminated. If there is no exact match between the CS entries and the name, the PIT is consulted (step 3). If it contains an exact match between one of its entries and the name in the Interest packet, the source interface of the packet is added to the list of interfaces with the same Interest. The Interest packet will then be discarded. If the CS and the PIT don't provide any information, the FIB is consulted (step 4). If a match between one of its entries and the Interest name prefix is found, this packet is transmitted to the interfaces indicated in the FIB related to this prefix (step 5). A new entry is also added to the PIT containing the Interest packet (step 6). This entry may be deleted after the expiration of the Interest lifetime. If no match is found, the Interest packet is discarded.

Once an Interest packet arrives at a network node holding a copy of the desired content, the corresponding Data packet is sent to the requester through the reverse path. Indeed, when a data packet is received (step 7), a search for its name is performed in the PIT. If a match is found, this Data packet is sent to all requesting interfaces

Figure 4. Interest and Data packets Transmission in NDN

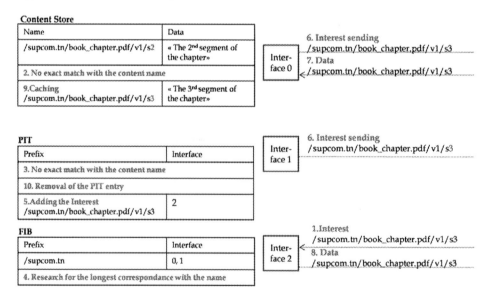

(step 8). This packet is also stored in the CS (step 9) and the entry corresponding to its name is removed from the PIT (step 10).

The routing of Interest packets can be done in a similar way as the IP routing, based on classical routing algorithms. However, instead of announcing IP prefixes, an NDN router advertises the names' prefixes that it can send.

The Caching and Permanent Storage

NDN natively supports on-path caching. Each router stores in its content store (CS) all data packets that it routes to their final destinations. This permits to respond to future requests.

To ensure content availability, NDN implements a new communication element called *repo*, ensuring the permanent storage of any type of NDN data (Afanasyev 2013).

SECURITY IN ICN

To improve performance in the ICN approach, the in-network caching is natively supported. However, with this property, security can no longer be tied to a particular location and it cannot be ensured by using traditional mechanisms. Indeed, mechanisms incorporated into the content and independent of its location must be used. A new content-oriented security model is needed and must provide the following security services (Smetters & Jacobson, 2009; Pyhnen & Stranberg, 2011):

- **Access Control:** Access for reading, writing (production) and management of content, reserved for authorized entities.
- **Data Confidentiality:** Restriction of data reading to authorized entities.
- **Availability:** Accessibility of content published in the network for authorized entities, according to predefined performance.
- **Data Integrity:** The non-alteration of the data.
- **Name Authenticity:** The correspondence between the received data and the name indicated by the requester.
- **Producer Identification and Authentication:** Knowledge and validation of the producer identity.
- **Relevance:** Satisfaction of the expressed demand by the received content.

To ensure access control and confidentiality, sensitive data can be encrypted and the keys used in their encryption and decryption must be known only by authorized entities. On the other hand, availability is reinforced by the communication model adopted in the ICN approach. Indeed, this model prevents the majority of denial of service attacks of the current Internet; the recovery of content must be preceded by a request, which prevents the sending of unsolicited content. In addition, hosts aren't directly addressable, which prevents the targeting of a particular host (AbdAllah et al., 2015).

Other security services are essentially based on the integration of cryptographic into the content and on an adequate naming system (Dannewitz et al., 2010).

The Impact of Naming on Security

Each ICN architecture relies on its own mechanisms to ensure security. These mechanisms strongly depend on the adopted naming system and the data signature (Ghodsi et al., 2011a). In the literature, there are two main naming approaches in the ICN (Bari et al., 2012). The first one is based on human-readable and hierarchical names and it has been proposed in NDN. The second one uses self-certifying and flat names and has been proposed in several architectures such as NetInf. To study the impact of each naming approach on security, an analysis of NetInf and NDN security is performed. This analysis will permit the deduction of the requirements that the naming system must satisfy to enhance security.

Security in NetInf

In NetInf, an NDO is composed (1) of a name having the form P: L, (2) data and (3) metadata. This metadata includes the data signature and the public key necessary for its verification.

To ensure the received data integrity, a requester verifies the signature using the public key embedded in the metadata. To trust this key K_{pub}, its hash is included in the name ($P = h (K_{pub})$). The signature and the link established between the name and the producer public key ensure the data integrity without any trusted third party. However, the name authenticity can't be verified. An attack can be launched as follows:

- A requester demands an NDO named *P: L*, with $P = h(K_{pub})$. If no attack is launched, he will recover the first NDO shown in Figure 5 (a).
- However, an attacker intercepts this request and has a copy of another NDO *<P: L', data1, metadata1>*, signed by the producer of the desired content, using the corresponding private key K_{priv}. This NDO corresponds to the 2nd NDO shown in Figure 5 (b).
- He forges an NDO with the same name *P: L* but the false data *data1* and the metadata *metadata1* previously stored (3rd NDO in Figure 5(c)).

Figure 5. The different NDOs illustrating a name authenticity attack in NetInf

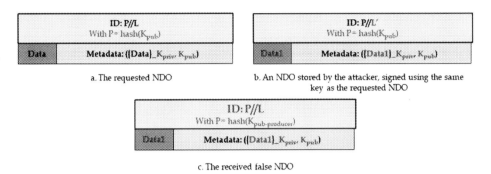

a. The requested NDO

b. An NDO stored by the attacker, signed using the same key as the requested NDO

c. The received false NDO

- When receiving the content, the requester checks the signature using K_{pub}. However, he can't perceive the attack.

If a link between the content name and the data existed, this attack would be detected. Otherwise, producer identification and authentication are independent of the naming system.

Relevance is also not taken into consideration. Indeed, as the content names are incomprehensible, a requester can't decide if the name used during his request corresponds to that of the desired content. He can easily use a false name. He retrieves non-altered data, but that don't match those desired. A system similar to the Domain Name System (DNS), which is used to match illegible self-certifying names with human-readable ones, can be used. However, this system transforms the security problem of the correspondence between a name and the associated data into a security problem of correspondence between (1) an unreadable name and (2) a meaningful name.

Security in NDN

The security in NDN is essentially based on the integration of a digital signature linking the name to the data in each Data packet. Indeed, this signature is calculated on the whole packet (content name, metadata, data and signature information), using the private key of the producer.

The signature verification ensures that the received data have not been altered (data integrity) and that they correspond to the name expressed in the Interest packet, since this name is the same as that of the Data packet (authenticity of the names). It also ensures the authentication of the producer since it is calculated using his private key. However, the producer's public key is required to perform this verification and it can be retrieved as an NDN data. To establish trust in this key, a Public Key Infrastructure (PKI) can be used. But, this solution is vulnerable to a potential attack, illustrated in Figure 6. This attack can be launched as follows (Hamdane et al., 2012):

- A requester sends an Interest packet (1st packet in Figure 6).
- By intercepting this packet, an attacker produces false data.
- He links these data to the name of the requested ones, through a digital signature calculated using his own private key $K_{priv\text{-}attacker}$. He sends to the requester a Data packet (2nd packet in Figure 6), containing the same name, false data, information about his own key (in the *KeyLocator* field) and the calculated digital signature.
- Upon receiving this Data packet, the requester uses the received information, indicated in *KeyLocator* field, in order to retrieve the attacker public key (3rd packet in Figure 6).
- He receives a Data packet (4th packet in Figure 6), including the requested public key and signed by a valid Certification Authority (CA). This packet acts as a certificate issued by the CA.
- The requester checks the signature of this last packet and uses the attacker public key to check the signature of the first packet. He can't perceive the attack since the Data packet seems legitimate, with a valid signature.

Figure 6. Attack in NDN when using a PKI

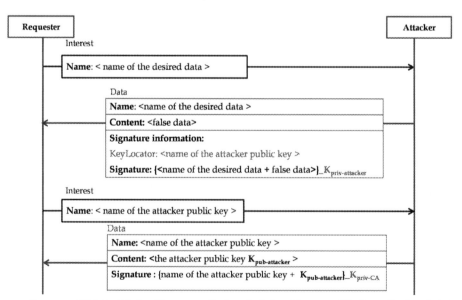

$K_{pub\text{-}attacker}$: attacker public key; $K_{priv\text{-}attacker}$: attacker private key; $K_{priv\text{-}CA}$: certification authority private key

The requester initially only knows the content name. However, he needs the producer's public key to verify the signature. A link between the name and the corresponding public key is then necessary to overcome the identified attack.

On the other hand, in NDN, the names are human-readable and often carry significant information about the associated data. With this information, a requester can judge whether content with that name matches the desired ones. The link established between the name and the expressive information on the content ensures then the relevance (Smetters & Jacobson, 2009). In addition, NDN doesn't impose any obligation in the choice of a name. This flexibility permits the integration of information about the real identity of the producer. The link established between the name and these information ensures consequently the producer identification.

Requirements on the ICN Naming System

In ICN, the adopted naming system has an important role in security. Table 2 highlights this role. It summarizes the mechanisms related to names, used to provide security services in both naming approaches.

To conclude, data integrity, name authenticity and producer authentication can be ensured, if the name establishes a first link with the producer public key and a second link with data using a digital signature. The first link is established only in

Table 2. The impact of naming on security in the ICN approach

		NetInf	NDN
Naming		Flat name composed by: • $P = Hash (K_{pub})$ with K_{pub}: producer public key • Label L	Hierarchical name composed by: • Globally Routable Part • Organizational part • Numbers of version and segment
Security	**Data integrity**	+ Ensured: a data signature in the metadata, a the public key hash in the name => A link established between the **name** and the **producer public key**	+ Ensured: a link between the name and the content by means of a signature => Need a link between the **name** and the **producer public key**
	Name authenticity	- Not ensured: a name can correspond to several content signed using the same key =>Need a link between the **name** and the **content**	
	Producer authentication	Independent of the naming system	
	Producer identification	Independent of the naming system	+ Ensured: => Need links between (1) the **name** and the **producer public key** and between (2) the **name** and **information about the producer identity**
	Relevance	- Not ensured => Need a link between the **name** and **information about the content**	+ Ensured => Need a link between the **name** and **significant information about the content**

self-certifying names while the second is established only in human-readable and hierarchical names. On the other hand, the producer identification requires a link between the name and the real identity of the producer. The relevance requires a link between the name and significant information about the content. These two links can be established only in human-readable and hierarchical names.

A hybrid naming system, combining both approaches and providing the required links, will improve security (Hamdane et al., 2014). In this system, the name must contain valid and understandable information about the identity of the producer and the associated content. It must link to this content through a digital signature. Finally, it must be self-certifying ensuring a direct link with the public key of the producer.

To meet these requirements, an extension of the naming system is proposed in (Hamdane et al., 2014). It is essentially based on Identity Based Cryptography (IBC), where any unique string can form a valid public key. The corresponding private key is generated by a trusted server called Public Key Generator (PKG), based on its secret key, its public parameters and the public key (Gorantla et al., 2005). The encryption, decryption, signature and verification operations require in addition to the keys, the PKG public parameters. Hamdane et al. (2014) propose the integration of the naming extension into the NDN and NetInf architectures, representing the two naming approaches.

Naming System Adaptation

Naming System Adaptation in NetInf

To meet the requirements of the naming system, the IBC is integrated into NetInf. The set up PKG, responsible for the generation of private keys (K_{priv}), is associated with the NRS. This PKG is also responsible for the secure distribution of each K_{priv} to his owner.

In addition, the name structure is retained. The label L is composed of the producer identifier and information on the published data. This part acts as an IBC public key. The authenticator A is equal to the cryptographic hash of the Label L for dynamic data and it is equal to the hash of the content and the PKG public parameters for static content. Metadata includes the public parameters *params* as well as a digital signature. This signature is no longer computed only on data as in classic NetInf, but also on the name and *params*.

In the naming system adaptation proposed for NetInf, information on producer identity included in the name ensure its identification. Expressive information, related to content, guarantees relevance, since a requester can use it to decide whether the content with that name is the desired one. In addition, the signature included in the metadata not only ensures data integrity and the authentication of the producer as in NetInf classic, but also name authenticity; it is calculated on the name and data, thus ensuring a link between them. A requester can therefore verify if the received data correspond to the name given, by checking this link.

Naming System Adaptation in NDN

Hierarchical Identity Based Cryptography (HIBC) represents the hierarchical variant of the IBC. In this variant, a PKG root generates only the private keys of the PKGs in its domain. It delegates the generation of other private keys to lower level PKGs. This PKG root also generates the public parameters, used by the other PKGs as well as in the different cryptographic operations.

HIBC is more suited to naming system adaptation in NDN, given the hierarchical structure of names. Indeed, each component of the name (delimited by '/') is associated with a PKG. This PKG is responsible for the identity uniqueness at this level as well as the distribution of the generated private keys to their owners.

In addition, names are still composed of a globally routable name, an organizational name and a versioning and segmentation part. However, the organizational part includes information about the associated data and the producer identity. The obtained name identifies the content as well as its producer. It acts as an HIBC public key for this content (Hamdane et al., 2017).

The proposed security extension maintains the same name structure in NDN, which keeps the same global architecture and the same routing and caching mechanisms. Moreover, it better meets the security requirements. Indeed, the integration of information about the producer identity ensures his identification. The addition of meaningful information about the data ensures relevance. The use of the name as an HIBC public key and the digital signature ensure both data integrity, name authenticity and producer authentication.

To trust in the root PKG public parameters, a trust model for NDN's current testbed can be deployed. In this model, the root PKG is directly attached to the root of the testbed. This PKG is responsible for generating sites' private keys and public parameters *params*. These parameters are trusted by all entities and are preconfigured in all applications (Bian et al., 2013). The sites represent the PKGs of the next level. They generate in turn the private keys of their users. Each user corresponds to a next level PKG. It generates the private keys used in the signature of the Data packets that they publish. To verify the signature of a received Data packet, a requester must no longer retrieve and then check all public keys and certificates in a trusted chain as in a PKI (Bian et al., 2013). He needs only the content name of the content taken directly from the packet, and the preconfigured root PKG public parameters.

E-GOVERNMENT SECURITY OVER NDN

The security aspect represents an important requirement in electronic services and especially in e-government ones. A minimal set of services must be ensured. It corresponds to integrity, confidentiality and availability (Priyambodo et al., 2017). Other security aspects like authentication are also important in several situations. However, the use the actual Internet, as a medium to provide e-government services, doesn't satisfy such security aspects. The used host to host security model, based on securing the host storing content and the communication channel used to retrieve it, is vulnerable and lacks in security (Priyambodo and Suprihanto 2016). A content-oriented security model, based on the integration of security mechanisms in the content, represents an interesting and a more adequate model for e-government. Such a model has been proposed in the ICN approach, representing a major candidate for the Internet of the future architecture.

Several studies have proposed the use of the ICN for the implementation of new services and have demonstrated the benefits of such use compared to the current Internet. Most of these studies use the NDN, since it represents the most emergent ICN architecture.

An advanced information centric platform for supporting the typical ICT services of a Smart City was even proposed in (Piro et al., 2014). This platform fits with all upcoming wireless technologies and it also enhances the security aspect. To demonstrate the relevance of the proposed platform for e-government services, a use case, over the NDN architecture, is illustrated. This use case details the management of a start-up event of a new business in a foreign country. To prove that the ICN approach can improve the security of e-government services, this use case is detailed and it is enhanced by integrating in addition the adaptation of the naming system based on the IBC.

A Use Case of an E-Government Service Over NDN: Starting of a New Business in a Foreign Country

To set up an e-government service in (Piro et al., 2014), 3 phases are necessary. The first one represents the Discovering phase. It allows retrieving the necessary information about the portals supporting the required administrative procedures. The second phase is that of the Security Initialization. It aims to create a secure communication. The last phase is related to the Service Usage.

The security services to be provided depend on the corresponding phase. Indeed, during the discovery phase, the availability, the data integrity, the name authenticity, the producer identification and authentication and the relevance must be ensured. In the last two phases, in addition to the aforementioned services, confidentiality must be ensured given the sensitivity of the exchanged data. For availability, NDN communication model design is more resilient to denial of service attacks compared to the current Internet. Contents are sent only as a response to a corresponding Interest packet. In addition, targeting a particular destination is difficult since it is not directly addressable.

Discovery Phase

To discover the portal set up for the administrative procedures needed to start a business in Country Y, a requester sends an Interest packet with the Content Name:

```
/domain/PublicAdmin/BusinessManagement/Discover/CountryY
```

The name structure corresponds to that of the naming adaptation integrating HIBC. Indeed, the *'/domain'* part is globally routable name.

The *'/PublicAdmin/BusinessManagement/Discover/CountryY'* part represents an organizational name. It includes information about the producer identity *'/PublicAdmin'*, that can contain the identifier of the manager of the public administration, responsible for the content production under this namespace. It also includes information about the associated data (*'BusinessManagement/Discover/CountryY'*).

A network Node, having the requested information, intercepts the packet. It sends the corresponding Data packet as an answer. This node can correspond to the *repo*, ensuring the permanent storage of these data or another router, closer to the requester and storing this information in its cache.

By receiving this Data packet, the requester verifies the signature, based on the content name used as HIBC public key, as well as the root PKG public parameters initially preconfigured. Thus, the integrity of the received information, the name authenticity and the producer authentication are ensured. Also, information about the manager of the public administration permit the producer identification. The relevance is finally ensured since the content name is significant.

Security Initialization

Once all the necessary information about the e-government portal is collected, the Secure Initialization phase can start. A key that can be used in data encryption is negotiated between the user (citizen) and the producer, using a well-known key agreement mechanism such as Diffie-Hellman. The exchanged packets during this negotiation are illustrated in Figure 7.

Figure 7. Example of the Key agreement procedure of an e-government service over NDN

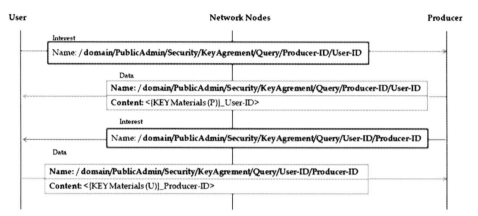

Producer-ID: the HIBC producer public key; User-ID: the HIBC user public key

Indeed, the user sends an Interest packet, requesting the producer key materials, needed to establish a shared key (1st packet). He indicates in the User-ID part his identity, which corresponds to his HIBC public key. This key is used by the producer to encrypt his key materials, before sending it to the user (2nd packet). This producer requests in turn the corresponding user key materials (3rd packet). He receives these values, encrypted using his ID indicated in the content name (4th packet).

By receiving this Data packet, the requester verifies the signature, based on the content name used as HIBC public key, as well as the root PKG public parameters initially preconfigured. Thus, the integrity of the received information, the name authenticity and the producer authentication are ensured. Also, the information about the administrator, permit the producer identification. The relevance is finally ensured since the content name is significant. As in the Discovery phase, the naming adaptation using HIBC is integrated. The Data packet signatures are verified using the content name as an HIBC public key and the preconfigured public parameters. This ensures the key materials integrity, the name authenticity and the producer authentication. Producer identification and relevance are also ensured due to the integration of information about the producer and the data in packets' content name. Finally, Data encryption ensures confidentiality.

Service Usage

To initiate the procedure to start-up a business, the user sends an Interest packet with the following name:

```
/domain/PublicAdmin/BusinessManageemnt/Query/StartNewBusiness/
            EncryptedUser-ID/EncryptedBusinessDetails
```

This name contains all the details needed to accomplish the task as well as the hash of his User-ID (used as an HIBC public key), encrypted using the key established during the Security Initialization phase. Upon receiving this request, the e-government portal formalizes the administrative procedure. It responds with a Data packet that includes the document to feedback to the citizen. If the portal needs additional information to accomplish the administrative procedure, it sends to the citizen an Interest packet named:

```
        /domain/PublicAdmin/BusinessManageemnt/
Query/StartNewBusiness/EncriptedUser-ID/AdditionalInfo.
```

The citizen responds with a Data packet including required information, encrypted with the negotiated key. As in the first two phases, data integrity, producer identification and authentication, name authenticity and relevance are ensured, using signatures and the naming system adaptation. In addition, the encryption of sensitive data such as Business Details, using the derived key, ensures confidentiality. Finally the ID of the user encryption preserves his anonymity.

CONCLUSION

Despite its great importance, e-government faces many challenges. With the use the Internet as a medium of providing these services, security represents one of the most important challenges. Indeed, the host to host security model, used in the current Internet, remains vulnerable, and this despite the various proposed corrections. The Information Centric Networking approach represents a radical solution for the security challenge and also for the other ones. It adopts a more adequate security model. This model is content-oriented, and it relies on the integration of security mechanisms in the content itself and in its naming system.

In this chapter, the different aspects of the ICN were presented. The security in this approach was then analyzed. Finally, a case study of an ICN was provided. It demonstrates that the ICN meets the security requirements in e-government services.

REFERENCES

AbdAllah, E. G., Hassanein, H. S., & Zulkernine, M. (2015). A survey of security attacks in information-centric networking. *IEEE Communications Surveys and Tutorials, 17*(3), 1441–1454. doi:10.1109/COMST.2015.2392629

Abdullahi, I., Arif, S., & Hassan, S. (2015). Survey on caching approaches in information centric networking. *Journal of Network and Computer Applications, 56*, 48–59. doi:10.1016/j.jnca.2015.06.011

Afanasyev, A. (2013). *Addressing Operational Challenges in Named Data Networking Through NDNS Distributed Database* (PhD thesis). University of California, Los Angeles, CA.

Bari, M., Rahman Chowdhury, S., Ahmed, R., Boutaba, R., & Mathieu, B. (2012). A survey of naming and routing in information-centric networks. *Communications Magazine, IEEE, 50*(12), 44–53. doi:10.1109/MCOM.2012.6384450

Bian, C., Zhu, Z., Afanasyev, A., Uzun, E., and Zhang, L. (2013). *Deploying key management on ndn testbed.* UCLA, Peking University and PARC, Tech.Rep.

Burke, J., Horn, A., & Marianantoni, A. (2012). *Authenticated lighting control using named data networking.* UCLA, NDN Technical Report NDN-0011.

Dannewitz, C. (2013). *NETINF Network of Information, An Information-Centric Networking Architecture for the Future Internet* (PhD thesis). Faculty of Computer Science, Electrical Engineering and Mathematics, University of Paderborn, Germany.

Dannewitz, C., Golic, J., Ohlman, B., & Ahlgren, B. (2010). Secure naming for a network of information. In *Proceedings of the 29th Conference on Computer Communications Workshops (INFOCOM)* (pp. 1-6). IEEE. 10.1109/INFCOMW.2010.5466661

Dannewitz, C., Kutscher, D., Ohlman, B., Farrell, S., Ahlgren, B., & Karl, H. (2013). Network of information (netinf)-an information-centric networking architecture. *Computer Communications, 36*(7), 721–735. doi:10.1016/j.comcom.2013.01.009

Dierks, T. (2008). *The transport layer security (tls) protocol version 1.2.* Rfc 5246, Internet Engineering Task Force.

Frankel, S., & Krishnan, S. (2011). *Ip security (ipsec) and internet key exchange (ike) document roadmap.* Rfc 6071, Internet Engineering Task Force.

Ghodsi, A., Koponen, T., Rajahalme, J., Sarolahti, P., & Shenker, S. (2011a). Naming in content-oriented architectures. In *Proceedings of the ACM SIGCOMM workshop on Information-centric networking* (pp. 1-6). ACM.

Ghodsi, A., Shenker, S., Koponen, T., Singla, A., Raghavan, B., & Wilcox, J. (2011b). Information-centric networking: seeing the forest for the trees. In *Proceedings of the 10th ACM Workshop on Hot Topics in Networks* (p. 1). ACM. 10.1145/2070562.2070563

Gorantla, M. C., Gangishetti, R., & Saxena, A. (2005). A survey on id-based cryptographic primitives. *IACR Cryptology ePrint Archive*, 94.

Hadi, F., & Muhaya, F. T. B. (2011). Essentials for the e-government security. In *Information Society (i-Society), 2011 International Conference on* (pp. 237-240). IEEE.

Hamdane, B., Boussada, R., Elhdhili, M. E., & El Fatmi, S. G. (2017). Hierarchical identity based cryptography for security and trust in named data networking. In *26th International Conference on Enabling Technologies: Infrastructure for Collaborative En-terprises (WETICE)*. IEEE. 10.1109/WETICE.2017.33

Hamdane, B., Guemara El Fatmi, S., & Serhrouchni, A. (2014). A novel name-based security mechanism for information-centric networking. In *Proceedings of the Wireless Communications and Networking Conference (WCNC)* (pp. 2928-2933). IEEE. 10.1109/WCNC.2014.6952919

Hamdane, B., Serhrouchni, A., Fadlallah, A., & Guemara El Fatmi, S. (2012). Named-data security scheme for named data networking. In *Proceedings of the Third International Conference on the Network of the Future (NoF)* (pp. 1-7). IFIP - IEEE. 10.1109/NOF.2012.6464002

Jacobson, V., Smetters, D. K., Thornton, J. D., Plass, M. F., Briggs, N. H., & Braynard, R. L. (2009). Networking named content. In *Proceedings of the 5th international conference on Emerging networking experiments and technologies* (pp. 1-12). ACM.

Kauffmann, B., & Peltier, J.-F. (2013). Final netinf architecture. *4WARD EU FP7 Project, Deliverable D.3.3 v1. 1.*

Kutscher, D., Eum, S., Pentikousis, K., Psaras, I., Corujo, D., Saucez, D., Schmidt, T., and Waehlisch, M. (2016). *Icn research challenges, draft-irtf-icnrg-challenges-06*. Technical report, ICNRG, Internet-Draft, Expires, September 20.

Kutscher, D., Farrell, S., & Davies, E. (2012). *The netinf protocol-draft-kutscher-icnrg-netinf-proto-01*. Technical report, Internet Draft, IETF, Expires, August 14.

Lagutin, D. (2010). *Securing the Internet with digital signatures* (PhD thesis). Aalto University, Department of Computer Science and Engineering.

Pan, J., Paul, S., & Jain, R. (2011). A survey of the research on future internet architectures. *Communications Magazine, IEEE, 49*(7), 26–36. doi:10.1109/MCOM.2011.5936152

Peltier, W. Y., & Simon, G. (2012). *Information-centric networking: current research activities and challenges. In Media Networks: Architectures* (p. 141). Applications, and Standards.

Piro, G., Cianci, I., Grieco, L. A., Boggia, G., & Camarda, P. (2014). Information centric services in smart cities. *Journal of Systems and Software, 88*, 169–188. doi:10.1016/j.jss.2013.10.029

Priyambodo, T. K., & Suprihanto, D. (2016). *Information security on egovernment as information-centric networks*. Academic Press.

Priyambodo, T. K., Venant, U., Irawan, T., & Waas, D. V. (2017). A comprehensive review of e-government security. *Asian Journal of Information Technology, 16*(2-5), 282–286.

Pyhnen, P., & Stranberg, O. (2011). *The network of information: Architecture and applications*. 4WARD EU FP7 Project, DeliverableD.B.1 v1. 0.

Smetters, D. K., & Jacobson, V. (2009). *Securing network content*. PARC Tech Report TR-2009-1, Xerox Palo Alto Research Center-PARC.

Sulaiman, H. A., Othman, M. A., Othman, M. F. I., Rahim, Y. A., & Pee, N. C. (2015). Advanced Computer and Communication Engineering Technology. In *Proceedings of ICOCOE 2015* (vol. 362). Springer.

Sunde, L. (2013). *Netinf node for bluetooth enabled android devices* (Master's thesis). Uppsala Universitet, Department of Information Technology, Uppsala, Sweden.

Vasilakos, A. V., Li, Z., Simon, G., & You, W. (2015). Information centric network: Research challenges and opportunities. *Journal of Network and Computer Applications, 52*, 1–10. doi:10.1016/j.jnca.2015.02.001

Wang, L., Hoque, A., Yi, C., Alyyan, A., & Zhang, B. (2012). *Ospfn: An ospf based routing protocol for named data networking.* University of Memphis and University of Arizona, Tech. Rep.

Weiler, S., & Blacka, D. (2013). *Clarifications and implementation notes for dns security (dnssec).* Rfc 6840, Internet Engineering Task Force.

Xylomenos, G., Ververidis, C. N., Siris, V. A., Fotiou, N., Tsilopoulos, C., Vasilakos, X., ... Polyzos, G. C. (2014). A survey of information-centric networking research. *IEEE Communications Surveys and Tutorials, 16*(2), 1024–1049. doi:10.1109/SURV.2013.070813.00063

Yaqub, M. A., Ahmed, S. H., Bouk, S. H., & Kim, D. (2016). Information-centric networks (icn). In *Content-Centric Networks* (pp. 19–33). Springer. doi:10.1007/978-981-10-0066-9_2

Yu, Y., Afanasyev, A., Zhu, Z., & Zhang, L. (2014). *Ndn technical memo: Naming conventions. Technical report.* UCLA.

Zhang, L., Afanasyev, A., Burke, J., Jacobson, V., Crowley, P., & Papadopoulos, C. (2014). Named data networking. *Computer Communication Review, 44*(3), 66–73. doi:10.1145/2656877.2656887

Chapter 4

The Role of Social Marketing in Preventing the Spread of Non–Communicable Diseases:
Case of Tunisia

Ines Mezghani Daoud
Carthage University, Tunisia

Marwa Meddeb
Carthage University, Tunisia

ABSTRACT

Non-communicable diseases (NCDs) such as obesity, diabetes, cardiovascular diseases, and cancers have become a major health concern for most countries around the world. Different elements such as social, biological, and environmental cause the NCDs. But the only way that one can intentionally modify to avoid these diseases is the desire to reduce risk factors for physical activity, tobacco, and diet. Several prevention strategies have been launched worldwide thorough governmental programs by implementing policies/laws. However, these programs don't integrate active communicate participation and support with the social community. This chapter aims to bring out the priority of enhancing the level of public awareness of NCDs. To ensure public responsiveness, the focus of this research is to create an effective solution to prevent risky behavior. The authors focus on the construction of "Sahtek," a social media solution developed on the fundamentals of social marketing, to better coach and promote awareness of NCDs prevention.

DOI: 10.4018/978-1-5225-5984-9.ch004

INTRODUCTION

Non-Communicable Diseases (NCDs) is a real burden to health systems in all regions of the world, and mainly in low and middle-income countries. It represents one of the most pressing challenges facing the world today. The total number of deaths attributed to the NCDs is projected to rise over the coming decade in case of absent significant interventions (World economic forum, 2011). The NCDs, known as the invisible epidemic, poses unique governance challenges: the causes are multifactorial, the affected populations diffuse, and effective responses require sustained multi-sectorial cooperation. Scientific evidence shows that unhealthy diet, physical inactivity, the lack of knowledge and the negative attitudes of the public enhance negative risk factors of NCDs. To avoid more expensive treatment, innovative global governance for health is urgently needed to engage civil society and individuals in the global response to the NCD crisis. Preventive strategy is fundamental to tackle the onset of disease, it occurs under health education, environmental measures and social policy. The ultimate goal is to bring about a change in behaviour or factors affecting community or individuals so that diseases will be prevented from developing. Although national responses are crucially important, community and personal initiatives are badly needed. As global health governance mechanisms aren't be able to rein in the rise in NCDs, several studies suggest that principles and techniques of social marketing may help to enhance the global awareness of NCDs. Effectively tackling NCDs and their key risk factors requires a detailed understanding of the current status and progress at Tunisia level. Feasible and cost effective interventions must be implemented to reduce the burden and impact of NCDs now and in the future.

This chapter will review growing complexity in global governance for NCDs. In the absence, as yet, of a universal standard to advance multi-sectorial global health governance, the chapter will explore whether current governance mechanisms in Tunisia are capable of addressing the determinants of NCDs. This work emphasizes integrated prevention by targeting the two main risk factors: unhealthy diet and physical inactivity. In this process, the chapter proposes to find ways to increase public awareness of NCDs and support NCD prevention and control efforts by using social media solution. Social networks proposed initiatives for the global governance of NCDs, and the challenges and opportunities confronting health actors in their efforts to implement healthy lifestyle to all. For this, the specific objectives of the chapter are first to propose a social media solution with effective preventive and control policy on diet, physical activity and health, second to promote the adoption of more healthful behaviour and finally to promote the multi-stakeholder engagement.

BACKGROUND: NON-COMMUNICABLE DISEASES

A non-communicable disease is a medical condition or disease that is not transmissible from an infected individual to another (NIH, 2007). It is defined as disease of long term; mostly gradual development and it is the main cause of adult mortality and morbidity worldwide (WHO, 2005a). In fact, in the last decade, NCDs have shown an unexpectable evolution and a rapid spread. These can be perceived clearly, as shown in Figure 1, that NCDs are the leading causes of death worldwide, killing more persons each year than all other causes combined.

In 2017, a large study conducted by the World Health Organization (WHO, 2017) has shown a clear increase in mortality from NCDs globally in the last thirty years. These pathologies were principally cardiovascular diseases (stroke and heart attacks), chronic respiratory (asthma and chronic obstructive pulmonary disease), cancers and diabetes. All theses examples are the leading causes of what could be considered nowadays as the invisible epidemic. These NCDs provoke 39.5 million deaths in 2015 and the premature deaths of 15 million people aged 30 to 70 years annually. The prevalence of NCDs is rapidly increasing; while the prevalence of infectious diseases is largely decelerate (Figure 2). It is expected that evolution of non-communicable disease by 2030 will cause "almost three-quarters as many deaths as communicable, maternal, perinatal, and nutritional diseases by 2020, and to exceed them as the most common causes of death by 2030" (WHO, 2010).

Tunisia, as shown in Figure 3, doesn't escape to this global phenomenon (WHO, 2015), the burden of NCDs causes 82,3% of all deaths. Cardiovascular diseases account for 49.2%, cancers 12.3%, respiratory diseases 5.0% and diabetes 4.9% of all deaths. As a result, 17.0% of adults aged 30–70 are expected to die from the four main NCDs.

Figure 1. Causes of worldwide mortality

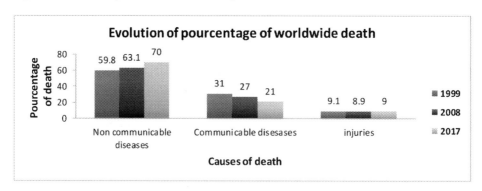

Figure 2. Projected global deaths for selected causes, 2004 – 2030

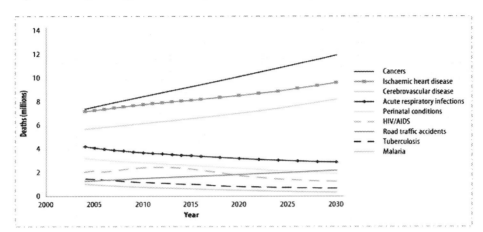

Figure 3. Proportional mortality in Tunisia

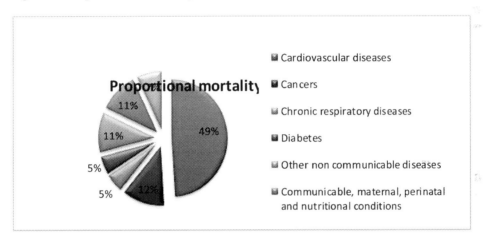

It is not unexpected therefore that this scourge has inspired research's interest and that the fields of research into this widespread are several and diverse. Most of these researches are in medicine, pharmacy and public health. These various studies are providing curatives actions based on heavy medical treatments, which represent a high cost to the society. NCDs are a major public health preoccupation that strains global economies. The spending associated to healing care and pain and suffering due to NCDs will double between 2010 and 2030. The global cost of NCDs was 6.3 trillion US dollars in 2010, which is expected to increase to $13 trillion by 2030 (World economic forum, 2011).

To bring down the burden of this short-term strategy, the world health organization underscores the importance to apply a holistic approach with multi level policies. This long-term approach combines preventives policies, community-driven initiatives and individual-level prevention to reduce root causes of NCDs. To achieve this global change, a new approach of healthy lifestyle initiatives is needed. Effective communication and meaningful practices set partnerships among stakeholders is essential. Consequently, it is fundamental to identify the different stakeholders, their roles, who they impact and connectivity one to another (Table1) (Griffiths et al, 2007).

Stakeholder association is crucial for rising the percentage of people adopting healthy behaviours. To ensure connectivity, coordination of all efforts among key stakeholders, adequate integration and collaboration is essential to implement healthy initiatives. Social marketing through social media offers a new opportunity for key stakeholders to share, to organize and to coordinate interventions. Social marketing aims to influence or encourage people to adopt specific behaviours, which are widely recognized as being beneficial through coordination efforts between the various stakeholders. The marketing research has also suggested the inclusion of an

Table 1. Key healthy lifestyle stakeholders and their overarching roles

Stakeholder	Overarching Roles
Professional organizations	*Advocacy, championing healthy lifestyle thought leaders, dissemination of scientific knowledge and practice guidelines, professional meetings*
Educational systems	*Providing an appropriate healthy lifestyle curriculum at all levels of education, creating a healthy lifestyle environment within the educational setting*
Government	*Creating, supporting, and implementing legislation and programs that support healthy lifestyle initiatives on a population level*
Health care organizations	*Integrating healthy lifestyle interventions into the medical model as a standard of care*
Insurance industry	*Providing mechanisms for coverage of healthy lifestyle initiatives*
Nonprofit and community organizations	*Advocacy; creating, supporting, and implementing healthy lifestyle initiatives*
Media outlets	*Disseminating credible healthy lifestyle information to the lay public*
Mobile health and technology companies	*Bringing technological inventions/advances that support healthy lifestyle initiatives to market*
Employers	*Creating a healthy lifestyle environment within the workplace, offering healthy lifestyle programming to employees*
Food industry	*Making healthy food choices available, providing health-conscious nutrition labeling*
Health and fitness industry	*Providing an infrastructure and professionals capable of offering healthy lifestyle programming to the public*
Individuals and families	*Consumers of healthy lifestyle initiatives*

Table 2. Tunisian national system response to NCDs

Tunisian National System Response to NCDs	
Has an operational NCD unit/branch or department within the Ministry of Health, or equivalent	No
Has an operational multi-sectoral national policy, strategy or action plan that integrates several NCDs and shared risk factors	No
Has an operational policy, strategy or action plan to reduce the harmful use of alcohol	No
Has an operational policy, strategy or action plan to reduce physical inactivity and/or promote physical activity	No
Has an operational policy, strategy or action plan to reduce the burden of tobacco use	Yes
Has an operational policy, strategy or action plan to reduce unhealthy diet and/or promote healthy diets	No
Has evidence-based national guidelines/protocols/standards for the management of major NCDs through a primary care approach	No
Has an NCD surveillance and monitoring system in place to enable reporting against the nine global NCD targets	No
Has a national, population-based cancer registry	No

additional P, dedicate to partnership between stakeholder, to the 4 Ps of marketing: product, place, price, and promotion (Lee & Kotler, 2011). This partnership offers a new perspective through policy change to improve healthy lifestyle, to reduce NCD burden, and to drive individual, community, social and economic development.

ISSUES, CONTROVERSIES AND PROBLEMS: CURRENT NCD PREVENTION MECHANISMS AND ITS EFFECTIVENESS IN TUNISIA

Tunisia face multiple health and developmental challenges, especially after the Arabic spring revolution. NCDs tend to receive lesser political attention than to issues with visible and immediate government impact. The results of the research conducted by the World Health Organization (WHO, 2014) shown in Table 2, confirm that there are no significant policies or programs have been made to tackle the problem of NCDs in Tunisia level. However, the only governmental policies are centered on education and/or laws in reducing the use of tobacco.

No policies are actually planned or implemented in Tunisia to prevent the spread of NCDs. The fact that there is a lack of local advocacy and limited community participation and there is no urban-level research evidence available to local policymakers and stakeholders. As a result, the chapter proposes to use the social marketing; wich applies commercial marketing strategies to promote public health, as a strategic perspective to change the behaviour of target stakeholders. Moreover the interaction through social media can be used as a tool to raise public health awareness of public information and stakeholder engagement to NCDs.

Social Marketing

The social marketing was introduced by kotler and Zaltman in (1971) as "design, implementation, and control of programs calculated to influence the acceptability of social ideas, and involving considerations of product, planning, pricing, communication, distribution and marketing research". In the last years, changes in social marketing have been made, by integrating several features (Fench et al, 2010). First, rely on techniques and principles of commercial marketing specially 4Ps in social marketing campaign. Second, focus on behaviour change "to create, to communicate and deliver value in order to influence target audience behaviours".

Kotler and Lee (2008) highlight four main fields of researchers that social marketing have focused on: health promotion (e.g. tobacco use, drinking, obesity, cancer, blood pressure), environmental protection (e.g. water conservation, litter, forest destruction), injury prevention (e.g. women abuse, suicide, road accident), and community mobilization (e.g. organ or blood donation, vote). Social marketers strategies encompass traditional mass media, but also interactive and digital media to enhance community level outreach public's attention.

In many countries, social marketing researches and strategies are nowadays, at the top of health development and especially in the prevention of NCDs (Douglas et al., 2009). In the United States, social marketing is increasingly being promoted as a fundamental key strategy for prompting voluntary lifestyle behaviors such as smoking, drinking, drug use, and diet (Stead et al, 2007). In the United Kingdom, the advantages of social marketing were recognized by the department of Health, as a key success factor "to build public awareness and change behavior" (Gracia-Marco et al, 2012). Besides these strategies, many social marketing campaigns have been launched and developed such as "let's move" (United States) supported by Michelle Obama, "Manger bouger" (France) or "Change4Life" (United Kingdom). All these campaigns apply social marketing strategies to transform lifestyle and environmental factors supporting diet and physical activity to reduce the proliferation of NCDs.

Social Marketing through community-based approaches is becoming increasingly relevant. It allows shaping markets that are more efficient and decrease the obstacles and increase motivations to behaviours that improve the quality of life for individuals and society (Newton-Wards et al, 2004, Andreason, 1994). The use of traditional media such as newspapers, magazines, radio, and television are not a powerful method to reach individuals or community (Brooks, 2000). While, in the digital age, modern mass media, that public are passionate about like Social Media offers a number of benefits including extension of richer and responsive messages to a larger audience, convenience, cost reduction and competitive pricing.

In fact, the access for health information is problematic to low income or low education citizen. The Internet provides an incontestable way to implement and spread health related information with nationwide impact. Nowadays, Internet is without contest an important method to disseminate healthy lifestyle information's to the masses. Internet world stats estimate in June 2017 that the number of Internet users in the world is about 3,88 billion users. The same stats indicate that more than 64% of Internet users accessing social media service on line. Advances in social media are an exclusive way to prevent the spread of NCD and to change mind-sets to promote a Healthy Lifestyle.

Social Media in Health Care

There is a continuing spread of the use of social media generally (Boyd et al 2008) and especially in health care contexts (Thackeray et al, 2008, Dawson, 2010). Several research highlight opportunities that social media offers among health professional (Hu et al, 2010, Sanford, 2010), patient (Liang et al, 2011; Denecke et al, 2009) and the general public (Liang et al, 2011, Kaplan, 2010) to create posts, share, like, and comment on health care content through multisensory communication. Before focusing on social media for health communication, it is important to outline, first, the characteristics of social media. Kaplan and Haenlein, (2010) defined social media as "a group of Internet-based applications that build on the ideological and technological foundations of Web 2.0, and that allow the creation and exchange of user generated content". Social media encompasses interactive web and mobile platforms through where individuals and communities can share, co-create, or exchange information, ideas, photos, or videos within a virtual network. Besides, it offers opportunities for public health to communicate about health issues, including the prevention of NCDs by using social media platforms.

Social media allows users to create peer-to-peer discussion in a way not allowed by traditional media. It can be categorised in several ways to show the different range of social media platforms, such as collaborative projects (eg, Wikipedia), content communities (eg, YouTube) and social networking sites (eg, Facebook) (Kaplan and Haenlein, 2010). The main practices of social media concentrate on rising exchanges with others, and gathering, sharing, and obtaining health messages (Freeman & Chapman, 2007). Various benefits of using social media for health communication were reported. A major advantage of social media for health communication is the accessibility and widening access of health information to a large audience, regardless of race, age, ethnicity, education or locality (Chou at al, 2009).

Moen et al, (2009) explain, present patterns of cooperation tend to create an asymmetric relationship between health care provider and patient. This underlines a real need for health providers to develop the role within social media in the health communication. Sedereviciute et al (2011) have suggested that stakeholders need to recognize and understand the social media landscape by developing appropriate strategies. Specially, work out how often and when they should enter into conversations, and be aware of what others are doing and act accordingly.

This development of social media is because they are clear, understandable, accessible and affordable. Social media also encourages interaction, communication, and expansion of health-related content by way of multiple channels including Facebook, Twitter, Google, Pinterest and Instagram. According to "Statista, 2017", Social Media statistics indicate an enormous evolution in 2017 as shown in Figure 4. This clear shift is attributed towards mobile platforms. Smartphone, tablet apps and mobile web access have facilitated the constant presence of users. The incontestable leader of social media is Facebook by surpassing the 2 billions active users monthly.

Given the widespread use of social media, even among population and groups, there are opportunities to leverage these popular online platforms to support prevention of NCDs. Social media platforms such as Facebook has been gradually used for health prevention and supporting public health efforts, as demonstrated in a recent review of 73 studies (Capurro et al, 2014). To be efficient, the archetype NCDs prevention solution should be developed to reach large audiences with being accessible any times and inexpensive. It should include individuals, families, communities and organizations while inducing voluntary behavioral changes, to truly bring about transformation within individuals.

In January 2017, despite its small size, Tunisia ranks 4th in Africa in terms of the number of Internet users. 56% of the global population accessed the Internet with 7.7 million users. Facebook is extremely popular. 6,31 million Tunisians use

Figure 4. Most famous mass media

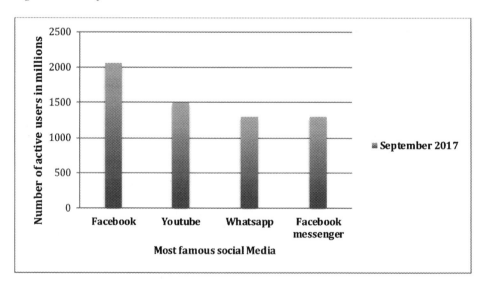

Facebook for a penetration rate of 50,5%, making Tunisia the second country in Africa in terms of Facebook users (Tunisia digital summit, 2017). These statistics show an obvious increase of Internet usage and validate the use of Facebook as a solution to support the implementation of a Tunisian health policy and to promote the prevention of NCDs.

This chapter intends the creation of "Sahtek", a Facebook page developed on the fundamentals of Social Marketing, to better support awareness of Non-Communicable Disease prevention. The fundamental contribution of this solution is to motivate individuals to take preventive behaviours against NCDs before it is too late. The choice of this type of social media has been motivated by the fact that Facebook offers an influential platform that promotes exposure to health information. It allows the exchange of information easily, flexibly and quickly (Mozas-Moral et al., 2016).

The Facebook platform "Sahtek" considers three distinctive dimensions: intensity, richness, and responsiveness of Facebook activity.

First, intensity is measured by the network size. It is obtained by dividing the number of posts and comments on "Sahtek" Facebook page with the number of fans of that page. A developed flow of posts and comments could represent an opportunity to improve users' awareness and engagement (Vlachvei & Notta, 2015).

The next dimension is richness, obtained qualitatively by the posts made by administer and also the quality of their Facebook page activities. It is measured by the ratio of the number of posts, including videos, photos, or links and the total number of posts. The researchers suggest that messages containing text, pictures, or videos have a higher capacity to deliver information (Daft & Lengel, 1986). In particular, this capacity is amplified if messages include not only text but also pictures. Messages that include pictures and videos require less processing effort because they are easier to understand than messages containing static pictures (Larkin & Simon, 1987, Park & Hopkins, 1992). Evolution from text-only messages to those that contain pictures and video allows more valuable communication to users. These contents are more likely to be detected and shared by users, because they are more engaging and informative (Emerson, 2012).

The third and last dimension is responsiveness. It is obtained qualitatively by the degree of interaction between Sahtek Facebook page and users. It measured by dividing the number of comments made by Sahtek Facebook page and the total number of comments.

York, 2012 explain that the higher the value of responsiveness, or interactivity, the greater is the exchange of information on NCDs prevention. The following section explores how "Sahtek" has been created so as to incorporate the needs of all stakeholders.

SOLUTION AND RECOMMENDATIONS: CREATION OF "SAHTEK"

"Sahtek" is Facebook solution, which helps individuals, families or communities to learn how to avoid the behavioural risk factors of NCDs, through interaction with healthcare professionals as well as sports coach. Former to the development of "Sahtek", the stakeholder needs were gathered through Focus brainstorming, Focus Group Discussions (FGD), interviews, and self-analysis of existing healthcare based Social Networks in Tunisia. After analysis of the results, it was definite that "Sahetek" will be developed as a Facebook solution developed on the fundamentals of Social Marketing.

This choice is motivated by the accessibility, the deployability and the cost effective of social media solution. Users of "sahtek" need minimal system requirement as Internet connection and hardware with basic personal computer or smart device. Sahtek is accessible for a range of devices as long as it is Internet enabled.

Features of "SAHTEK"

Information is available to guests of "sahtek", it is essential that visitors are provided adequate information before they can become a member of the page. Therefore, a visitor is able to gather the following information before signing up as a member:

- A presentation of "Sahtek",
- Current membership of "Sahtek",
- Information on NCDs and their behavioural risks,
- The team of healthcare professionals (doctors, dieticians and Physical coach),
- In what ways "Sahtek" can help the visitor in the prevention of NCDs,
- Demonstration video describing the main features of sahtek,
- The team that manages "Sahtek" and ways in which they can be contacted.

Logo of "Sahtek"

A logo is an essential element of communication. It is used in various communication media, both to reinforce the image and to offer a personality to the brand, but also to identify and recognize it. It is a graphical representation that immediately identifies companies, products, services or campaigns in a unique way. A logo should make sense in the mind of the target by conveying a simple and memorable message.

The utility of the logo is various as attract and target the audience, promote the image of the importance of NCDs prevention, give identity to the prevention campaign, federate users around the same symbol of adoption a healthy lifestyle and reinforce the impact of messages and opinions of society. The Figure 5 demonstrates the key features of Logo "Sahtek".

- **Name:** The name Sahtek means, on the one hand, the adoption of an active lifestyle by increasing physical activity and reducing sedentary time.
- **Keywords:** Logo "sahtek" is perceived by the patient as a balance, a change, a health, a well-being, a healthy diet, a sport and a lifestyle.
- **Shape:** The first half of the apple refers to healthy diet and the second half represents a person in good shape. It supposes that it is essential to eat healthy to be in good health.
- **Choice of Colours:** First, green is about hope, well-being, balance, happiness, energy, patience, optimism, youth, and concentration. It symbolizes growth, stability, calm and nature, health, success, freshness, confidence, or security. Green is popular in the field of energy, finance, food, technology and medicines. Second, blue evokes the color of nature, the sea and the sky. In shades of darkness, it reveals truth, trust, loyalty, intelligence and security. In lighter tones, it is associated with freedom, dream and youth. Blue suggests regeneration, the need for evolution, transformation and the need for change. It is popular in the field of energy, medicine, technology, health, and agriculture.

Figure 5. The logo of Sahtek

- **The Slogan:** Is the catch of our brand. This short phrase easily memorized, intended to hit the spirits and make a promise to the customer: "koul metwezen w koun sportif." Translated from Arabic as "eat balanced and be sporty". This slogan aims at counterbalance the current Tunisians behaviors by changing their eating habits, plus their sedentary lifestyle, which are responsible for NCDs.

Facebook Content of "Sahtek"

To increase users' awareness of NCDs with the opportunity to communicate efficiently, it is crucial to focus on the quality of the messages and posts. The content of the different posts emphasis sport activity the perception and the choice of food and the importance of sport activity. The style of writing was friendly to reach the maximum of users. The Table 3 summarize the different posts and pictures created for the first 2 weeks.

In Tunisia, according to a study made by MEDIANET in 2016, the effectiveness of publications on Facebook is during the period between 10h and 15h with a peak at 11h (Figure 6). It is more relevant to post the publications in this time interval.

The current study examined preventive and health-related predictors of NCDs by the use of Facebook in an effort to better understand who is accessing and being reached through these emerging communication channels. The results showed that this form of social media have distinctly different use patterns and user characteristics, hence different health communication implications. Among the forms of social media, Facebook by far attract the most users in Tunisian context, making them an obvious target for maximizing the reach and impact of health communication and NCDs prevention. Furthermore, with increasing prevalence of personal wireless devices, communication scientists commonly expect the popularity of social networking applications to continue to grow worldwide.

Compared to social media, a much smaller percentage of Tunisian Internet users have reported writing in a blog, twitter or Instagram suggesting a lower prevalence of these media. However, reading and commenting on Facebook may have been a more reliable measure of Internet penetration due to its higher popularity in Tunisian context. Moreover, Facebook presents a tremendous opportunity for NCDs prevention. Particularly so, because Facebook users have been observed to act as important communication stakeholders, not only are they information disseminators, but they play a crucial role in developing the awareness of NCDs through Facebook content and comments.

A key finding of this study offers new and important implications for NCD communication in this digital age: among Internet users, Facebook is found to

Table 3. Sahtek's Facebook content for the first 2 weeks

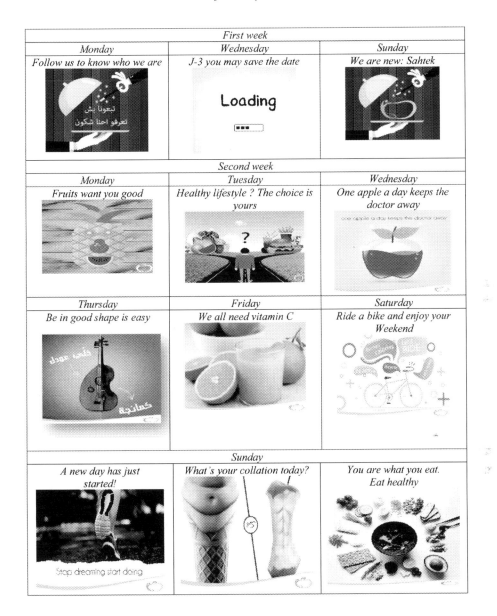

penetrate the Tunisian population regardless of education, race, ethnicity, or health care access. Considering implications of NCDs prevention communication efforts, the results of this study suggest that in the future, social media promise to be a way to reach the target population regardless of socioeconomic and health-

Figure 6. The effectiveness of publications on Facebook in Tunisia

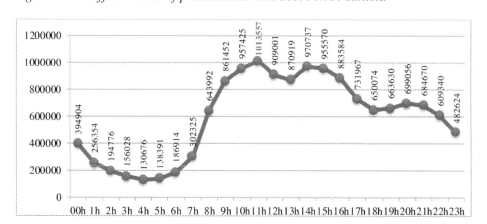

related characteristics. If stakeholders efforts can enable wilder and more equitable Internet access (eg, increasing broadband access or Free wireless mobile access), thus reducing the digital divide, the potential for impacting the health and NCDs prevention behaviour of the general Tunisian population through social media will be remarkable.

FUTURE RESEARCH DIRECTIONS

Despite all efforts to complete this study, a number of limitations need to be highlighted. To these limits, we will associate future paths of research. In the first place, this Facebook solution can be sustained by value added services such as online consultation with doctors or physical trainer or the incorporation of other social networks Twitter or google +. A second limitation is choosing a single online environment such as Facebook. Our study may not be representative of all communities developed on Facebook social network. Thus, future studies should investigate other communities in order to have a rich understanding about the NCDs prevention in Tunisia case. Future research may take into consideration the users individual factors as gender, age, and perceived risk of adopting a sedentary lifestyle. A third limitation concerns the longitude of the study whose practices of NCDs are dynamic and their effects will change with time. Therefore, a longitudinal and in depth study will be necessary in order to fellow the changes of individual's behaviours and to uncover the variable behind the spread of NCDs in Tunisian context to better target their spread.

CONCLUSION

NCDs are the prominent cause of death worldwide. Preventive action must be taken to stop the number of deaths through NCDs. Several biological, environmental and social factors are the main cause of this spread. Specially, the lifestyle adopted by people provokes the majority of theses diseases. The best NCD prevention action must influence a wide audience to change their behaviours before it is too late. Social marketing is a strategic key to incite individual's voluntary behavioural changes with the support of social community. Nowadays, traditional social marketing campaigns are insufficient. Therefore, it is fundamental to reinforce them through modern media such as social media.

It is in this context that Sahtek was developed as a Facebook solution based on the fundamental of social marketing. Sahtek's ultimate contribution is to enhance the awareness and inspire individuals to adopt a healthy lifestyle. The facebook page incites populations to actively getting involved in physical activity programs, improved access to information for physical activity and substantial reductions in the intake of sault and unhealthy food. It provides personalized and specific plans and programs through consulting with healthcare professionals.

REFERENCES

Andreasen, A. (1994). Social marketing: Its definition and domain. *Journal of Public Policy & Marketing, 13*(1), 108–114.

Arena, R., Guazzi, M., & Mianov, L. (2015). Healthy lifestyle interventions to combat non-communicable disease. *European Heart Journal*, 2097–2109. doi:10.1093/eurheartj/ehv207 PMID:26524498

Atun, J., Jaffar, S., Nishtar, S., Knaul, F. M., Barreto, M. L., Nyirenda, M., ... Piot, P. (2013). Improving responsiveness of health systems to non-communicable diseases. *Lancet, 381*(9867), 690–697. doi:10.1016/S0140-6736(13)60063-X PMID:23410609

Bayo-Moriones, A., Billon, M., & Lera-Lopez, F. (2013). Perceived performance effects of ICT in manufacturing SMEs. *Industrial Management & Data Systems, 113*(1), 117–135. doi:10.1108/02635571311289700

Boyd, D., & Ellison, B. (2008). Social network sites: Definition, history, and scholarship. *Computer Medicine Communication, 13*(1), 210–230. doi:10.1111/j.1083-6101.2007.00393.x

Brooks R. (2000). *The basics of social marketing: how to use marketing change behaviours*. University of Washington.

Capurro, D., Cole, K., Echavarria, M., Joe, J., Neogi, T., & Turner, A. M. (2014). The Use of Social Networking Sites for Public Health Practice and Research: A Systematic Review. *Journal of Medical Internet Research, 16*(3), e79. doi:10.2196/jmir.2679 PMID:24642014

Chou, W. Y., Hunt, Y. M., Beckjord, E. B., Moser, R. P., & Hesse, B. W. (2009). Social media use in the United States: Implications for health communication. *Journal of Medical Internet Research, 11*(4), e48. doi:10.2196/jmir.1249 PMID:19945947

Daft, R. L., & Lengel, R. H. (1986). Organizational information requirements, media richness and structural design. *Management Science, 32*(5), 554–571. doi:10.1287/mnsc.32.5.554

Dawson, J. (2010). *Doctors join patients in going online for health information*. New Media Age.

Denecke, K., & Nejdl, W. (2009). How valuable is medical social media data? Content analysis of the medical web. *Inform Sciences, 179*(12), 1870–1880. doi:10.1016/j.ins.2009.01.025

Douglas, E. (2009). Childhood Obesity Prevention in South Africa: Media, Social Influences, and Social Marketing Opportunities. *Social Marketing Quarterly, 15*, 22-48.

Emerson, M. F. (2012). Social media marketing from A to Z. *The New York Times*.

Fench, J., Blair-Stevens, C., Merritt, R., & McVey, D. (2010). *Social Marketing and Public health, theory and practice*. Oxford University Press.

Freeman, B., & Chapman, S. (2007). Is "YouTube" telling or selling you something? Tobacco content on the YouTube video-sharing website. *Tobacco Control, 16*(3), 207–210. doi:10.1136/tc.2007.020024 PMID:17565142

Gracia-Marco, L., Moreno, L., & Vicente-Rodríguez, G. (2012). Impact of Social Marketing in the Prevention of Childhood Obesity. *An Advanced in nutrition, an International Review Journal*, 6115-6155.

Grier, S., & Bryant, C. (2005). Social marketing in public health. *Annual Review of Public Health, 26*(1), 319–339. doi:10.1146/annurev.publhealth.26.021304.144610 PMID:15760292

Griffiths, J., Maggs, H., & George, E. (2007). *Stakeholder Involvement.* Background paper prepared for the WHO/WEF Joint Event on Preventing Noncommunicable Diseases in the Workplace.

Hu, Y., & Sundar, S. (2010). Effects of online health sources on credibility and behavioral Intentions. *Communication Research, 37*(1), 105–132. doi:10.1177/0093650209351512

Kaplan, A. M., & Haenlein, M. (2010). Users of the world unite! The challenges and opportunities of social media. *Business Horizons, 53*(1), 59–68. doi:10.1016/j.bushor.2009.09.003

Kietzmann, J. H., Hermkens, K., McCarthy, I. P., & Silvestre, B. S. (2011). Social media? Get serious! Understanding the functional building blocks of social media. *Business Horizons, 54*(3), 241–251. doi:10.1016/j.bushor.2011.01.005

Kotler, P., & Lee, N. (2008). *Social Marketing: Influencing Behaviors for Good.* Sage Publications.

Kotler, P., & Zaltman, G. (1971). Social marketing: An approach to planned social change. *Journal of Marketing, 35*(3), 3–12. doi:10.2307/1249783 PMID:12276120

Larkin, J. H., & Simon, H. A. (1987). Why a diagram is (sometimes) worth ten thousand words. *Cognitive Science, 11*(1), 65–100. doi:10.1111/j.1551-6708.1987.tb00863.x

Lee, N., & Kotler, P. (2011). *Social Marketing, influencing behaviors for good* (4th ed.). Sage Publications, Inc.

Liang, B., & Scammon, D. L. (2011). E-Word-of-Mouth on health social networking sites: An opportunity for tailored health communication. *Journal of Consumer Behaviour, 10*(6), 322–331. doi:10.1002/cb.378

Newton-Ward, Andreasen, & Hastings. (2004). Positioning Social Marketing. *Social Marketing Quarterly, 10*(3), 17-22.

Moen, A., Smørdal, O., & Sem, I. (2009). Web-based resources for peer support - opportunities and challenges. *Studies Health Technology Information*, 302–306.

Mozas-Moral, A., Bernal-Jurado, E., Medina-Viruel, M. J., & Fernández-Uclés, D. (2016). Factors for success in online social networks: An fsQCA approach. *Journal of Business Research, 69*(11), 5261–5264. doi:10.1016/j.jbusres.2016.04.122

National Institutes of Health. (2007). *Understanding Emerging and Re-emerging Infectious Diseases.* Author.

Nordqvist, C., Hanberger, L., Timpka, T., & Nordfeldt, S. (2009). Health professionals' attitudes towards using a Web 2.0 portal for child and adolescent diabetes care: Qualitative study. *Journal of Medical Internet Research, 11*(2). PMID:19403464

Park, O. C., & Hopkins, R. (1992). Instructional conditions for using dynamic visual displays: A review. *Instructional Science, 21*(6), 427–449. doi:10.1007/BF00118557

Sanford, A. A. (2010). "I Can Air My Feelings Instead of Eating Them": Blogging as Social Support for the Morbidly Obese. *Communication Studies, 61*(5), 567–584. doi:10.1080/10510974.2010.514676

Sedereviciute, K., & Valentini, C. (2011). Towards a more holistic stakeholder analysis approach. Mapping known and undiscovered stakeholders from social media. *International Journal of Strategic Communication, 5*(4), 221–239. doi:10.1080/1553118X.2011.592170

Stead, M., Gordon, R., Angus, K., & McDermott, L. (2007). A systematic review of social marketing effectiveness. *Health Education, 107*(2), 126–191. doi:10.1108/09654280710731548

Thackeray, R., Neiger, B. L., Hanson, C. L., & McKenzie, J. F. (2008). Enhancing promotional strategies within social marketing programs: Use of Web 2.0 social media. *Health Promotion Practice, 9*(4), 338–343. doi:10.1177/1524839908325335 PMID:18936268

Vlachvei, A., & Notta, O. (2015). Greek Food Manufacturing Firms' Social Media Efforts: Evidence from Facebook. *Procedia: Social and Behavioral Sciences, 175*(1), 308–313.

Wakefiled, M., Loken, B., & Hornik, R. (2014). *Use of mass media campaigns to change health behaviour.* HHS Author manuscripts.

World economic forum and Harvard school of public health. (2011). *The global economic burden of Non communicable diseases.* Author.

World Health Organization. (2005a). *Preventable hospital infections are a major cause of death and disability for patients.* WHO.

World Health Organization. (2010). *Global statue report on non communicable disease.* WHO.

World Health Organization. (2015). *Health profile.* Tunisia: WHO.

World Health Organization. (2017). *Non-communicable disease Progress Monitor*. WHO.

The Statistics Portal. Most Famous Social Networking Sites as of January 2018. (n.d.). Retrieved from https://www.statista.com/statistics/272014/global-social-networks-ranked-by-number-of-users/

Medianet. (n.d.). *Social Media in Africa: Key Statistical Indicators*. Retrieved from http://blog.medianet.com.tn/blog/chiffres-cles-sur-les-reseaux-sociaux-en-afrique-facebook-linkedin-instagram-presentes-lafrican

Chapter 5
Strengthening Cybersecurity in Singapore:
Challenges, Responses, and the Way Forward

Ching Yuen Luk
Nanyang Technological University, Singapore

ABSTRACT

This chapter uses a historical perspective to examine the development trajectory of e-government in Singapore, the trends and patterns of cybercrimes and cyber-attacks, and the measures taken by the government to combat cybercrimes and cyber-attacks. It shows that the government has adopted a proactive, holistic, and cooperative approach to cybersecurity in order to tackle the ever-increasing cybersecurity challenges. It has regularly reviewed and improved cybersecurity measures to ensure their effectiveness and strengthened its defense capabilities over time through coordinating national efforts with public and private sectors and cooperating with regional and international counterparts. The chase for a perfect cybersecurity system or strategy is both impossible and unnecessary. However, it is important and necessary to establish a cybersecurity system or formulate a cybersecurity strategy that can monitor, detect, respond to, recover from, and prevent cyber-attacks in a timely manner, and make the nation stronger, safer, and more secure.

DOI: 10.4018/978-1-5225-5984-9.ch005

INTRODUCTION

Singapore is one of the most connected countries in the world. Due to the government's continuous effort to upgrade information technology (IT) infrastructure and implement e-government strategies, information and communications technology (ICT) serves as a powerful tool to modernize the civil service and enhance administrative efficiency, facilitate economic growth and foster interaction between citizens and government. However, Singapore's growing dependence on IT has made it become targets of cyber attacks in recent years. Singapore is likely to remain a prime target for cyber attacks for years to come, especially when it transforms into a Smart Nation and prioritizes digital economy. For these reasons, the government has put cybersecurity at the top of the agenda and is racing against time to build a safe, secure and trusted cyber environment. While there are some studies examining development of e-government in Singapore during a specific period of time, there is the lack of studies on the trends of cybercrimes and cyber attacks in the nation and the government's responses to such crimes and attacks. In order to fill the existing research gaps, this study uses a historical and policy perspectives to examine the development trajectory of e-government in Singapore, the trends and patterns of cybercrimes and cyber attacks, and the measures taken by the government to combat cybercrimes and cyber attacks.

BACKGROUND

Cybersecurity "refers to security issues related to digital assets connected to the Internet" (Thompson, 2017, p.84). It refers to the use of people, process and technology to "prevent, detect, and recover from damage to confidentiality, integrity, and availability of information in cyberspace" (Bayuk et al., 2012, p.3). Such damage is usually caused by cyber attacks or cyberterrorism. Being regarded as a non-traditional threat, cyberterrorism refers to premeditated, unlawful attacks against computer systems, networks, and data stored therein to intimidate or coerce a government or civilian population in furtherance of political, economic, social, religious or ideological objectives (Denning, 2000, p.29; Everard, 2008, p.119; Theohary and Rollins, 2015, p.1). Such attack is carried out anonymously and remotely through computer viruses, computer worms, denial-of-service (DoS) attacks, distributed denial of service (DDoS) attacks (Tehrani, 2017, pp.55-61), Domain Name System (DNS) attacks, malicious software such as Trojan horses, phishing or spamming. It causes different types and levels of damage, including stealing, erasing, or altering information (Al-Rodhan, 2011, p.37), deleting or corrupting stored data (Fidler, 2016, p. 480), denying services, remotely taking control of a system or devices connected to the Internet of Things, paralyzing targeted critical infrastructure such as power systems, government or business operations, causing substantial financial loss, spreading misinformation, and increasing anxiety, stress, insecurity and threat perception of the general public (Gross et al, 2016, p.286). The damages caused by cyber attacks and the serious national security threat presented by cyber attacks have provoked considerable alarms among governments and various sectors of society. Governments worldwide have put cybersecurity at the top of their agenda and formulated cybersecurity policy or carried out cybersecurity measures to combat cyber attacks. The Singapore government is no exception.

THE DEVELOPMENT TRAJECTORY OF E-GOVERNMENT IN SINGAPORE

Singapore became an independent sovereign state on 9 August 1965. At that time, Singapore was a third-world nation with no natural resources, limited capital and poor infrastructure. In order to develop the economy, the government adopted an export-led industrialization strategy to attract foreign investment in labour-intensive manufacturing (Van Dijck & Verbruggen, 1987, p.406). In the late 1970s, the government realized that IT was a key to improve its economic competitiveness. It restructured manufacturing production towards capital, technology and skill-intensive activities (Van Dijck & Verbruggen, 1987, p.406). Since 1980, the government has promoted infocomm development through a series of national Inforcomm Plans and electronic government (e-government) Masterplans so as to facilitate socio-economic development and increase efficiency in government agencies.

Singapore's e-government has gone through different stages of development over time. It has evolved in tandem with each national Inforcomm Plan (Ministry of Finance & Infocomm Development Authority of Singapore, 2006, p.12) to provide better public service delivery and improve interaction between the government and various sectors of society. Since 1980, the government has launched five e-government Masterplans, which are supported by six national Infocomm Plans. Being the first e-government Masterplan, the Civil Service Computerisation Programme (CSCP) (1980-1999) was supported by three National Infocomm Plans: The National Computerization Plan (1980-1985), The National IT Plan (1986-1991), and A Vision of an Intelligent Island: The IT2000 Report (hereafter IT2000) (1992-1999). National Computer Board (NCB) was established as a central agency to oversee the implementation of the CSCP. From 1980 to 1985, the focus of the CSCP was on transforming a labour-intensive, paper-based work environment into a capital-intensive, automated work environment through computerization (Tan et al., 2013, pp.2-3). Training programmes were implemented for civil servants to gain the necessary computer knowledge and foreign professionals were recruited to solve the problem of inadequate ICT manpower in the civil service. Computerization greatly improved operational efficiency in the civil service. From 1986 to 1991, the focus of the CSCP was on using networking technologies to bring about the fusion of computer and communications. Electronic Data Interchange (EDI) was employed to allow government agencies, private companies and professional bodies to exchange data and documents electronically in a structured format (Hioe, 2001). For example, TradeNet, LawNet and MediNet were developed based on EDI to provide one stop services for the trading, legal and health care communities. EDI eliminated manual document handling procedures, thereby reducing administrative costs and turnaround time as well as achieving greater data accuracy, efficiency and productivity.

When it came to the 1990s, the focus of the CSCP was shifted to using the Internet as a new channel to engage citizens and civil servants. In March 1995, the Singapore INFOMAP (http://www.sg), which was Singapore's national website, was launched to provide the Singapore Yearbook and other government publications (Ministry of Information and the Arts, 1995, p.3). Following that, the Government Resources on the Internet (GRIN) network was established to make the Internet available to the entire civil service (Wong et al., 2003, p.350). GRIN facilitated the online presence of government agencies. In 1996, about 50 government websites were established and a government intranet was also established to "link up more than 16,000 computers across government ministries and statutory boards" (Lee, 1996). In July 1997, Singapore ONE (a.k.a. One Network for Everyone) was launched to deliver interactive, multimedia applications and services to everyone in Singapore through a nation-wide broadband network. By 2001, more than 200 multimedia applications had been deployed over Singapore ONE, such as real-time news and video-on-demand (Khoong, 2001). Singapore ONE could be accessible from homes, schools, workplaces, community centres, public libraries, or shopping malls (National Computer Board, 1997). The implementation of the Singapore ONE was regarded by the government as a concrete move to transform Singapore into an Intelligent Island (National Computer Board, 1997).

In 2000, the government launched the fourth National Infocomm Plan known as Infocomm 21. Infocomm 21 aimed at transforming Singapore into a prosperous E-economy and an infocomm-savvy e-Society (Infocomm Development Authority of Singapore, 2000, p.5). The first e-Government Action Plan (eGAP I), which was developed as part of Infocomm 21, was launched to deliver integrated and customer-oriented electronic services to citizens and businesses respectively via the eCitizen Portal (www.ecitizen.gov.sg) and the G2B Portal (www.business.gov.sg), allow faster and secure access to the government network via developing Broadband Infrastructure for Government (BIG) and Government Access Infrastructure (GATE), and promoting e-learning in the civil service via the provision of InfoComm

Education Programme (IEP) and Technology Experimentation Programme (TEP) (Ministry of Finance & Infocomm Development Authority of Singapore, 2003, pp.6-8). In 2003, the government launched the fifth National Infocomm Plan known as Connected Singapore. Connected Singapore aimed to leverage ICTs to achieve pervasive wireless connectivity, create new economic opportunities, and achieve higher efficiency, effectiveness and customer satisfaction in the government and business sectors (Infocomm Development Authority of Singapore, 2003, pp.8-18). The second Government Action Plan (eGAP II), which was developed as part of Connected Singapore, was launched to provide citizens with more integrated and personalized e-government services, foster citizen engagement through online consultation portal, and facilitate inter-operability and information sharing across agencies through The Service-Wide Technical Architecture (SWTA) (Ministry of Finance & Infocomm Development Authority of Singapore, 2003, pp.2-5).

In 2006, the government launched the sixth National Infocomm Plan known as the Intelligent Nation (iN2015) Masterplan. The iN2015 Masterplan was a 10-year masterplan with the aim of using ICT to turn Singapore into a digitally inclusive society and a more competitive economy (Infocomm Development Authority of Singapore, 2010, p.3). Following the direction of the iN2015 Masterplan, the fourth e-government Masterplan known as iGov 2010 was launched to (1) increase reach and richness of e-services; (2) increase citizens' mindshare in e-engagement; (3) enhance capacity and synergy in government; and (4) enhance national competitiveness advantage (Ministry of Finance & Infocomm Development Authority of Singapore, 2006, p.4). In 2011, the fifth e-government Masterplan known as eGov 2015 was launched to increase the interaction among the government, citizens and businesses through three strategic thrusts: (1) co-creating for greater value, where users were empowered to co-create new services by using available government datasets; (2) connecting for active participation, where new channels such as crowdsourcing tools were used to engage citizens and tap on their views; and (3) catalysing Whole-of-Government transformation, where public infrastructure and services were transformed through cloud computing and the Government Business Analytics programme (Ministry of Finance et al., 2011, pp.6-15).

After more than three decades of development, e-government in Singapore has become more and more sophisticated. As a result, Singapore has a remarkable performance in e-government and high ranking in international e-government surveys (See Table 1 in Appendix 1 and Table 2 in Appendix 2). For example, it ranked fourth in United Nations E-government Survey 2016 (United Nations, 2016, p.111) and has been ranked first in Waseda–IAC International E-Government Ranking Survey for three consecutive years from 2015-2017. Singapore is well regarded as one of the regional and world leaders in e-government. To further embrace the benefits of digital transformation, the government in November 2014 launched the

Smart Nation initiatives, with an aim to merge information technology into five key domains: public sector services, business productivity, transport, home and environment, and health and enabled ageing (Smart Nation Singapore, 2017). It is anticipated that the use of the latest technologies can increase citizens' everyday convenience and improve their quality of life, facilitate greater business efficacy and support innovation in different areas (GovTech, 2017).

THE PROBLEMS OF CYBERCRIME AND CYBER ATTACKS IN SINGAPORE

However, Singapore's growing dependence on information technology to develop the economy and society not only increases its vulnerability to cybercrime, but also increases its vulnerability to cyberterrorism with potentially catastrophic consequences. Over the past decade, cybercrime in Singapore has been increasing in frequency and severity. Singaporeans have become targets of cyber criminals due to their increasing reliance on the Internet to obtain information, have online shopping and transaction, and connect with friends (Cyber Security Agency of Singapore, 2017a, p.26). They fall victim to different types of cybercrime, including e-commerce scam, Internet love scam, email impersonation scam, credit-for-sex scam, multiple payment online purchase scan, phony PayPal email scam, and cyber extortion (Singapore Police Force, 2015; Singapore Police Force, 2017b). In Singapore, e-commerce scam, Internet love scam and credit-for-sex were the top three categories of online cheating cases (Cyber Security Agency of Singapore, 2017a, p.26). In 2016, there were 2,105 e-commerce scam cases and caused the loss of S$1.5 million (Singapore Police Force, 2017a, p.7). Internet love scam has become more frequent and caused substantial financial losses of S$24 million in 2016 (Singapore Police Force, 2017a) (See Table 3 in Appendix 3). In the first half of 2017, there were 349 cases of Internet love scam, causing the loss of S$22.1 million (Singapore Police Force, 2017b, p.3).

Police investigations revealed that scammers befriended their victims through social media platforms and online dating (Singapore Police Force, 2011, p.6). Most of these scammers were foreigners who used various cons such as being detained by Customs to dupe victims of their money. The borderless nature of the Internet makes cybercrimes difficult to solve (Sun, 2017 August 29). The continuous rise in cybercrime has become a major concern for the police and law enforcement agencies.

Meanwhile, the nation's increasing use of the Internet also creates opportunities for attackers to cause disruption or destruction. In fact, Singapore has been the target of cyber attacks for more than a decade. Four waves of Trojan email attacks were launched against civil servants in several ministries between 2004 and 2005 (Loh,

2010, p.43). In 2009, Singapore became the target of Trojan e-mail attacks again when the Asia-Pacific Economic Cooperation (APEC) meetings were held in the nation. At least seven waves of Trojan e-mail attacks were launched against members of the APEC Organising Committee and delegates of various APEC countries to infiltrate their computers and extract privileged information (Loh, 2010, p.44). "The malware used in these attacks were highly sophisticated and stealthy enough to evade the detection of most anti-virus programs" (Loh, 2010, p.45). Besides, the establishment of anti-tracking operation set-ups indicated that the perpetrators were both technically savvy and security conscious. In recent years, cyber attacks in Singapore have become more frequent and come in different forms, inflicting varying levels of damage and status. They have provoked considerable alarm in many government agencies and received extensive media attention. In 2013, a wave of cyber attacks occurred in Singapore. A hacker who went by the moniker "The Messiah" performed a series of high-profile attacks from March to November 2013 (Ng, 2015 January 23). He hacked into the Fuji Xerox web server to steal bank statements belonging to 647 premium clients of Standard Chartered Bank (Sreedharan, 2013 December 7). Besides, he hacked into the websites of People's Action Party Community Foundation (PCF), the Ang Mo Kio Town Council, Singapore's newspaper *Straits Times*, and a fan site for popstar Sun Ho (Ng, 2015 January 23). He also posted an online video threatening that the infamous hacker group Anonymous, which he claimed to be part of, would "go to war" with the Singapore Government by having aggressive cyber intrusion if the government implemented the internet licensing framework (Lee, 2013). The hacker was arrested in early November. However, another wave of cyber attacks was launched against the nation in the same month, defacing the websites of Seletar Airport, Prime Minister's Office, the Istana, which was the official residence of President Tony Tan, and 13 schools. Meanwhile, the website of the Singapore Art Museum was breached twice in November, leading to its data containing personal information of over 4,000 individuals being illegally published on an overseas website (Kok, 2013 November 30).

In early 2014, there was a security breach of the IT system of the Ministry of Foreign Affairs. But the affected devices were immediately isolated and security measures were appropriately implemented to further strengthen the network. In June the same year, SingPass accounts, which were set up for Singapore residents to perform online transactions with government agencies, were breached (Ng, 2014 June 5). A total number of 1,560 SingPass accounts were breached while 419 of these users had their passwords illegally reset (Ng, 2014 June 5). Consequently, security measures were strengthened by introducing two-factor authentication for access to e-government services (TODAY, 2017 May 12). In March 2015, a cyber attack was launched against the website of Curtin University's Singapore campus.

The defaced website displayed a smiley emoticon and a militant group's flag with the message "Hacked by Islamic State (ISIS) — we are everywhere" (TODAY, 2015 March 10). As a result, the website was taken offline for a day and then restored after resolving the security breach. In 2016, cyber attacks of website defacements and phishing attacks were launched against the government sector while e-mail scams, phishing and ransomware attacks were launched against individuals and small and medium enterprises (SMEs) (Cyber Security Agency of Singapore, 2017a, p.5). Ransomware attacks were launched against the healthcare sector, which made patient data inaccessible to medical practitioners (Cyber Security Agency of Singapore, 2017a, p.4). A total number of 19 CryptoLocker and Locky ransomware cases from individuals and SMEs were reported to the Cyber Security Agency of Singapore (CSA) (Cyber Security Agency of Singapore, 2017a, p.6). Meanwhile, over 60 command and control servers, nearly 1,800 website defacements, and over 2,500 phishing URLs were detected in Singapore in 2016 (Cyber Security Agency of Singapore, 2017a, p.6). The statistics indicated that cyber attacks in Singapore have become more frequent, widespread and severe.

In February 2017, a cyber attack was launched against the I-net system of the Ministry of Defence (MINDEF), which resulted in the theft of the personal data of 850 national servicemen and employees from MINDEF (Lee, 2017 March 1). The stolen personal data included National Registration Identity Card (NRIC) numbers, dates of birth, and telephone numbers (Chua, 2017 April 3). Based on the investigation, MINDEF's Deputy Secretary for Technology said that this was a targeted and well-panned attack with the aim of accessing official secrets (Loke, 2017 February 28). But no classified military data was lost in the attack because the data was stored on a separate system that was not connected to the Internet (Loke, 2017 February 28). In April 2017, advanced persistent threat (APT) attacks were launched against the National University of Singapore (NUS) and Nanyang Technological University, with the aim of stealing government information and research documents. Investigations by the CSA indicated that the attacks on these two universities were not coordinated because "they did not originate from the same place, and were not conducted by the same people" (Ong, 2017 May 12). In May the same year, the WannaCry ransomware attack, which locked users' files unless they paid a designated sum in virtual currency, were launched against the digital directory service at some shopping malls in Singapore (Channel NewsAsia, 2017 May 14). But no money or bitcoins were paid to the hackers and the affected systems were fixed and fully restored the following day (Channel NewsAsia, 2017 May 14). While the WannaCry ransomware attack had infected over 230,000 computers in about 150 countries (Mullin and Lake, 2017 August 4), the scale of the attack was moderate in Singapore without affecting any government agencies and critical information infrastructure (Toh, 2017 May 13).

Since cyber attacks are increasing in frequency, scale, diversity, and sophistication and have a much broader target, they inflict wide-ranging damage on the victim and have far-reaching impact on the economy and society. It is apparent that no country, institutions or individuals can be completely immune to cyber attacks. Singapore is likely to remain a prime target for cyber attacks for years to come, especially when it transforms into a Smart Nation and boosts the digital economy. In fact, Singapore in 2014 ranked fifth in Cyber Vulnerability Index (CVI) in the survey conducted by Deloitte, indicating that it was nine times more vulnerable to cyber attack than other Asia-Pacific economies (Deloitte, 2016, pp.19-20). Hence, the government needs to be more vigilant and devote more time and resources to strengthening its cyber security.

CYBERSECURITY MEASURES IN SINGAPORE

The Implementation of Infocomm Security Masterplans

The formulation and implementation of Infocomm Security Masterplans represents the government's continuous commitment and unremitting efforts to provide a secure and reliable infocomm environment that is vital to the functioning of the economy and society. Infocomm Security Masterplan provides a strategic roadmap for strengthening the nation's cybersecurity. It is reviewed regularly to ensure its relevance and applicability so that the nation can keep pace with the constantly changing cyber threat landscape and address evolving cybersecurity challenges. In February 2005, the first Infocomm Security Masterplan was developed through a multi-agency effort under the guidance of the National Infocomm Security Committee (NISC) (Infocomm Development Authority of Singapore, 2005). It was a three-year Masterplan having a budget of S$38 million to build new capabilities within the public sector to manage internal and external cyber threats and enhance the overall cybersecurity of the nation (Infocomm Development Authority of Singapore, 2005). One of the key initiatives was the establishment of National Cyberthreat Monitoring Centre (NCMC), which consisted of the Cyber-Watch Centre (CWC) to provide the 24-hour monitoring of critical IT installations in the public sector and Threat Analysis Centre (TAC) to analyse cyber-threat data.

In 2008, the second Infocomm Security Masterplan was implemented to protect CIIs in the nation and enhance the competencies of public sector, private sector and the general public against cyber threats (Infocomm Development Authority of Singapore, 2008). It was a five-year Masterplan having the budget of S$70 million to carry out key initiatives (Infocomm Development Authority of Singapore, 2008). Sector-specific infocomm security programmes were developed to assess and develop customised solutions that could meet unique security requirements of CII owners (Infocomm Development Authority of Singapore, 2008). Meanwhile, Cyber Security Awareness Alliance was formed to raise awareness and adoption of good cyber security practices among businesses and individuals through seminars and workshops (Infocomm Development Authority of Singapore, 2008). It co-organized some well received initiatives such as National Infocomms Security Competition and Infocomm Security Seminar (Ministry of Home Affairs, 2014). In 2013, a five-year National Cyber Security Masterplan 2018 (NCSM2018) was implemented to increase the level of maturity and sophistication of Singapore's infocomm security (Infocomm Development Authority of Singapore, 2013a, p.4). Some of the key initiatives that the government undertook included (a) the implementation of the CII Protection Assessment programme and the National Cyber Security Exercise programme to enhance security and resilience of CIIs to deal with sophisticated cyber attacks; (b) upgrading the detection capabilities of CWC and the analysis capabilities of TAC via advanced techniques and technologies; (c) raising cybersecurity security awareness and promoting the adoption of appropriate security measures amongst businesses and individuals through the implementation of the Cyber Security Awareness and Outreach programme; and (d) increasing the number and skill levels of cybersecurity professionals through the implementation of the National Cybersecurity R&D Programme and the establishment of the DigiSAFE Cyber Security Centre (Infocomm Development Authority of Singapore, 2013a, pp.12-7). In July 2016, National Cybercrime Action Plan (NCAP) was implemented to deter, detect and disrupt cybercriminal activities effectively. The government's strategies to combat cybercrime could be grouped into four priority areas, which included (a) educating and empowering the public to stay safe in cyberspace through outreach programme and a one-stop self-help portal; (b) enhancing the government's capabilities to combat cybercrime through the use of the latest technologies and strengthening coordination between Singapore Police Force (SPF) and government agencies; (c) strengthening cybersecurity legislation; and (d) strengthening local partnerships and international engagements (Ministry of Home Affairs, 2016, pp. 2-3).

The Establishment of New Institutions to Handle Cybersecurity-Related Issues

The growing volume and sophistication of cyber attacks poses a serious threat to national security, public safety, and the economic and social well-being of a nation. New institutions need to be established to handle cyber threats and attacks more effectively. They possess legal authorities, financial resources, specialized expertise, skills, technologies and equipment required for monitoring, detecting, responding to, recovering from and preventing cyber attacks. Over the past two decades, the government has established different institutions to handle cybersecurity-related issues. In October 1997, the Singapore Computer Emergency Response Team (SingCERT) was established by the Infocomm Development Authority of Singapore (IDA), in collaboration with NUS to "facilitate the detection, resolution and prevention of security related incidents on the Internet" (The Singapore Computer Emergency Response Team, 2015). Beyond its work in Singapore, SingCERT collaborated with foreign CERTs to manage cyber incidents across borders. It was a founding member of the Asia Pacific Computer Emergency Response Team (APCERT) in 2002 to support the cooperation between national CERTS in the Asia Pacific region (Tan, 2004). In 2007, the CWC was established by IDA. It was staffed with 12 security professionals comprising security engineers and analysts and adopted new security tools such as security event correlation (Yu, 2006) to provide alerts on cyber attacks for the relevant government agencies so that appropriate preventive measures could be taken in a timely manner (Infocomm Development Authority of Singapore, 2013b). In 2014, the CWC enhanced its detection capabilities to detect network data loss and malware threat through the use of advanced technology such as intrusion detection sensors and intelligence feeds (Infocomm Development Authority of Singapore, 2013b). In the first half of 2018, the government will call a tender for the first Government Security Operation Centre (SOC), which will replace the CWC to detect cyber threats through the use of artificial intelligence and the analytics smarts (Tham, 2017 May 25).

In 2009, the Singapore Infocomm Technology Security Authority (SITSA) was established under the Internal Security Department of the Ministry of Home Affairs (MHA) as a specialist authority to safeguard Singapore's national security against external threats, such as cyber-attacks and cyber-espionage (Cyber Security Agency of Singapore, 2016a, p.7). Its main responsibilities included protecting CII in the water, energy, transportation and finance sectors against cyber attacks, raising the level of readiness to counter cyber-attacks against the nation, and creating a process for monitoring and reporting security incidents (Lemon, 2009). Recognizing that there was a lack of skilled cyber security professionals in the nation, the government in November 2014 set up a Cyber Security Lab (CSL) within the Home Team Academy (Phneah, 2013), which is one of the seven departments of the MHA. Its main responsibility was to enhance the capabilities of officers, CII regulators and operators in preventing, detecting and responding to cyberthreats through training (Phneah, 2013). Courses were split into three levels: basic, intermediate, and advanced (Ng, 2014). The curriculum covered a wide range of topics, including cyber security fundamentals, malware analysis and digital forensics (Networks Asia, 2016). Apart from teaching individual cyber skills, CSL also taught team-based cyber skills through group dynamic exercises (Ng, 2014). The first batch of training participants came from various sectors, including Monetary Authority of

Singapore, Infocomm Development Authority, the Land Transport Authority and the Energy Market Authority (Ng, 2014). Besides, CSL was responsible for forging closer public-private sector collaboration in the protection of CII (Phneah, 2013).

In April 2015, CSA was established as a national agency under the Prime Minister's Office and was managed administratively by the Ministry of Communications and Information (MCI) (Cyber Security Agency of Singapore, 2016a, p.7). It subsumed SingCERT and SITSA to "provide centralised supervision over the nation's key cyber security functions" (Ng, 2015), "lead the cyber security master plan" (Tan, 2015 January 28) and "carry out both cybersecurity capability development and crisis management across all CII sectors" (The Ministry of Communications and Information and the Cyber Security Agency of Singapore, 2017, p.1). CSA's responsibilities included coordinating public- and private-sector efforts against cyber threats (Ng, 2015) and enhancing the cybersecurity awareness of the general public through outreach programmes (Cyber Security Agency of Singapore, 2017b). It was also "empowered to develop and enforce cybersecurity regulations, policies, and practices" (Cyber Security Agency of Singapore, 2016a, p.7). For example, CSA in late 2015 commenced work on a new Cybersecurity Bill and in July 2017 released the Bill for public consultation. CSA has been working closely with the Smart Nation Programme Office (SNPO) to ensure that there will be cybersecurity-by-design for the Smart Nation project (Kwang, 2015 August 4). In 2015, the Cybercrime Command was established by the SPF as a unit within the Criminal Investigation Department (Bhunia, 2017a) to "develop specialist expertise in cyber investigation, digital forensics and cybercrime policy, and also to improve Police readiness for, and response to, emerging cyber threats" (Bhunia, 2017a). Besides, it oversees full-time Cybercrime Response Teams (CRTs) (Networks Asia, 2016), which was set up by the SPF in all six of its frontline Police Divisions in December 2015 to enhance cybercrime response capabilities (Bhunia, 2017a). CRTs "have a level of proficiency and expertise in investigations and digital forensics" (Networks Asia, 2016). In February 2017, the Cybercrime Command created the "Alliance of Public-Private Cybercrime Stakeholders" to forge active collaboration between law enforcement and the private sector and enhance cybercrime awareness in the private sector to detect, deter and prevent cybercrime (Ministry of Home Affairs, 2017a). The Alliance serves as a new public-private industry platform to allow 40 partners from global IT companies, the financial industry, E-commerce platforms, remittance agencies and telecommunications service sector to strengthen communication with the police and they convene biannually to share updates on cybercrime (Cashshield, 2017). It helps accelerate the pace at which the public and private sectors can take preventive measures or collective action against cybercrimes, especially those that are transnational in nature (Tan, 2017 July 5).

Developing a Robust Legislative Framework

Cybercrime legislation is an integral component of a national cybersecurity strategy. The advent of the Internet gave rise to new forms of crime (Leung, 2003, p.4) that could no longer be addressed by existing legislation. As a result, new and proper legislation is enacted to specifically investigate, prosecute and adjudicate cybercrime. It clearly defines the acts constituting offences and corresponding penalties that can create a strong deterrent effect. To remain effective, cybercrime legislation is regularly reviewed and updated to keep up with the rapidly evolving cybercrime landscape. In Singapore, the landmark Computer Misuse Act (CMA) was enacted in 1993 to introduce "specific offences and penalties targeted at computer crimes" (Kor, 2017). Being modelled after the United Kingdom's Computer Misuse Act 1990, the CMA criminalized unauthorized access to computer material, unauthorized modification of computer material, unauthorized access with intent to commit an offence involving property, fraud, dishonesty or which causes bodily harm, unauthorized use or interception of computer service, and abetments (Singapore Statutes Online, 1993). In 1998, the Computer Misuse (Amendment) Act was introduced to "provide for enhanced penalties proportionate to the different levels of potential and actual harm caused" (Zhou, 2011), criminalize unauthorized obstruction of use of computer and unauthorized disclosure of access code, grant police officer the power to access decrypted data when conducting an investigation, and make it an offence to obstruct the lawful exercise of the powers of a police officer or refuse to assist a police officer in an investigation (Singapore Statutes Online, 1998). In 2003, CMA was amended to fight against cyberterrorism by allowing "police to take pre-emptive action based on credible information before hackers strike to protect computer networks from unauthorized entry" (CNN.com, 2003 November 11). "In 2013, the CMA was amended to include cybersecurity measures and renamed the Computer Misuse and Cybersecurity Act (CMCA)" (Ministry of Home Affairs, 2017b). The CMCA empowered the Minister of Home Affairs to issue a certificate to authorise or direct any person or organisation to take measures necessary to prevent, detect or counter cyber threats to Singapore's national security, essential services, defence or foreign relations (Chang, 2013, p.13). Anyone convicted for obstruction or non-compliance could face a fine of up to S$50,000 or imprisonment for up to 10 years or both (Chang, 2013, p.14). In April 2017, the CMCA was amended to handle the evolving tactics of cybercriminals, the transnational nature and increasing scale of cybercrime (Ministry of Home Affairs, 2017b). There were four key amendments. Firstly, it criminalized the act of obtaining, retaining, supplying and transmitting personal information obtained through cybercrime (OrionW LLC, 2017). Secondly, it criminalized the act of obtaining or retaining certain specified items which could be used to commit a computer crime (OrionW LLC, 2017). Thirdly, it extended the territorial scope of the CMCA by criminalizing cybercrimes committed overseas (OrionW LLC, 2017). Fourthly, it allowed prosecutors to amalgamate cybercrime charges in certain circumstances (OrionW LLC, 2017).

After several amendments, the range and scope of CMA provisions have been progressively enhanced to cope with the changing tides of cyber-crime and technology (Kor, 2017). Nevertheless, the government recognized that the CMCA alone was not enough to deal with the rapidly evolving cybersecurity landscape of Singapore, especially when cyber attacks had become more frequent, sophisticated and impactful (Cyber Security Agency of Singapore, 2017c). A new cybersecurity legislation was needed to allow the government to take pro-active measures to protect CII across the public and private sectors, facilitate sharing of cybersecurity information across critical sectors and respond to cyber threats in an expedient manner (Cyber Security Agency of Singapore, 2017c). For this reason, a proposed Cybersecurity Bill was released in July 2017 for public consultation that ended in early August. It is expected that the new Cybersecurity Bill will be introduced to Parliament in 2018.

Strengthening Regional and International Cooperation

Given the cross-border nature and complexity of cybercrime and cyber threats, no single country can successfully combat cybercrime or cyber threats alone using the traditional siloed approach. Meanwhile, the shortage of cyber security workforce presents a challenge to combat cybercrime or cyber threats in a timely and efficient manner. Jurisdictional issues also present a challenge to combat cybercrime and cyber threats because perpetrators or organized crime gangs are located overseas. Under these circumstances, bringing perpetrators to justice requires coordinated effort and collaborative response from governments, law enforcement agencies, and stakeholders in different regions. It is only by having collective efforts and strengthening international cooperation that capacity building, the sharing of cyber threat intelligence, the collection of evidence and the training of cybersecurity professionals can be facilitated to combat cybercrime and cyber threats more effectively. On the international front, Singapore has been actively enhancing strategic partnership with Western counterparts in the area of cyber security. For example, Singapore and the United States in August 2016 signed a cybersecurity Memorandum of Understanding (MOU) to formalise their commitment to work together in key areas that included regular information exchanges between CERTS in two places, conducting joint cybersecurity exercises, sharing of best practices on CII protection, and coordination in cyber incident response (Cyber Security Agency of Singapore, 2016b). Singapore also had bilateral agreement with France, the United Kingdom, the Netherlands, Australia and Germany, which covered cybersecurity cooperation in key areas including regular information exchanges, sharing of best practices, and cyber security talent development (Bhunia, 2017b). On the regional front, Singapore has been continuously forging closer cybersecurity cooperation with other Asian countries (Infocomm Development Authority of Singapore, 2013a, pp.23-4). For example, Singapore and India in 2015 signed a cybersecurity MOU to establish formal cooperation in key areas such as cooperation between CERTS in these two places, sharing of best practices and joint training and research (Bhunia, 2017b). In September 2017, Singapore and Japan signed a Memorandum of Cooperation to strengthen cybersecurity awareness, information exchanges, sharing of best practices and joint regional capacity building (Tan, 2017 September 19). Meanwhile, Singapore has been actively contributing to cybersecurity capability building in the Association of Southeast Asian Nations (ASEAN) region through the annual ASEAN CERT Incident Drill (ACID), ASEAN Network Security Action Council (ANSAC), and ASEAN cybersecurity and cybercrime workshops (Cyber Security Agency of Singapore, 2016a, p.45). In September 2017, Singapore announced that it would use S$1.5 million from the ASEAN Cyber Capacity Building Programme (ACCP) it set up in 2016 to train incident responders and operators in the ASEAN region for the next three years (Bhunia, 2017c). It is expected that up to 18 candidates will be trained and equipped with knowledge about "security operations centre (SOC) operations and management, and other relevant technical areas of cybersecurity" (Bhunia, 2017c) so that they will be able to monitor and respond to cyber threats effectively. Singapore's devotion to strengthening regional coordination and cybersecurity capability building has contributed to stronger regional cohesion and ensured a safe and secure cyberspace.

Raising Cybersecurity Awareness Among Businesses and Individuals

Cybersecurity is a shared responsibility. To avoid becoming easy targets for cyber criminals, businesses and individuals are also responsible for engaging in appropriate online behaviour and taking precautionary measures to protect their computers. Nevertheless, enterprises in Singapore have yet to adopt sufficient cybersecurity practices to address relevant cybersecurity risks and protect their data assets such as customer information, financial information and intellectual property. In 2017, a survey conducted by Accenture revealed that one in four cyberattacks resulted in an actual security breach in large enterprises in Singapore, which equated two to three effective attacks per month for the average company (Accenture, 2017a, p.4; Accenture, 2017b). Nevertheless, it took months or more than a year for large enterprises to detect such security breach (Accenture, 2017a, p.4). While facing frequent cyberattacks, only 41 percent of large enterprises surveyed would invest extra money to protect customer data, which was 3 percent lower than the global average (Accenture, 2017a, p.5). Besides, only 31 percent of large enterprises surveyed would invest extra money to mitigate against financial losses caused by security breach, and only 8 percent of large enterprises surveyed would invest in cybersecurity training, which was much lower than the global average of 17 percent (Accenture, 2017a, p.5). Meanwhile, SMEs that accounted for 99 percent of the nation's enterprises and 50 percent of the nation's Gross Domestic Product (GDP) (www.gov.sg, 2017) did not have sufficient cybersecurity measures due to the lack of awareness, cost, and the shortage of IT staff (Channel NewAsia, 2016 April 11). In fact, adopting a proactive approach to cybersecurity matters to large enterprises and SMEs because any security breach can lead to incalculable losses in terms of finance, reputation, consumer trust and loyalty. A proactive approach to cybersecurity requires enterprises to regularly conduct cybersecurity risk assessment in order to find out and address security vulnerabilities in computer systems in advance. This can also help enterprises identify cybersecurity priorities when facing budget constraints and the shortage of IT staff. For enterprises that do not have cybersecurity budget constraint, they can adopt data breach prevention tools to ensure data safety. For enterprises that have budget constraint, they can adopt a more cost-effective but often overlooked approach to cybersecurity by regularly updating software patches. They can also sign up for alerts and advisories at the website of SingCERT (www. csa.gov.sg/singcert) on how to pre-empt cyber incidents (Lee, 2017 May 30).

Meanwhile, it is also important to strengthen the cyber defence capability of enterprises by providing on-site or online cybersecurity training for their employees. Cybersecurity training should be provided on a regular basis and make it compulsory for all the employees. It can raise the cybersecurity awareness of employees and ensure that they stay alert for the latest cyber security threats. Employees should be instructed to use strong password and change it frequently. They should also be instructed to report any suspicious links or emails they receive to IT staff. In October 2015, the government introduced a free plug-and-play digital Employee Cyber Security Kit (ECS Kit) to help enterprises "achieve a structured employee education program with minimal time, investment and manpower" (Hui, 2015 Oct 27). The ECS Kit took employees through the five stages of behavioural change in the Transtheoretical Model: awareness, design, knowledge, action and reinforcement (Networks Asia, 2015). The CSA also reaches out to SMEs to promote the awareness and adoption of cyber security practices by regularly holding talks and conferences (Lee, 2017 May 30).

There is also a pressing need to enhance cybersecurity awareness among individuals and change their attitudes and behaviours towards cybersecurity. Both international and local surveys indicate that Singaporeans do not take enough precautionary measures to protect their computing devices. Internationally, the Global Digital Assets survey conducted by McAfee showed that while 73 percent

Singaporeans surveyed were familiar with online security risks such as identify theft or monetary theft, about 87 percent of Singaporeans surveyed did not take any precautionary measures to protect their tablets and about 69 percent of Singaporeans surveyed did not install any security software to protect their smartphones (Precious Communications, 2013). Another problem was that 50 percent of Singaporeans surveyed used the same password for all websites (Precious Communications, 2013). This undermined password security and put their online accounts at risk because hackers could easily gain access to all of their accounts on every website as long as hackers could crack the password. Locally, Cybersecurity Public Awareness Survey conducted by the CSA in August 2016 indicated that many Singaporeans had not integrated good cyber hygiene practices into their daily routines although they agreed that individuals were responsible for cybersecurity. According to the survey, 73 percent of 2,000 respondents surveyed agreed that all Singaporeans had a role to play in cybersecurity (Cyber Security Agency of Singapore, 2017d, p.12). While 86 percent of respondents surveyed created strong password by using a combination of letters, numbers and symbols (Cyber Security Agency of Singapore, 2017d, p.6), many of them did not store their passwords securely. While 33 percent of respondents stored passwords on their computers or wrote down passwords on paper, 31 percent of respondents used the same password for work and personal accounts (Cyber Security Agency of Singapore, 2017d, p.7). These storage methods were not secured at all because anyone who had physical access to that paper or the computers could steal passwords easily and compromise victims' online accounts. Besides, passwords stored in the computers could also be stolen by hackers easily if no encryption was used. The survey also found that 24 percent of respondents did not enable Two-Factor Authentication (2FA) when the option was available because they thought that it was time consuming and unnecessary (Cyber Security Agency of Singapore, 2017d, p.7). According to the survey, 41 percent of respondents did not conduct virus scan on files or devices before opening because most of them thought that it was time consuming to do so (Cyber Security Agency of Singapore, 2017d, p.11). In addition, 32 percent of respondents did not install security applications on their mobile phones because they thought that such applications were unnecessary and took up too much storage space (Cyber Security Agency of Singapore, 2017d, p.4). Both the international and local survey results showed that the government needs to raise cybersecurity awareness among individuals and introduce good cyber hygiene practices to them through different channels. Recognizing that it is important to establish good cyber hygiene at an early age, the government produced and distributed a series of activity book to educate primary school students on cyber safety and personal data protection (GoSafeOnline, 2017). The books contained fun and engaging activities such as word search and maze for students to learn about cybersecurity knowledge in an interesting way (Cyber Security Agency of

Singapore and Personal Data Protection Commission, 2016). They also contained parent-child activities to encourage parents to engage in meaningful conversations with their children about cyber safety and reinforce the values children have learnt in the book. Besides, the government made use of television program to cultivate a cybersecurity-conscious culture and educate ordinary citizens on cyber crime prevention. Episodes covering cybercrimes such as ransomware were produced and broadcast on free-to-air television channels (Cyber Security Agency of Singapore, 2017a, p.38). The government also established the GoSafeOnline and SingCERT websites to provide Internet users with up-to-date cybersecurity news, resources and tips to protect their computing devices from cyber threats (Cyber Security Agency of Singapore, 2017a, p.38).

FINDINGS AND DISCUSSION

The case study of Singapore shows that the government has adopted a proactive, holistic and cooperative approach to cybersecurity in order to tackle ever-increasing cybersecurity challenges. It has regularly reviewed and updated cybersecurity measures to ensure their effectiveness and strengthened its defence capabilities over time through coordinating national effort with public and private sectors and cooperating with regional and international counterparts. The government has demonstrated strong political will and long-term commitment to combating cyber attacks and ensuring a safe and secure cyberspace. The chase for a perfect cybersecurity system or strategy is both impossible and unnecessary. However, it is important and necessary to establish a cybersecurity system or formulate a cybersecurity strategy that can mitigate and avoid cyber risks or threats, detect and respond to cyber attacks in a timely manner, and strike a balance between cybersecurity and efficiency. Besides, cybersecurity is a shared responsibility. The government alone is insufficient to tackle an unprecedented increase in volume, sophistication and severity of cyber attacks. The business sector and individuals also play an important role in cybersecurity.

FUTURE RESEARCH DIRECTIONS

The development of cybersecurity strategy or measures is an ongoing effort. At the time of this study, the new Cybersecurity Bill has not been introduced to Parliament. Future studies can examine the impact of new cybersecurity legislation on combating cyber attacks in the nation or compare the new cybersecurity legislation with cybersecurity legislation in other Asian or Western countries. Future studies can also examine citizens' views on cybersecurity measures or their cybersecurity awareness so that the government can find ways to strengthen current measures or introduce new measures to protect citizens from cyber attacks.

CONCLUSION

To conclude, the government in Singapore has made unremitting efforts to combat cybercrime and cyber attacks. Facing the increasing volume and sophistication of cyber attacks, the government has demonstrated strong political will and determination to introduce, review and improve cybersecurity measures so that the nation has a safe and trusted cyberspace and maintains high cybersecurity standards, which are vital to the economic and social well-being of the nation. Looking forward, the government's commitment to carrying out cybersecurity measures will make the nation stronger, safer and more secure.

REFERENCES

Accenture. (2017a). *Building Confidence: Facing the Cybersecurity Conundrum in Singapore*. Retrieved November 18, 2017, from https://www.accenture.com/t20170406T010037Z__w__/sg-en/_acnmedia/PDF-38/Accenture-Facing-Cybersecurity-Conundrum-Singapore.pdf

Accenture. (2017b). *Accenture Survey: One in Four Cyberattacks in Singapore Result in a Security Breach, Yet Most Organisations Remain Confident in Their Ability to Protect Themselves*. Retrieved November 18, 2017, from https://www.accenture.com/sg-en/company-newsroom-accenture-survey-one-four-cyberattacks

Al-Rodhan, N. R. F. (2011). *The Politics of Emerging Strategic Technologies: Implications for Geopolitics, Human Enhancement and Human Destiny*. London: Palgrave Macmillan. doi:10.1057/9780230304949

Bayuk, J. L., Healey, J., Rohmeyer, P., Sachs, M. H., Schmidt, J., & Weiss, J. (2012). *Cyber Security Policy Guidebook*. Hoboken, NJ: Wiley. doi:10.1002/9781118241530

Bhunia, P. (2017a). *Public-Private Alliance Launched by Singapore Police Cybercrime Command*. Retrieved November 6, 2017, from http://opengovasia.com/articles/7778-public-private-alliance-launched-by-singapore-police-cybercrime-command

Bhunia, P. (2017b). *Singapore Enters into Seventh Bilateral Agreement on Cybersecurity Cooperation.* Retrieved November 13, 2017, from http://opengovasia.com/articles/7785-singapore-enters-into-seventh-bilateral-agreement-on-cybersecurity-cooperation

Bhunia, P. (2017c). *New Steps from Singapore Government to Build Cybersecurity Capabilities in Singapore and ASEAN Region in Collaboration with Industry.* Retrieved November 13, 2017, from http://opengovasia.com/articles/8020-new-steps-from-singapore-government-to-build-cybersecurity-capabilities-in-singapore-and-asean-region-in-collaboration-with-industry

Cashshield. (2017). *A Pact Against CyberCrime: CashShield and the Singapore Police Force Join Forces to Secure the Digital World.* Retrieved November 6, 2017, from http://www.cashshield.com/a-pact-against-cybercrime-cashshield-and-the-singapore-police-force-join-forces-to-secure-the-digital-world/

Chang, W. (2013). *Amendments to Singapore's Computer Misuse Act.* Retrieved November 4, 2017, from http://www.cnplaw.com/en/media/files/services/EFPLP.pdf

Channel NewAsia. (2015, May 11). *Cyber Security Agency, IDA Maintain High Level of Vigilance over Govt Networks: Yaacob.* Retrieved October 26, 2017, from http://www.channelnewsasia.com/news/singapore/cyber-security-agency-ida-maintain-high-level-of-vigilance-over--8264556

Channel NewAsia. (2016, April 11). *New Cybersecurity Act to be Tabled in 2017: Yaacob Ibrahim.* Retrieved November 18, 2017, from http://www.channelnewsasia.com/news/singapore/new-cybersecurity-act-to-be-tabled-in-2017-yaacob-ibrahim-8088054

Channel NewsAsia. (2017, May 14). *Tiong Bahru Plaza's Digital Directory Hit by Global Ransomware Attack: Mall Operator.* Retrieved October 30, 2017, from http://www.channelnewsasia.com/news/singapore/tiong-bahru-plaza-s-digital-directory-hit-by-global-ransomware-8846096

CNN.com. (2003, November 11). *Singapore Clamps Down on Hackers.* Retrieved November 4, 2017, from http://edition.cnn.com/2003/TECH/internet/11/11/singapore.internet.reut/

Cyber Security Agency of Singapore. (2016a). *Singapore's Cybersecurity Strategy.* Retrieved November 5, 2017, from https://www.csa.gov.sg/news/publications/singapore-cybersecurity-strategy

Cyber Security Agency of Singapore. (2016b). *Singapore Strengthens Partnership with the United States*. Retrieved November 13, 2017, from https://www.csa.gov.sg/news/press-releases/singapore-us-mou

Cyber Security Agency of Singapore. (2017a). *Singapore Cyber Landscape 2016*. Retrieved October 29, 2017, from https://www.csa.gov.sg/~/media/csa/documents/publications/singaporecyberlandscape2016.ashx?la=en

Cyber Security Agency of Singapore. (2017b). *Our Organisation*. Retrieved November 5, 2017, from https://www.csa.gov.sg/about-us/our-organisation

Cyber Security Agency of Singapore. (2017c). *MCI and CSA Seek Public Feedback on Proposed Cybersecurity Bill*. Retrieved November 4, 2017, from https://www.csa.gov.sg/news/press-releases/mci-and-csa-seek-public-feedback-on-proposed-cybersecurity-bill#sthash.g9mjneAk.dpuf

Cyber Security Agency of Singapore. (2017d). *Cybersecurity Public Awareness Survey 2016 Key Findings*. Retrieved November 15, 2017, from https://www.csa.gov.sg/~/media/csa/documents/key_findings/key%20findings-cybersecurity%20public%20awareness%20survey%202016.ashx?la=en

Cyber Security Agency of Singapore, & Personal Data Protection Commission. (2016). *Cyber Safety Issue 2*. Retrieved November 18, 2017, from https://www.csa.gov.sg/gosafeonline/~/media/gso/images/activity_book/cyber_security_activity_book_2.ashx?la=en

Deloitte. (2016). *Asia-Pacific Defense Outlook 2016: Defense in Four Domains*. Retrieved July 25, 2017 from https://www2.deloitte.com/content/dam/Deloitte/global/Documents/Public-Sector/gx-ps-ap-defense-outlook-2016-160216.pdf

Denning, D. E. (2000). Cyberterrorism: The Logic Bomb versus the Truck Bomb. *Global Dialogue*, 2(4), 29–37.

Everard, P. (2008). NATO and Cyber Terrorism. In Centre of Excellence Defence Against Terrorism (Ed.), Responses to Cyber Terrorism (pp. 118-126). IOS Press.

Fidler, D. P. (2016). Cyberspace, Terrorism and International Law. *Journal of Conflict and Security Law*, 21(3), 475–493. doi:10.1093/jcsl/krw013

GoSafeOnline. (2017). *Cyber Safety Activity Book*. Retrieved November 18, 2017, from https://www.csa.gov.sg/gosafeonline/resources/activity-book

GovTech. (2017). *Opening GOH Address by Dr. Janil Puthucheary for GovInsider Innovation Labs World Conference 2017*. Retrieved October 25, 2017, from https://www.tech.gov.sg/media-room/speeches/2017/09/opening-goh-address-by-dr-janil-puthucheary-for-govinsider-innovation-labs-world-conference-2017

Gross, M. L., Canetti, D., & Vashdi, D. R. (2016). The Psychological Effects of Cyber Terrorism. *Bulletin of the Atomic Scientists*, *72*(5), 284–291. doi:10.1080/00963402.2016.1216502 PMID:28366962

Hioe, W. (2001). *National Infocomm Strategy and Policy: Singapore's Experience*. Retrieved October 18, 2017, from http://www.unapcict.org

Hui, C. (2015, Oct 27). *Cyber Security in Businesses Gets a Boost with New Employee Kit*. Retrieved November 18, 2017, from http://www.channelnewsasia.com/news/business/cyber-security-in-businesses-gets-a-boost-with-new-employee-kit-8234376

Infocomm Development Authority of Singapore. (2000). *Infocomm 21: Singapore Where the Digital Future Is*. Retrieved August 31, 2017, from https://www.imda.gov.sg/about/corporate-publications/past-publications/past-infocomm-plans

Infocomm Development Authority of Singapore. (2003). *Connected Singapore: Unleashing Potential, Realizing Possibilities, through Infocomm*. Retrieved August 31, 2017, from https://www.tech.gov.sg/-/media/GovTech/About-us/Corporate-Publications/Past-infocomm-plans/Connected.pdf?la=en

Infocomm Development Authority of Singapore. (2005). *Three-year Infocomm Security Masterplan Unveiled*. Retrieved November 12, 2017, from https://www.imda.gov.sg/about/newsroom/archived/ida/media-releases/2005/20050712110643

Infocomm Development Authority of Singapore. (2008). *Plan Aims to Bolster National Readiness to Counter Cyber Threats*. Retrieved November 12, 2017, from https://www.tech.gov.sg/media-room/media-releases/2008/04/new-s70m-masterplan-to-boost-singapores-infocomm-s

Infocomm Development Authority of Singapore. (2010). *Realising the iN2015 Vision: Singapore: An Intelligent Nation, A Global City, Powered by Infocomm*. Retrieved August 31, 2017, from https://www.tech.gov.sg/-/media/GovTech/About-us/Corporate-Publications/PDFs/iN2015-Reports/realisingthevisionin2015.pdf

Infocomm Development Authority of Singapore. (2013a). *National Cyber Security Masterplan 2018*. Retrieved November 12, 2017, from https://www.itu.int/en/ITU-D/Cybersecurity/Documents/National_Strategies_Repository/Singapore_2013_AnnexA.pdf

Infocomm Development Authority of Singapore. (2013b). *Enhanced Cyber-Watch Centre to Strengthen Infocomm Security.* Retrieved November 6, 2017, from https://www.tech.gov.sg/-/media/GovTech/Media-Room/Media-Releases/2013/5/AnnexDpdf.pdf

Khoong, H. Y. (2001). *Khoong Hock Yun, Assistant Chief Executive, Infocomm Development, IDA Singapore – Speech CIAPR Forum - Singapore Day Symposium, Grand Hyatt Shanghai, China.* Retrieved October 19, 2017, from https://www.imda.gov.sg/about/newsroom/archived/ida/speeches/2001/20061212150610

Kok, X. H. (2013 November 30). MOM Site Duplicated, Art Museum Site Breached. *Today.* Retrieved October 26, 2017, from http://www.todayonline.com/singapore/mom-site-duplicated-art-museum-site-breached

Kor, V. (2017). *Cybersecurity: A Concentric Approach.* Retrieved November 4, 2017, from https://www.tech.gov.sg/TechNews/Opinions/2017/04/07/08/06/Cybersecurity-A-Concentric-Approach

Kwang, K. (2015, August 4). Internet 'Was Not Designed for Safety': Cyber Security Agency Chief. *Channel NewsAsia.* Retrieved November 6, 2017, from http://www.channelnewsasia.com/news/singapore/internet--was-not-designed-for-safety--cyber-security-agency-chi-8237784

Lee, C. (2017, May 30). *Cyber Security Resources, Grants Available to SMEs.* Retrieved November 18, 2017, from http://www.todayonline.com/voices/cyber-security-resources-grants-available-smes

Lee, H. L. (1996). *Speech - Launch of the Singapore Government Internet Web Site and Intranet.* Retrieved August 30, 2017, from https://www.imda.gov.sg/about/newsroom/archived/ida/speeches/1996/20050728144718

Lee, T. (2013). *'Anonymous' Hackers Threaten War with Singapore Government.* Retrieved October 26, 2017, from https://www.techinasia.com/youtube-anonymous-hacker-group-threatens-war-singapore-govt-video-removed-viral

Lee, U. (2017 March 1). *Mindef's Internet System Breached in Cyberattack.* Retrieved October 26, 2017, from http://www.businesstimes.com.sg/technology/mindefs-internet-system-breached-in-cyberattack

Lemon, S. (2009). *Singapore to Form National Cyber-Security Agency.* Retrieved November 5, 2017, from https://www.cio.com/article/2424366/government/singapore-to-form-national-cyber-security-agency.html

Leung, E. (2003). *Speech by the Secretary for Justice at Internet Law Symposium.* Retrieved November 19, 2017, from http://www.doj.gov.hk/eng/archive/pdf/sj260903e.pdf

Loh, P. J. (2010). APEC Trojan Email Attacks. *Home Team Journal, 2,* 43-6. Retrieved October 26, 2017, from https://www.mha.gov.sg/HTA/Documents/Home%20Team%20Journal%20Issue%202.pdf

Loke, K. F. (2017, February 28). *MINDEF Internet System Breached; Data Stolen from National Servicemen, Employees.* Retrieved October 26, 2017, from http://www.channelnewsasia.com/news/singapore/mindef-internet-system-breached-data-stolen-from-national-servic-7617146

Ministry of Finance, Ministry of Information, Communications and the Arts, & Infocomm Development Authority of Singapore. (2011). *E-government Masterplan 2011-2015: Collaborative Government.* Retrieved August 31, 2017, from https://www.tech.gov.sg/-/media/GovTech/About-us/Corporate-Publications/eGov/eGovBOOK1115.pdf?la=en

Ministry of Finance, & Infocomm Development Authority of Singapore. (2003). *Singapore E-government.* Retrieved August 31, 2017, from https://www.tech.gov.sg/-/media/GovTech/About-us/Corporate-Publications/eGov/eGap-II.pdf?la=en

Ministry of Finance, & Infocomm Development Authority of Singapore. (2006). *iGov2010: From Integrating Service to Integrating Government.* Retrieved August 31, 2017, from https://www.tech.gov.sg/-/media/GovTech/About-us/Corporate-Publications/eGov/iGov.pdf?la=en

Ministry of Home Affairs. (2014). *2014 National Security Conference at Suntec Singapore Convention & Exhibition Centre - Opening Address by Mr S Iswaran, Minister, Prime Minister's office, Second Minister for Home Affairs and Trade & Industry.* Retrieved November 12, 2017, from https://www.mha.gov.sg/Newsroom/speeches/Pages/2014-National-Security-Conference-at-Suntec-Singapore-Convention---Exhibition-Centre---Opening-Address-by-Mr-S-Iswaran,-Min.aspx

Ministry of Home Affairs. (2016). *National Cybercrime Action Plan.* Retrieved November 12, 2017, from https://www.mha.gov.sg/Newsroom/press-releases/PublishingImages/Pages/Launch-of-the-National-Cybercrime-Action-Plan-at-RSA-Conference-Asia-Pacific-Japan/NCAP%20Document.pdf

Ministry of Home Affairs. (2017a). *Official Launch of Interpol World 2017 – Speech by Mr Desmond Lee, Second Minister for Home Affairs and Second Minister for National Development*. Retrieved November 6, 2017, from https://www.mha.gov.sg/newsroom/speeches/Pages/Official-Launch-of-Interpol-World-2017-%E2%80%93-Speech-by-Mr-Desmond-Lee.aspx

Ministry of Home Affairs. (2017b). *Computer Misuse and Cybersecurity (Amendment) Bill*. Retrieved November 4, 2017, from https://www.mha.gov.sg/Newsroom/press-releases/Pages/Computer-Misuse-and-Cybersecurity-(Amendment)-Bill-.aspx

Ministry of Information and the Arts. (1995). *Speech by BG (NS) George Yeo, Minister for Information & the Arts and Minister of Health, at the Launch of SINGAPORE INFOMAP on Wednesday, 8 March 1995 at 10.00 am*. Retrieved October 19, 2017, from http://www.nas.gov.sg/archivesonline/data/pdfdoc/yybg19950308s.pdf

Mullin, G., & Lake, E. (2017, August 4). What Is Wannacry Ransomware? Malware Used to Cripple NHS in 2017 Cyber Attack. *The Sun*. Retrieved October 30, 2017, from https://www.thesun.co.uk/tech/3562470/wannacry-ransomware-nhs-cyber-attack-hackers-virus/

National Computer Board. (1997). *National Computer Board Annual Report 1996/1997*. Retrieved August 30, 2017, from https://www.imda.gov.sg/about/newsroom/archived/ida/speeches/1997/20050728143225

Networks Asia. (2015). *Singapore Business Federation unveils Employee Cyber Security Kit for SMBs*. Retrieved November 18, 2017, from https://www.networksasia.net/article/singapore-business-federation-unveils-employee-cyber-security-kit-smbs.1446085033

Networks Asia. (2016). *Singapore Launches National Cybercrime Action Plan*. Retrieved November 6, 2017, from https://www.networksasia.net/article/singapore-launches-national-cybercrime-action-plan.1469025526?source=transform-security&qt-breaking_news_most_read=0

Ng, J. (2014). *Staying Ahead of Digital Criminals through Robust Cyber Security Training*. Retrieved November 11, 2017, from https://www.hometeam.sg/article.aspx?news_sid=20141113RNtrYzE8rlqH

Ng, J. (2015). *New Cyber Security Agency Set to Lead the way in Combating Emerging Cyber Threats*. Retrieved November 5, 2017, from https://www.hometeam.sg/article.aspx?news_sid=201501282Uakllrzrg7S

Ng, J. Y. (2014 June 5). 1,560 SingPass User Accounts Breached. *Today*. Retrieved October 29, 2017, from http://www.todayonline.com/singapore/1560-singpass-user-accounts-breached

Ng, K. (2015 January 23). Hacker 'Messiah' Pleads Guilty to 39 Computer Misuse Charges. *Today*. Retrieved October 26, 2017, from http://www.todayonline.com/singapore/hacker-messiah-pleads-guilty-cyberattacks

Ong, J. (2017 May 12). *NUS, NTU Networks Hit by 'Sophisticated' Cyber Attacks.* Retrieved October 29, 2017, from http://www.channelnewsasia.com/news/singapore/·nus-ntu-networks-hit-by-sophisticated-cyber-attacks-8840596

Orion, W. LLC (2017). *Amendments to the Computer Misuse and Cybersecurity Act.* Retrieved November 4, 2017, from http://www.orionw.com/blog/news/security/amendments-to-the-computer-misuse-and-cybersecurity-act

Phneah, E. (2013). *Singapore to Open Cyber Security Lab to Train Law Enforcers.* Retrieved November 6, 2017, from http://www.zdnet.com/article/singapore-to-open-cyber-security-lab-to-train-law-enforcers/

Precious Communications. (2013). *McAfee Survey Reveals Average Internet User in Singapore Has S$57,500 Of Under-Protected 'Digital Assets'.* Retrieved November 16, 2017, from http://www.mynewsdesk.com/sg/preciouscommunications/pressreleases/mcafee-survey-reveals-average-internet-user-in-singapore-has-s-57-500-of-under-protected-digital-assets-871659

Singapore Police Force. (2011). *Annual Crime Brief 2011.* Retrieved November 1, 2017, from https://www.police.gov.sg/news-and-publications/statistics?page=2

Singapore Police Force. (2015). *Annual Crime Brief 2014.* Retrieved November 1, 2017, from https://www.police.gov.sg/news-and-publications/statistics?page=1

Singapore Police Force. (2016). *Annual Crime Brief 2015.* Retrieved November 1, 2017, from https://www.police.gov.sg/news-and-publications/statistics?page=1

Singapore Police Force. (2017a). *Annual Crime Brief 2016.* Retrieved November 1, 2017, from https://www.police.gov.sg/news-and-publications/statistics?page=1

Singapore Police Force. (2017b). *Mid-year Crime Statistics for January to June 2017.* Retrieved November 1, 2017, from https://www.police.gov.sg/news-and-publications/statistics?page=1

Singapore Statutes Online. (1993). *Computer Misuse Act 1993*. Retrieved November 4, 2017, from http://160.96.185.113/aol/search/display/view.w3p;page=0;query=DocId%3A%228a3534de-991c-4e0e-88c5-4ffa712e72af%22%20Status%3Apublished%20Depth%3A0%20%20TransactionTime%3A%2216%2F02%2F2017%22;rec=0;whole=yes

Singapore Statutes Online. (1998). *Computer Misuse (Amendment) Act 1998*. Retrieved November 4, 2017, from http://statutes.agc.gov.sg/

Smart Nation Singapore. (2017). *Enablers*. Retrieved October 25, 2017, from https://www.smartnation.sg/about-smart-nation/enablers

Sreedharan, S. (2013, December 7). 647 StanChart Clients' Bank Statements Stolen. *Today*. Retrieved October 26, 2017, from http://www.todayonline.com/singapore/647-stanchart-clients-bank-statements-stolen?page=1

Sun, D. (2017, August 29). *More Falling for Online Love Scams*. Retrieved November 1, 2017, from http://www.tnp.sg/news/singapore/more-falling-online-love-scams

Tan, B., Ling, P. S., & Cha, V. (2013). The Evolution of Singapore's Infocomm Plans: Singapore's E-government Journey from 1980 to 2007. In G. Pan (Ed.), *Dynamics of Governing IT Innovation in Singapore: A Case Book* (pp. 1–39). World Scientific. doi:10.1142/9789814417839_0001

Tan, C. Y. (2004). *Taking the Lead on Regional Infocomm Security*. Retrieved November 5, 2017, from https://www.tech.gov.sg/media-room/speeches/2004/10/taking-the-lead-on-regional-infocomm-security

Tan, T. M. (2017, July 5). Private Sector, Police Tie up to Fight Cyber Criminals. *Straits Times*. Retrieved November 6, 2017, from http://www.straitstimes.com/singapore/courts-crime/private-sector-police-tie-up-to-fight-cyber-criminals

Tan, W. (2015, January 28). New National Agency to Tackle Cyber Threats. *Today*. Retrieved November 5, 2017, from http://www.todayonline.com/singapore/new-national-agency-tackle-cyber-threats

Tan, W. (2017, September 19). *S'pore Gives S$1.5m to Boost ASEAN Cyber Security*. Retrieved November 13, 2017, from http://www.todayonline.com/business/spore-gives-s15m-boost-asean-cyber-security

Tehrani, P. M. (2017). *Cyberterrorism: The Legal and Enforcement Issues*. World Scientific Publishing Europe Ltd. doi:10.1142/q0063

Tham, I. (2017, May 25). New Govt Centre to Detect Cyber Threats. *Straits Times*. Retrieved November 6, 2017, from http://www.straitstimes.com/tech/new-govt-centre-to-detect-cyber-threats

The Ministry of Communications, & Information and the Cyber Security Agency of Singapore. (2017). *Public Consultation Paper on the Draft Cybersecurity Bill*. Retrieved November 5, 2017, from https://www.csa.gov.sg/~/media/csa/cybersecurity_bill/consult_document.ashx?la=en

The Singapore Computer Emergency Response Team. (2015). *Frequently Asked Questions*. Retrieved November 5, 2017, from https://www.csa.gov.sg/singcert/about-us/faqs

Theohary, C. A., & Rollins, J. W. (2015). *Cyberwarfare and Cyberterrorism: In Brief*. Retrieved October 25, 2017, from https://fas.org/sgp/crs/natsec/R43955.pdf

Thompson, E. (2017). *Building a HIPAA-Compliant Cybersecurity Program: Using NIST 800-30 and CSF to Secure Protected Health Information*. Apress. doi:10.1007/978-1-4842-3060-2

TODAY. (2015, March 10). *Curtin Singapore's Website Defaced by Hackers Claiming to Represent ISIS*. Retrieved October 29, 2017, from http://www.todayonline.com/singapore/curtin-singapores-website-defaced-hackers-claiming-represent-isis

TODAY. (2017, May 12). *NUS-NTU Hack: Other Recent Cyber Breaches in Singapore*. Retrieved October 26, 2017, from http://www.todayonline.com/singapore/recent-cyber-security-attacks

Toh, E. M. (2017 May 13). Global Cyber Attack: Don't Pay the Ransom, Says S'pore's Cyber Security Agency. *Today*. Retrieved October 30, 2017, from http://www.todayonline.com/singapore/singapores-govt-agencies-and-critical-infrastructure-not-affected-global-cyber-attack-csa

United Nations. (2003). *UN Global E-government Survey 2003*. Retrieved October 23, 2017, from https://publicadministration.un.org/egovkb/Portals/egovkb/Documents/un/2003-Survey/Complete-Survey.pdf

United Nations. (2004). *United Nations Global E-government Readiness Report 2004: Towards Access for Opportunity*. Retrieved October 23, 2017, from https://publicadministration.un.org/egovkb/Portals/egovkb/Documents/un/2004-Survey/Complete-Survey.pdf

United Nations. (2005). *United Nations Global E-government Readiness Report 2005: From E-government to E-inclusion.* Retrieved October 23, 2017, from https://publicadministration.un.org/egovkb/Portals/egovkb/Documents/un/2005-Survey/Complete-survey.pdf

United Nations. (2008). *UN E-government Survey 2008: From E-government to Connected Governance.* Retrieved October 23, 2017, from https://publicadministration.un.org/egovkb/Portals/egovkb/Documents/un/2008-Survey/Complete-survey.pdf

United Nations. (2010). *United Nations E-government Survey 2010: Leveraging E-government at a Time of Financial and Economic Crisis.* Retrieved October 23, 2017, from https://publicadministration.un.org/egovkb/Portals/egovkb/Documents/un/2010-Survey/Complete-survey.pdf

United Nations. (2012). *United Nations E-government Survey 2012: E-government for the People.* Retrieved October 23, 2017, from https://publicadministration.un.org/egovkb/Portals/egovkb/Documents/un/2012-Survey/Complete-Survey.pdf

United Nations. (2014). *United Nations E-government Survey 2014: E-government for the Future We Want.* Retrieved October 23, 2017, from https://publicadministration.un.org/egovkb/Portals/egovkb/Documents/un/2014-Survey/E-Gov_Complete_Survey-2014.pdf

United Nations. (2016). *United Nations E-government Survey 2016: E-government in Support of Sustainable Development.* Retrieved October 23, 2017, from http://workspace.unpan.org/sites/Internet/Documents/UNPAN97453.pdf

United Nations Division for Public Economics and Public Administration, & American Society for Public Administration. (2002). *Benchmarking E-government: A Global Perspective.* Retrieved October 23, 2017, from https://publicadministration.un.org/egovkb/Portals/egovkb/Documents/un/English.pdf

Van Dijck, P., & Verbruggen, H. (1987). The Case of Singapore. In H. Linnemann (Ed.), *Export-oriented Industrialization in Developing Countries* (pp. 381–415). Singapore: Singapore University Press.

Waseda University, & International Academy of CIO. (2014). *WASEDA – IAC 10th International E-Government Ranking 2014.* Retrieved October 23, 2017, from http://www.e-gov.waseda.ac.jp/pdf/2014_e-gov_press_release.pdf

Waseda University, & International Academy of CIO. (2015). *2015 WASEDA – IAC International E-Government Ranking Survey*. Retrieved October 23, 2017, from http://www.e-gov.waseda.ac.jp/pdf/2015_Waseda_IAC_E-Government_Press_Release.pdf

Waseda University, & International Academy of CIO. (2016). *The 12th Waseda - IAC International e-Government Rankings Survey 2016 Report*. Retrieved October 23, 2017, from http://www.e-gov.waseda.ac.jp/pdf/2016_E-Gov_Press_Release.pdf

Waseda University, & International Academy of CIO. (2017). *THE 13TH WASEDA – IAC International Digital Government Rankings 2017 Report*. Retrieved October 23, 2017, from http://www.e-gov.waseda.ac.jp/pdf/2017_Digital-Government_Ranking_Press_Release.pdf

Wong, Y. Y. J., Gerber, R., & Toh, K. A. (2003). A Comparative Study of Diffusion of Web-based Education (WBE) in Singapore and Australia. In A. Aggarwal (Ed.), *Web-Based Education: Learning from Experience* (pp. 347–370). Hershey, PA: IGI Global. doi:10.4018/978-1-59140-102-5.ch021

Yu, E. (2006). *S'pore: New Center to Monitor Govt Systems*. Retrieved November 6, 2017, from http://www.zdnet.com/article/spore-new-center-to-monitor-govt-systems-2039419454/

Zhou, J. (2011). Singapore Law on Information Technology. *IT Connect*, 20. Retrieved November 4, 2017, from http://enewsletter.ntu.edu.sg/itconnect/2011-08/Pages/SingaporeLawOnIT.aspx

KEY TERMS AND DEFINITIONS

Computer Misuse Act: A legislation that is enacted to specifically investigate, prosecute and adjudicate cybercrime in Singapore.

Critical Information Infrastructure: Networks or information and communications systems that deliver essential services such as electricity, telecommunications and transportation.

Cyber Security Agency of Singapore: A national agency to oversee cybersecurity strategy and agencies' cybersecurity operations, and enhance public awareness of cybersecurity through education and outreach.

Infocomm Security Masterplan: A strategic roadmap for strengthening cybersecurity in Singapore.

Singapore Computer Emergency Response Team: It is a group of experts that detects, resolves, and prevents security-related incidents on the internet.

SingPass: A security measure that is used in Singapore for verification of identity when people have online transaction with government agencies.

Smart Nation: An initiative launched by the Singaporean government in 2014 to solve problems, create more opportunities and make society more connected through the extensive use of information technology.

APPENDIX 1

Table 1. Singapore's E-government Ranking in United Nations E-government Survey

Year	Ranking
2001	4
2003	12
2004	8
2005	7
2008	23
2010	11
2012	10
2014	3
2016	4

(Data Source: United Nations E-government Survey, 2001-2016)

APPENDIX 2

Table 2. Singapore's E-government Ranking in WASEDA – IAC International E-Government Ranking Survey

Year	Ranking
2005	3
2006	3
2007	2
2008	2
2009	1
2010	1
2011	1
2012	1
2013	1
2014	2
2015	1
2016	1
2017	1

(Data Source: WASEDA – IAC International E-Government Ranking Survey, 2014-2017)

APPENDIX 3

Table 3. Internet Love Scams in Singapore (2010- 2016)

	2010	2011	2012	2013	2014	2015	2016
No. of cases	21	62	--	81	198	385	636
The amount of money cheated	S$824,000	S$2.3 million	--	S$5.8 million	S$8.8 million	S$12 million	S$24 million

(Data Source: Singapore Police Force, 2011; Singapore Police Force, 2015; Singapore Police Force, 2016; Singapore Police Force, 2017a)

Chapter 6
E–Governance and Corruption Impasse in Nigeria:
A Developmental Expedition Synopsis

Opeyemi Idowu Aluko
University of Ilorin, Nigeria

Gabriel Temitope Aderinola
University of Ilorin, Nigeria

ABSTRACT

E-governance is a technological innovation that brings governance to the fore of integrity and accountability. It requires high technological commitment so as to bring the government closer to the people. Corruption on the other hand is a bane to growth and development in any country. E-governance is a corrective measure to corruption which prevents government officials from shady activities due to its transparency nature. The connection between e-governance and corruption is analyzed in this chapter, and Nigeria is selected as a case study in developing countries. The chapter concludes on the premise that e-governance reduces the strength of corruption in any country and more investment is needed to enhance this development.

INTRODUCTION

E-government is a concept that has its etiology in the nineteen century. It refers to the use of information and communication technology (ICT) to promote more efficient and cost effective government, facilitate more convenient government services, allow

DOI: 10.4018/978-1-5225-5984-9.ch006

greater government access to information, and make government more accountable to the citizens. E-government is the use of ICT by government agencies to transform relations with citizens (government to citizen) (G2C), businesses (government to business) (G2B), government organizations (government to government) (G2G) and employees (government to employee) (G2E). ICTs have a lot of advantages of improving service delivery to citizens, interacting with business and industry, increasing public accessibility to information, fostering more efficient government management, increasing transparency and accountability and eventually reducing corruption and costs of governance.

Corruption on the other hand is a vice that delimitate the efficiency and effectiveness of service delivery within the public or private sector. It has the tendency to destroy or shut down the whole government and private sector existence to becoming a state of anarchy. ICT can reduce corruption by promoting good governance, strengthening reform initiatives, reducing the potential for corrupt behavior, strengthening relations between government employees and citizens, allowing tracking activities, monitoring and controlling behavior of government employees by the citizens, enhancing the effectiveness of internal control and management of corrupt behavior by promoting government transparency and accountability (Bhatnagar, 2003; Shim & Eom, 2008; Anderson, 2009; Mauro, 1997). In fact, Lupu and Lazar (2015) found that a 1% increase in the use of e-government reduces corruption by over 6.7% in the EU/ non EU countries.

Corruption has been a major issue in Nigeria because of the negative impact on the people, government and drawbacks on economic development and national progress (Emechele, 2009; Ajie & Wokekoro, 2012). It pervades all facets of the country's public and private sector (Inokoba & Ibegu, 2011) with devastating consequences of poverty, decaying infrastructures, unemployment, poor budget implementation and performance, low standard of living (Odo, 2015). Corruption has seriously affected every sector of the economy and hampered sustainable development in education, health, employment, power and electricity generation, transportation, legislature, judiciary, civil service, politics, electoral process and other major sectors of the economy (Ezigbo, 2006). It has hindered economic growth and development (Cookey, 2005), foreign direct investment (Cooker, Ugwu & Adams, 2012) and resulted in poor human development indices and massive poverty of Nigerians (Action Aid, 2015). Corruption increases the rate of injustice, disregards rule of law and destabilizes society by creating social tensions, increases the crime rate, violence and terrorism. It also acts as a barrier to advancing any innovations (OECD, 2010). Ribadu, (2007) argued that corruption is Nigeria's worst problem responsible for its woes, instability in the Niger Delta, debt overhang, barrier to democratic elections and impediment to flow of foreign direct investment (FDI). In fact, the misfortune and woes of Nigeria has been linked to the pervasive, endemic corruption. Nigeria has been ranked among the most corrupt countries in the world by the Transparency International (TI) since late 1990s (Ribadu, 2003; Action Aid, 2015). The World Bank studies showed that nearly $1 trillion USD was paid in bribes annually and in some countries such as Nigeria, Kenya and Venezuela the bribe paid was up to 12% of gross domestic product (Nwabuzor, 2005).

The formulation of the new national ICT policy in 2001 began with the establishment of the National Information Technology Development Agency (NITDA). This was expected to promote e-governance initiatives. However, there were problems due to the unavailability and poor telecommunication facilities, electricity power supply and other enabling infrastructure for e-government activity. Little wonder, the e-governance activity in Nigeria is poor and rank low (Yusuf, 2006; Adeyemo, 2011; Oye, 2013).

Some of e-governance initiatives and utility in the recent times include: registration of teachers, e-passport and visa application, voters registration, tax payment, land registration and e-payment, online registration of examinations and the monthly publishing of the allocation to States and local governments by the Ministry of Finance to enable citizens and civil societies engage their governments on their use of public funds. The use of card reader and in the last general elections has brought some measure of credibility and sanity into Nigerian elections, e-wallet in the distribution of fertilizers to farmers and the cashless policy introduced by the Central Bank of Nigeria. The introduction of Integrated Payroll and Personnel Information System (IPPIS), the adoption of Bank Verification Number (BVN) and the cashless policy in the banking sector have helped to checkmate the activities of 'ghost' workers in Nigeria and also save billions of Naira for the government (Enofe, Ogbaisi & Mboto, 2015).

Conceptualizing E-Governance

The term governance needs to be understood before we move on to e-governance. The concept of 'governance' is as old as human civilization. In essence, the term 'governance' refers to the process of decision-making and the process by which decisions are implemented (or not implemented). The word 'governance' can be used in several contexts such as corporate governance, international governance, national governance and local governance. Governance is not the exclusive preserve of the government. It extends to civil society and the private sector. It covers every institution and organization from family to the state.

It involves exercise of political, economic and administrative authority to manage the affairs in and the manner in which power is exercised in the management of a country's economic and social resources for development. It can be better understood as the complex mechanisms, processes, relationships and institutions through which citizens and groups articulate their interests, exercise their rights and obligations and mediate their differences. Boeninger (1992), opined that it is the capacities of a system to exercise authority, win legitimacy, adjudicate conflicts as well as carry out programme implementation.

E-governance concept originated at the beginning of 21st century, mostly as a copy of e-commerce into public sector. All intentions were directed towards the presence of the public services on the Internet. In the early years of its development, e-governance follows the evolutionary e-business evolving model, which in particular means that in the early days of e-governance evolvement, primary focus of the e-services was simple appearance of graphic user interfaces with no interactions. Early enthusiasm during the mean time weakened but such experiences brought crucial acknowledgments (United Nations, 2008). Today, the development of electronic public services enters in the new phase, which is mostly determined by reengineering of existing processes of public government. Public sector by its nature (based on information and communications) is ideal for international increase of efficiency and quality (Fang, 2002; Mario, et al 2009).

The term is used in a loose manner to describe the legacy of any kind of use of information and communication technology within the public sector. It represents the use of internet to deliver information and services by the government (Bhatnagar, 2003). The United Nations Department of Economic and Social Affairs define e-governance as utilizing the internet and the world-wide-web for delivering government information and services to citizens (United Nations, 2008). Therefore, e-governance is the use of information and communication technologies (ICT) to transform government by making it more accessible, effective and accountable.

E-governance refers to the use of information technologies (such as the Internet, the World Wide Web, and mobile computing) by government agencies that can transform their relationship with citizens, businesses, different areas of government, and other governments. These technologies help deliver government services to citizens, improve interactions with businesses and industries, and provide access to information (Moon, 2002). E-governance is also the use of emerging information and communication technologies to facilitate the processes of government and public administration (Drucker, 2001).

In contemporary governance, Basu (2004) states that "e-governance refers to the use by government agencies of information technologies that have the ability to transform relations with citizens, businesses and other arms of government". This will result to a less corrupt society, increased transparency, greater convenience, revenue growth and cost reductions. According to Chatfield (2009), e-governance refers to the use of information and communication technologies, particularly the internet, to deliver government information and services. E-governance is understood as the use of ICT to promote more efficient and cost effective government, facilitate more convenient government services, allow greater government access to information, and make government more accountable to the citizens (World Bank, 1992). For the purpose of this paper, the definition of e-governance provided in the European Commission (2003) will be adopted: "the use of information and communication technologies in public administrations combined with organizational change and new skills in order to improve public services and democratic processes and strengthen support to public policies".

The aim of e-governance is to allow the public to initiate a request for a particular government service without going to a government office or having direct contact with a government employee. The service is delivered through government web sites (Brannen, 2001; Moon, 2002). E-governance comprises of an alignment of ICT infrastructures, institutional reform, business processes and service content towards provision of high-quality and value added services to the citizens and businesses. Wimmer and Traunmuller (2001) contend that the main objectives of e-governance should include the following: (1) restructuring administrative functions and processes; (2) reducing and overcoming barriers to coordination and cooperation within the public administration; and (3) the monitoring of government performance.

A major goal of e-governance projects in developed economies is to enhance productivity of both public and private sectors through the leveraging of ICT. E-governance has captured the interest of developing countries. There has been a considerable demonstration effect of the constructive difference that e-governance has made in advanced economies in the delivery of services, provision of information and internal administration of the public sector. A country's ICT infrastructure and its openness to public sector reform play an important role in determining the types of applications and kind of goals for which e-governance is implemented (Bhatnagar, 2003). A country's willingness to adopt basic public sector reform must determine the breadth and scope of e-governance applications. Many times e-governance applications are used as a catalyst and enabler to further reform. E-governance projects are funded with the expectation that these applications will increase efficiency, and bring about more transparency and accountability to citizens.

An Analysis of Corruption

Corruption is the process of circumventing formally agreed, official schedules or implicit rules for decision-making (in the public or private sector) by use of personal inducements in order to achieve institutional and/or personal objectives. Corruption can be defined as a process by which the virtue of the citizen is undermined and eventually destroyed (Otalor and Eiya, 2013). Corruption can also be defined as the use of public office or the use of official position, rank or status by an office bearer for his own personal benefit Myint (2000) in Otalor and Eiya (2013). While activities such as fraud and embezzlement can be undertaken by an official alone and without involvement of a second party, others such as bribery, extortion and influence peddling involve two parties – the giver and taker in a corrupt deal.

Two party type of corruption can arise under a variety of circumstances such as: government contracts, government benefits, government revenue, time savings and regulatory avoidance, Influencing outcomes of legal and regulatory processes (Otalor and Eiya, 2013). Corruption or "corrupt" behavior has broadly been defined as the violation of established rules for personal gain and profit", or "efforts to secure wealth or power through illegal means – private gain at public expense; or a misuse of public power for private benefit or a behavior which deviates from the formal duties of a public role, because of private gain (Sen, 1999; Lipset and Lenz, 2000; Nye, 1967). This definition includes such behavior as bribery (use of a reward to pervert the judgment of a person in a position of trust); nepotism (bestowal of patronage by reason of inscriptive relationship rather than merit); and misappropriation (illegal appropriation of public resources for private uses (Banfield, 1961 in Otalor and Eiya, 2013).

Corruption has also been looked at as the abuse of public office for private gains through rent seeking activities when an official accepts, solicits, or extorts a bribe. Public office is also abused when private agents actively offer bribes to circumvent public policies and processes for competitive advantage and profit or even if no bribery occurs, through patronage and nepotism, the theft of state assets or the diversion of state resources (World Bank 1997). Corruption requires a multifaceted attack. It requires, for example, a set of regulations against corrupt practices, a code of conduct for employees and vendors, awareness raising campaigns, training of staff, internal controls, sanctions and incentives, protection of whistleblowers and an open approach towards information reporting (Otalor and Eiya, 2013).

Corruption is one of the greatest challenges of the contemporary world. It respects no national boundaries and deepens poverty around the globe by distorting political, economic and social life. Corruption undermines good government, fundamentally distorts public policy, leads to the misallocation of resources, harms the private sector and particularly hurts the poor citizens who bear the heavy economic and social costs of corruption (Stapenhurst, Johnston and Pellizo, 2006).

The Effect of Corruption on Economic Development

Some researchers have defined corruption as an act in which the power of public office is used for personal gain in a manner that contravenes the rules of the game (Jain, 2001; Tanzi, 1998) while others have defined it as the abuse of public power for private benefit (Rose-Ackerman, 1999). For example, as Tanzi (1998) opines, although the definition of corruption suggests that it is the abuse of public power for private benefit, it cannot be concluded that corruption does not exist in the private sector. Tanzi (1998) goes on to state that it exists in large private enterprises, especially in procurement and hiring issues. In the public sector, it can raise public expenditure and lower the amount of tax received, thereby increasing fiscal deficits and creating macro-economic instability (Mauro, 1997; Bhargava and Bolongaita, 2004).

Scholarship on corruption in the past decade (Aides and Di Tella, 1999; Aidt, 2003; Elliot, 1997; Jain, 2001; Mauro, 1997; Svensson, 2005; Tanzi, 1998) has indicated that corruption discourages investment, limits economic growth, alters the composition of government spending, usually undercuts a nation's mission of reducing poverty and hinders improvement in the quality of life for the rural and poor segments of developing countries (Bhargava and Bolongaita, 2004). Using indices of government corruption, along with country level economic data, Mauro (1997), documents that the amount of corruption is negatively linked to the level of investment and economic growth. The analysis further indicates that when the corruption index improved by one standard deviation, the country's investment rate increased by more than 4 percentage points and the annual growth rate of per capita GDP increased by over a half percentage point.

Similarly, analysis of country data from the data bases of world organizations such as the International Monetary Fund and the World Bank provide further evidence that corruption worsens income inequality and poverty (Gupta et al., 1998; Bhargava and Bolongaita, 2004; Tanzi and Davoodi, 1997) and hurts the poor most of all. Although, the argument that bribery may be viewed as payment of speed and efficiency for the rich, in countries with high levels of corruption the poor have to bribe even for access to basic services. Since they pay a higher proportion of their income on bribes, income inequality is exacerbated (Vittal, 2003). Thus, as Bhargava and Bolongaita (2004) contend, controlling corruption is then nothing less than promoting economic development, increasing country competitiveness, improving social conditions, and reducing poverty. However, dismantling corruption is no easy task. Most of the efforts in the past decade to address corruption typically began with an analysis of the underlying causes or enablers of corruption.

From an economic perspective, corruption arises from economic rent, which refers to "…the extra amount paid (over what would be paid for the best alternative use) to somebody or for something useful whose supply is limited either by nature or through human ingenuity" (Mauro, 1997:2). According to this author, seeking economic rents by creating artificial limitations is an underlying source of corruption. Trade restrictions may be viewed as government induced sources of rent. Similarly, government subsidies, price controls, and multiple exchange rates are all potential sources of rent-seeking activities. In addition, restricted natural resources, low wages in civil service, and sociological divisions (such as ethnic divisions and loyalties) also enable corruption.

Analyzing the financial crises that occurred in Indonesia, Korea, and Thailand in the late 1990s, Bhargava and Bolongaita (2004) suggest that corruption was partly responsible. The authors claim that a lack of transparency and a weak banking system that was not prepared for financial liberalization, led to the financial crises. In addition, in his analysis of the causes of corruption, Tanzi (1998) distinguishes between the factors that affect demand for corruption and those that affect supply of corruption. He concludes that the circumstances that affect demand include regulations that restrict or create artificial limitations of goods and services, certain characteristics of tax systems, certain spending decisions, and price controls resulting in goods at below market prices. On the other hand, the factors that affect supply of corruption include rigid bureaucratic traditions, low level of public sector wages, weak or ineffectual penalty systems, institutional controls, lack of transparency of rule processes, and examples of corruption set by leaders. Although many policy analysts emphasize the public sector as a primary enabler of corruption (e.g., Mauro, 1997; Tanzi, 1998; Kauffman et al., 2000), similar conditions of discretionary power and lack of accountability occur in the private sector too. As Tanzi (1998) describes, privatization can create its own conditions to enable corruption, through payment of commissions to get access to markets and insider information not available to others that promote corruption in response to market competition.

Maor (2004) investigates two hypotheses related to transparency and accountability by a comparative analysis of five anticorruption mechanisms in the United States, the Soviet Union, Italy, and Australia (Queensland and New South Wales). First, he examines corruption investigations of senior officeholders following the creation of anticorruption mechanisms (e.g., commissions, special prosecutors, independent counsels, investigating judges) and hypothesizes that the outcome of this process is a concerted move by targeted political executives to undermine the credibility of anticorruption mechanisms and, when deemed necessary, to terminate their operation, and second, the extent to which the prosecutors are successful depends on both institutions and media accessibility the more centralized and fused political power is, and the less media accessible the government is, the harder it will be to carry out an investigation.

The hypotheses are strongly supported by the research and suggest that transparency and accountability are imperative to combat corruption. Kim et al. (2009) documented and evaluated an anti-corruption system called OPEN (Online Procedures Enhancement for civil application) in the Seoul Metropolitan Government. They utilized institutional theory and incorporated three distinctive (yet interrelated) dimensions of institutionalization (regulatory/coercive, cognitive/mimetic, and normative), and four anticorruption strategies embedded in the system to investigate how an e-government system for anticorruption in a local government has evolved. They found that in implementing such a system, the regulatory dimension was most effective, and (as in many IS implementations) strong leadership was crucial to its success.

Thus, we argue from the preceding discussion, that the conditions that promote public officials' discretionary and monopoly power to extract economic rents are core enablers of corruption. In addition, unless public officials face clear consequences for demanding and extracting economic rents, it is difficult to mitigate corruption, especially in developing countries where informality of bureaucratic processes and the lack of enforceable consequences maintain discretionary power. Clearly, then the discretionary and monopoly power of public officials to extract economic rents has to be dismantled and public institutions have to be to strengthened in order to enable accountability and transparency. If corruption is to be mitigated, the critical question remains: how can its enablers be targeted? In the next section, we argue that IT enabled e-government can improve the transparency of the bureaucratic process and therefore, promote accountability.

The Nexus Between E-Governance and Corruption and Security Frameworks

E-government has become an umbrella term covering all use of information technology in government (Torres et al., 2006) and includes IT-based sharing of information and conducting transactions within the government (G2G), between government and businesses (G2B), and between government and citizen (G2C). As noted by Singh et al., (2010:256), e-government "…entails streamlining operational processes, transcribing information held by government agencies into electronic form, linking disparate databases, and improving ease of access to services for members of the public". E-government has also been promoted as a strategy of public sector reform, with a focus on how it can improve the managerial process (Kudo, 2010).

Extant research on the evolution of e-government (West, 2004; Caba et al., 2005; Torres et al., 2006; Christou and Simpson, 2009) focus on the numerous factors that influence the growth of e-government in the past decade and found that income levels, strength of institutions and the commitment of the government to promoting e-government were the most important factors. Other studies focus on the factors that determine the level of development of e-government (Kim, 2007; Siau and Long, 2006) and suggest that one of the most important factors was the economic growth of the country. Rodriguez et al. (2011) examine socio-economic factors (economic development. technological development, and education) and characteristics of public agencies (organizational complexity, institutional capacity, degree of leverage, administrative effectiveness and control of corruption) to examine the influence of such factors on the development of e-government.

Their results differ from earlier studies and suggest that economic growth was not an important factor but the characteristics of public agencies such as effectiveness and fulfillment of programs and public policies efficiently, effectively and responsibly were necessary for the implementation and development of e-government. They also conclude that the control of corruption does not encourage the development of e-government. Finally, Bertot et al. (2010) study the potential impacts of ICT (specifically e-government and social media) on cultural attitudes about transparency. They suggest that a culture of openness must be embedded within the governance system. In addition, this must be combined with technical and social capabilities to truly implement e-government transparency initiatives (Bertot et al., 2010).

Literature that focus on e-government initiatives to target corruption, (Hopper et al., 2009) suggest that electronic delivery of services (e.g., submitting internet applications and tax returns for computer processing) can reduce corruption by reducing interactions with officials, speeding up decisions, and reducing human errors. Similarly, in reviewing the literature to identify the potential role of e-government in reducing corruption, Singh et al., (2010) emphasize that e-government eliminates discretion from the equation by removing intermediary services and allowing citizens to conduct transactions themselves. Andersen and Rand (2006) also study the relation between corruption and e-government and examine a cross-section of countries from the 1997 to 2002 period.

The security frameworks in well-designed ICT policies are likely to be effective in the fight against corruption. Shim and Eom (2008) opined that the impacts of bureaucratic professionalism, bureaucratic quality and law enforcement through the use of national level data and find that both e-government and traditional anti-corruption factors have a positive impact on reducing corruption. The security frameworks as observed by Shim and Eom (2009) is that ICT and social capital curb corruption and ICT has the potential to reduce unnecessary human intervention in government work processes, the technology reduces the need to monitor corrupt behavior. They uses panels of datasets from various sources and concluded that ICT is an effective tool for reducing corruption and social capital also has positive effects on reducing corruption, although the relationship between social capital and ICT is inconclusive.

To summarize, in the setup of the security frameworks as an important strategy for dismantling corruption is the easy access to information for all citizens by providing e-government initiatives. This can result in greater transparency that reduces the ability of the public sector official to demand bribes. Thus, e-government cannot just only provide greater information to the population but also remove the discretion of the public official and allow citizens to conduct transactions themselves which, in turn, could lead to a reduction in corruption.

E-Governance and War Against Corruption in Nigeria

Introduction of e-governance in the country has played and is playing a vital role(s) in the herculean war against the cancer of corruption in the Nigeria. Through e-governance public and private sectors adopted measures that strangulated corruption to a comatose degree in certain sectors and in some instances annihilated it permanently. It started at the Federal Government level and private sector, State and Local Governments followed suit.

Before the advent of e-governance in Nigeria, understanding the real workforce in the three tiers of authorities (Federal, State, and Local Governments) was a mystery and hard like rocket science. Personnel in Administration in league with their colleagues in Finance inflate the workforce with ghost workers running into hundreds of thousands. And perpetrators of such crime created a system where most staff are not paid in the banks using workers functioning accounts, they pay cash using their ministries cashiers. The amount oozing through this channel into the pockets of these fraudsters surpasses the real salary bills government pay to workers. Successive governments battled with this menace through setting up special staff audit committees and what they called "TABLE PAYMENT" and physical appearance of staff without getting to the root of the matter.

The palaver lingered until the introduction of Integrated Payroll and Personnel Information System (IPPIS) by the three tiers of governments across the nation. Recently, the Federal Government made further discovery of ghost workers after scrutinizing 215 Ministries, Departments, and Agencies. About 45,000 ghost workers were uncovered making the Federal government to save 100b in salaries of the said workers alone. Similar scenarios unfolded at state and Local Government levels, many told stories of how the introduction of Integrated Payroll and Personnel Information System saved them billions in salaries only (www.cnknigeria.com 14/2/2013).

Introduction of e-governance and transaction in financial transactions like e-mail, e-verification of payment, e-transfers etc eliminated corrupt practices bordering following of files and cheques from one desk to the other and from one accounting officer to another. It has been established that the unfortunate culture of physical following of files and other contract papers breeds unholy cum corrupt practices between the contractors, internal monitors, and the banks. E-measures ended some of those practices and cleansed the system to some level of decency. (www.negst.com. php). Public officers were left with working on papers and pushing their assessments without knowing owners or seeing them. The pace of files and assessment papers movement instilled confidence in the heart of owner thereby making them resist temptation of seeking of avenues to bribe their ways through.

The financial sub-sector witnessed extensive cleansing impact of e-governance. Their integrated data system and interconnectivity checkmated fraudulent practices.

It also scaled down unnecessary delays associated with clearing of transactions, which take days or weeks before customers get them or services are delivered. With the introduction of e-payments, cheques and other payment orders are ready within minutes or hours (depending on the nature or quantum of the transaction). Before this period papers in form of orders and cheques are physically carried from one branch to headquarters and down to the branch of customers. This snail space shuttle instigates people to break laid down rules just to get services in time. Breaking due process comes with palm greasing of the officers in charge of the process.

Introduction of automatic teller machines helped immensely because people transfer or withdraw cash without necessarily going through the ritual of signing cheques and queuing in long lines in branches where their accounts is. Such long queues often make people corrupt the process by cutting corners using bank staff who are products of the same corrupt system.

Recruitments and examinations in schools, ministries, departments, and parastatals are electronically done. Candidates apply online; write examination online via buying well secured scratch cards and their scripts marked electronically. Within days results of examinations are out and candidates told his fate. The practice was not like that before now; they were slow, esoteric, and manipulated due to excessive involvement of personnel rather than machines. This process also nips in the bud inconsistencies associated with age and other academic claims by candidates, issues very essential for recruitments. In each recruitment exercise especially into Nigerian Armed Forces, so many candidates are rejected or recruitment offer withdrawn because of phantom claims that contradicted regulations associated with the recruitments which are noticed due to employment of e-governance.

E-governance has helped the country's most active anti graft body Economic and Financial Crimes Commission (EFCC) in tracking financial fraudsters and international money launderers. EFCC partnered with other global crime fighting bodies and law enforcement agencies of other countries to trace inflow and outflow of monies and the possible sources. Through their eagle eye operations, many top government functionaries and captain of industries were caught in money laundering and other financially related crimes at home and abroad. E-measures like instant sending of alerts messages which includes photos and other claims of customers by banks to EFCC on individual's withdrawals that are up to Five Hundred Thousand Naira (N500,000) and One Million Naira (N1, 000, 000) for cooperate bodies. This measure instigated massive arrests of fraudsters and money launderers even before they left bank premises. And those who succeeded in escaping arrest from banks, proper investigations are carried out and most times clues are gotten that ultimately leads to arrest and prosecution. It is not an easy task for money launderers to head straight banks because of almost 100% risk involved in such acts. Bank staffers abetting fraudulent and subversive practices have developed cold feet or resisting the temptation because of the high risk and possibility of falling into the net of EFCC.

Nigeria's electoral body Independent National Electoral Commission (INEC) boarded the e-governance plane by introducing biometric registration of voters and compilation of results (www.nigeriaintel.com). Before this era, electoral register are compiled manually which was open to various forms of manipulations in terms of double registrations in the same centre and in other centers. There was also the problem of results compilation and delay in doing so. But today election results are transferred through their well organized site from either the Local Government or Zonal collation centers to their state offices or national headquarters in Abuja. This stopped the menace of election officials changing figures on transit. Elections results now reach headquarters within seconds. This has reduced to the minimum corrupt practices of politicians of violating electoral laws that promotes credible electoral contests. INEC has a well functioning website with information of their electoral calendars, results of previous elections, and everything that has to do with them.

With the transfer of the country's capital from the coastal city of Lagos to the Abuja land became an issues. Black marketers and other racketeers started trading in none existing lands or selling same plots of land to various people. Another level of corruption perpetrated by public officers in the lands department of Federal Capital Authority is selling of green zones and other strategic locations not earmarked for residential or commercial purposes. Criminals involved in this unholy business of lands buying and selling became super rich and their heinous business running into a multi-billion Naira empire. The former minister of FCT took a bold step of establishing Abuja Geographic Information System (AGIS) in 2003. AGIS was to: provide a comprehensive, all-inclusive, state-of-the Art, foolproof, computerized, Geospatial data infrastructure for the FCT; and computerize the cadastral and land registry for the FCC (Federal Capital City), the Area councils and the satellite Towns of the Federal Capital Territory. Integrating the entire lands of Federal Capital Territory into a single data bank sent the illegal land cartel involved in duping people and causing monumental legal tussles in various FCT courts between individuals and between government and citizens. AGIS was able to tell buyers whether such lands exist for sale and what each piece of land stands for. Cases of developing lands outside the original master plan stopped in a nick of time.

Many State's Boards of Internal Revenue have developed functional data base of monitoring individuals and cooperate taxes by knowing when they are due for payment. Corrupt ways of declaring profit and loss at the end of each financial year just to evade taxes or get complete tax holidays have been drastically reduced. Recklessness associated with revenue collectors whose trademark was siphoning of public monies because of improper records has made way for a more transparent collection and remittance procedure. States Chief Accounting officers now tied most of the revenue accounts with alerts showing payments and withdrawals from such accounts. And they can with a simple pressing of a computer key stop illegal withdrawals or query unauthorized withdrawals from key signatories to such accounts. Apart from boosting the revenue base of governments, this has scaled down the level of corruption in the system.

Some State's Governors developed a syndicate accounting system that linked accounts of all states ministries and parastatals to single alarm system that tell them withdrawals and deposit of monies. This trap has made fraudsters within the civil service especially men and women in the Account Department deter from the usual style of open robbery of the treasury in league with top brass of the civil service. Fraudsters now have to think twice before attempting to dip their thieving fingers into the common treasure. The North East State of Gombe is a classical example of where this integration of all accounts within the State to a single alert in the governor's handset is working. Governor Dankwambo's style is replicated in many States now and the system has checkmated fraud from public servants.

Challenges of E-Governance in Fighting Corruption in Nigeria

There is no contesting the fact that introduction of e-governance have massively downsized the level of corruption in the public and private sectors. The indices show that there is improvement in the cleansing processes in the system. Local and international anti graft watch dogs gave introduction of e-governance much of the credit in the war. Through this remarkable improvement confidence is gradually returning and local and international investors are taking the risk of investing in the country and donors are once more reconsidering making their facilities available to government and businessmen in the country. This is by no means piquing that the cancer of corruption has been cut off or successfully healed through the introduction of e-governance.

Despite the tremendous boom in ICT in the country a commanding sizeable number of people are not in the world of ICT. Those outside the ICT curve are not only those without Western education, we have highly placed government functionaries without a simple knowledge of operating a PC, the best they can do is handle a small cell phone. This low level of knowledge of is still giving criminals some rooms to wangle through their heinous schemes due to the gullibility of the people. Many are still falling on the booby trap of fraudsters because of lack of knowledge to simply verify bogus claims of criminals.

Content management by government and organization is another cog in the wheel of progress. Ministries and parastatals web sites are sometimes dead zone with outdated information to satisfy the need of the moment. The problem is not only associated with lack of latest equipments or gadgets but the knowledge of simple information management by officers in charge of such units. And since they can't manage theirs, they can't also help out in answering questions forwarded to them by either law enforcement officers or other anti graft bodies. This is also affecting the inter-agency connectivity in synergizing effort is so hard like rocket science. There are cases where criminals manipulate sites or break into control systems of government sites and manipulate information for heinous reasons. Many a times people received messages from official government sites or addresses just to later realize that such message though coming from them are not genuine.

Nigeria is a very large country with a three different physical geography. Till today, most parts are yet to be connected to the Global system for mobile communications and other ICT facilities. Even some Local Government Areas which are headquarters of the lowest layer of administration are not connected. By this a large part of the country is not incorporated into e-governance, making those corrupt practices concomitant in the system glow. Manual means of verification and transmission of messages that encourages corruption is still the standing order. People still follow files and lobby for their speedy movement from one desk to the other and files are still shuttled by messengers within and outside their areas of administrative jurisdictions. At this level of authority government clients that is contractors are still in the usual game of corrupting public officials and getting things don't outside laid down set rules and procedures.

Power supply is one of Nigeria's serious problems next to corruption, though corruption created the problem of power supply. Solving this problem is still a far cry and affecting effectiveness of its contribution on the war on corruption. Shortage of power supply is so chronic that most States spends days without seeing power. The federal capital territory is not left out of the problem. E-governance can't be effective because it is a process that uses power round the clock. And once there is no power for a second, much is lost and the system's capacity to perform is given complicated fractures. Instances abound where banks were forced to halt because of lack of power, business were put on slow motion, and delivery of services delayed all because of lack of power. Consequent upon these CCTV cameras that supposed to pick pictures of criminals on streets and within business premises are rendered useless and ineffectual. And other sundry means of gathering information are suffering thus sometimes making corrupt practices flow with impunity.

Another problem associated with this is weak financial muscle of government at all layers of authority and the private sectors. There is no doubt Nigeria is one of African's strongest economy and the continent's largest market due to its population. However, protracted corruption in the public and private sectors, policy vacillations, and misplaced priorities has rendered the country financially week. This has denied the country the needed capacity to install all equipment needed for a robust e-governance, training of personnel to man the equipment and the political will to implement laws enacted by the parliament in response to e-governance in the country. Much of the problem now does not know what to do but having the strength to do what is needful.

CONCLUSION AND RECOMMENDATION

In this paper, we have looked at the various meanings of e-governance. As we can see, e-governance is more than just a government on the website but as a strategic framework to curb corruption. The strategies of e-governance can enable government and citizens to engage and partner with each other and other stakeholders. We also discussed the objectives of e-governance as well as the types of service delivery in e-governance. E-governance as we observe from our discussion may enhance access to government by citizens. It may increase access by those who work within government and those who work with government. It facilitates good governance for all stakeholders. The chapter strongly believes that the NITDA Act directives could send positive signals of the country's commitment to fighting corruptions. The international rating agencies are watching such steps aimed to improve Nigeria's corruption rating. The onus therefore, lies on government to monitor the process to ensure that its benefits are not eroded. Consequently, the following are recommended:

It is imperative and significant to have a mechanism to tackle the practice whereby public sector payments are made through names other than the authentic payees (contractors, suppliers or vendors). This would reduce the incidences of induced or "forced kind gestures" from any quarter. We however, urge caution here because fraud committed on electronic platforms are usually colossal and could go on for a longtime unnoticed due to the skewed format for software programming. The chapter recommends a security framework measure of regular internal and external e-governance transaction auditing to reveal any existing systemic fraud and forestall new fraud initiatives. The electronic platform must be made to identify all partners to any transactions. This is to reduce the rising incidence of anonymity that plays a critical role in corruption.

REFERENCES

Action Aid. (2015). *Corruption and Poverty in Nigeria: A Report*. Abuja, Nigeria: Action Aid.

Adeyemo, A. B. (2011). E-government Implementation in Nigeria: An Assessment of Nigeria's Global e-governance Ranking. *Journal of Internet and Information System*, 2(1), 11–19.

Aides, A., & Di Tella, R. (1999). Rents, Competition, and Corruption. *American Economic Review, 89*(4), 982-993. 10.1257/aer.89.4.982

Aidt, T. S. (2003). Economic Analysis of Corruption: A Survey. *Economics Journal, 113*, 632-652. 10.1046/j.0013-0133.2003.00171.x

Ajie, H. A. & Wokekoro, O. E. (2012). The Impact of Corruption on Sustainable Economic Growth and Development in Nigeria. *International Journal of Economic Development Research and Investment, 3*(1), 91-109.

Andersen, T., & Rand, J. (2006). *Does E-Government Reduce Corruption.* University of Copenhagen, Department of Economics, Working Paper.

Anderson, T. B. (2009). E-government as an Anti-Corruption Strategy. *Information Economics and Policy, 21*(3), 201–210. doi:10.1016/j.infoecopol.2008.11.003

Basu, S. (2004). E-governance and Developing Countries: An Overview. *International Review of Law Computers, 18*(1).

Bertot, J., Jaeger, P., & Grimes, J. (2010). Using ICT to Create A Culture of Transparency: E-Government and Social Media as Openness and Anti-Corruption Tools for Societies. *Government Information Quarterly, 27*(3), 264–271. doi:10.1016/j.giq.2010.03.001

Bhargava, V., & Bolongaita, E. (2004). *Challenging Corruption in Asia: Case Studies and A Framework for Action.* The International Bank for Reconstruction and Development/ The World Bank. Working Paper No. 27580.

Bhatnagar, S. (2003). E-government and Access to Information. In R. Hodess, T. Inowlocki, T. Wolfe, & T. International (Eds.), Global Corruption Report 2003, (pp. 24-32). Academic Press.

Brannen, A. (2001). E-governance in California: Providing Services to Citizens through the Internet. *Spectrum (Lexington, Ky.), 74*(2).

Caba, C., Lopez, A. M., & Rodriguez, M. P. (2005). Citizen's access to on-line governmental financial information: Practices in the European Union Countries. *Government Information Quarterly, 22*(2), 258-276. 10.1016/j.giq.2005.02.002

Chatfield, A. T. (2009). Public Service Reform through e-Government: A Case Study of e-Tax in Japan. *Electronic Journal of E-Government, 7*(2).

Christou, G., & Simpson, S. (2009). New Governance: the Internet, and Country Code Top-Level Domains in Europe. *Governance: an International Journal of Policy, Administration and Institutions, 22*(4), 599-624. 10.1111/j.1468-0491.2009.01455.x

Coker, .A., Ugwu, D.U., & Adams, J.A. (2012). Corruption and Direct Foreign Investments in Nigeria: Challenges of Implementing Anti-corruption Programmes under Obasanjo, 1999–2007. *Global Advanced Research Journal of History, Political Science and International Relations, 1*(4), 79-88.

Cookey, P. (2005, February). Corruption Stalls Nigeria's Development -World Bank. *Financial Standard*, 9.

Elliott, K. A. (1997). *Corruption and the Global Economy*. Washington, DC: Institute for International Economics.

Emechele, O. J. (2009). *A Critical Review of the Role of Economic and Financial Crime Commission (EFCC) in Public Sector Accountability* (Unpublished Thesis). Madonna University, Okija.

Enofe, A. O., Ogbaisi, S. A., & Mboto, O. H. (2015). E-governance and Corruption in Nigeria. *International Journal of Multidisciplinary Research and Development, 2*(8), 640–645.

European Commission. (2003). The Role of e-governance for Europe's Future. Communication from the Commission to the Council, the European Parliament, the European Economic and Social Committee and the Committee of the Regions, Brussels.

Ezigbo, O. (2007, February). Nigerian Image Still not Good, says World Bank. *This Day*.

Fang, Z. (2002). E-governance in Digital Era: Concept, Practice and Development. *International Journal of the Computer, the Internet and Management, 10*(2).

Gupta, S., Davoodi, H., & Alonso-Terme, R. (1998). *Does Corruption Affect Income Inequality and Poverty*. International Monetary Fund. Working Paper. Retrieved from http://bit.ly/V8Ojq8

Hopper, T., Tsamenyi, M, Uddin, S., & Wickramasinghe, D. (2009). Management accounting in less developed countries: what is known and needs knowing. *Accounting, Auditing and Accountability Journal, 22*(3), 469-514. 10.1108/09513570910945697

Hu, G., Pan, W., Lu, M., & Wang, J. (2009). The Widely Shared Definition of E-Government: An Exploratory Study. *The Electronic Library*, 27.

Inokoba, P.A. & Ibegu, W.T. (2011). Economic and Financial Crime Commission (EFCC) and Political Corruption Implication for the Consolidation of Democracy in Nigeria. *Anthropologist, 13*(4).

Jain, A. K. (2001). Corruption: a Review. *Journal of Economic Surveys, 15*, 72-121. 10.1111/1467-6419.00133

Kaufmann, D., Kraay, A., & Zoida-Lobaton, P. (2000). Governance Matters: from measurement to action. *Finance and Development: World Bank Policy Research, 37*(2). Retrieved from http://bit.ly/XYS9S9

Kim, C. (2007). A cross-national analysis of global E-government. *Public Organization Review, 7*(10), 317-329. 10.100711115-007-0040-5

Kim, S., Kim, H. J., & Lee, H. (2009). An Institutional Analysis of an E-174 Government System for Anti-Corruption: The Case of Open. *Government Information Quarterly, 26*(1), 42–50. doi:10.1016/j.giq.2008.09.002

Kudo, H. (2010). E-Governance As Strategy Of Public Sector Reform: Peculiarity Of Japanese IT Policy And Its Institutional Origin. *Financial Accountability & Management, 26*(1), 65-84. 10.1111/j.1468-0408.2009.00491.x

Lupu, D., & Lazar, C. (2015). Influence of E-Government on the Level of Corruption in Some EU and Non-EU States. *Procedia Economics and Finance, 20*, 365–371. doi:10.1016/S2212-5671(15)00085-4

Maor, M. (2004). Feeling the Heat? Anticorruption Mechanisms in Comparative Perspective. *Governance: An International Journal of Policy, Administration and Institutions, 17*(11), 1-28. 10.1111/j.09521895.2004.00235.x

Mario, S. (2009). E-governance in Transition Economies. *World Academy of Science, Engineering and Technology*.

Mauro, P. (1997). Corruption and Growth. *The Quarterly Journal of Economics, 110*(3), 681–712. doi:10.2307/2946696

Moon, M. J. (2002). The Evolution of E-governance Among Municipalities: Rhetoric or Reality? *Public Administration Review, 62*(4), 424–433. doi:10.1111/0033-3352.00196

Nwabuzor, A. (2005). Corruption and Development: New Initiatives in Economic Openness and Strengthened Rule of Law. *Ethics, 59*(1), 121–138.

Odo, L. U. (2015). The Impact and Consequences of Corruption on the Nigerian Society and economy. *International Journal of Arts and Humanities, 4*(1), 177–190.

OECD. (2010). *The OECD Innovation Strategy. Getting a head start on Tomorrow*. OECD Publishing.

Otalor, J. I., & Eiya, O. (2013). Combating Corruption in Nigeria: The Role of the Public Sector Auditor. *Research Journal of Finance and Accounting, 4*(4), 123-124. Retrieved from www.iiste.org

Oye, N. D. (2013). Reducing Corruption in African Developing Countries: The Relevance of E-Governance. *Greener Journal of Social Sciences, 3*(1), 6–13. doi:10.15580/GJSS.2013.1.103112183

Ribadu, N. (2003). *Economic Crime and Corruption in Nigeria: The Causes, Effects, and Efforts aimed at combating these vices in Nigeria.* Paper presented at the Monaco World Summit 5th International Summit on Transnational Crime Monte Carlo.

Ribadu, N. (2007). Corruption Drains Africa of $140bn Annually. *Punch Nigeria.* Retrieved from http://www.efccnigeria.org/index.php?option=comcontent=view&id-1347&Itemid=2

Rodriguez-Dominguez, L., Sanchez, I. M. G., & Alvarez, I. G. (2011). From Emerging to Connected E-Government: The Effects of Socioeconomics and Internal Administration Characteristics. *The International Journal of Digital Accounting Research, 11*(1), 85–109. Retrieved from http://bit.ly/TTJjzE

Rose-Ackerman, S. (1999). *Corruption and Government: Causes, Consequences and Reform.* Cambridge, UK: Cambridge University Press. doi:10.1017/CBO9781139175098

Shim, D. C., & Eom, T. H. (2008). E-Government and Anti-Corruption: Empirical Analysis of International Data. *International Journal of Public Administration, 31*(3), 298–331. doi:10.1080/01900690701590553

Shim, D. C., & Eom, T. H. (2009). Anti-Corruption Effects of Information Communication Technology (ICT) and Social Capital. *International Review of Administrative Sciences, 75*(1), 99–116. doi:10.1177/0020852308099508

Siau, K., & Long, Y. (2006). Using Social Development Lenses to Understand E-Government Development. *Journal of Global Information Management, 14*(1), 47-62. 10.4018/jgim.2006010103

Singh, G., Pathak, R., Naz, R., & Belwal, R. (2010). E-Governance for Improved Public Sector Service Delivery in India, Ethiopia and Fiji. *International Journal of Public Sector Management, 23*(3), 254-275. 10.1108/09513551011032473

Stapenhurst, R., Johnston, N., & Pelizzo, R. (2006). *The Role of Parliament in Curbing Corruption.* World Bank Institute of Development Studies. doi:10.1596/978-0-8213-6723-0

Svensson, J. (2005). Eight Questions about Corruption. *Journal of Economic Perspectives, 19*(3), 19-42. Retrieved from, 10.1257/089533005774357860

Tanzi, V. (1998). *Corruption around the World: Causes, Consequences, Scope and Cures.* International Monetary Fund. Working Paper 98/63. Retrieved from http://bit.ly/5BIhBw

Tanzi, V., & Davoodi, H. (1997). *Corruption, Public Investment and Growth.* International Monetary Fund. Working Paper 97/139.

Torres, L., Pina, V., & Acerate, B. (2006). E-Governance Developments in European Union Cities: Reshaping Government's Relationship with Citizens. *Governance: An International Journal of Policy, Administration, and Institutions, 19*(2), 277-302. 10.1111/j.1468-0491.2006.00315.x

United Nations. (2008). *United Nations e-governance Survey 2008 – From e-governance to Connected Governance.* New York: Department of Economic and Social Affairs, Division for Public Administration and Development Management.

Vittal, N. (2003). *Corruption in India.* New Delhi, India: Academic Foundation.

West, D. (2004). E-Government and the Transformation of Service Delivery and Citizen Attitudes. *Public Administration Review, 64*(1), 15-27. 10.1111/j.1540-6210.2004.00343.x

Wimmer, M., & Traunmuller, R. (2001). Trends in Electronic Government: Managing Distributed Knowledge. In *Proceedings of the 11th International Workshop on Database Expert Systems Applications*, Springer.

World Bank. (1992). *Governance and Development.* Washington, DC: World Bank.

Yildiz, M. (2004). E-governance Research: Reviewing the Literature, Limitations, and Ways Forward. *Government Information Quarterly*, 24.

Yusuf, O. (2006). *Solutions for E-Government Development in Nigeria.* Accenture EIU Government Research.

Chapter 7

Cyber Crime and Challenges of Securing Nigeria's Cyber-Space Against Criminal Attacks

Benjamin Enahoro Assay
Delta State Polytechnic Ogwashi-Uku, Nigeria

ABSTRACT

The growing menace of cyber-related crimes in Nigeria is giving the government and other stakeholders in the information and communication technology sector a cause to worry. Apart from taking a toll on the nation's economic sphere, it has also affected the image of the country negatively especially when viewed against the backdrop of the recent ranking of Nigeria as third in global internet crimes behind United Kingdom and the United States. This scenario, no doubt, requires urgent attention. This chapter, therefore, proffer solutions and recommend ways to make the country's cyberspace free from incessant criminal attacks.

INTRODUCTION

Unarguably, information and communication technology has revolutionized the world in which we live. It is credited with playing a leading role in stimulating economic growth in most modern economies. Apart from creating millions of new jobs, it is also an important enabler of innovation and development (Kvochko, 2013).

In societies where it has been fully deployed, available evidence (Ursula, 2010; Fair, 2013) shows that its impact can be felt in all aspects of a nation's life. Hence, Williams and Sawyer (2015 p. 4) aver that "information technology affects almost all aspects of our lives, including education, health, finance, recreation and entertainment, government, jobs and careers, and your personal life". Information

DOI: 10.4018/978-1-5225-5984-9.ch007

and communication technology (ICT) therefore offers limitless opportunities for individuals, organizations and nations to attain greater heights in areas that were otherwise difficult.

Information and communication technology systems are now as basic to humans as life necessities such as shelter, water and electricity. Many individuals, corporate organizations and government agencies depend on ICT and computer networks to perform simple as well as complex tasks from social networking and research to business and commerce.

Today, the cyberspace has become increasingly important to the ICT world because of the momentum Internet transactions are gaining everyday. From business, industry, government to not-for-profit organizations, the Internet has simplified business processes such as sorting, summarizing, coding, editing, customized and generic report generation in a real-time processing mode. However, it has also brought unintended consequences such as criminal activities, spamming, credit card frauds, Automatic Teller Machine (ATM) frauds, phishing, identity theft and a blossoming haven for cybercriminal miscreants to perpetrate their insidious acts.

It is sad to note that there are delinquents who roam the cyberspace, with negative intentions. The cyberspace, more than ever before, has become more vulnerable as businesses, agencies and individuals are being threatened by cybercriminals not only in Nigeria but around the world. The exceptional outbreak of cybercrime in Nigeria in recent times is quite alarming, and the negative impact on the economy of the country is highly disturbing.

This chapter thus examines cybercrime and the challenges of securing Nigeria's cyberspace against criminal attacks. The objectives of the chapter are:

1. To show the dangers cybercriminals pose to individuals, organizations, the Nigerian economy and other parts of the world.
2. To point out how the activities of a few Nigerians who engage in cybercrime is affecting the reputation of the country.
3. To come out with recommendations that will help to put an end to activities of cybercriminals in Nigeria and beyond.

BACKGROUND

Overview of Cybercrime

Cybercrime, also known as computer crime is increasingly becoming a worrisome phenomenon the world had to contend with in this information age. Williams and Sawyer (2015, p. 464) assert that "because of the opening of borders, the growth of low-cost international transportation, and the rise of the Internet, crime in general has become globalized, and computer crime is a big part of it".

Cybercrime, or computer oriented crime, is crime that involves a computer and a network (Moore, 2005). The computer may have been used in the commission of a crime, or it may be the target (Warren and Jay, 2002). Maitanmi et al. (2013, p. 45) describe cybercrime as any "illegal behavior committed by means of, or in relation to, a computer system or network, including such crimes as illegal possession and offering or distributing information". According to them, it also refers to all activities done with criminal intent in cyberspace. These fall into three categories: (1) crimes against persons, (2) crimes against business and non-business organizations, and (3) crimes against the government.

Similarly, Azeez (2013) sees it as an illegal activity which is mainly committed using a computer or Internet. In this activity, a computer or Internet is the major location of crime. According to him, it is mainly committed by hackers and it may be of various types like hacking or stealing data from online server or computer. Ngugi (2005) refers to it as a crime committed with the help of a computer through a communication device or a transmission media called the cyberspace and global network called the network. Cyberspace is the notional environment in which communication over computer networks occurs. It encompasses not only the online world and the Internet in particular but also the whole wired and wireless world of communications in general – the nonphysical terrain created by computer and communication systems (Williams and Sawyer, 2015).

The Indian Law Institute (2000) defines cybercrime as a crime committed on the Internet using the computer as either a tool or a targeted victim. It involves both the computer and the person behind it as victims, depending on which of the two is the main target. Hence, the computer could be looked at as either a target or a tool. For example, hacking involves attacking the computer's information and other resources. When the individual is the main target of cybercrime, the computer can be considered as the tool rather than the target.

Halder and Jaishankar (2011) also define cybercrime as offences that are committed against individuals or groups of individuals with a criminal motive to intentionally harm the reputation of the victim or cause physical or mental harm, or loss, to the victim directly or indirectly, using modern telecommunication networks such as Internet (networks including but not limited to chat rooms, emails, notice boards and groups) and mobile phones (Bluetooth/SMS/MMS). Issues surrounding these types of crimes have become high-profile, particularly those involving hacking, copyright infringement, unwarranted mass-surveillance, child pornography, and child grooming. There are also problems of privacy when confidential information is intercepted or disclosed, lawfully or otherwise. Internationally, both government and non-state actors engage in cybercrimes, including espionage, financial theft, and other cross-border crimes. Activity crossing international borders and involving the interests of at least one nation is sometimes referred to as cyber-warfare (Wikipedia, n.d.).

Criminals who perform illegal activities on the Internet (hacking, phishing, spamming, child pornography, hate-crimes etc.) are often referred to as hackers (Technopedia, n.d.). These crimes generally involve less technical expertise as the damage done manifests itself in the real world and human weaknesses are generally exploited (Quarshie and Martin - Odoom, 2012).

It is obvious from the foregoing that cybercrime is a computer related crime that involves a computer and a network – connected device, such as a mobile phone. It is aided by various forms of computer technology such as the use of online social networks to bully others or sending sexually explicit digital photos with a smart (Find Law, n.d.)

The Department of Justice of the United States classifies cybercrime into: (1) crimes in which the computing device is the target, for example, to gain network access; (2) crimes in which the computer is used as a weapon, for example, to launch a denial of service (DoS) attack; and (3) crimes in which the computer is used as an accessory to a crime, for example, using a computer to store illegally–obtained data (www.searchsecurity.techtarget.com/definition).

Cybercrimes have increased in sophistication and frequency over the years. As a result, individuals, business organizations and government bodies are all affected by cybercrime. Morgan (2016) notes that cybercrime may threaten a person or a nation's security and financial health. Therefore it is the responsibility of everyone to put an end to the menace.

Types of Cybercrimes

Any crime that is committed over the Internet is referred to as a cybercrime. Cybercrimes are of various types but the most common ones are discussed below:

Spam and Phishing

Spamming and phishing are two very common types of cybercrimes. There is not much one can do to control them. Spam is basically unwanted emails and messages. They use spambots. Phishing is a method where cyber criminals offer a bait so that you take it and give out the information they want. The bait can be in form of a business proposal, announcement of a lottery to which one never subscribed, and anything that promises one money for nothing or a small favour. Phishing has its variants, notably among them are Tabnabbing, Tabjacking, and Vishing and Smishing (The Windows Club, n.d).

An alarming 91 per cent of hacking attempts begin with some kind of phishing attack, which uses email and social engineering to gain access to confidential data. Mimecast, an international firm that specializes in cloud-based email management for Microsoft Exchange and Microsoft office 365 said recently that hackers always attempt to dupe recipients by luring them to open an attachment, click on a link, divulge confidential information or even wire money to a fraudulent account (Ajanaku, 2017). The reason phishing attacks are often successful is that it usually appears to come from a known or trusted source, impersonating a c-level executive. As such, phishing email attacks can be remarkably difficult to identify, and even when employees are trained on how to spot a possible phishing attack or CEO fraud, 23 per cent of phishing emails are still open.

With the potential for phishing scams to cause disruption to business operations, damage to reputation and loss of business costing millions of dollars, organizations urgently need a sophisticated solution for preventing a phishising attack. Mimecast Managing Director, Brandon Bekker however warned:

It is not just about potential monetary loss, as this can often be recovered – it is reputational damage that is very difficult to recover from. The world is changing and email has become a successful place for cybercriminals to operate as it is far easier to hack a person than a system. (Ajanaku, 2017, 2017, p. 13).

Social Engineering

Social engineering is a method used by cybercriminals to make direct contact with people using emails or cell phones. They strive to gain the confidence of their victims and once they succeed at doing that, they get the information they need. This information can be about a person, his money, his company, where he works or anything that can be of interest to the cybercriminals. Social engineering makes phishing attacks effective. Dr. Bright Gameli Mawudor, Head of Cyber Security Solutions, Internet Solutions, Kenya, blamed the success of phishing attacks on human tendency to open any email they come across.

Mawudor, who spoke on social engineering and how it works at the second Annual Afrisecure Cyber Security summit held in Johannesburg, South Africa with the theme 'Mimecast: Anatomy of an Email-Borne Attack' enthused: "As human beings, we are very open especially on social media, and all this information is incredibly valuable to hackers. We are the problem. People are the problem. It is human nature that makes people so vulnerable – the desire to be helpful, have the tendency to trust people we do not know, and have a fear of getting into trouble, which are all traits that social engineers are able to capitalize on" Cyanre, n.d.).

Social engineers are able to create confidence that they are who they say they are and that they are legitimately seeking information. Ajanaku (2017) affirms that even people who do not consider themselves to be trusting by nature are vulnerable when presented with the right story, the right voice, the right speech pattern, the right body language, and so forth.

Hacking

This is a type of crime whereby a person's computer is broken into so that his personal or sensitive information can be accessed. Through their hacking activities, hackers are able to access someone else's, personal information over the Internet. In the process, they may shut down or misuse websites or computer networks (government of the Netherlands, n.d.) In the United States, hacking is classified as a felony and punishable as such. This is different from ethical hacking, which many organizations use to check their Internet security protection. In hacking, the criminal uses a variety of software to enter a person's computer and the person may not be aware that his computer is being accessed from a remote location (Cross Domain Solutions, n.d.). The only way to protect oneself from a hacker is to regularly change one's password and have a strong firewall in place that will prevent outsiders from accessing one's computer from a remote location. It is also necessary to put a password on one's wireless network so that no one else can access any of the information that is sent and received over the network.

Identity Theft

This is perhaps the most devastating type of cybercrime. It has become a major problem with people using the Internet for cash transactions and banking services. Those who use the worldwide web for purchases are at a higher risk of having their identity stolen (Supportz, n.d.). In this cybercrime, a criminal accesses data about a person's bank account, credit and debit card numbers, social security information, and other sensitive information to siphon money or to buy things online in the victim's name. This can result to major financial losses and a ruined reputation for the victim, and the criminal is not always caught.

Cyber Stalking

Cyber stalking is yet another common type of cybercrime. Stalkers subject their victims to a barrage of threatening online messages and emails. Bullies often use this tactic to attack fellow students. The stalkers know their victims and instead of resorting to official stalking, they use the Internet to stalk. However, if they notice that cyber-stalking is not having the desired effect, they begin offline stalking along with cyber-stalking to make the victim's life more miserable. Cyber stalking is a serious crime, especially if it evolves into real-world stalking (Cross Domain Solutions, n.d.)

Theft

On a regular basis, a lot of theft occurs online, especially when it comes to artistic works in the form of writing, music, movies, games and software. These criminals infringe upon another person's copyrighted materials by stealing them and claiming them as their own or selling them for profit without permission from the owners of the works (Supportz, n.d.). There are even peer sharing websites which encourage software piracy and illegal downloading, especially over file sharing networks but these websites are now being targeted by law enforcement agencies such as the Federal Bureau of Investigations (Cross Domain Solutions, n.d.)

Malicious Software

These are Internet-based software or programmes that are used to disrupt a network. The software is used to gain access to a system to steal sensitive information or data or causing damage to software present in the system (Cross Domain Solutions, n.d.). The only way to protect oneself is to visit trusted websites and have an updated antivirus programme installed.

Child Soliciting and Abuse

In this type of cybercrime, criminals solicit minors via chat rooms for the purpose of child pornography. Child pornography refers to any content that depicts sexually explicit activities involving a child. Visual depictions include photographs, videos, digital or computer generated images indistinguishable from an actual minor. These images and videos that involve the documentation of an actual crime scene are then circulated for personal consumption (We Are Thorn, n.d.).

Child pornography exploits children for sexual stimulation (Finkelhor, 1994; Helga and Wynne, 1999; Milner and O'Domel, 2007; Sheldon and Howitt, 2007; Klain, Heather and Molly, 2001). It may be produced with the direct involvement or sexual assault of a child (also known as child sexual abuse images) or it may be simulated child pornography (Wells, Finkelhor, Wolak and Mitchel, 2007; National Centre for Missing and Exploited children, 2005; Crosson-Tower, 2005). Abuse of the child occurs during the sexual acts or lascivious exhibitions of genitals or pubic areas which are recorded in the production of child pornography (Finkelhor, 1994; Hobs, Helga and Wynne, 1999; Sheldon and Howitt, 2007; Klain, Heather and Molly, 2001; Wortley and Smallbone, n.d; Fournier de Saint Maur, 1999). Child pornography may use a variety of media (National Centre for Missing and Exploited Children, 2005) including writings (Akdeniz, 2008; Criminal Code of Canada, 2004; CBC News, 2002), magazines, photos, sculpture, drawing, cartoon, painting, film, video (National Centre for Missing and Exploited Children, 2005), animation, sound recording (Akdeniz, 2008) and video games (digiknow, 2013).

Laws regarding child pornography generally include sexual images involving prepubescents, pubescent or post-pubescent minors and computer-generated images that appear to involve them (Wells, Finkelhor, Wolak and Mitchell, 2007). Most possessors of child pornography who are arrested are found to possess images of prepubescent children, possessors of pornographic images of post-pubescent minors are less likely to be prosecuted, even though those images also fall within the statutes (Wells, Finkelhor, Wolak and Mitchell, 2007).

Producers of child pornography strive to avoid prosecution by distributing their material across national borders, though this issue is increasingly being addressed with regular arrests of suspects from a number of countries occurring over the last few years (Wells, Finkelhor, Wolak and Mitchell, 2007; National Centre for Missing and Exploited Children, 2005). The prepubescent pornography is viewed and collected by pedophiles for a variety of purposes, ranging from private sexual uses, trading with other pedophiles, preparing children for sexual abuse as part of the process known as 'child growing', or enticement leading to entrapment for sexual exploitation such as production of new child pornography or child prostitution (Crosson-Tower, 2005; Wortley and Smallbone, n.d; Levesque, 1999). Children themselves also sometimes produce child pornography on their own initiative or by the coercion of an adult (ECPAT, 2015).

In most jurisdictions of the world, child pornography is illegal and therefore censored (World Congress against CSEC, 2012). Ninety-four of 187 Interpol member states had laws specifically addressing child pornography as of 2008, though this does not include nations that ban all pornography regardless of intent to distribute (Model Legislation and Global Review, 2008). Both distribution and possession are now criminal offences in almost all Western countries. A wide movement is working to globalize the criminalization of child pornography, including major international organizations such as the United Nations and the European Commission (Akdeniz, 2008; World Congress against Commercial Sexual Exploitation of Children, 2012).

Motives of Cybercrime

Perpetrators of cybercrime do so for several reasons ranging from financial, espionage to ego. A Symantec report revealed that cybercrime has surpassed illegal drug trafficking as a criminal money-maker, as 1 in 5 persons will become victim. (Symantec, n.d.). Similarly, another research firm, Verizon (2017) found that 89 percent of breaches had a financial or espionage. Mr. Andy Archibald, deputy director, cybercrime unit of the National Crime Agency also confirms that the main motivation for cybercrime is financial gain.

In Nigeria, cybercriminals to date have been consistently implicated in money-oriented rather than psychosocial and geopolitical cybercrimes. Emerging evidence shows that perpetrators of cybercrimes in Nigeria focus exclusively on cyber-fraud (Ojedokun and Eraye, 2012; Smith, 2008; Tade and Aliyu, 2011; Adogame, 2007; Doyon-Martin, 2015; Chawki et al., 2015b; Akpome, 2015; Ellis, 2016; Ibrahim, 2016).

Wherever the rate of return on investment is high and the risk is low, people are bound to take advantage of the prevailing situation. This is exactly what happens in cybercrime. Accessing sensitive information and data and using it means a rich harvest of returns for the criminals who engage in cybercrime and apprehending such criminals is often difficult. As a result, there has been a steady rise in cybercrime across the world.

Socio-Economic Impact of Cybercrime

The social impact of cybercrime in Nigeria is damning, and is felt both locally and abroad. At home, cybercrime has thrown up a set of young people known as "yahoo boys" who frequently roam the cyberspace with the intention to defraud their victims. Buoyed by unemployment and the get-rich quick syndrome in the Nigerian society, the fraudsters who openly flaunt their proceeds of crime are increasingly taking advantage of the rise in online transactions, electronic shopping, e-commerce, electronic messaging systems and the weak implementation of the Cybercrimes Act 2015 to engage in all manner of crimes. Instead of their source of wealth being questioned, society glorifies the cybercriminals and this seems to be encouraging more and more young people to take to cybercrime.

At the international level, cybercrime has earned Nigeria a very negative reputation (Okeshola and Adeta, 2013 p, 98) as the country is seen as a breeding ground for cybercriminals. Confidence in the nation's economy is being eroded by the activities of these miscreants. Perpetual tourists and investors are equally scared and the image of genuine Nigerians is marred (Martins Library, n.d). Nigeria cannot afford to have her reputation tarnished by being associated with cybercrime if it must compete favorably in today's global economy. Something urgent must therefore be done to stem this ugly trend.

The economic cost of cybercrimes is quite enormous. In fact, cybercrime imposes a huge financial burden on individuals, organizations and nations. Available statistics put the cost of cybercrime globally at over $700 billion annually and it is projected to rise to about $2 trillion by 2019 (Morgan, 2016). Due to the rapid digitization of consumer lives and company records, the number of incidents of cybercrime in 2016 grew by 38 percent as against the number reported in 2015 (Adepetun, 2016).

A report by cyber-security ventures has predicted that global annual cybercrime cost will grow to about $6 trillion by 2021. The report released by the Cyberseurity Experts Association of Nigeria (CSEAN) stated that the menace would soon include destruction of data, stolen money, lost production and theft of intellectual property. Others include theft of personal and financial data, embezzlement, fraud, post-attack, disruption to the normal course of business, forensic investigation, destruction and deletion of hacked data and systems, including reputational harm. According to Remi Afon, CSEAN President, the estimate does not include the cost incurred for unreported crime (Adanikin et al, 2016).

Nigeria's cybercrime estimates show that between2012 and 2014, the country lost N64 billion to cyber-crimes while N127 billion is lost annually to the menace. This is even as Ultrascan, a Dutch investigation research firm found that the cost of cybercrime originating from Nigeria globally is valued at $9.3 billion (World Stage Group, n.d.)

Cybercrime Statistics in Nigeria

There is no denying the fact that cybercrime is increasing at an alarming rate in Nigeria. Palo Alto Networks, a U.S network and enterprise security company, disclosed recently that cybercriminals operating in Nigeria have evolved from silly spray-and-pray email spam campaigns into more refined con games that target large business organizations with malware and fetch princely sums totaling millions of dollars.

According to a report compiled by threat research team unit 42 of the tech company, the researchers analyzed over 8,400 malware samples originating from Nigerian scams from July 2014 to June 2016, pinpointing roughly 100 individual actors or groups behind these campaigns. The report said that "the frequency of malware attacks jumped wildly in this time, from fewer than 100 attacks in July 2014 to a range 5,000 to 8,000 per month – peaking in May 2016 with nearly 19,000 incidents".

The tech security company further disclosed that "Nigerian actors have demonstrated a clear growth in size, scope, complexity and capability over the past two years and as a direct result, they should now be regarded as a formidable threat to business worldwide".

Palo Alto said that because Nigerians have the reputation of using cheap commodity malware tools that are readily available in the underground market, Nigerian scammers still seem to be the:Rodney Dangerfeld of the cybercriminal world- in part. However, this does not reflect a lack of internet – savvy. Rather, they have learned how to successfully apply simple malware tools with precision in order to create substantial losses ranging from tens of thousands up to millions of dollars for victim organizations, and they have broadened their scope well beyond targeting unsuspecting individuals", the report reads. The company identified five of the scammers' most popular malware tools as Predator Pain, ISR Stealer, Keybase, ISP Software and Pony, each of which enables attackers to remotely access or steal credentials from infected machines.

According to the tech company, relying on inexpensive commodity tools actually affords the scammers a key advantage: they can instead allocate the bulk of their budget toward the latest, state-of-the-art cryptors that obfuscate the malware in order to evade anti-virus solutions. It also noted that just because commodity malware is inexpensive does not mean it is effective at what it does. In fact, "if you were to compare that tool to something built by a very sophisticated-nation-state, that tool is probably more sophisticated", particularly from a development perspective, Ryan Olson, Intelligence Director at Palo Alto Networks said.

The report further said that the Nigerian scammers have also shifted from "carpet bombing" random individuals with spam to coordinating "surgical spear-phishing strikes" against specific business targets. Instead of relying on bizarre tales of political intrigue and lost fortunes to tempt recipients with improbable get-rich-quick schemes, these scammers now carefully craft emails that offer credible value propositions to their targets. Many of these emails rely on Business Emails Compromise and Business Email Spoofing techniques to make the emails appear as if they are originating from a trusted and plausible source.

In the samples Palo Alto studied, malware attacks most frequently targeted the high-tech, higher education and manufacturing industries. In addition to using email, it also said the Nigerian scammers propagated their malware through fraudulent websites that sometimes impersonate the sites of legitimate companies and organizations. The tech company also took a closer look at the individuals and entities behind these campaigns, leveraging threat intelligence and advanced analytics to link threat actors' domain registration details with their Facebook and

Google+ social media profiles. In doing so, the researchers found that many of the perpetrators live comfortably, are primary range in age from late teens to mid- 40s.

By mapping out this Nigerian social network, unit 42 was able to link Nigerian actors to additional malware tools, including the Nanocore remote access Trojan Hawkeye Keylogger, Aegis Crypter and Orway Crypter. Moreover, the researchers were able to identify a select few individuals who "appear to serve as the connective tissue between various subsets of Nigerian actors and the tools they use". These key links could potentially be suppliers of malware tools or perhaps even cybercriminal bosses (Technology Times, n.d.).

Nigeria's Cybercrimes Act 2015

Nigeria's Cybercrimes Act was passed into law to address the challenges posed by cybercriminals after the bill went through a rigorous process of the 6th chambers of the National Assembly. The Act which was assented to by former President Goodluck Jonathan on May 15, 2015 has the following broad objectives:

1. Provide an effective and unified legal, regulatory and institutional framework for the prohibition, prevention, detection, prosecution and punishment of cybercrimes in Nigeria;
2. Ensure the protection of national information infrastructure; and
3. Promote cybersecurity and the protection of computer systems and networks, electronic communications, data and computer programs, intellectual property and privacy rights.

The Act listed offences and penalties including unlawful access to computers, unlawful operation of cyber-cafes, system interference, intercepting electronic messages, emails, e-money transfer, tampering with critical infrastructure, computer-related forgery, among others as punishable offences. The law imposes, for instance, seven years imprisonment for offenders of all kinds and additional seven years for online crimes that result in physical harm, and life imprisonment for those that lead to death. However the major problem with this law lies in its enforcement. Some of the "yahoo boys" still throng cyber-café premises to "transact" their business with the owners looking away. Yet the law criminalizes internet café owners who knowingly allow their premises to be used to commit crimes. Others who use their personal computer systems to perpetrate the crime do so without being caught, and cybercrimes continue to flourish in the Nigerian society unhindered.

MAIN FOCUS OF THE CHAPTER

Issues

Cybercrime has become a growing concern for government, information security professionals, individuals and organizations not only in Nigeria but across the globe. Over the past 20 years, immoral cyberspace users have continued to use the Internet to commit crimes; thus evoking mixed feelings of admiration and fear in the general populace along with a growing unease about the state of cyber and personal security. Piqued by the unending activities of cybercriminals and the havoc they have wrecked on Nigeria, the Senate, recently disclosed that Nigeria has lost about $450 million to 3500 cyber-attacks on its information and communications technology (ICT) space, representing about 70 percent of hacking attempts in the country.

The activities of the cybercriminals have not only affected the economy of Nigeria negatively, it has also brought a collective shame on the people as the country is often cited as a breeding ground for most of these nefarious practices because of the illegal activities of some of its citizens. In the last few years, many criminal elements in Nigeria have been using the modern telecommunication networks such as the Internet and mobile phones to commit all manner of crimes that give Nigeria a negative image globally. Of late, Nigerian cyber hackers and cyber criminals were accused of masterminding a grand theft of information and money running into billions of dollars worldwide. According to information and communication technology experts, the Nigerians were able to carry out the heist by sending phishing emails to commercial organizations and industrial enterprises, which they later steal dry. The Federal Bureau of Investigation (FBI) estimates that these phishing attacks have cost companies over $3 billion as the numbers of affected companies exceed 22,143.

Controversies

The apparent failure of the cybercrimes Act to address the growing challenges posed by cybercriminals has sparked series of reactions from the Nigerian public. While some put the blame squarely on the doorstep of the government for its inability to tackle the criminals head on, others blame the lapses in the enforcement of the Act for the continued increase in cybercrime in Nigeria. As the controversy rages, there appears be no end in sight of the nefarious activities of the cybercriminals.

The Cybercrimes Act was passed into law in 2015 to address all issues associated with cybercrimes in Nigeria. The law criminalizes a variety of offences – from ATM Card Skimming and identity theft to possession of child pornography. It imposes for instance, seven years imprisonment for offenders of all kinds and additional seven years for online crimes that result in physical harm, and life imprisonment for those that lead to death. But like almost every law in the country, there is the problem of enforcement. The perpetrators of cybercrime ("yahoo boys"), still daily throng cybercafé premises to transact their business with the owners looking away. Yet the law criminalizes Internet café owners who knowingly allow their premises to be used to commit crimes.

Problems

Indeed, there is an upsurge of cybercrime in Nigeria. The country is ranked third in global Internet crime after the United States of America and United Kingdom while 7.5 percent of the world's hackers are said to be Nigerians. Committed mostly by the young, often called "yahoo" boys, a precursor of the infamous '419' email scammers, the fraudsters are increasingly taking advantage of the rise in online transactions, electronic shopping, e-commerce and the electronic messaging systems to engage in all manner of crimes.

The Central Bank of Nigeria (CBN) reported last year (2016) that 70 per cent of attempted or successful fraud/forgery cases in the Nigerian banking system were perpetrated via the electronic channels. Between 2000 and 2013, banks in the country lost N159 billion to electronic frauds and cybercrime. In 2014, bank customers lost about N6 billion in Nigeria. In addition, the damage to business from the theft of intellectual property is exceedingly high.

Experts in the information and technology industry have raised the alarm that the growing Internet of Things (IoT) would soon snowball into further increase in cybercrime. They have argued that the massive growth in global cyber threats in recent times was inadvertently aided by the significant rise in exploitation of IoT technologies.

According to Wikipedia, IoT is the network of physical devices, vehicles, home appliances, and other items embedded with electronics, software, sensors, actuators, and network connectivity, which enable the objects to connect and exchange data. Each item is uniquely identifiable through its embedded computing system but is able to inter-operate within the existing Internet infrastructure.

It is estimated that the IoT will consist of about 30 billion objects by 2020. United States Consul-General in Nigeria, Mr. John Bray, who spoke during the 2017 Cybersecurity Awareness event in Lagos predicted that the global Internet community would lose $6 trillion to cybercrime with IoT (Olaleye, 2017).

SOLUTIONS AND RECOMMENDATIONS

Solutions

There is no doubt that cybercrime has become a national threat in Nigeria. With increased access to the Internet being facilitated by telecommunications companies across the country, industry experts and civil society groups have raised the alarm over the danger, which the gradual ubiquitous access to the Internet without necessary regulations and enforcement of cyber security laws portends for the country.

In view of the current national drive towards electronic transactions and more and more access to the Internet, the following solutions are hereby proposed.

1. There should be a robust, sustained collaboration and awareness creation among various stakeholders in Nigeria and beyond to stem the tide of cybercrimes globally
2. A special unit of the police should be created, properly trained and equipped to handle all cybercrime related issues in the country.
3. The relevant laws proposed by the National Assembly should be applied by the Nigeria Government and enforced by the police.
4. The Nigeria Government should build a cyber army of security experts to defend the country's cyberspace. Nigeria needs nothing less than one million cyber security experts in the next three years to cope with the challenges of cyber security. Countries such as North Korea currently boasts of 15,000 well-trained cybersecurity experts, China has over 25 million cyber commandos while India is targeting 5 million cyber security experts to defend their cyber space.
5. Individuals should be encouraged not to share their Personal Identification number (PIN), bank account, email access code with unknown persons. They should ignore any email requiring financial and other confidential information.

Recommendations

In view of the issues and problems articulated in this chapter, the following recommendations are pertinent.

1. The National Assembly should convoke a national stakeholders conference on cyber-security that would help stimulate a collective reflection among relevant stakeholders and articulate a national and broad-based approach to keep the country ahead of cybercrime challenges.

2.   There is need to have a stronger cyber-gateway which will filter processes going and coming into the country's cyberspace.

3.   There is also need for the government to develop, invest, and deploy innovative technologies to manage information security in Nigeria. An example of such innovative technology is the "Quantum Encryption" recently developed by China to fight online fraud and identity theft, hacking attacks and other cybercrimes, which are threats to global economy.

4.   To successfully tackle cyber-security related issues, organizations should focus on developing 'human firewalls' to stop cybercrimes from occurring. Most organizations focus mainly on security solutions, but continue to fail because they rely on data that is gathered after an attack rather than preventing the attack from happening in the first place.

FUTURE RESEARCH DIRECTIONS

Cybercrime has assumed a worrisome dimension in Nigeria, hence stakeholders are unanimous in their call for a concerted effort in dealing with the malaise in order to secure Nigeria's cyberspace. Nigeria's cyberspace had become very porous and the system lacked a well coordinated, structured and effective approach to cybercrime control.

In line with the focus of the book which has to do with Security Frameworks in Contemporary Electronic Government, it is expedient that government and stakeholders in the ICT industry evolve policies that would help curtail the growing influence of cybercrime in Nigeria and the rest of the world. To effectively checkmate the activities of cybercriminals, the relevant stakeholders need to come together to deal decisively with all cybercrime related issues. The nation can only benefit maximally, if all those concern tread this path.

The stakeholder engagement model will be useful here. Stakeholder engagement is the process by which an organization involves people who may be affected by the decisions it makes, or can influence the implantation of its decisions. They may support or oppose the decisions, be influential in the organization or within the community in which it operates, hold relevant official position or be affected in the long term (Wikipedia, n.d.) It is a tool used by mature private and public sector organizations, especially when they want to develop understanding and agree to solutions on complex issues or issues of concern (Stakeholder Mapping, n.d.)

The term stakeholder engagement has however emerged as a means of describing a broader, more inclusive public participation process. When executed effectively, stakeholder engagement can be used to improve communication, obtain wider support, gather useful data and ideas, enhance agency reputation, and provide for more sustainable decision making (Perm Newsletter, 2012). A robust stakeholder engagement model is vital for organizations, governments and other entities to be able to understand and respond to legitimate stakeholder concerns such as cybercrime. Cybercrime is a complex issue of public concern not only to Nigeria but the entire world.

Fighting cybercrime is the responsibility of everyone. It is important to understand that no one person or institution can have the requisite capacity to deal with cybersecurity. Cybersecurity is not an event but rather a process. Seck (2014) notes that it is not simply a matter of passing legislation, or something that belongs to lawyers only. As a result, all segment of society including members of parliament, lawyers, the judiciary, intelligence/military, civil society, media, young people and members of the public should be involved in efforts to deal with cyber-security at the earliest available opportunity. It is important to engage all stakeholders to ensure that they understand the issues and processes involved.

As the key stakeholders are engaged, it is imperative to monitor the implementation of the policies put in place to address cyber-security breaches from time to time in order to realize the set targets. This will form the direction of future research in this domain. Proper monitoring of the implementation of cyber-security policies will ensure that obstacles that make it difficult to protect Nigeria's cyberspace against criminal attacks are removed.

CONCLUSION

There is no doubt that cybercrime has taken a dangerous dimension in Nigeria as it has exposed entities and businesses to multiplicity of risks. Even government servers are currently being threatened. Cybercrime is having an increasingly alarming toll on Nigeria's financial, economic, security, information and communication technology systems. Acts of online fraud, identity theft, cyber-bulling, etc., have become regular feature of our daily life.

This ugly trend has prompted calls for increase awareness campaign among the populace, strict enforcement of the Cybercrime Act 2015, a robust network security including appropriate network architecture and software, use of encryption, data protection legislation, information security standards and other tools of threat protection and detection.

It is heartwarming to note that the upper chamber of the nation's National Assembly (Senate) has unveiled plans to initiate Cybercrime Bill to fight criminality in technology and safeguard Nigeria's cyberspace. The decision of the Senate is hinged on series of incidences of cyber-attacks around the world and the failure of the Cybercrimes Act 2015 to address the challenges of cyber-security in the country.

Cyberspace contributes significantly to achieving countries' national development goals, and so international organizations, national security services, operators, intelligence and data protection agencies, as well as citizens all have a role to play in making cyberspace safer and more resilient.

REFERENCES

Adepetun, A. (2016, November 9). Is cybercrime proving difficult to tackle? *The Guardian*, p. 36.

Adogame, A. (2007). *The 419 code as business unusual: Youth and the unfolding of the advance fee fraud online discourse.* International Sociology Association. Retrieved from http://www.isa-sociology.org/publ/e-bulletin/E-bulletin7.pdf

Ajanaku, L. (2017, October 31). Why phishing attacks remain effective. *Nation (New York, N.Y.)*, 13.

Akdeniz, Y. (2008). *Internet child pornography and the law: National and international responses.* Farnham, UK: Ashgate Publishing Limited.

Akpome, A. (2015). What is Nigeria? unsettling the myth of exceptionalism. *Africa Spectrum, 50*(1), 65–78.

Azeez, K. (2013, August 15). Concerns mount over poor cyber security. *National Mirror*, p. 35.

CBC News. (2002, March 26). *Sharpe not guilty of possessing written child pornography.* CBC News.

Chawki, M., Darwish, A., Khan, M. A., & Iyagi, S. (2015b). 419 scam: An evaluation of cybercrime and criminal code in Nigeria. In *Cybercrime, Digital Forensics and Jurisdiction. Studies in Computational Intelligence* (Vol. 593). New York: Springer, Cham. doi:10.1007/978-3-319-15150-2_9

Criminal Code of Canada. (2004). Definition of child pornography. Section 163.1. Electronic Frontier.

Cross Domain Solutions. Cyber Crimes. (n.d.). Retrieved from http:www.crossdomatinsolutions.com/cyber-crime/

Crosson-Tower, C. (2005). *Understanding child abuse and neglect.* Boston: Allyn and Bacon.

Cyanre. SA Cyber Crimes. (n.d.). Retrieved from http://www.cyanre.co.za/tag/ Sa-cyber-crime

Digiknow. (2013). *Child porn video game rated PG in Australia.* Author.

Doyon-Martin, J. (2015). Cybercrime in West Africa as a result of transboundary e-waste. *Journal of Applied Security Research, 10*(2), 207–220. doi:10.1080/1936 1610.2015.1004511

ECPAT (2015). *End child pornography.* ECPAT.

Ellis, S. (2016). *This present darkness: A history of Nigerian organized crime.* Oxford, UK: Oxford University Press.

Fair, O. (2013). *The importance of technology in economic and social development.* Retrieved from https://www.fairobserver.com/regionafrica -technology-economic-and-soical-development/

Find Law. Cyber Crimes. (n.d.). Retrieved from www.criminal.findlaw.com/criminal-charges/cyber-crimes.html

Finkelhor, D. (1994). Current information on the scope and nature of child sexual abuse. *The Future of Children, 4*(2), 31–53. doi:10.2307/1602522 PMID:7804768

Forbes. (2016). *Cyber Crime Costs Projected To Reach $2 Trillion by 2019.* Retrieved from https://www.forbes.com/sites/stevemorgan/2016/01/17/cyber-crime-costs-projected-to-reach-2-trillion-by-2019/

Fournier de Saint Maur, A. (1999, January). Sexual abuse of children on the Internet: A new challenge for INTERPOL. In *Expert meeting on sexual abuse of children, child pornography and paedophilia on the Internet: An international challenge.* UNESCO.

Government of the Netherlands. Cyber Crimes. (n.d.). Retrieved from https://www. government.nl/topics/ cybercrime/forms-of-cybercrime

Halder, D., & Jaishankar, K. (2011). *Cybercrime and the victimization of women: Laws, rights, and regulations.* Hershey, PA: IGI Global.

Ibrahim, S. (2016). Causes of socioeconomic cybercrime in Nigeria (Parents' Perspectives). In *Proceedings of the 4th International Conference on Cybercrime and computer Forensics.* Canada, Vancouver: IEEE Xplore Publishing.

Indian Law Institute. (2000). *Introduction to cyberlaw.* Available at www.ili.ac.in/e-learnCL.html

Klain, E. J., Heather, J. D., & Molly, A. H. (2001). *Child pornography: The criminal justice system response*. National Centre for Missing and Exploited Children.

Kvochko, E. (2013). *Five ways technology can help the economy*. Available at https://www.weforum.org/agenda/2013/04/five-ways-technology-can-help-the-economy/

Levesque, R. J. R. (1999). *Sexual abuse of children: A human rights perspective*. Bloomington, IN: Indian University Press.

Maitanmi, O., Ogunlere, S., Ayinde, S., & Adekunle, Y. (2013). Impact of cybercrimes on Nigerian economy. *International Journal of Engineering Science*, 2(4), 45–51.

MappingS. (n.d.). Retrieved from http://www.stakeholdermapping.com/smm-maturity-maturity-model/

Martins Library. (n.d.). Retrieved from https://martins.library.blogspot.com/2013/08/

Milner, C., & O'Donnel, I. (2007). *Child pornography: Crime, computers and society*. Milton Park: Willan Publishing Limited.

Model Legislation and Global Review. (2008). *Child pornography*. Available at https://www.issuelab.org/resource/child-pornography-model-legislation-global-review.html

Moore, R. (2005). *Cybercrime: Investigating high technology computer crime*. Cleveland, MI: Anderson Publishing.

Morgan, S. (2016). *Cybercrime costs projected to reach $2 trillion by 2019*. Retrieved from https://www.forbes.com/sites/stevemorgan/ 2016/01/17/cybercrime-costs-porjected-to-reach-2-trillion-by-2019/

National Center for Missing and Exploited Children. (2015). *Child pornography*. Available at www.missingkids.com/dam/documents

Ngugi, M. (2005). *Law on cybercrime overdue*. Available at www.crimeresearch.org

Ojedokun, U.A., & Eraye, M.C. (2012). Socioeconomic lifestyles of the yahoo-boys: A case study of perceptions of university students in Nigeria. *International Journal of Cyber Criminology, 6*(2), 1001-1013.

Okeshola, F.B., & Adeta, A.K. (2013). The nature, causes and consequences of cybercrime in tertiary institutions in Zaria, Kaduna State, Nigeria. *American International Journal of Contemporary Research, 3*(9).

Olaleye, O. (2017, November 1). Cybercrime: Experts proffer solutions as IoT grows. *Daily Sun*, p. 33.

PermNewsletter. (2012, April). *Understanding the importance of stakeholder engagement*. Retrieved from https://www.cansr.msu.du/uploads/files

Quarshie, H.O., & Martin-Odoom, A. (2012). Fighting cybercrime in Africa. *Computer Science and Engineering, 2*(6), 98-100. Doi:105923/j.computer.20120206.03

Seck, M. (2014). *Tackling the challenges of cybersecurity in Africa. Policy Brief.* United Nations Economic Commission for Africa.

Sheldon, K., & Howitt, D. (2007). *Sex offenders and the Internet*. John Wiley and Sons.

Smith, D. J. (2008). *A culture of corruption: Everyday deception and popular discontent in Nigeria*. Princeton, NJ: Princeton University Press.

Supportz. The Five Most Common Types of Cyber Crime. (n.d.). Retrieved from http://supportz.com/the-five-most-common-types-ofcyber-crime/

Syemantic. Newsroom. (n.d.). Retrieved from https://www.symantec.com/about/newsroom /press-releases/2009/symantec09/1001

Tade, O., & Aliyu, I. (2011). Social organization of Internet fraud among university undergraduates in Nigeria. *International Journal of Cyber Criminology, 5*(2), 860–875.

Technology Times. Cyber Crime in Nigeria. (n.d.). Retrieved from http://www.technologytimes.ng/cyber-crime-in-nigeria-increasing-at-alarming-rate/

Technopedia. Dictionary. (n.d.). Retrieved from https://www.techopedia.com/dictonary/

The Nation. (2016). *Cost of cyber crime to hit $6 trillion annually – Report*. Retrieved from www.thenationonlineng.net/cost-cyber-crime-hit-6-trillion-annually-report/

ThornW. A.PornographyC.StatsA. (n.d.). Retrieved from https://www.wearethorn.org/child-pornography-and-abuse-statistics/ http://www.missingkids.com/en_us/documents/CP_ Legislation_Report.pdf

Ursala, S. (2010). *Importance of the role of ICT for development*. Retrieved from https://www.adb.org/news/speeches/importance-role-ict-development

Verizon. (2017). *Data breach investigation report paints a bleak picture of the current state of cybersecurity*. Retrieved from www.silicon.co.uk/security/verizon-cyber-attacks-210499

Warren, G., & Jay, G. H. (2002). *Computer forensics: Incident response essentials.* Boston: Addison-Wesley.

Wells, M., Finkelhor, D., Wolak, J., & Mitchell, K. (2007). Defining child pornography: Law enforcement dilemmas in investigations of Internet child pornography possession. *Police Practice and Research, 8*(3), 269–282. doi:10.1080/15614260701450765

Wikipedia. (n.d.). *Cyercrime.* Retrieved from https:/en.m.wikipedia.org/wiki/cybercrime

Wikipedia. Internet of Things. (n.d.). Retrieved from https://en.m.wikipedia.org/wiki/Internetofthings

Wikipedia. Stakeholder Engagement. (n.d.). Retrieved from https://en.m.wikipedia.org/wiki/stateholder-engagement

Williams, B.K., & Sawyer, S.C. (n.d.). *Using information technology* (11th ed.). New York: McGraw Hill.

World Congress Against CSEC. (2002). *Child pornography.* Author.

World Stage Group. (n.d.). Retrieved from www.worldstagegroup.com/worldstagenew/Index.php? active=news&newscid=256138&catid=2

Wortley, R., & Smallbone, S. (n.d.). Child pornography on the Internet. *Problem Oriented Guides for Police, 41*, 14-16.

KEY TERMS AND DEFINITIONS

ATM Fraud: ATM fraud refers to fraud with the use of an ATM card whereby the perpetrator of the crime uses the card to immediately withdraw funds from a consumer account using PIN based transactions at the automated teller machine.

Cyberattack: Is a deliberate exploitation of computer systems, technology-dependent enterprises and networks. Cyberattacks use malicious code to alter compute code, logic or data, resulting in disruptive consequences that can compromise data and lead to cybercrimes, such as information and identity theft.

Cybercriminal: A cybercriminal is an individual who commits cybercrimes, where he/she makes use of the computer either as a tool or as a target or as both. Cybercriminals use computers in three broad ways: select computer as their target, uses computer as their weapon and uses computer as their accessory.

Cyberworld: Is the world of inter-computer communication; a real or virtual world of information in cyberspace.

Hacking: Is the use of a computer or other technological device or system in order to gain unauthorized access to data held by another person or organization.

Information and Communication Technology: ICT refers to technologies that provide access to information through telecommunications. It is similar to information (IT) but focuses primarily on communication technologies. This includes the internet, wireless networks, cell phones, and other communication mediums.

Internet: Is a global computer network that provides a variety of information and communication facilities, and consists of interconnected networks using standardized communication protocols.

Internet Fraud: Internet fraud is a type of fraud which makes use of the Internet to defraud victims or take advantage of them. It ranges from e-mail spam to online scams.

Internet of Things: Is a computing concept that describes the idea of everyday physical objects being connected to the Internet and being able to identify themselves to other devices.

Telecommunications Device: It means: (1) a device that is able to transmit telephonic, electronic, digital, cellular, or radio communications, or (2) a part of a device that is able to transmit telephonic, electronic, digital, cellular, or radio communications, regardless of whether the part itself is able to transmit. It includes a cellular telephone, digital telephone, picture telephone, and modem equipped device.

Chapter 8
Internet Service Provider Liability in Relation to P2P Sites:
The Pirate Bay Case

Nisha Dhanraj Dewani
Jamia Millia Islamia University, India

ABSTRACT

Different systems require different levels of security according to the services they provide to their users. Cyberspace is the alliance of various networks together connected through internet service providers (ISPs). However, the alliance of these networks often faces security issues. Some use the internet as a path for illegal activities such as breaching of others computer or networks, damaging and stealing information, and blocking or denying legitimate users from services they subscribe. So, the purpose of this chapter is to review the responsibilities of ISPs in securing their customers' network, and find out whether there are legal provisions, or liabilities that are bindings on the ISPs to provide security for their customers. What protections are envisaged under the umbrella of safe harbors? Are ISPs responsible for end users' network security? The Swedish Court recently found The Pirate Bay (TPB) guilty of making copyright works available. Finally, this chapter will analyze the issues raised in the TPB along with ISPs liability.

DOI: 10.4018/978-1-5225-5984-9.ch008

INTRODUCTION

The internet entity is extremely dependent on information and network security. The entire enterprise of the information society becomes crucial when internet content is disseminated, hosted and placed through online intermediaries. In this relation, an ISP's position can be called a gateway to the Internet which host of legal and ethical duties. The ability of unidentified users to freely exchange information over the Internet creates legal responsibilities for ISPs to act in the public's interest. Customers rely on the Internet for personal communication, information, and to conduct business, giving ISPs an obligation to deliver reliable service and access to the websites and services their customers depend upon. On the other hand, the online activity affects innovation and free speech. Even most creative expression today takes place over communications networks owned by private enterprises. The intermediaries have to block their users or unwanted online content in order to repress dispute, hate speech, privacy violations and the like (Min, 2012). Therefore online intermediary liability has become very controversial in relation to copyright material due to unauthorized downloading of digital music, film and video since the beginning of the P2P revolution; and the arrival of "Web 2.0" interactive user generated or mediated content (UGC or UMC) sites such as eBay, YouTube, Facebook etc. The problem of the liability of Internet intermediaries for content authored by or activities carried out by third parties known at first as the issue of "ISP liability. Recently among the top most internet piracy battles The Pirate Bay (TPB), probably the largest and most famous BitTorrent piracy site on the Web. It offers millions of movies, music, software and TV shows that can be downloaded for free. The decision stopped people from accessing the site as a consequence of such a judgment. Then TPB wrapped up the code that runs its entire Web site, and offered it as a free downloadable file for anyone to copy and install their own servers. People started locating hundreds of new versions of the site, and the piracy continues unrelieved. Therefore, it is a challenge to deal with the problems generated in and by the digital environment by such acts by P2P site holders (Michael, 2009).

Peer- to- Peer Technology

Liability for copyright infringement committed online via P2P file sharing frequently occurs across different jurisdictions, creating private international law challenges (Strowel, 2009). The Napster, Gnutella, and Kazaa are superlative examples of P2P technology. P2P has gained tremendous public attention through Napster which is a system supporting music sharing on the Web. It is an emerging and interesting research technology with a promising product base. Intel P2P working group gave the definition of P2P as "The sharing of computer resources and services by direct exchange between systems". This thus gives P2P systems two main key characteristics:

- **Scalability:** There is no algorithmic, or technical limitation of the size of the system, e.g. the complexity of the system should be somewhat constant regardless of number of nodes in the system.
- **Reliability:** The malfunction on any given node will not affect the whole system (or maybe even any other nodes).

P2P networks can be roughly classified into two types:

1. **"Pure P2P Networks":** The Gnutella and Freenet are examples of a pure P2P network where all participating peers are equivalent, and each peer plays both the role of client and of server. The system does not rely on a central server to help control, coordinate, or manage the exchanges among the peers.
2. **"Hybrid P2P Networks":** In a hybrid P2P network, a central server exists to perform certain "administrative" functions to facilitate P2P services. For example, in Napster, a server helps peers to "search for particular files and initiate a direct transfer between the clients". Only a catalogue of available files is kept on the server, while the actual files are scattered across the peers on the network. Another example is BitTorrent (BT), where a central server called a tracker helps coordinate communication among BT peers in order to complete a download (Kan, 2001).

SECURITY THREAD AND P2P

Undoubtedly Napster's huge success planted the seed for today's P2P catastrophe and many programs like Morpheus, Kaaza, Grokster, Gnutella and FastTrack followed its lead after eliminating the root cause because of which Napster had to be shut down. A P2P network treats every user as a peer. In file sharing protocols such as BT, each peer contributes to service performance by uploading files to other peers while downloading. It provides a conduit for files stored in the user machine to be uploaded to other foreign peers. As P2P networks facilitate file transfer and sharing, malicious code can exploit this conduit to propagate to other peers. For example, a worm called VBS. Gnutella was detected in 2000 which propagated across the Gnutella file sharing network by making and sharing a copy of itself in the Gnutella program directory. On the other hand, When a file is downloaded using the P2P software, it is not possible to know who created the file or whether it is trustworthy.

In addition to the risks of viruses or malicious code attached with the file, the person downloading the file might also be exposed to criminal and/or civil litigation if any illegal content is downloaded to a company machine. In addition to general security risks, the use of P2P applications in a company network situation could generate an unnecessarily large amount of network traffic, monopolising network bandwidth that should be available for other business applications.

Research Methodology

This research is based on doctrinal method. The primary and secondary sources used for this research. Various national and international legislations and statutes have been considered as primary source. Secondary sources are Books, Articles, Journals, Periodicals, News papers of national and international agencies and World Wide Web. The main reason of using this type of method was to review available research on the ISPs' responsibilities in provision of security to their subscribers, and find out whether there are legal provisions for liabilities that are bindings on the ISPs to provide such service to their customers.

Internet Service Provider (ISPs)

Hathaway and Savage (2012) said in their report that "ISPs own and operate a critical infrastructure that facilitates the delivery of essential goods and services. Also when a new ISP connects to the Internet it implicitly agrees to certain terms concerning the transmission of packets, sharing of routing information, resolution of domain names, reporting on the status of the Internet, and handling emergencies. Therefore there should be an explicit duty to comply with technical aspects of Internet participation (Shaibu, 2013). In this aspect, there are 8 duties of ISPs:-

1. Duty to provide a reliable and accessible conduit for traffic and services.
2. Duty to provide authentic and authoritative routing information.
3. Duty to provide authentic and authoritative naming information.
4. Duty to report anonymized security incident statistics to the public.
5. Duty to educate customers about threats.
6. Duty to inform customers of apparent infections in their infrastructure.
7. Duty to warn other ISPs of imminent danger and help in emergencies.
8. Duty to avoid aiding and abetting criminal activity.

The first three duties contain the basic functions, the projected services that an ISP should undertake as part of their contribution in the worldwide internet. The next four duties generally come outside of a regulatory regime, yet in many ways fall within our unwritten expectations or ISPs' social responsibility to maintain the security and integrity of the Internet as a global platform for communication and commerce. These duties are echoed in a recent OECD communiqué entitled, "Principles for Internet Policy Making (OECD, 2011).

According to Jennie Ness, a Regional IP Attaché at U.S. Commercial Service reported that the Functions of ISPs include: 1. Transitory communications (serving as an information carrier): ISP acts as a mere data conduit, transmitting digital information from one point on a network to another at a user's request. 2. System caching: Retaining copies, for a limited time, of material that has been made available online by a person other than the ISP. Caching is technologically necessary to ensure Internet speed and efficiency, particularly in terms of providing rapid access to popular content without overloading servers. 3. Storage of information on systems or networks at direction of users (hosting): Allowing users to post materials and host website for users and 4. Information location tools (searching): ISP provides Internet search engines and Hyperlinks Internet directories.

Issues Relating to ISPs Liability

According to the Organization for Economic Cooperation and Development ("OECD"), Internet intermediaries can be classified into three categories:

- Internet service providers,
- Search engines,
- Participative networked platforms.

The issues i.e., what are the liabilities of intermediaries, to what extent they are liable and limitations and exemptions are major not just for the ISP community, but also for a wider continuum of Internet hosts, e.g., universities, traditional media organizations going 'digital' (e.g. the BBC, the Times), software providers such as Microsoft or Sun, libraries and archives, chat rooms and 'weblog' sites, individuals setting up personal Web 'home pages' and for the emerging social networking sites. Besides Confronted with the problem of liability, courts, in cases concerning Internet intermediaries, doctrinally moved away, as reflected in the Cubby, Inc. v. CompuServe, Inc. and Stratton Oakmont, Inc. v. Prodigy Services Co. cases. The court in Cubby ruled that Compuserve was a "distributor" and could not be held liable for defamatory material if it had no knowledge of the illegal contents uploaded by its users. However in Stratton, the intermediary was ruled as a "publisher" and thus was held liable, regardless of whether it had knowledge of the contents. Beyond Cubby and Stratton, which centered on defamatory smug, cases involving copyright infringements issues faced similar conflicts. On the other hand, Religious

Technology Center v. Netcom and Playboy Enterprises v. Frena are two examples of such cases. In Netcom, the court ruled that Netcom could not be held liable for infringing materials posted by its clients. However in Frena, George Frena, the operator of a subscription computer bulletin board service, was held liable for the infringing photos uploaded by subscribers. Undoubtedly there are slight variations in decided cases but the basic questions are the same: Should Internet intermediaries are held liable for unlawful contents that originate from third parties? If so, what kind of liability should be imposed? The conflicts between these cases have caused serious confusion about how to solve these problems. The below are given some issues related to intermediaries liabilities.

Limited Liability

The immunity of ISPs from content liability around the world is reflected under the laws such as the US copyright statute, DMCA and ECD based mainly at the time on three factors:

1.   Lack of effective legal or tangible control;
2.   The inequity of striking liability upon a mere intermediary ("shooting the messenger"), and;
3.   Consequences of public interest if unlimited liability was, nonetheless, imposed.

It is argued that ISPs cannot manually check the legality of all the material which passed through their server, without impossible amounts of delay and expense in case of factual impracticality and legal restraint. Also it may hurt the privacy and confidentiality of their loyal subscribers. They want to remain as carrier for the purposes akin to confidentiality, postal services, and customer services under the umbrella of no liability (Clark & Tsiaparas, 2002).

As the regulation of content on the internet is a litigious issue at present and no more so than when it involves issues of jurisdiction. In France v. Yahoo! Case, Nazi memorabilia was accessible to French citizens via web links of www.fr.yahoo. com. The French court thus ordered Yahoo! Inc to prevent such content from being available. The French court justified the imposition of French law in the Yahoo! Inc case because, in spite of the fact the site was based and hosted in the USA, the effects of the content were felt in France. This implies that content providers must consider the laws of all countries where content is accessible while posting content to sites. Further to determine whether Yahoo! Inc was capable of enforcing the injunction. The expert panel opined that Yahoo! Inc could prevent French-based web users from accessing the American on-line content to a possible degree. So Yahoo! Inc was ordered to take all measures possible to restrict access, which included blocking French users' access through filtering software. However the difficulty was identifying French users. The panel suggested some ways to accomplish this: - Approximately 70% of French internet users can be identified from their IP address. For the remainder of internet users whose IP address makes their location unclear, Yahoo! Inc could require the user to enter in their nationality. With the combination of an IP address and nationality disclosure it was estimated that mostly people could be possibly found, without placing any real imposition on Yahoo! Inc. Therefore even with the imposition of such processes, some French citizens would still be able to access the material in contravention of the French law.

CONFUSION BETWEEN MESSENGER AND CONTENT PROVIDER

It is always argued that ISPs are mere "passive messengers" and not content providers, and thus that it would be inequitable to hold them liable. In case of *Sony v Universal Studios* also known as the "Betamax case", where the Supreme Court of the United States was of the opinion that

If one provides means to accomplish an act of infringement is not sufficient to hold the person liable in the absence of any constructive knowledge of such infringement.

Besides above, every day plenty data flows comes though the servers; therefore, it is impossible to check that all the data that flows through it is not an infringement. Moreover, it is impossible to achieve 100% accuracy even post-screening.

Unwanted Economic Consequences

Finally the ISP industry argued that they could not endure the burden of full liability for content authored by others. Since the promotion of e-commerce and the information society depended on a reliable and expanding Internet infrastructure, an immunity regime was in the public interest. Without it, the ISP industry might be rendered uneconomic. In Europe this count was even sturdier as the US online industry already had a start, but unlimited liability on EC online intermediaries would encourage them to migrate to more sympathetic jurisdiction. By the year 2000, finally a rough compromise had emerged in both Europe and the United States among the various stakeholders. ISPs should in principle be guaranteed freedom from liability for content authored by third parties, so long as they were prepared to cooperate when asked to remove or block access to identified illegal or infringing content. Such an immunity or "safe harbor," was implemented in Europe in the ECD, and in the

United States, in the 1998 DMCA (as respects copyright infringing material only). These regimes were to prove of critical importance in allowing the growth of the innovation, e-commerce and fledgling user generated content (UGC) industries.

Global Regimes of "Safe Harbors" or ISP / Intermediary Immunities

The legal frameworks for Internet intermediaries are dealing either with the liability of intermediaries across all types of content, such as the OECD, or regulation which lays down rules for special domains (copyright, protection of children, personal data, counterfeiting, domain names, online gambling, etc). Examples of the latter include the US Internet gambling law, the UK Defamation Act 1996, S 1, the US DMCA and the French 'Code monétaire et financier' for online fraud with a payment card.

Related Laws

EC E-Commerce Directive 2002, Arts 12-15; covers all types of civil or criminal liability except gambling and (oddly) privacy/DP; "horizontal" provision; almost total immunity for acting as mere conduit, for caching; controversy around the hosting provisions (Art 14).

Article 2 of the e-Commerce Directive, borrowing the definition contained in Article 1(2) of Directive 98/34/EC as amended by Directive 98/48/EC, considers a service provider as any natural or legal person delivering 'any service normally provided for remuneration, at a distance, by electronic means and at the individual request of a recipient of services' and a recipient of services as 'any natural or legal person who, for professional ends or otherwise, uses an information society service, in particular for the purposes of seeking information or making it accessible'.

Further for the purposes of analyzing the liability of ISPs for user-generated content, the activity to be taken into account consists in hosting. The definition provided for by Article 14 of the e-Commerce Directive comprises an information society service 'that consists of the storage of information provided by a recipient of the service'. In that situation, the Directive exempts the ISPs from liability regarding the content generated by users under two conditions: (a) the provider has no actual knowledge of the illegal information or (b) it acts expeditiously to remove or to disable access to the information after obtaining such knowledge.

According to recital 42 of the e-Commerce Directive, exemptions from liability cover only cases where the activity of the ISP 'is of a mere technical, automatic and passive nature, which implies that the information society service provider has neither knowledge nor control over the information which is transmitted or stored.'

The ECJ has interpreted these provisions in the case Google v Louis Vuitton, a preliminary reference raised from the French *Cour de Cassation*. The ECJ characterized the role of the host provider as follow:

It comes from recital 42 in the preamble to Directive 2000/31 that the exemptions from liability established in that directive cover only cases in which the activity of the information society service provider is 'of a mere technical, automatic and passive nature', which implies that that service provider 'has neither knowledge nor control over the information which is transmitted or stored.

In 2011, the ECJ adopted a similar position in the Scarlet v Sabam case, concerning an injunction to an ISP (Scarlet), to prevent its users from sending or receiving protected content. According to the judges, 'Directives 2000/31, 2001/29, 2004/48, 95/46 and 2002/58, read together and construed in the light of the requirements stemming from the protection of the applicable fundamental rights, must be interpreted as precluding an injunction made against an ISP which requires it to install the contested filtering system.'

In USA, the Communications Decency Act (CDA) and the Digital Millennium Copyright Act (DMCA), enacted in 1996 and 1998 respectively, followed by the E.U.'s E-Commerce Directive (ECD), setup a legal framework that provided extensive freedom or "safe harbor" to Internet intermediaries from illegal third-party content. The approach of USA poles apart from that of the EU, which 'expressly chose not to focus exclusively on copyright, but rather to tackle the issue of ISP liability in a so-called horizontal manner that is, drafting the safe harbours to cover intermediaries' liability for any kind of illegal content provided by their users, whether it constituted copyright infringement, trademark infringement, defamation, unfair competition, hate speech or any other type of illicit material.

U.S. Safe Harbor Provisions

The provision for safe Harbors is Section 512 of the U.S. copyright legislation that limits ISPs' copyright liability in certain circumstances for four activities:

1. Transitory digital network communications
2. Temporary caching (section 512(b))
3. Hosting of an end-user's material on a network or ISP's system (section 512(c))
4. Provision of information location tools, such as hyperlinks (section 512(d)).

To comply with the safe harbors as per section 512 is not mandatory. An ISP that does not come within the safe harbors is not automatically liable for copyright infringement. Instead, infringement must be proven on general principles (section 512(n)). Limited Immunity of ISP that comes within the safe harbor provisions obtains immunity from monetary penalties from copyright holders and very limited forms of injunctive relief for secondary copyright infringement. Since the DMCA was enacted in 1998, no ISP that has qualified for the safe harbors has been subject to monetary damages or injunction. ISPs must adopt and reasonably implement a policy that provides for termination, in appropriate circumstances, of repeat infringers (section 512(i)). In addition thereto, the third and fourth safe harbors also require ISPs to remove or block access to material residing on their system upon receipt of an appropriate "takedown" notice from a rights holder or an authorized agent of a rights holder.

In 2016, The American Vimeo case, also broadens the exemption for internet service providers (ISPs) in cases of copyright infringement by platform users. In this case, there was a collective claim by several right holders of musical recordings. According to these right holders, musical recordings had been used without permission in a total of 199 videos, all of which were posted by users of the platform. According to the federal judge, a federal safe harbor law, the Digital Millennium Copyright Act, did not create liability for video-sharing websites as long as they remove the infringing material once they receive notice of it.

But these regimes are in crisis. Right holders seem to be in a constant tug of war with ISPs. The approach of USA is to solve the problem by encouraging right holders to make use of the notice-and-take-down system, practically blocking the way to effectively challenge intermediaries in court. The EU legislation however seems to be in the opposite direction. Based on the Google France case, the ECJ does not seem to find liability for ISPs problematic per se. Moreover, if the Proposal for a Directive is adopted in its current wording, service providers will have a larger responsibility in battling copyright infringement. Where the United States seems to find for the ISPs, the European Union places emphasis on protection of the right holders (Leon, 2016).

A recent Fourth Circuit decision in BMG Rights Mgmt LLC v. Cox Communications Inc. 2018, affirmed summary judgment that an internet service provider, an ISP, was not entitled to claim Digital Millenium Copyright Act (DMCA) immunity from copyright infringement for third-party postings through its service, opening up the company to massive copyright liability. The *Cox* decision teaches several important lessons to companies who wish to use the DMCA to avoid copyright liability.

- Create a policy that has a realistic protocol to weed out infringers. Cox's 13-strikes-and-you're-out policy seemed designed more to avoid actually removing any subscribers than weeding out copyright infringers.

- Take real steps to implement the policy. Nothing is worse than adopting a policy on (digital) paper and then not following through – that is a sure sign to a court that the policy is likely a sham.
- Don't ignore whole classes of takedown notices. Cox did this because BMG used an outside vendor to send takedown notices that included settlement demands. While such demands seem abusive and Cox understandably wanted to avoid burdening its customers with these kinds of letters, its solution of simply ignoring them was a major factor in losing its immunity.
- The repeat infringer policy cannot be limited to persons determined to be infringing by a court. The Fourth Circuit expressly rejected that construction of the DMCA advanced by Cox.

PART II

The Case Study of Pirate Bay

The Pirate Bay (TPB) was one of the world's most trendy pirated music and content sites, offering free access to millions of copyrighted songs and thousands of copyrighted Hollywood movies. It claimed that it is the world's largest BitTorrent tracker. In June 2013, TPB reported that it had over six million registered users. It

Figure 1.

is in the top 500 Web sites in the world in terms of global traffic, with about 20% of the visitors coming from the United States.

The history of the Pirate Bay (TPB) as a company started in the 2003 and is connected with the Swedish anti-copyright organization Piratebyrån. In 2004 TPB separated its services from the anti-copyright organization and in 2005 the company started to administer the world wide accessible website. This means the website was rewritten into other languages, the computing power was increased, trackers functions were improved and the website changed its commercial site into more advertising-friendly environment. In order to run operations of TPB, a new company was set up called Random Media. The p2p technology was widely used over the Internet network. The same was applied in connection with the application of distribution of data, where sharing data might be legally purchased or not copyright protected, or on the other hand acquired from pirated copies and shared illegally. The conclusion concerning the source of digital data is often difficult to determine in the cyber space and this is the strategy where TPB was built on (Sara, 2011).

As demonstrated above it was self-proclaimed largest BitTorrent tracker in the world. Thus it could be reduced to a logical conclusion that the nature of BitTorrent protocol allowed users to download any content at extremely high speeds and that resulted in the technology's widespead public use for piracy. But such an open contravention of international copyright law did not go unnoticed for long. On May 31, 2006, the Swedish police arrived at The Pirate Bay office with a search warrant and confiscated enough servers to appear to mark the demise of the site, but the crafty effervescent pirates were back online in just three days which further adapted about the fact of the menace created by them. But this was not the end of the legal battle against The Pirate Bay. On January 31, 2008, Swedish Prosecutors filed charges of copyright infringement against the website's captains namely Fredrik Neij, Gottfrid Svartholm Warg, Peter Sunde and Carl Lundstrom. The defendants, three of which were administrators or otherwise closely linked to the website and one of which was alleged to be the financier of the service, were prosecuted under the Swedish Penal Code and Copyright Act.

TPB Focused on 3 Major Areas of Issues

- The legality of running a torrent tracker search engine which contains torrents that point to unlicensed copyright protected material,
- The scope of the safe harbor for service providers created by the e-Commerce Directive and its Swedish implementation, and
- The applicable damages calculation mechanisms and principles.

According to the original description of the alleged offence presented as part of the charges, Pirate Bay consisted of three components; an index portal, a database and a tracker function. The tracker feature creates a 'peer-to-peer' network of users who want to share the same file. All components were necessary for the users of the service to share files between them. Besides the technology used in The Pirate Bay was BitTorrent protocol, created by Bram Cohen and commercialised by BitTorrent Inc, allowed users to easily download large files, such as movies, over the internet by breaking up the files into many pieces. The key underlying technological idea was that the availability of pieces from numerous sources speeds up transfer as compared to retrieving the file from a single source. Information on these pieces was provided by small so-called torrent files which are indexed, tracked and to some extent also stored on the Pirate Bay website. In addition to ''regular'' BitTorrent downloading through trackers, the BitTorrent protocol also supported so-called DHT (Distributed Hash Table) downloading in which the users' BitTorrent clients were in direct communication with each other, thus eliminating the need for a centralized tracker (Mikko, 2009).

Investigation in TPB Case

The prosecutor claimed that the defendants had contributed to copyright infringement on the basis of 3 grounds:-

- A complete database was offered that was linked to a catalogue of torrent files pointing to infringing content.
- Options were offered for search and download of the torrent files, and
- A tracker functionality feature through which the file-sharing users could contact each other.

The charges also stated that the majority of the files found via Pirate Bay contain unlicensed copyrighted works and that the service is financed by advertisements, thus fulfilling the precondition for commercial exploitation of copyrighted works. However, the court found that the witness' statements and parts of the defendants' e-mail correspondence showed that the most popular torrent files pointed almost exclusively to infringing materials. Also, all 33 works that were at issue and the fact that they had been downloaded numerous times indicated that infringing material was very popular and generated a lot of traffic on the Pirate Bay website. Besides the results of the studies were startling—70 to 80 per cent of all torrent files on Pirate Bay pointed to material that was legally shared online (Mikko, 2009).

Subjective Knowledge and TPB

The most important legal question in this case was whether someone can be found guilty of contribution to an offence that he/she is unaware of?

According to the prosecution, the defendants assisted in offering (infringing) copyright protected works to the public. However, the defendants claimed that they were totally unaware that any of the 33 works at issue were illegally distributed via Pirate Bay between July 2005 and May 2006 and no contribution could, thus, have taken place. Then the prosecutor showed E-mail correspondence that provided some evidence that the defendants knew that TPB assisted copyright infringement. The court found that the defendants 'had the intent to bring about the existence of copyright-protected material on the website. On the other hand, the contributory liability arises when a person either physically or mentally has had an influence on the coming into being or the committing of a crime. Contributory liability does, thus, not require that the contribution is such that the criminal act would not have been undertaken without it. Liability for contribution can therefore arise even for persons who have only marginally contributed to the crime being committed. Consequently, in order for a person to be liable for contribution, a main offence must exist (Micheal, 2009).

Safe Harbor Provisions and TPB

The question whether the Swedish Act on Electronic Commerce and other Information Society Services and the EC's e-Commerce Directive ''safe harbors'' were applicable to Pirate Bay, as the defendants claimed that the service was just an intermediary. To discuss the above, it's important to focus on the chief questions given below:

- Whether Pirate Bay is a service provider as described in the Act on Electronic Commerce and the e-Commerce Directive.
- Whether the services it provided could be deemed to fall within the scope of the Act and the Directive.

According to the services provided by Pirate Bay clearly fulfilled the criteria for information society services set forth in the Directive. The non-liability provisions which are found in sections 16 to 19 of the Act on Electronic Commerce and correspond to Arts 12 to 14 of the e-Commerce Directive. On the basis of the same, it was found that the services provided by Pirate Bay did not fall within the scope of ss. 16 or 17 of the Act. Instead, it was found that Pirate Bay provided a service where a user could upload and store torrent files on the website, and the service was, consequently, deemed to be a ''hosting'' service in accordance with section.18 of the Act and article 14 of the Directive. According to the provision, a service provider shall not be liable for the information stored at the request of a user, under the condition that the provider does not have actual knowledge of the illegal or infringing activity and, as regards damage claims, is not aware of facts or circumstances from which the activity is apparent. Further, in order to fulfill the prerequisites set out in the provision, the provider must, upon obtaining knowledge of such activity, act expeditiously to remove or disable access to the illegal or infringing material. The defendants in this case uploaded torrent files on the website that directed users to copyright-protected works made available without the owners' authorization. Also the defendants had neither put any heed to request made by complainants nor took any actions to remove infringing content. Thus they are not afforded the protection of the non-liability provisions. Also the defendants had knowingly ignored the copyrighted material was made available through the website and found that their act was intentional. The fact that the defendants were unaware of the infringing nature of the specific works that were at issue was deemed irrelevant, as the defendants had shown total indifference to the fact that copyright infringing material was shared via Pirate Bay.

Relief

The plaintiffs were divided into three groups in claiming damages: the Swedish music industry, the Nordic film industry and the international film industry. The court found guilty to all four accused Peter Sunde, Fredrik Neij, Gottfrid Svartholm and Carl Lundström and sentenced to serve one year in prison "assisting in making copyright content available." All the defendants appealed the verdict, and in November 2010 the appellate court reduced the prison sentences, but increased damages. The total damages claim was 101.9 million Swedish kronor ($13.0 million, 9.7 million) with interest, of which the international film industry's claim was some 93 million kronor.

CONCLUSION

Until the Geneva Treaties provided the communication to the public right copyright law struggled to provide a coherent response to file sharing of music and films. Liability for uploaders was established but in practical terms this was not effective. Visiting liability on telecommunications networks and ISP's was not possible in the light of the international consensus that such entities should enjoy a measure of immunity (Clark, 2007). The liability of intermediaries has been widely discussed in other cases also i.e., Viacom, Inc v Youtube, Inc in the United States and between eBay and LVMH. In eBay case, the online auction website was found liable for offering a sales platform for counterfeit goods and ordered to pay damages to LVMH. Besides above, the Tribunal de Commerce in Paris agreed that web hosts should have immunity on basis of the e-Commerce Directive, but did not find eBay's activities to fall within that category. However, an even more recent French court decision in L'Or´eal v eBay seems to rebut this line of reasoning, as eBay was found to fulfill the prerequisites set out for safe harbors in the e-Commerce Directive. In the UK proceedings between eBay and L'Or´eal the question of safe harbor provision was forwarded to the European Court of Justice, whose preliminary ruling cleared the legal situation to some extent. Despite the controversy on the definition of an internet intermediary, it is clear these high-profile cases all involve a service provider, which, at least seemingly, tried to respond to takedown requests and did not openly insult the copyright holders, as was the case with Pirate Bay. Thus it is suggested that more and more research and policy work should be conducted to scrutinize how ISPs could be called to the chain of security responsibilities of the internet. For example, if ISPs could provide adequate security for their networks, this can reduce the cyber attacks. Furthermore, ISPs are technically capable and more knowledgeable to provide internet security, as such making them responsible for the Internet security could be of benefit since they control the gateway.

Suggestion

Some measures and precautions required to be taken by the concerned ones specially the ISPs, Internet users etc are suggested below:

- The ISPs must ensure that the information transacted by the subscribers is secure and protected.
- The ISPs should not be judged from the physical world legal liability requirements.
- There is a need to harmonize the different cyber security laws prevailing in different countries and to bring absolute uniformity in them so as to easily trace and stop the bad material flowing through them.
- The complete and updated list of the ISP's subscribers must be available in a password protected portion of the ISP's website. This is for the use of authorized Intelligence Agencies.
- The provision should be made where government can take over the service, equipment and networks of ISPs in case of emergency, war etc.
- ISPs must ensure privacy of communication on their networks.
- ISPs must maintain a log of all users connected and the service they are using (mail, telnet, http etc.). ISPs can definitely bar undesirable information, if it desires.

- Indirect liability, imposed upon ISP, is desirable to a certain extent since it discourages them from handling material which is incriminating in nature.
- The police officers, investigating officers, prosecuting officers and the judicial officers need to be trained more vigorously and made well equipped to handle the situation in a more efficient manner so that the evidence relating to the cyber crimes is not destroyed and the offenders are traced, prosecuted and convicted effectively.

REFERENCES

BMG Rights Mgmt LLC v. Cox Communications Inc. (4th Cir. 2018)

Capitol Records, LLC, et al. v. Vimeo, LLC (2d Cir. June 16, 2016)

Clark. (2007). Illegal downloads: sharing out online liability: sharing files, sharing risks. *Journal of Intellectual Property Law & Practice, 2*, 402-409.

Clark, J. A., & Tsiaparas, A. (2002). Bandwidth-On-Demand Networks - A Solution to Peer-To-Peer File Sharing. *BT Technology Journal, 20*(1), 53–55. doi:10.1023/A:1014518008964

Cubby Inc. v. CompuServe Inc., 776 F. Supp. 135 (S.D.N.Y. 1991).

Google v. Louis Vuitton OJ C134, 22.5.2010.

Hasina. (2009). Decentralised P2P technology: Can the unruly be ruled? *International Review of Law, Computers & Technology, 23*, 123-124.

Hathawat & Sawage. (2012, March). *Duties of ISPs, Cyber Dialogue.* Available on https://www.belfercenter.org/sites/default/files/legacy/files/cyberdialogue2012_hathaway-savage.pdf

Jennifer, N. (2007, July). *Internet Service Provider Liability.* Paper presented at ASEAN- USPTO Workshop on Digital Copyright and Copyright Collective Management, Bangkok. Retrieved from http://asean.org/wp content/uploads/images/2012/Economic/sectoral_aem/service/agreement/ASEAN-USPTO%20Workshop%20on%20Digital%20Copyright%20and%20Copyright.pdf

L'Oreal v. eBay [2009] EWHC 1094 (Ch).

LICRA et UEJF v. Yahoo! Inc and Yahoo France, 20 November 2000, Tribunal de Grande Instance de Paris, Superior Court of Paris) p14.

LVMH v. eBay TC Paris, 1ere Ch B, June 30, 2008.

Manner, Siniketo, & Polland. (2009). *The Pirate Bay Ruling—When The Fun and Games End.* Retrieved from file:///C:/Users/DLL/Desktop/the-pirate-bay-ruling.pdf

Marshman, S. D. (2011). Giving a country of Pirates a chance: Using the three step test to accommodate the shifting of national attitudes on Copyright Protection. *The George Washington International Law Review, 43*(4), 707.

OECD. (2011). *Communiqué on Principles for Internet Policy Making.* Delivered at an OECD High-Level Meeting, The Internet Economy: Generating Innovation and Growth, Paris, France.

Playboy Enterprises v. Frena 839 F. Supp. 1552 (M.D. Fla. 1993)

Religious Technology Center v. Netcom Online Communication Services, Inc., 907 F.Supp. 1361 (N.D. Cal. 1995).

Scarlet v. Sabam (2011) C-70/10 para. 54.

Sony v. Universal Studios; 464 U.S. 417 (1984)

Stratton Oakmont Inc. v. Prodigy Services Co., 1995 WL 323710 (N.Y. Sup. Ct. 1995).

Strowel, A. (2009). *Peer-to-peer File Sharing and Secondary Liability in Copyright Law.* Cheltenham, UK: Edward Elgar Publishing. doi:10.4337/9781848449442

Usman, S. H. (2013). A Review of Responsibilities of Internet Service Providers Toward Their Customers' Network Security. *Journal of Theoretical and Applied Information Technolog, 49*(1), 70–78.

Viacom Inc v. YouTube Inc No.1:07-cv-02103 (S.D.N. *Y.*), (2008)

Yan, M. (2012). The law surrounding the facilitation of online copyright infringement. *European Intellectual Property Review, 34*(2), 122–126.

Chapter 9
Trust and Reputation in Digital Environments:
A Judicial Inkling on E-Governance and M-Governance

Opeyemi Idowu Aluko
University of Ilorin, Nigeria

ABSTRACT

The trend of e-governance and m-governance in governance is increasing rapidly and the instrument of governance is getting closer to the citizens. This chapter considers the trust and reputation of the digital environment of e-governance and m-governance in the world from the existing legal and judicial inkling. How sufficient are the international policies and benchmarks on the use of information communication technology (ICT) for e-governance and m-governance within and among nations to be trusted and judged to be of good repute among the users and has it been able to promote the use of e-governance and m-governance among the nations of the world? The theoretical framework that this chapter hinges on is the actor network theory (ANT). It emerged from a line of research broadly referred to as the social shaping of technology. The methodology adopted focuses on the United Nation survey data on e-governance from 2005-2016. The data collected is analyzed based on regional and economic groupings for e-government development index (EGDI) of Africa, Americas, Asia, Europe, and Oceania.

DOI: 10.4018/978-1-5225-5984-9.ch009

INTRODUCTION

The developments in the Information and Communications Technology (ICT) world have made it possible for citizens to interact with the government remotely in a convenient manner without physically visiting any government office. In the context and perspective of Electronic Service Delivery (2011), e-Governance is about the making use of ICT in systems of governance for a wide range participation and an intense involvement of citizens, institutions, civil society groups and the private sector in the decision making process of governance. Therefore the need for government process to re-engineer governance using Information Technology to simplify and make the governance processes more efficient which is critical for transformation to take place by making the delivery of government services more effective across various government domains.

The United Nations defines e-Government as the use of ICT and its application by the government for the provision of information and public services to the people. There is no doubt about the multitude of definition and at the same time no fixed definition of e-Governance. Several different agencies have tried to define this term according to their own objectives and requirements. The term 'e-Government' is also used in place of 'e-Governance'. The Organization for Economic Co-Operation and Development (OECD 2005) and Kyem (2016) perceived e-Government to be the use of information and communication technologies, and particularly the internet, as a tool to achieve better government.

The World Bank (2015); Banerjee, Duflo, Imbert, Mathew and Pande (2016) also opined that e-Government refers to the use by government agencies of information technologies gadgets and utilities (such as Wide Area Networks, the Internet, and mobile computing) that have the ability to transform relations with citizens, businesses, and other arms of government. E-Government aims to make the interaction between government and citizens (G2C), government and business enterprises (G2B), and inter-agency relationships within the government sector (G2G) more friendly, convenient, transparent, and inexpensive.

E-Governance and m-Governance is also described by Agrawal, Sethi and Mittal (2015) and Meijer (2015) as a process of reform in the way government works, shares information, engages citizens and delivers services to external and internal clients for the benefit of both government and the clients that they serve. Specifically, E-Government sectors harnesses information technologies such as Wide Area Network (WAN), Internet, World Wide Web (www) and mobile computing to reach out to citizens, businesses and other arms of the government. E-Governance has vast objectives but potent among them include to make government administration more transparent, speedy and accountable, in order to addressing the society's needs and expectations through efficient public services and effective interaction between the people, business groups, sub nationalities and the entire government structure.

It is important to note that United Nations e-Governance survey (2016) revealed that E-government has grown rapidly over the past 15 years, since the first attempt of the United Nations to benchmark e-government in 2001. In the 2016 Survey, 29 countries score "very-high", with e-government development index (EGDI) values in the range of 0.75 to 1.00, as compared to only 10 countries in 2003. Since 2014, all 193 Member States of the UN have delivered some form of online presence. E-government is now ubiquitous in many more countries, a stark contrast in comparison to 2003 – when 18 countries or about ten percent (10%) of countries globally were without any online presence. Fifty one percent (51%) of countries had "low-EGDI" or "medium EGDI" values in 2016, as compared to over seventy three percent (73%) of countries in 2003 (United Nations Survey 2016a; 2016b).

The issue of trust in the transmission of data, information and classified materials through the electronic means is a major concern in the twenty first century. Top government secrets are in great jeopardy of being tracked and attacked by online hackers, spies of both state and personal categories and secret informants of anti state machineries. Classified information of important personalities are also under threat of been leaked through the mobile internet usage, accessibilities and electronic governance structures (Dash, Sethi, and Gupta 2016). These critical issues have created suspicion in the reputation, reliability and security of life and personal effects information of both the government and individuals. There is therefore the need to secure the digital environments. The digital environments include the e-Governance and m-Governance gadgets and technologies. The judicial and legal inclination at the global level usually at the United Nations level is a major determinant to the general trust by member states in the use of the e-governance technology. The judicial or legal backings to it uses should be a top down strategy. The top side is the United Nations judicial regulation which will trickle down to all member states. The United Nations agency should have a judicial regulation which will be implemented by all member states.

This chapter considers the trust and reputation of the digital environment of e-governance and m-governance in the world from the existing legal and judicial inkling. How sufficient is the international policies and judicial benchmarks on the use of ICT for e-Governance and m-Governance within and among nations to be trusted and judged to be of good repute among the users. Has the existing the international policies and judicial benchmarks on the use of ICT for e-Governance and m-Governance been able to promote the use of e-Governance and m-Governance among the nations of the world? The theoretical framework that this chapter hinge on is the Actor Network theory (ANT). It emerged from a line of research broadly referred to as the Social Shaping of Technology. This theory is used to explain how important electronic networking in governance is to the growth, good governance and sustainable development of a nation.

The chapter uses the United Nation survey data on e-Governance from 2005-2016. The data collected is analysed based on Regional and Economic Groupings for E-Government Development Index (EGDI) of Africa, Americas, Asia, Europe and Oceania. The descriptive statistics and graphical analysis of the findings depicts the prospect of the e-governance and m-governance in the light of the prevailing judicial and legal inklings in the global spectrum. This leads to the prospect that if the judicial inklings of countries on e-governance are more entrenched, the EGDI will be higher and development will be faster in such countries.

PROSPECTS OF E-GOVERNANCE AND M-GOVERNANCE IN GLOBAL GOVERNANCE

Government policies cannot be successful without the right and adequate judicial backings. This is because the level of its implementation will be low and the empowerment of the personnel to perform a duty will not be legally supported. Therefore, e-governance prospects can be strengthened by a judicial process to be enacted by each state. This should be backed up by the United Nations resolution to support the use of e-governance and m-governance for effective public service delivery.

E-Governance offers many benefits and advantages for the government, corporate sector and the society at large. These include reduced cost in terms of travelling, reduction in administrative cost of operation in terms of printing documents, control measures, resources (re)distribution, and centralized data centres. It also enhances transparency, anti-corruption and accountability in governance. This is as the direct result of less human interactions, less fraud, and ease of tracking public procurement contracts. The citizens get empowered through access to information by sharing of knowledge on specific field of operation and policy making networking. Integrated E-Government portal improves customer satisfaction whereby through a single point all or most government services are assessed by all citizens without discrimination. On the large scale more efficiency is promoted in governance processes and government management.

The challenges of e-Governance are also numerous. These include undefined rules and procedures with legal implications on the use of e-data and transmission from one person to the other and inadequate e-laws. The infrastructure (telecommunication and power) availability in most developing regions of the world is another limitation to e-governance. Another challenge is the access to right information and the interdepartmental collaboration networking which may be poor or not existing in many governmental agencies coupled with inadequacy of trained human resources, weak ICT penetration in remote areas and standardization and inter-operability problems.

There are a lot of expectations which government, other service providers and the service consumers are inclined to derive from the digital environments of e-governance and m-governance provided the trust and reputation of the digital transmission of information and data are guaranteed and secured from externalities (United Nations 2001; 2012; 2014; 2016a). A few of the expectations include; better customer services, empowerment through access to information and convenience, ease access to government services and an increased ICT literacy of both the government agencies and the general public. Other utility benefits include; an enhanced internet usage, cheaper internet rates, improved transparency and accountability and better collaboration among all stakeholders.

PROSPECT OF E-GOVERNANCE AND M-GOVERNANCE IN THE PREVAILING JUDICIAL AND LEGAL INKLINGS IN THE GLOBAL SPECTRUM

How sufficient is e-governance and m-governance to be trusted and judged to be of good repute among the users and has the prospects of e-Governance and m-Governance attracts and promotes the patronage among the nations of the world? E-Governance and M-Governance has a great deal of prospect among the various regions of the world. This e-governance prospect is determined by the availability of judicial backup to support the use. Also the level of the implementation and entrenchment of such enabling judicial support in each country determines the level of e-governance popularity and usability among the citizenry.

E-government can consistently improve the quality of life of the citizens and can create a sharp reduction of costs and enhance timeliness if there is an enabling judicial support for its utilization. E-government will eventually transform the processes and structures of government to create a public administration devoid of rigid hierarchical rigmarole, empowering civil servants to serve citizens better and to be more responsive to their needs. E-government must be given serious consideration also in the developing countries not only for its potential for stronger institutional capacity building, but also for better service delivery to citizens and business. This has the potential of increasing local social and economic development. It also reduces corruption by increasing transparency and social control (United Nations 2008; 2010).

Wide-ranging e-government development index remain at, or near the top of most countries policy agendas especially in developed countries. For many nations in Africa, America, Asia, Europe and Oceania regions of the world, digitizing service deliveries like filing personal income taxes online or paying value added taxes (VATs) electronically represents a marked departure from the traditional paper-based way of doing business. For some countries, such departures have culminated in success (United Nations 2004; 2005). For others, the challenge is formidable, but not yet insurmountable. E-government potentially empowers individual citizens by providing them with an alternative channel for accessing information and services and having a direct interaction with the government. It also gives the individual citizen another opportunity of becoming an active participant in the governing process.

It provides the citizens with new choices and goal that resonates throughout many of the national e-government strategic plans. When there is an enabling judicial environment, the overall expected outcomes of e-governance and m-government include the following; open communication, enhanced transparency, increased social inclusion and citizen participation, democratic enrichment and superior governance. These outcomes are more than a mere potential but an extant.

The Principles of E-Government includes building services around citizens, choices to make government and its services more accessible. It facilitate social inclusion by providing information responsibly and uses government resources effectively and efficiently. Over the years 2001 till 2016, the global E-government leaders in the world include; USA 3.11, Australia 2.60, New Zealand 2.59, Singapore 2.58, Norway 2.55, Canada 2.52, UK 2.52, Netherlands 2.51, Denmark 2.47 and Germany 2.46. The results of the E-government Index tend to reflect the level of judicial enablement given to it and a country's economic, social and democratic level of development. Industrialized nations, whose citizens enjoy the benefits of abundant resources, superior access to information and a more participatory relationship with their governments, rank higher in the E-governance Development Index (EGDI) (United Nations 2014; 2016a).

There are yet barriers to e-government effectiveness and efficiency across the regions of the world. The most intriguing problems, however, are always the ones created from the politics of organizational change and poor judicial reinforcement of the e-governance policies. If change-related issues get the kind of consideration they warrant, then implementing e-government programs will be a much less complicated exercise. Doubtful decision-makers and reluctant public sector managers need to understand and appreciate the value that can be created when technology is used to redesign workflow from an enterprise perspective.

Barriers to E-Government

See Table 1.

Table 1. Barriers to e-government

INSTITUTIONAL / OPERATIONAL	MANAGERIAL	POLICY / PLANNING
Technology and infrastructure costs / factors	Lack of capacity to manage large scale IT projects	Lack of Coordination and or Strategic Planning such as judicial enablement
Lack of resources to support 24 / 7 operations	Lack of conviction of top or middle mangers	Lack of comprehensiveness and continuity of policies / Programmes
Lack of innovative incentives in the public sector. Particularly regarding IT	Management Expectations vs. Management Realities	Absence of Policy guidelines
Organizational / cultural Dichotomies	Doubts and resistance by Leadership	Organizational / cultural dichotomies
Lack of institutional support	Opposition by professional or union interests	Local governments and municipalities if left far behind become bottlenecks
Information mismanagement Reluctance to share among depts. Misuse of sensitive data	Obsolete legal frameworks to innovate and incorporate private sector	Lack of comprehensiveness and continuity of policies and programmes
Absence of Policy guidelines	Information mismanagement Reluctance to share among depts. Misuse of sensitive data	Opposition by professional or union interests

Source: European Union the Use of Information and Communication Technology in the Public Administration of the EU Member States 35th Conference of the Directors-General of the Public Service of the Member States of the European Union Strasbourg, November 2001

THEORETICAL FRAMEWORK

Actor Network Theory (ANT)

Actors are legal rational being who are backed up with some levels of judicial enablements to interact between the people and the government using the e-governance interface. Actor-Network theory (ANT) emerged from a line of research broadly referred to as the Social Shaping of Technology designed by R. Williams and D. Edge (1996). This theory is based on actors or reactant that form networking bond with each other. Actors may be human or non human and constitute the interests and ability to maintain networks of allied interests, their ability to convince others to join their network, and to embody any emerging technology with their interests and priorities. Technology in ANT is a network that includes within it components structures like hardware and software, the people who designed these artefacts, the people who have built and assembled them and the large groups, organisations, and bodies that maintain these networks.

ANT, therefore, is a theory of the social, or what constitutes the social cross networks. It is a theory that strives majorly in an environment with adequate judicial enablement that has provides the elements that are used to understand and reconstitute social space. It is not a presupposed existing sociology that can be used to explain and understand the workings of technology and people. For example, the issue of power in ANT can be understood as the influence of a collective on the actions of some (Stanforth 2006).

ANT has the following concepts; Actor: An actor or reactant is a human or a component or part of a technology. Actor-network: This is a network, or a linking of people, technology components, organisations, technology bodies who have related interests bonded by adequate judicial interregnum. Enrolment and translation: these are the processes of creating a network of actors that have related interests; this enrolment may happen by the use of persuasion or translating interests. This environment includes majorly the judicial, economic and the political environments. Delegates: These are actors who represent, or speak for a particular interest. These actors may be components such as software or embedded hardware that has certain priorities and processing logic built into. Irreversibility: This is the idea that certain interests that have been embodied in the actors. (Delegates) may be permanent (or permanent to a degree) and cannot be reversed.

ANT analysis proceeds by understanding the actors in a particular setting, say the design and evolution of a particular technology. The analysis examines the networks that the actors form and reform, attempting to enrol others to their own networks and hence aligning them with their own interests. In relations to e-governance and m-governance the interconnections between actors, networking components such as software and embedded hardware with their processing logics makes communication to be faster, safer and economical within public establishments.

The government as an actor needs to have a judicial backup so as to reinforce its operational strength and ensures maximum compliance and multi network their clients for effective service delivery to the public. The government needs to make such services much more easily accessible, with little risks and much efficiency and effectiveness. The ANT requires necessary domestication through judicial laws and regulations from the United Nation so as to ensure that the government as the principal service deliverer is visible and solvent to the general public. Whenever there is a right and adequate judicial inclination in the government service delivery and networking, this will prevent the breakdown of administration due to poor visibility of government activities, inadequate accessibility of such services delivered and misleading propaganda. The problems of multiple taxations on service rendered or services not rendered are also reduced to the minimum whenever action networking is applied in e-governance and m-governance.

METHODOLOGY, DATA PRESENTATIONS AND DISCUSSION OF FINDINGS

This study uses the data from the United Nation survey database on e-Governance from 2005-2016. The data collected is analysed based on Regional and Economic Groupings for E-Government Development Index (EGDI) of Africa, Americas, Asia, Europe and Oceania. Descriptive statistics and graphical analysis is used to present and discourse the data. The finding shows that countries with more entrenched judicial inklings on e-governance have higher EGDI and development are faster in such countries.

E-Government Development Index (EGDI)

Table 1 and Figure 1 show the various regions of the world and their corresponding E-governance and development index from 2005 to 2010 (2005,2008 and 2010 respectively). This indicates the extent of E-governance compliance and the resultant technological development in the region. In 2005, Africa region of the world has a very low e-governance development index of 0.24, this fall short of the world average and it implies that the continent is not fully compliant with e-governance. This means that there are inadequate or poor judicial backings for the entrenching the use of e-governance mechanism in African countries. Americas region of the world e-governance development index is very high and this shows their levels of technological compliance. It EGDI index in 2005 is 0.56 and it is above the world average of 0.47. This means that there are adequate or good judicial backings for entrenching the use of e-governance mechanism in the American countries. The regions of Asian and Oceania has the e-governance compliance index of 0.45 and 0.43 respectively which were slightly below the world average but at the same time more compliance than Africa. Europe has a remarkable high EGDI of 0.61 and the most compliance in e-governance in the world.

Table 2.

Continent/Year	2005	2008	2010	2012	2014	2016
Africa	0.28	0.29	0.27	0.28	0.27	0.29
Americas	0.56	0.56	0.48	0.54	0.51	0.52
Asia	0.45	0.46	0.44	0.45	0.50	0.51
Europe	0.61	0.66	0.62	0.72	0.69	0.72
Oceania	0.43	0.29	0.42	0.42	0.41	0.41
World Average	0.47	0.21	0.44	0.22	0.47	0.49

Source: United Nations Department of Economic and Social Affairs 2005-2016

Figure 1. EGDI of World Regions and the World Average

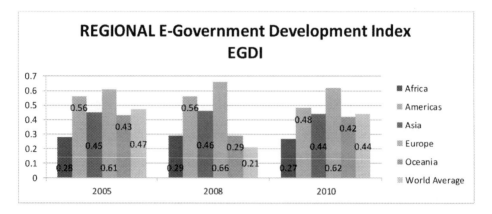

In 2008, Africa region of the world has a low e-governance development index of 0.29, but this is slightly higher than the world average of 0.21. This implies that the continent is getting more compliance with e-governance and the judicial backings are getting more entrenched by states for the use of e-government mechanism. In Americas region of the world, e-governance development index remains very high and this shows their levels of technological compliance and the availability of judicial provisions to entrench its uses. The region's EGDI index in 2008 was 0.56 and much more above the world average of 0.21. The regions of Asian and Oceania has the e-governance compliance index is 0.46 and 0.29 respectively. Asian EGDI shows a little improvement from 2005 index. This is because there was an improvement in the laws enabling the use of e-governance technology. The Oceania fell drastically in comparativeness to 2005 index due to low compliance to the available laws regulating the use of e-government interfaces. However both region indexes were higher than the world average of 0.21. Europe however still has a remarkable high EGDI of 0.66 and the most compliance in e-governance in the world because there was a sustainable improvement in the laws enabling the use of e-governance technology.

The 2010 e-governance development index shows a general improvement across all the regions of the world. However, Africa region of the world still has a low e-governance development index of 0.27, and the judicial inclination enabling the use of e-governance is at the low ebb thus it has a lower EGDI to the world average of 0.44. This implies that the continent is slightly stagnant in developing e-governance compliance environment. Americas region of the world e-governance development index remains very high and this shows their levels of technological compliance and trust. The trust level is due to an environment enabled by adequate judicial inclination. It EGDI in 2010 is 0.48 and slightly above the world average of 0.44 but lower than the 2008 index. The regions of Asian and Oceania has the e-governance compliance index is 0.44 and 0.42 respectively. Both Asian and Oceania regions shows a slightly decreased EGDI in comparativeness with 2008 index. However both region indexes were at par and or below the world average of 0.44 respectively. This shows a reduction in the trust and reputation in e-governance technology due to low judicial enabling environment. Europe however still has a remarkable high EGDI of 0.62 a little drops in relation with 2008 high record of 0.66. Nevertheless the region remains the most compliance in e-governance in the world. The trust and reputation in the e-governance technology usage is high due to the enabling judicial environments.

Table 1 and Figure 2 show the various regions of the world and their corresponding E-governance and development index from 2012 to 2016 (2012, 2014 and 2016 respectively). This indicates the extent of E-governance compliance trust and reputation of the e-governance technology, the resultant technological development in the region and the extent of the judicial enabling environment. In 2012, Africa region of the world has an improved e-governance development index of 0.28, this is higher than the world average of 0.22 and it implies that the continent is getting more compliant with e-governance trend in the world. Also, the level of trust and reputation in the e-governance technology has improved due to the judicial environment which is becoming more interactive. Americas region of the world e-governance development index is very high and this shows their levels of technological compliance. It EGDI index in 2012 is 0.54 and above the world average of 0.22. This is as a result of

Figure 2. EGDI of World Regions and the World Average

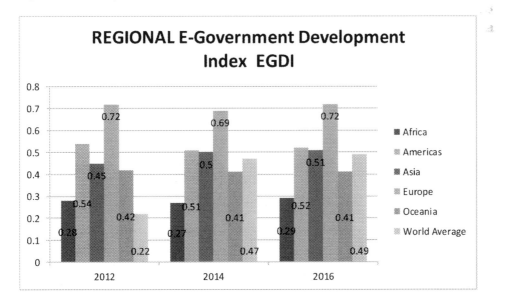

sustainable trust and reputation in the technological usage in governance and the virile judicial environment. The regions of Asian and Oceania has the e-governance compliance index of 0.45 and 0.42 respectively. These were higher than the world average and at the same time more compliance than Africa region. Europe has a remarkable high EGDI of 0.72 and the most compliance in e-governance in the world due to a high and sustainable trust and reputation in the e-governance earn from the enabling judicial environment.

In 2014, Africa region of the world has a reduced e-governance development index of 0.27; this is drastically lower than the world average of 0.47. This implies that the continent has more to do in getting more compliance with e-governance. There is a need to build up the trust and reputation of the e-governance technology through the right and adequate judicial inclination. Americas region of the world e-governance development index remains very high and this shows their levels of trust and reputation the citizens have on the technology provisions and the corresponding judicial supports. It EGDI index in 2014 is 0.51 and much more above the world average of 0.22. This indicates fallout from the 2012 development index of 0.54. The regions of Asian and Oceania has the e-governance compliance index of 0.50 and 0.41 respectively. Asian EGDI shows a little improvement from 2012 index while Oceania fell slightly in comparativeness to 2012 index. However both region indexes were higher than the world average of 0.47 except Oceania region. Europe however still maintains a remarkable high EGDI of 0.69 and the most compliance in e-governance in the world.

The 2016 e-governance development index shows a general improvement across all the regions of the world. It generally revealed that the judicial environments have improved to support e-governance usage therefore boosting the levels of trust and reputation in the e-governance technology compliance. Africa region of the world however still retains a low e-governance development index of 0.29 which is lower than the world average of 0.49. This implies that there is an inadequate trust in the reputation of the digital governance therefore continent is slightly stagnant in developing e-governance compliance community. Americas region of the world e-governance development index remains very high and this shows their levels of trust in the reputations of their technology and e-governance compliance. It EGDI in 2016 is 0.52 and slightly above the world average of 0.49 which is an improvement over the 2014 index. The regions of Asian and Oceania has the e-governance compliance index of 0.51 and 0.41 respectively. Both Asian and Oceania regions shows a stagnancy in EGDI in comparativeness with 2014 index. However both region indexes were at par and or below the world average of 0.49 respectively. Europe however still has a remarkable all time high EGDI of 0.72 a little bit higher than 2014 record of 0.69. The region remains the most compliance in e-governance in the world.

TRUST AND REPUTATION, INTERNATIONAL BENCHMARKS AND JUDICIAL INKLING ON E-GOVERNANCE AND M-GOVERNANCE

Regional legal framework for cyber laws covering electronic transaction, electronic signature and authentications, data protection and privacy, consumer protection and computer crime operational efficiency of any e-government framework requires an adequate back up support of necessary legislation on data security, network security, cyber crime, information systems and electronic transactions. These legislation or judicial support is necessary for the build up of trust and reputation in the uptake and utilization of the technology in governance and administration. These legislation needs to emanate from the apex of world governance—the United Nations General Assembly so that many countries may easily adopt the resolutions in their domestic policies.

Series of workshops and training has taken place: stakeholder's workshop, Nairobi (2005); Workshop on Cyber Laws and e-Justice, Kampala April 2006 and Information Security, April 2006 Workshops examined key legal and regulatory issues and identify priorities for cooperation among others. The formation of a regional taskforce to spearhead the development and implementation of the regional legal framework for cyber laws and of cyber laws review of the existing laws and bills of partner states can be undertaken and subsequently a regional legal framework for harmonization of cyber laws to be developed.

Interoperability Framework for e-Governance (IFEG) in global context encompass agreed approach to be adopted by the public agencies that wish to work together towards the joint delivery of public services using ICT to achieve above mentioned goals, namely exchange of data, meaning of exchanged data and agreed process. An IFEG involves a common structure which comprises a set of standards and guidelines; the structure can be used by the public agencies to specify the preferred way that all stake-holders interact with each other to share the information. It is synonymous to speaking a common language.

The interoperability levels relate to the sharing of information in IFEG which is base on mutual trust mainly classified into organisational Interoperability (like process-re-engineering including Government-Orders, Process Changes, and organisational Structures). Semantic Interoperability (Enabling data to be interpreted & processed with the same command and meaning, etc.) and technical interoperability (like technical issues in interconnecting ICT systems and services, information storage and archival, protocols for information exchange and networking and security).

In general, technical legal interoperability is considered as suitable to guard e-governance operability and usability security through classifying the standards into various layers or domains (for example Presentation domain, Network domain,

Data Interchange domain and laws) in earlier versions of IFEG/GIF documents which can be domesticated by various countries. The Legal frame work also entails issues like Copy Right, content regulation, privacy, freedom of information and electronic identities. These are context-sensitive. Legal factors include legal-power assigned to system for data protection and privacy information of the citizen, governance and related issues.

CONCLUSION

E-governance in every clime facilitates the interactions between citizens, government organizations and elected officials and how the internet can improve the governing and policy making process. The core area is the use of technology (particularly the web) to cause transformation in the governing process. E-government policy and laws must focus on the demand side of the equation, instead of just focusing on the supply side of e-government services delivery. The demand side is the need for effective service delivery and good governance and on areas of applications which are likely to generate high returns for sustainable development and to benefit the majority of citizens (e.g. in education), rather than those primarily driven by efficiency considerations. Therefore, there must be a sufficient level of trust in the service provision in the digital environment in terms of e-governance reputation by the provision of judicial assurance and security for the end users of such services.

E-government policies aimed at increasing user uptake, it ought to be guided by the simple question: 'how to get people to use e-government services'. This leads to questions of relevance of e-government content to users, motivational factors (especially convenience), as well as usability and other usage-influencing factors. The links between e-service delivery, usage and sustainable development are mediated and influenced by fundamentals like education, skills and digital infrastructure. Therefore, governments wishing to succeed in e-government would therefore do well to invest in strengthening these particular fundamentals, including broadband, improve capacity to effectively seek citizen feedback, monitor, track and analyze usage trends, so as to prioritize service digitization and integrate relevant data into policy.

Users' feedback can also provide important information as well as data for integration into policy efforts to increase service usage. E-government promotion and awareness campaigns, evaluation needs to be an integral part of a policy effort to increase e-government uptake, which is also an important part of educating the public about the benefits of e-government, thereby helping to increase user uptake. Finally, the government has a unique platform to maintain trust and reputation in the governance. This can be easily achieved when there are enabling laws and judicial environment that can strengthens their action network. The action network must exceed that of a vendor machine that merely receive taxes and provide any services in a faster, cheaper, stress free, to an efficient and effective level reasonable to achieve development in the country.

REFERENCES

Agrawal, S., Sethi, P., & Mittal, M. (2015). E-Governance: An Analysis of Citizens' Perception. *IUP Journal of Information Technology, 11*(3), 34.

Banerjee, A., Duflo, E., Imbert, C., Mathew, S., & Pande, R. (2016). *E-governance, Accountability, and Leakage in Public Programs: Experimental Evidence from a Financial Management Reform in India (No. w22803)*. National Bureau of Economic Research India. doi:10.3386/w22803

Dash, S. S., Sethi, I. P. S., & Gupta, O. P. (2016,). Measuring performance outcome of e-Governance projects through eTaal. In *Computing for Sustainable Global Development (INDIACom), 2016 3rd International Conference on* (pp. 23-27). Academic Press.

E-Government in Support of Sustainable Development United Nations New York. (n.d.). Retrieved from www.publicadministration.un.org

Kyem, P. A. (2016). Mobile Phone Expansion and Opportunities for e-Governance in Africa. *The Electronic Journal on Information Systems in Developing Countries*, 75.

Meijer, A. (2015). E-governance innovation: Barriers and strategies. *Government Information Quarterly, 32*(2), 198–206. doi:10.1016/j.giq.2015.01.001

Organization for Economic Co-Operation and Development (OECD). (2005). *e-Government for Better Government.* Retrieved from http://www.oecd.org/gov/digital-government/egovernmentforbettergovernment.htm#HTO

The Electronic Delivery of Services Bill (EDS). (2011). *Bill 2011 Draft 16th November 2011*. Retrieved from http://meity.gov.in/sites/upload_files/dit/files/Electronic_Delivery_of_Services_Bill_2011_16thNov_Legal_17112011.pdf

United Nations. (2001). *Benchmarking E-government: A Global Perspective Assessing the UN Member States Assessing the Progress of the UN Member States United Nations Division for Public Economics and Public Administration*. American Society for Public Administration.

United Nations. (2004). *UN Global E-Government Readiness Report 2004: Towards Access for Opportunity*. Department of Economic and Social Affairs Division for Public Administration and Development Management United Nations.

United Nations. (2005). *UN Global E-government Readiness Report 2005 From E-government to E-inclusion. Department of Economic and Social Affairs Division for Public Administration and Development Management*. United Nations.

United Nations. (2008). *From e-Government to Connected Governance e-Government Survey 2008. Department of Economic and Social Affairs Division for Public Administration and Development Management*. United Nations.

United Nations. (2010). *United Nations E-Government Survey 2010 Leveraging e-government at a time of financial and economic crisis UN Publishing Section*. Author.

United Nations. (2012). *United Nations E-Government Survey 2012 United Nations E-Government Survey 2012 E-Government for the People*. Department of Economic and Social Affairs United Nations.

United Nations. (2014). *United Nations E-Government Survey: E-Government For The Future We Want*. Department of Economic and Social Affairs.

United Nations. (2016a). *E-Government Survey Department of Economic and Social Affairs*. Author.

United Nations E-Government Survey. (2016b). *E-Government in Support of Sustainable Development*. United Nations. Retrieved from http://www.un.org/desa https://publicadministration.un.org

Williams, R., & Edge, D. (1996). The social shaping of technology. *Research Policy*, 25.

World Bank. (2015). *e-Government*. Retrieved from http://www.worldbank.org/en/topic/ict/brief/e-government Assessed on 28/6/2017

Chapter 10

DBMS Log Analytics for Detecting Insider Threats in Contemporary Organizations

Muhammad Imran Khan
Insight Centre for Data Analytics, Ireland

Simon N. Foley
IMT Atlantique, France

Barry O'Sullivan
University College Cork, Ireland

ABSTRACT

Insiders are legitimate users of a system; however, they pose a threat because of their granted access privileges. Anomaly-based intrusion detection approaches have been shown to be effective in the detection of insiders' malicious behavior. Database management systems (DBMS) are the core of any contemporary organization enabling them to store and manage their data. Yet insiders may misuse their privileges to access stored data via a DBMS with malicious intentions. In this chapter, a taxonomy of anomalous DBMS access detection systems is presented. Secondly, an anomaly-based mechanism that detects insider attacks within a DBMS framework is proposed whereby a model of normative behavior of insiders n-grams are used to capture normal query patterns in a log of SQL queries generated from a synthetic banking application system. It is demonstrated that n-grams do capture the short-term correlations inherent in the application. This chapter also outlines challenges pertaining to the design of more effective anomaly-based intrusion detection systems to detect insider attacks.

DOI: 10.4018/978-1-5225-5984-9.ch010

INTRODUCTION

Database Management Systems (DBMS) are at the heart of contemporary organizations. Contemporary organizations deploy DBMS to store and manage access to their application data. There exist traditional security controls including role-based access and authentication that control privileges to stored data. However, there is still the concern of insider threats within the DBMS framework whereby legitimate users of the system misuse their access privileges to access stored data with malicious intentions. For example, there are number of reported incidents (Carr, 2008; Report, 2007) where hospital staff, without cause, looked up the medical records of celebrity patients. It has been reported in a recent survey that 89% of respondent organizations are vulnerable to insider attacks (Insider Threat Report, Insider Threat Security Statistics, Vormetric, 2015). Another survey reports that malicious insiders are the cause of the costliest cybercrimes (2015 Cost of Cyber Crime: Global, 2015).

In order to detect insider attacks, intrusion detection systems can be deployed. An intrusion detection system can be further classified into either anomaly detection systems or misuse detection systems (Kemmerer & Vigna, 2002). Misuse detection systems look for well-known attack patterns that are a priori defined. Thus, misuse detection systems can detect previously known or existing attacks. In contrast to misuse detection systems, anomaly detection systems (Forrest, Hofmeyr, & Somayaji, 2008; Forrest, Hofmeyr, Somayaji, & Longstaff, 1996; Laszka, Abbas, Sastry, Vorobeychik, & Koutsoukos, 2016; Pieczul & Foley, 2013) look for deviations from normal behavior. Anomaly detection systems have the potential to detect previously unknown, or *zero-day*, attacks (Jamrozik, von Styp-Rekowsky, & Zeller, 2016; Pieczul & Foley, 2016). We are interested in considering the challenge of detecting anomalous DBMS queries made by insiders; while the insider may hold the correct access permission to make the query. This article provides two contributions on this challenge. Firstly, a taxonomy for understanding DBMS anomaly detection systems is proposed. Secondly, an n-gram model for DBMS anomaly detection, that extends (Khan & Foley, 2016), is developed and evaluated.

Anomaly-based intrusion detection techniques have been shown to be effective in detecting insider attacks (Sallam et al., 2015). The basic building block of an anomaly detection technique is how it models normative behavior. Existing anomaly-based intrusion-detection technique considers a query in isolation in order to construct a model of normative behavior. We consider sequences of SQL queries made to a DBMS (Khan & Foley, 2016) whereby n-grams are used to capture normal query patterns.

The book chapter is organized as follows. Section 2 provides an introduction to the problem of insider threat. A taxonomy for anomalous DBMS-access detection systems is developed in Section 3. This provides a context for understanding the different approaches to defining and detecting anomalous activity that might arise from insider threat. Our focus is on learning normal behavior from DBMS logs and then checking subsequent accesses against these normal behavior profiles. The book chapter consider how techniques from the taxonomy can help in achieving this. Section 4 describes our approach, and its evaluation using a simulated banking style application is described in Section 5. Arising from this work, insights are provided on the challenges for future research on this topic in Section 6. Conclusions are presented in Section 7.

INSIDER THREATS

Threats to an organization can be classified as external (outsider attack) or internal (insider attack). External threats come from attackers outside of the organization who discover network and/or system vulnerabilities and use this information to penetrate the organization. Outside attackers may, for example, utilize social engineering techniques to accomplish a malicious goal, such as stealing confidential information, or making some resources unavailable using a Denial-of-Service attack. There is much existing research on dealing with external threats and many security defenses have been proposed, including host-based access controls, intrusion detection systems, and access control mechanisms (Chari & Cheng, 2003), (Jajodia, Samarati, Sapino, & Subrahmanian, 2001), (Bertino, Bettini, Ferrari, & Samarati, 1996). On the other hand, an insider is a person who belongs to an organization and is authorized to access a range of data and services. This section considers how the understanding and definition of Insider has evolved in the literature.

Defining Insiders and Insider Threats

One can find several definitions in the literature for an Insider, however there is no consensus on a single definition. This can present a challenge (Hunker & Probst, 2011), as a precise characterization of an insider and insider capabilities will enable the devising of solutions to detect insider attacks. In the 2008 paper, 'Defining the Insider Threat', Bishop and Gates consider three definitions of insiders. The first definition was from a RAND report (C. Y. Chung, Gertz, & Levitt, 2000) that defines an insider to be "*an already trusted person with access to sensitive information and information systems*". The second definition was also from the same RAND report which defines an insider to be "*someone with access, privilege, or knowledge of information systems and services*". The third definition, originating from (Patzakis, 2003), defines an insider to be '*anyone operating inside the security perimeter*'.

In the first definition, a person needs to be trusted in order to be called an insider, however, in the second definition, a person having knowledge of the system and services is also considered as an insider. The third definition is somewhat more generic in considering everyone within the security perimeter to be an insider.

Bishop and Gates (Bishop & Gates, 2008) provide a fourth, non-binary, definition for an insider. The first three definitions are regarded as binary definitions since if the person satisfies one of these definitions then that person is called an insider, otherwise the person is not an insider. The non-binary notion of an insider is based upon a measure of the damage the organization would suffer if entities such as resources, important documents, e-mails, source code, etc. are compromised or leaked. Each entity is assigned an impact value that specifies this measure of damage. Entities with the same impact value are grouped together in protection domain groups. These protection domain groups are then paired with groups of users having access to entities in protection domain groups. Users having access to protection domain groups with the highest impact-value poses the highest risk of insider threat. This model provides a spectrum on which one can identify the degree to which an insider poses a threat. We believe that such a model is useful in developing more fine-grained security mechanisms by taking into account the threat-level an insider pose. This proposed model for insider threat presented by Bishop & Gates is effective in understanding how threats may be traced and aggregated through a system when insiders are identified and given threat levels. However, it does not define what is meant by an insider.

In a 2008 cross-disciplinary workshop on "Countering Insider Threats" (Probst, Hunker, Bishop, & Gollmann, 2008), a more complete definition was proposed. An insider is defined as "*a person that has been legitimately empowered with the right to access, represent, or decide about one or more assets of the organization's structure*". Predd et. al. defined an insider threat as *[...] an insider's action that puts an organization or its resources at risk* (Predd, Pfleeger, Hun-ker, & Bulford, 2008).

The Impact of Insider Attack

The extent of the damage that can be done by an insider can be much worse than that of an external attack as Insiders hold authorization to use resources and services and have more information about the structure and working of the organization. A 2015 report titled Insider Threat Report by Vormetric (Insider Threat Report, Insider Threat Security Statistics, Vormetric, 2015), reported that globally 89% of the respondent organizations are at risk of insider attack, and that among these respondent organizations 34% of them felt extremely vulnerable to this kind of attack. From the respondent organizations 56% plan to increase their spending on tackling the challenge of insider threat. The 2015 Cost of Cyber Crime: Global from the Ponemon Institute (2015 Cost of Cyber Crime: Global, 2015) reported that the costliest cyber-crimes are caused by insiders. Information Systems Audit and Control Association (ISACA), in 2016 reported that, globally, insider threat was among the top three threats for 2016 (Audit & (ISACA), 2016). In the context of healthcare, it is reported that healthcare data breaches are mostly caused by insiders (Brenner, 2017).

Insider attacks are on the rise, as reported in a 2015 survey report (Grand Theft Data - Data exfiltration study: Actors, tactics, and detection, 2015) that 43% of data breaches were caused by internal factors as compared to 2004 where it was reported in (CERT, 2004) that 29% of the crimes were caused by insiders.

The reporting rate of insider attacks / incidents is very low for a variety of reasons including inconsequential impact, lack of evidence, loss of reputation and liability (CERT, 2014). However, now legislation is in place that directs organization to report data breaches such as a recently passed Privacy Amendment (Notifiable Data Breaches) Act 2016 in Australia (Australian Government, 2017) and EU's General Data Protection Regulation that come into effect from 2018 (Union, 2016). In 2013, Verizon reported that from data breaches that occurred in 2012 two-third of those breaches were from database or files (data at rest), one-third breaches involved data in memory (data in process) and none of the data breaches involved data at transit (Verizon, 2016).

INSIDER THREAT AND DATA MINING

This article focuses on the detection of insider threats in Data Base Management Systems. More specifically, we are interested in the detection of malicious queries that are made, by an organization insider, to applications that access the DBMS, or through direct accesses. Our hypothesis is that an Intrusion Detection Systems (IDS) can be used to detect these malicious queries made by an insider. Intrusion Detection Systems can be classified into misuse detection systems and anomaly detection systems (Kemmerer & Vigna, 2002). There has been a great deal of research on Intrusion Detection Systems reported in the literature (Barry & Chan, 2010) (Liao, Richard Lin, Lin, & Tung, 2013). This work has generally focussed on identifying malicious system operations (Creech & Hu, 2014), malicious network events (C. J. Chung, Khatkar, Xing, Lee, & Huang, 2013) or malicious application system events (Abed, Clancy, & Levy, 2015). In relative terms, there is little existing research on applying these techniques to detect malicious DBMS activity and this section reviews this research.

Misuse detection systems look for existing misuse patterns and are able to only detect previously known attacks. However, in contrast to misuse detection systems, anomaly detection systems look for a deviation from past or normal behavior. In principle, anomaly detection systems may have the potential to detect zero-days attacks, that is, attacks for which there is not a known pre-defined pattern. However, in practice, it is a challenge to determine a profile of normal behavior that yields good false positive/negative results. This section consider how data mining techniques can be applied to DBMS logs to learn profiles of normal behavior.

Taxonomy of Anomalous DBMS-Access Detection Systems

We introduce a taxonomy of mechanisms that detect anomalous access to a DBMS, with a focus on anomaly-detection mechanisms. Misuse detection systems require the specification of signatures of known attacks (Kemmerer & Vigna, 2002; Kumar & Spafford, 1994; Ning & Jajodia, 2004). This is contrasted with anomaly detection systems, where a profile of normal behavior is learned from a DBMS log of past queries. We classify anomaly detection systems according to set of features such as time of access, attributes in projection clause, relations/tables queried etc., used to generate profile of normal behavior and their properties.

Figure 1 identifies two approaches to detecting anomalous access in a DBMS. In the first approach, a record of the malicious access patterns is kept. If there is a match between any known malicious access pattern and an access pattern at run-time, then the run-time access can be characterized as malicious. This is the approach that underlies misuse detection systems. In the second approach, one builds a profile of normal access patterns based on logs of past behavior of the DBMS. Any access pattern that does not fall into the set of normal access patterns can be characterized as a malicious access to the DBMS. This is the underlying notion of anomaly detection system. The scope of this book chapter covers anomaly detection systems and, therefore, we focus on the classification of all such systems.

Anomaly-based intrusion detection techniques can be classified as syntax-centric (Hussain, Sallam, & Bertino, 2015), context-centric (Wu, Osborn, & Jin, 2009), and data-centric (Mathew, Petropoulos, Ngo, & Upadhyaya, 2010) (which is sometimes is referred as result-centric in the literature). With syntax-centric techniques the generated behavioral profiles are based on syntax features of the SQL query, for example, the attributes in a projection clause, the relations queried, the attributes in selection clause, or the type of SQL command. With data-centric or result-centric technique, the behavioral profiles are based on the data returned in response to an SQL query. For example, one could use the amount of information returned in response to a query or the returned values of attributes to generate profiles. With context-centric techniques the behavioral profiles are based on information related to the context of the query. For example, the time of access or the time at which the query was made, the user ID of the person making the query, or the number of

Figure 1. Taxonomy of anomalous DBMS-access detection systems. The proposed n-gram approach in this paper can be classified as a white-box anomaly detection system that uses syntax-centric features to generate profiles of normal behavior.

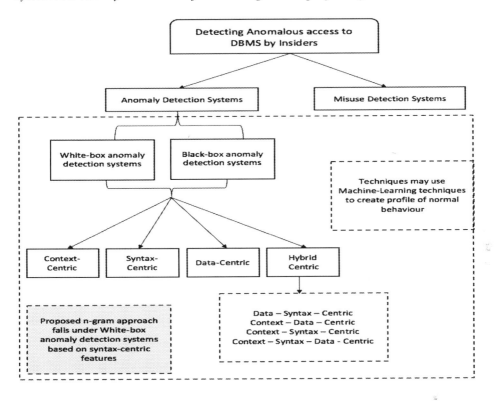

queries made in a specified time period. Any combination of the context, syntax and data-centric features, can be used in the generation of behavioral profiles. A hybrid mechanism, based on syntax and data-centric features, is proposed in (Sallam et al., 2016), and is described later in this section.

Anomaly detection techniques may deploy machine learning algorithms to generate behavioral profiles, for example as in (Sallam et al., 2016), where naive Bayesian classifiers and multi-labeling classifiers, were also deployed in the profile generation process. We discuss this approach under hybrid approaches (data-centric and syntax-centric) later in this section. Besides machine learning algorithms, an alternative data-mining technique used is based on n-grams, which we use in our proposed model. We deploy n-grams to generate behavioral profiles using syntax-centric features. The proposed approach is a white-box approach as it allows a security officer to understand and explain the anomaly. Also, the profiles in the proposed model can be manually updated.

Syntax-Centric Features-Based Techniques

Many of the existing approaches of anomalous DBMS-access detection use the syntax features of the queries to generate behavioral profiles (Hussain et al., 2015; Kul et al., 2016; Lee, Low, & Wong, 2002; Low, Lee, & Teoh, 2002; Sallam et al., 2016). In the following, a syntax-centric technique known as *DETANOM* (Hussain et al., 2015) is described.

Hussain et al. presented an anomaly detection technique used to detect malicious DBMS-access by application programs (Hussain et al., 2015). Like all anomaly detection techniques, this technique consists of two phases: a training phase and an anomaly detection phase. In order to generate a normal profile of an application, SQL queries executed by an application program are represented in the form of SQL query abstraction. These SQL query abstractions, in the literature, are also referred as SQL query fingerprint (Lee et al., 2002; Low et al., 2002), SQL query signature (Hussain et al., 2015) or SQL query skeleton (Kul et al., 2016).

A SQL query abstraction consists of the following elements, (c, t, r, q, n), where c is SQL command type, for instance SELECT. Attribute t is the list of attribute identifiers projected in the query. The list of attribute identifiers are relative to the relation to which they belong, for example, if a relation *Dublin* consists of an attribute name and the identifier for Dublin is 100 and the identifier for name is 5, then the corresponding value of t will be 100:5. Attribute r is the list of relation identifiers. Attribute q is the list of attribute identifiers in the WHERE clause and n is the number of predicates in the WHERE clause. The generation of a query abstraction is followed by the exploration of all execution paths of the application program accomplished by *Concolic execution (concolic testing)* which is a technique for program analysis (Majumdar & Sen, 2007; Sen, 2007; Sen, Marinov, & Agha, 2005). Concolic testing is used to discover all execution paths within a program by performing symbolic execution. Where symbolic execution is a way of testing / analyzing a source code of a computer program to identify inputs that results in the execution of different paths in the code.

In Concolic testing, first the input variables are determined. These selected input variables are then referred as symbolic variables while the remaining variables in the code are referred as concrete values. For the first time the program is executed with an initial random input, and this random input leads to the execution of a certain path in the code where the path conditions are true for these random inputs. For the next run, discovery of a new path in the code is desired thus the path condition which didn't hold true in previous execution with initial random input is negated and symbolic variable values are determined such that it satisfies the path condition which wasn't satisfied in previous run thus resulting in discovering a new branch /

execution path in program. This process is repeated till the maximum code coverage is achieved.

In the next step of *DETANOM*, branching condition is paired with the SQL query that falls under that branching condition which were discovered in the process of concolic testing. This branch condition – SQL query pair is referred to as *query record*. In the detection phase, a query is intercepted and its constraint is matched with the constraint in the corresponding a *query record*. If the constraint is satisfied, then that query abstraction is matched. In case of a mismatch, then the query is said to be malicious.

Data-Centric / Result-Centric Features-Based

Existing literature lacks anomaly detection techniques based on data-centric features, also known as result-centric features, in the context of detecting insider threats in a DBMS. Data-centric features include, the amount of information returned in response to a query or returned values of attributes. In this book chapter, we refer to those techniques that are based on data-centric features as data-centric techniques. A data-centric feature-based technique for the detection of insider attacks in a DBMS was proposed by Mathew et al. in 2010 (Mathew et al., 2010). To the authors' knowledge this is the first and only data-centric technique proposed to-date. In (Mathew et al., 2010), it is argued that syntax-centric features of a query alone are a poor discriminator of intent. Syntactically different queries (different in-terms of abstractions) can give the same result while syntactically similar queries (similar in-terms of abstractions) can yield different results, thus stemming an increase in false positives and false negatives respectively (Mathew et al., 2010). A false positive is when the query is legitimate but it is labeled as malicious and a false negative is when the query is malicious but it is labeled as legitimate.

In (Mathew et al., 2010), the user profiles are clusters that are specified in terms of an *S-Vector* that provides a statistical summary of results (tuples/rows) from columns accessed. An S-Vector represents statistical measurements for queried attributes in the relation. In case of numeric attributes, an S-Vector consists of maximum value, minimum value, standard deviation, median and mean for that each numeric attribute in the query. In case of non-numeric attributes, the S-Vector consists of the total count of values along with the number of distinct values. In detection phase, if the query belongs to the cluster then it is considered normal else it is considered as anomalous. As supervised learning methods, Euclidean k-means clustering, Support Vector Machines (SVM), Decision Tree Classifier, and Naive Bayes, were used. k-means clustering is a way of grouping similar data point / objects (S-Vector). In other words, objects that are more similar to each other forms a cluster of objects.

In *k*-means clustering, for a given data-set, value of *k* is chosen which is the desired number of clusters. Initially the first *k* data points are selected to form cluster centroids. In the next step, *Euclidean* distance is calculated between the next data point in the data set and cluster centroids. Subsequently this data point is assigned to the nearest cluster based on the Euclidean distance. This cluster centroid, to which the data point is assigned, is updated by calculating mean of cluster centroid and the assigned data point itself. The process is repeated until all the data points are assigned to some cluster. In case of Support Vector Machines (SVM), a decision boundary also known as hyperplane is drawn between two classes. The goal of the SVM is finding a wider decision boundary or in other words a decision boundary that is as far away possible for the data point in both the classes, this is achieved by tuning some parameters called regularization, gamma, kernel and margin (see (Bishop, 2006) and (Mathew et al., 2010) for more explanation). Decision tree classifier basically keeps on dividing the attributes into subparts such that in the end either the subparts have elements that are of same class or some other classification criteria is met. In Decision trees, first the entropy of the target attribute is computed followed by the splitting of data into subsets / branches with respect to different attributes. Then information gain is computed for each subset. The subset having the highest information gain is chosen as a decision node. The dataset is further divided with respect subsets based on the attributes. The process is repeated till a branch having an entropy of zero is reached, then this branch is called a leaf node. The whole process results in a tree like structure where the top most node is known as the root node. Naive Bayes Classification (NBC) is based on Bayes theorem. In NBC, prior probabilities are calculated for each class, where the classes have some existing data point. In the next step, conditional probabilities are calculated, that are probability of each attribute value given each class. In order to classify a new data point, posterior probabilities are computed that are the probabilities of a data point falling in a specific class, thus this probability is calculated for the new data point for each class. The new data point is assigned the class for which the calculated probability is higher (see (Bishop, 2006) for the theoretical details). As unsupervised methods, two detection techniques were constructed that is Cluster-Based Outlier Detection which was based on Euclidean distance clustering and *Attrib-Deviation* which used L_∞-norm as the distance function. In case of cluster-based outlier detection, the data points are represented in a multidimensional Euclidean vector space. A centroid for a cluster is selected where if the distance of a new data point is greater than certain user specified threshold than that data point is labeled as outlier.

Context-Centric Features-Based Techniques

As mentioned earlier, in context-centric techniques behavioral profiles are based on contextual features. As an example, contextual features include time at which the query was made, *user_ID* of the user who made the query, and the number of queries made by a user. The proposed approach in (Wu et al., 2009), though not purely context-centric, records features like Employee ID, Role ID, time, IP address, access type (direct or through application) and SQL query. This approach also employs a Naive Bayes classifier to generate normal profiles. The evaluation was carried out using a synthetically generated data-set.

Hybrid (Data-Centric and Syntax-Centric) Techniques

Data and syntax-centric features can be combined to construct behavioral profiles as shown in (Sallam et al., 2016). Machine learning techniques, in particular, Naïve Bayes classifiers and multi-labeling classifiers, were also deployed in profile generation process. User profiles are built in training phase from logs containing user / role activities. The approach transforms an SQL query into an SQL query abstraction called a *quadruplet*. A *Quadruplet Q* is composed of the following elements: $Q(C, P_R, P_A, S_R)$ where C is the command type; P_R is a list of relations accessed by the query, whereby accessed relations are represented by 1 and the one not accessed are represented by 0; P_A is a list of attributes accessed by query relative to the relation, where each attribute is represented by 1 if accessed and 0 if not; S_R represents the amount of selected information from the relation. This selected information can be a small portion, medium portion, large portion, or null, if the table is not accessed at all. This hybrid approach is demonstrated in two settings that is role-based anomaly detection and unsupervised anomaly detection. In first setting, Naive Bayes classification was used to predict the role of a user submitting queries. If there is a difference in the predicted role and actual role of that user who is making a query, then the query is marked as anomalous. Another classifier, multi-labeling classification, was used in case of an overlap of roles that results in more than one role. If the user's role is not among the predicted roles, then the query is marked as anomalous. In the second setting of unsupervised anomaly detection, no roles were considered. The *COBWEB* clustering algorithm was selected for this unsupervised anomaly detection setting. In *COBWEB*, a classification tree is created where the first node is the root node, afterwards the decision on where to insert a new data point is made by using category utility function (see (Fisher, 1987; Gennari et. al.,1989) for more details). A query is considered normal if the query made by a user belongs in the cluster of queries which also has queries that were made by the same user. In other words, the query will be treated as anomalous if a query made by a user falls into a cluster which does not contain any query made by this user.

Hybrid (Context-Centric and Data-Centric) Techniques

The approach proposed in (Gafny, Shabtai, Rokach, & Elovici, 2011) used context-centric and data-centric features. Normal profiles are constructed by discovering association rules between context-centric features and data-centric features using *frequent item-set mining* (Agrawal, Imieliński, & Swami, 1993). The approach in (Gafny et al., 2011) uses context-centric features like transaction execution time, day, geographical location, user role, and the type of action and data-centric features like customer name, customer type, place of work, address, and zip code. The generated rules take the form of a tree. In the detection phase, for an incoming query, context-centric features are extracted and rules conforming to these features are matched afterwards. The result is matched with the results associated with the retrieved rules.

Hybrid (Context-Centric and Syntax-Centric) Techniques

In (Costante et al., 2016) a white-box approach to detecting anomalies while accessing databases is presented that uses context-centric and syntax-centric features to construct behavioral profiles. The entire approach can be divided into six main phases, that is, (i) - data collection, (ii) - feature extraction, (iii) - feature aggregation (optional phase), (iv) - profiling, (v) - tuning phase, and (vi) - detection and feedback loop. In the first phase, that is of data collection, DBMS transactions are collected and stored for further processing. The second step is feature extraction. In this phase, a feature space f is generated. For demonstration, the selected feature space, in the original publication, was f = [client's ID, length of query, the query command, column set over which the query was executed, time stamp]. An example of this feature space looks like f = [alice, 30, INSERT, {Last_Name, DOB}, 16:00]. Thus, f has both contextual information, that is, client's ID and time, and syntax information, that is, query command and the column/attributes on which the query was executed. The feature extraction phase is followed by the optional phase of feature aggregation. The feature aggregation phase combines features together in order to achieve better detection. In the profiling phase, profiles are generated using extracted features. The authors introduced two ways to generate profiles: *single transaction profiling* and *transaction flow profiling*. In *single transaction profiling*, each transaction is treated independently of others. A notion of *bin* is introduced in the profiling phase, where a probability is calculated for a feature value that falls in that *bin*. These *bins* are represented in form of a histogram (see (Costante et al., 2016) for more details).

In *transaction flow profiling*, it is assumed that a single transaction may not be malicious however a combination of transactions can be. Thus, in order to detect these combinations of malicious transactions, a more expressive feature space is selected, e.g. the number of transactions submitted, the number of records, the number of bytes, the number of sensitive columns, etc. The features are recorded in defined scope. A scope can be based on setting start and end time. In the tuning phase, security experts are allowed to set thresholds for each feature's *bin*. The last phase is of detection and feedback, where after detection, safe behavior is added to the normal profile via feedback loop. For the purpose of evaluation two data-sets were used, one from an enterprise and the other one was a synthetic data-set.

PROPOSED N-GRAM-BASED APPROACH

The proposed approach considers *sequences* of SQL queries instead of simply considering a SQL statement in isolation, as majority of proposed approaches considers query in isolation (Hussain et al., 2015; Kul et al., 2016; Lee, Low, & Wong, 2002; Valeur et al., 2005; Low, Lee, & Teoh, 2002; Sallam et al., 2016). Precisely, *sequences* of SQL queries are basically *sequences* of query abstractions. The inspiration to adopt n-grams comes from some early work (Forrest et al., 2008, 1996; Hofmeyr, Forrest, & Somayaji, 1998) that considered the problem of modeling normal behavior of an application based on sequences of system calls made by processes. Where system calls were extracted from system a log followed by articulation in the form of sets of n-grams. These sets of n-grams define normal behavior of the application.

Past research has shown that n-grams capture short-range co-relation in application programs, for example, in sendmail (Forrest et al., 2008, 1996; Hofmeyr et al., 1998) along with its effectiveness in intrusion detection in general (Wressnegger et al., 2013).

Figures 2 and 3 show the architecture of the proposed n-gram-based anomaly detection approach. Similar to traditional anomaly detection approaches, the proposed approach also consists of training phase and detection phase.

Training Phase

The training phase consists of following steps: (i) - Availability of safe audit logs, (ii) - Generating SQL query abstraction, (iii) - Building a normative model of behavior (profile construction phase). These steps are described in following sections.

Figure 2. Training phase of the proposed n-gram-based approach. Where SQL query abstractions are generated from the Audit logs followed by the construction of normative profile.

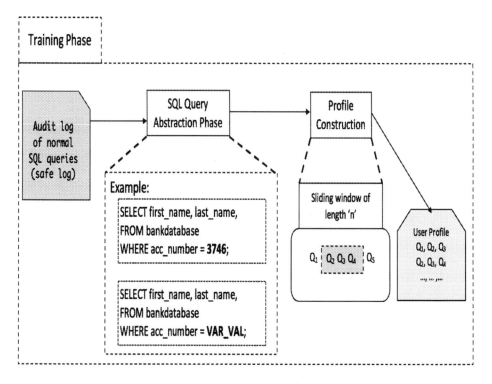

Availability of a Safe Audit Log

It is assumed that an audit log of SQL statements is available for the training phase. First and foremost, this audit log is free from any malicious query or transaction, notably free from sequences of malicious SQL queries. This audit log is referred to as a safe audit log. An audit log L is a sequence of SQL queries $\langle Q_1, Q_2, Q_3, ..., Q_n \rangle$, where each Q_i can be any of the SQL query command types, i.e. SELECT, UPDATE, INSERT or DELETE.

SQL Query Abstraction

There have been number of techniques proposed in the literature (Hussain et al., 2015; Kamra, Terzi, & Bertino, 2008; Kul et al., 2016; Sallam et al., 2015) that transformed the syntax of an SQL statement into a more abstract representation, as it is seen in previous sections. The SQL abstraction technique proposed in (Kul et al., 2016) is adopted for this work. This query abstraction technique replaces the constant values in a query Q_i with placeholders generating a query skeleton, which we denote as abs(Q_i) such that *abs(L)* is the mapping of abs(Q_i) over the elements Q_i of *L*. Figure 4 shows an example mapping of a query to query's abstractions.

Building a Normative Model of Behavior

The focus of this book chapter is building normative models from audit logs consisting of SQL queries resulted from insider/user interactions with application systems as a part of well-formed transactions that arise from normal operations and work-flows, both defined and undefined, of an organization. In this work, we have demonstrated that normative behavior can be constructed based on a variety of perspectives from the SQL log. Thus, *role projection* i.e. *role(L, R)* is considered, which returns the abstract log *abs(L)* containing those queries in *L* executed on behalf of users in the role *R*.

Figure 3. Detection phase of the proposed n-gram-based approach. In contrast to the training phase, in detection phase the SQL query abstractions are generated from the run-time audit log that can contain malicious queries.

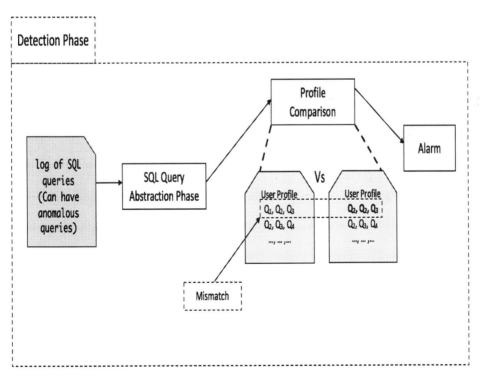

Figure 4. SQL log abstraction. This figure shows how query abstractions are generated using the technique (Kul et al., 2016).

Q_i	SQL statement	skeleton $abs(Q_i)$
Q_1	SELECT city FROM dba WHERE id = 2	SELECT city FROM dba WHERE id = VAR_VAL
Q_2	SELECT city FROM dba WHERE id = 9	SELECT city FROM dba WHERE id = VAR_VAL
Q_3	SELECT city FROM dba WHERE id = 3	SELECT city FROM dba WHERE id = VAR_VAL
Q_4	SELECT city FROM dba WHERE id = 3 AND Name = "Alice"	SELECT city FROM dba WHERE id = VAR_VAL AND Name = VAR_VAL

An n-gram based approach (Forrest et al., 1996) is used in order to investigate a normative model for user roles. N-gram-based models are suited to modeling short-range correlations between events in logs. N-grams are basically sub-sequences, of a given sequence of elements, generated by sliding a window of size '*n*'. When n = 2 the resulting sub-sequences / n-grams are known as *bi-grams* while in case of n = 3 the sub-sequences are known as *tri-grams*. A sequence consisting of '*j*' number of elements generates '*K*' number of n-grams such that $K = j-(n-1)$. Given a sequence L of SQL query (skeletons), $ngram(abs(L), n)$ is the set of all sub-sequences of size n that appear in $abs(L)$. For example, the 2-gram model for the (skeleton) log in Figure 4 is $\{\langle abs(Q_1), abs(Q_1)\rangle, \langle abs(Q_1), abs(Q_4)\rangle\}$. While it is important to note only unique n-grams are kept and duplicates are removed to have optimal normal profiles.

ANOMALOUS SQL STATEMENT DETECTION

In order to evaluate our proposed model, synthetic data-sets were generated. A banking-style application was developed that included typical banking transactions like opening an account, closing an account, transferring amount from one bank account to another account and depositing an amount to a bank account, withdrawal of an amount from a bank account. These transactions were carried out by insiders which in our case are bank employees. Each transaction consisted of multiple SQL queries. 10,000 random transactions were executed in the application system that resulted in the generation of an audit log consisting of around 28,000 SQL statements. The process was repeated twice in order to generate a baseline log of '*normal*' behavior Log_N, and to generate a test log, initially of normal activity L_A. Subsequently the test log L_A was perturbed by malicious/attacker activities simulating attacks for experiments as described below.

SQL anomalies can give rise to malicious data observation, malicious data modification, or deletion of data from a database. In this book chapter, the focus is on the detection of malicious data observation that arises from anomalous SQL queries. Intuitively, attacks pertaining malicious data observation is challenging to detect. A SQL query is malicious when a malicious insider queries the database without the need to know for any fair/justifiable/legitimate purpose. In this work, we considered different attack scenarios. In one scenario, the log L_A was perturbed by 50 malicious SQL queries, inserted into groups of 5 statements at 10 locations selected at random, resulting in logs L_{A1}. In the other scenario, the log L_A was perturbed by a single malicious SQL query inserted at random locations i.e. between two transaction and during a transaction resulting in logs L_{A2}, L_{A3}, L_{A4}, and L_{A5}, respectively.

In the attack scenarios, the anomalous statements had the same query abstraction/skeleton as the statements in the training log; this ensures that a detected mismatch is not based on the query abstraction alone, but on its correlation (or lack thereof) with other events in the log, i.e. *ngram(abs(L), n)*. Let's say $Set_i = ngram(abs(L), n)$. Let G_i be one of the sub-sequences from $Set_i = ngram(abs(L), n)$. For example, $G_1 = \{abs(Q_1), abs(Q_1)\}$. If Set_1 and Set_2 are compared then a mismatch will be when an n-gram G_1, exists in set Set_1 but does not exist in Set_2. Any malicious SQL query that has a different SQL query abstraction than that of those in the training log is easily detectable against unigram. Thus, for the experimentations the focus is to detect malicious SQL statements mimicking legitimate queries, however, these malicious SQL statements cannot be correlated to a legitimate transaction.

Figure 5 shows the number of mismatches that lead to the detection of inserted malicious queries as mentioned above in attack scenarios. In this study, it was observed that n-grams of size 2, 3 or 4 are effective to detect all the anomalous queries inserted using logs L_{A1}, L_{A2}, L_{A3}, L_{A4}, and L_{A5}.

N-gram profiles *ngram(role(Log_N, r), n)* and *ngram(role(Log_A, r), n)* were built from the synthetic logs, while different sizes of n-gram and different roles r were considered. Figure 6 depicts the number of mismatches arising when comparing the test (but normal) log *ngram(role(Log_A, r), n)* against baseline normal behavior for the role r that is *ngram(role(Log_N, r), n)*, for different values of n. As indicated in Figure 6 the number of false positives (mismatches) increases with the size of n,

Figure 5. Mismatches, with respect to the size of n-gram, indicating anomalous queries. For instance, there were 14 mismatches (while the size of n-gram was 3) when the attack where 50 malicious queries were made.

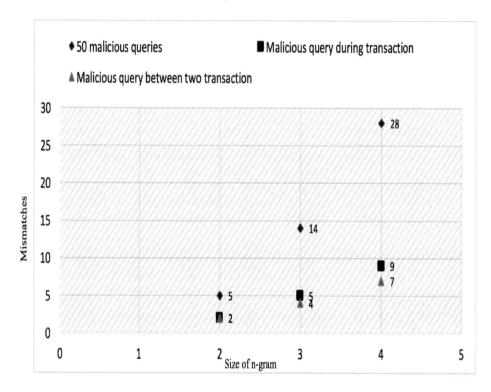

as expected. False positives are eventually being dealt with in a feedback loop after it is discovered. A n-grams that triggered false positive are added to normal profile. The reader is reminded that in using a synthetic data-set our characterization of normal behavior, though constrained by the shape of the transactions, is effectively random. From Figure 6 one can also extrapolate that any increase in the size of audit log with small length of n-gram will result in small variations in number of new n-grams beyond a certain point. This point is called point of saturation.

The proposed approach is white-box as it enables a security officer to inspect the sequence of SQL query abstractions that corresponds to SQL queries thus allowing a security officer to understand why this is an anomaly. For example, if an alarm is raised due to a contiguous sequence of SQL SELECT queries, then the security officer is able to inspect and infer why this sequence is labeled as an anomaly. The security officer also can check individually which records are being queries.

Anomaly Response

In the proposed work, mismatches are an indication of an anomaly and triggers an alert signal. Response to an alert signal can vary depending on the environment, in a sensitive environment like banking or military database systems, then intuitively an immediate response will be to stop the response of an anomalous query. In case of a more relaxed environment, a query can simply be labeled as anomalous and can be logged for later manual inspection by an information security officer or database administrator. Another way of dealing with a malicious query is to respond it with some noise; for example, this can be done by adding some extra values in returned data.

Use Cases

1. A well reputed international bank offers internship opportunity for university students. University students having a high sense of curiosity browsed through records of several clients. If the proposed n-gram approach was in place, any activity of this nature would be labeled as anomalous.
2. A similar use-case is in the medical domain, similar to real world privacy breaches reported in (Carr, 2008; Report, 2007). When hospital staff browse through records of a celebrity, using proposed n-gram based model is in place, these activities will be detected as anomalous.
3. A third use-case is when existing security mechanisms goes down, while proposed n-gram mechanism is in place. The proposed model is able to detect malicious accesses to DBMS while traditional security mechanism is down thus complementing existing mechanisms.

Scaling Up the N-Gram Model

There are two aspects of scaling up the n-gram model. The first aspect is of applicability of proposed n-grams-based on other data models, besides relational model, for instance deductive databases and object-oriented databases. The second aspect is the potential of the proposed approach to scale up when it comes to bigdata, this is an open question for our future work.

The proposed n-gram model basically considers abstraction of SQL queries (sequences of SQL query abstraction). Thus, in case of extending this model to object oriented databases (Elmasri & Navathe 2017), statements of Object Query Language (OQL) are the input to the proposed model. However, the main challenge is of discovering the right level of abstraction for OQL statements. The other case is of deductive databases (Elmasri & Navathe 2017). Deductive databases deal with

Figure 6. Discovered number of n-grams when comparing profiles. The zeros on the x-axis shows the comparison of normal profile with itself. The orange line shows the comparison between the baseline normal profile and test profile.

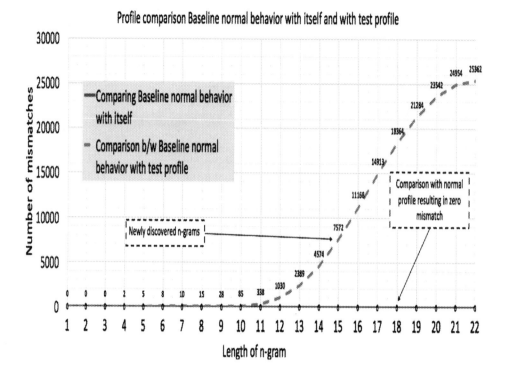

fact and rules while using datalog. In our future work, we plan to further investigate if the n-gram model has the potential to be translated for deductive databases. Additionally, a probe is desired to find a right level of abstraction for Object Query Language (OQL) statements along with the study on how the n-gram model evolves for object oriented databases.

CHALLENGES

In this section, an attempt is made to briefly present challenges that research community faces in this domain of research. Studies focused on these challenges are desirable to further the research on database intrusion detection systems.

Semantic-Centric Anomaly Detection Systems

Most proposed anomaly detection systems consider syntactic features to generate behavioral profiles. However, syntactically, a query can be written in many different ways. A much more effective approach will be to capture semantics in order to generate behavioral profiles. Thus, a semantic-based approach in generation of behavioral profiles is desirable.

Similarity Index for SQL Statements

How do one best compare two queries or query signatures? Should one consider semantics or just syntax? Is an exact match required or is an approximation sufficient? Answers to these questions are desirable. The literature lacks a query similarity index that measures how close two queries are syntactically as well as semantically.

Metrics to Measure Effectiveness

One of the challenges is of unavailability of standard metrics to measure the effectiveness of anomaly detection mechanisms. The availability of standard metrics will enable comparison of these mechanisms with each other.

Unavailability of Real-World Data-Sets

Real-world data-sets for the purpose of evaluation are not publicly available because an organization's data is considered to be sensitive in nature. Most of the existing mechanisms are evaluated on synthetic data-sets. Few existing mechanisms have used real-world data-set for evaluation of their models (Costante et al., 2016; Kul et al., 2016; Mathew et al., 2010). Another aspect of this challenge is the unavailability of standard data-sets.

Privacy Concerns

Modeling the insider's behavior requires that the activities of insiders must be logged. Privacy concerns are often raised by insiders; thus, a solution is desirable that considers privacy of an insider while modeling their behavior.

Explaining Anomalies

Up-till now, the majority of anomaly-based intrusion detection systems can be characterized as a black-box, in other words, a human may not be able to comprehend why the system labeled something as an anomaly. Explaining anomalies is just not a challenge within the context of database intrusion detection but it is a challenge in general in anomaly detection domain. In order to generate explanations for anomalies, systems that acts as white-box are desirable which will enable humans to easily comprehend why the anomaly arose and subsequently generate an explanation for that anomaly.

Application Specific Tuning

The combination of multiple context, syntax, data/result- centric features captures a much richer model of normative behavior. However, tuning profiles constructed based on these features is desirable with respect to the application. For instance, in the scenario of banking system, it is known that the bank entertains their clients until 5:00 PM, thus any query made after 5:00 PM that falls within the role of a bank teller is marked as an anomaly. Similarly, a limit is imposed on the amount of data returned by a query depending on the environment where the IDS is deployed. For example, in a banking system, the data returned in response to a bank teller's query usually involves very few records, thus if the number of records returned is exceeded then this deviation is considered an anomaly. However, in the scenario of a medical research where the amount of data returned in response of a query can be several hundreds of records, a different limit to the returned data is applicable.

CONCLUSION AND FUTURE WORK

To date, a considerable amount of development has been seen in terms of anomaly-based approaches to detecting insider attacks. In this book chapter, a taxonomy of anomaly-based intrusion detection systems is presented that will help in furthering research in this domain. Along with the taxonomy, a mechanism to detect insider threats was proposed whereby n-grams were used to construct a model for normative behavior for insiders which is extracted from logs of DBMS queries. Experiments were presented to judge the effectiveness of using an n-gram based scheme to detect query anomalies in DBMS logs and thereby identify insider attacks.

While limited to a synthetic application, the experiments show that it is possible to build a useful query abstraction and that n-grams of these queries can capture the short-term correlations inherent in the application. This book chapter also outlined the challenges faced by the research community in this domain of research.

The future work is to investigate other query abstractions along with an investigation into anomaly-based intrusion detection systems that explains anomalies. We also plan to further evaluate the approach using non-synthetic data-sets. We also plan to investigate the idea of scaling the proposed approach in current age of big data. Additionally, we plan to explore the fitness of proposed model for object oriented databases and deductive databases.

ACKNOWLEDGMENT

This work was supported, in part, by Science Foundation Ireland under grant SFI/12/RC/2289 which is co-funded under the European Regional Development Fund.

REFERENCES

Abed, A. S., Clancy, T. C., & Levy, D. S. (2015). Applying bag of system calls for anomalous behavior detection of applications in linux containers. In 2015 IEEE Globecom Workshops (p. 1-5). IEEE. doi:10.1109/GLOCOMW.2015.7414047

Agrawal, R., Imieliński, T., & Swami, A. (1993, June). Mining association rules between sets of items in large databases. *SIGMOD Rec., 22*(2), 207–216. doi:10.1145/170036.170072

Australian Government. F. R. o. L. (2017). *Privacy amendment (notifiable data breaches) act 2017*. Retrieved from https://www.legislation.gov.au/ Details/C2017A00012

Barry, B. I. A., & Chan, H. A. (2010). Intrusion detection systems. In P. Stavroulakis & M. Stamp (Eds.), Handbook of information and communication security (pp. 193–205). Berlin: Springer. doi:10.1007/978-3-642-04117-4_10

Bertino, E., Bettini, C., Ferrari, E., & Samarati, P. (1996, February). A temporal access control mechanism for database systems. *IEEE Transactions on Knowledge and Data Engineering, 8*(1), 67–80. doi:10.1109/69.485637

Bishop, C. M. (2006). *Pattern recognition and machine learning*. New York: Springer.

Bishop, M., & Gates, C. (2008). Defining the insider threat. In *Proceedings of the 4th annual workshop on cyber security and information intelligence research: Developing strategies to meet the cyber security and information intelligence challenges ahead* (pp. 15:1–15:3). New York: ACM. Retrieved from http://doi.acm. org/10.1145/1413140.1413158

Brenner, B. (2017). *Healthcare data breaches 'mostly caused by insiders'.* Retrieved 23-02-2017, from https://nakedsecurity.sophos.com/2017/ 02/23/healthcare-data-breaches-mostly-caused-by-insiders/

Carr, J. (2008). *Breach of Britney spears patient data reported, sc magazine for it security professionals.* Retrieved from https://www.scmagazine.com/ breach-of-britney-spears-patient-data-reported/article/ 554340/

CERT. (2004). *E-crime watch survey.* Retrieved from https://resources.sei .cmu. edu/asset_files/WhitePaper/2004_019_001_53391.pdf

CERT. (2014). *Us state of cybercrime survey.* Retrieved from https://resources.sei. cmu.edu/asset_files/Presentation/ 2014_017_001_298322.pdf

Chari, S. N., & Cheng, P.-C. (2003, May). Bluebox: A policy-driven, host-based intrusion detection system. *ACM Transactions on Information and System Security, 6*(2), 173–200. doi:10.1145/762476.762477

Chung, C. J., Khatkar, P., Xing, T., Lee, J., & Huang, D. (2013, July). Nice: Network intrusion detection and countermeasure selection in virtual net-work systems. *IEEE Transactions on Dependable and Secure Computing, 10*(4), 198–211. doi:10.1109/ TDSC.2013.8

Chung, C. Y., Gertz, M., & Levitt, K. (2000). Integrity and internal control information systems. Norwell, MA: Kluwer Academic Publishers. Retrieved from http://dl.acm. org/citation.cfm?id=342030.342078

2015. Cost of Cybercrime: Global (Tech. Rep.). (2015). Ponemon Institute.

Costante, E., den Hartog, J., Petkovic, M., Etalle, S., & Pechenizkiy, M. (2016). A white-box anomaly-based framework for database leakage detection. *Journal of Information Security and Applications.* Retrieved from http://www.sciencedirect. com/science/article/pii/S2214212616302629

Creech, G., & Hu, J. (2014, April). A semantic approach to host-based intrusion detection systems using contiguousand discontiguous system call patterns. *IEEE Transactions on Computers, 63*(4), 807–819. doi:10.1109/TC.2013.13

Elmasri, R., & Navathe, S. (2017). *Fundamentals of database systems*. 1272 Seiten: S.n.

Fisher, D. H. (1987). *Knowledge acquisition via incremental conceptual clustering*. Academic Press.

Forrest, S., Hofmeyr, S., & Somayaji, A. (2008, Dec). The evolution of system-call monitoring. In *2008 annual computer security applications conference (acsac)* (p. 418-430). Academic Press. 10.1109/ACSAC.2008.54

Forrest, S., Hofmeyr, S. A., Somayaji, A., & Longstaff, T. A. (1996, May). A sense of self for unix processes. In *Proceedings 1996 ieee symposium on security and privacy* (p. 120-128). IEEE. 10.1109/SECPRI.1996.502675

Gafny, M., Shabtai, A., Rokach, L., & Elovici, Y. (2011). Poster: Applying unsupervised context-based analysis for detecting unauthorized data disclosure. In *Proceedings of the 18th acm conference on computer and communications security* (pp. 765–768). New York, NY: ACM. doi:10.1145/2046707.2093488

Gennari, J. H., Langley, P., & Fisher, D. (1989). *Models of Incremental Concept Formation. Ft. Belvoir*. Defense Technical Information Center.

Grand theft data data exfiltration study: Actors, tactics, and detection (Tech.Rep.). (2015). Intel security and McAfee.

Hofmeyr, S. A., Forrest, S., & Somayaji, A. (1998, August). Intrusion detection using sequences of system calls. *J. Comput. Secur., 6*(3), 151–180. Retrieved from http://dl.acm.org/citation.cfm?id=1298081.1298084

Hunker, J., & Probst, C. W. (2011). Insiders and insider threats An overview of definitions and mitigation techniques. *Journal of Wireless Mobile Networks, Ubiquitous Computing and Dependable Applications*, 4–27.

Hussain, S. R., Sallam, A. M., & Bertino, E. (2015). Detanom:detecting anomalous database transactions by insiders. In Proc. 5th ACM codaspy (p. 25-35). San Antonio, TX: ACM.

Insider threat report, insider threat security statistics, vormetric (Tech. Rep.). (2015). Vormetric.

ISACA. (2016). *Isaca survey: 63% of it professionals are against governments having backdoor access to encrypted information systems*. Retrieved from www.isaca.org/About-ISACA/Press-room/ News-Releases/2016/Pages/ISACA-Cybersecurity-Snapshot-Survey.aspx

Jajodia, S., Samarati, P., Sapino, M. L., & Subrahmanian, V. S. (2001, June). Flexible support for multiple access control policies. *ACM Trans. Database Syst., 26*(2), 214–260. Retrieved from http://doi.acm.org/10.1145/383891.383894

Jamrozik, K., von Styp-Rekowsky, P., & Zeller, A. (2016, May). Mining sand-boxes. In *2016 ieee/acm 38th international conference on software engi-neering (icse)* (pp. 37-48). IEEE. doi: 10.1145/2884781.2884782

Kamra, A., Terzi, E., & Bertino, E. (2008, August). Detecting anomalous access patterns in relational databases. *The VLDB Journal, 17*(5), 1063–1077. doi: 10.100700778-007-0051-4

Kemmerer, R. A., & Vigna, G. (2002, April). Intrusion detection: A brief history and overview. *Computer, 35*(4), 27–30. doi:10.1109/MC.2002.1012428

Khan, M. I., & Foley, S. N. (2016). Detecting anomalous behavior in dbms logs. In International conference on risks and security of internet and systems (crisis2016). Roscoff, France: Academic Press.

Kul, G., Luong, D., Xie, T., Coonan, P., Chandola, V., Kennedy, O., & Upadhyaya, S. (2016). Ettu: Analyzing query intents in corporate databases. In *Proceedings of the 25th international conference companion on world wide web* (pp. 463–466). Geneva, Switzerland: International World Wide Web Conferences Steering Committee. 10.1145/2872518.2888608

Kumar, S., & Spafford, E. H. (1994). A pattern matching model for misuse in-trusion detection. *Proceedings of the 17th national computer security conference*, 11–21.

Laszka, A., Abbas, W., Sastry, S. S., Vorobeychik, Y., & Koutsoukos, X. (2016). Optimal thresholds for intrusion detection systems. In *Proceedings of the symposium and bootcamp on the science of security* (pp. 72–81). New York, NY: ACM. Retrieved from http://doi.acm.org/10.1145/2898375.2898399

Lee, S. Y., Low, W. L., & Wong, P. Y. (2002). Learning fingerprints for a database intrusion detection system. In *Proceedings of the 7th European symposium on research in computer security* (pp. 264–280). London: Springer-Verlag. doi:10.1007/3-540-45853-0_16

Liao, H.-J., Richard Lin, C.-H., Lin, Y.-C., & Tung, K.-Y. (2013, January). Review: Intrusion detection system: A comprehensive review. *Journal of Network and Computer Applications, 36*(1), 16–24. doi:10.1016/j.jnca.2012.09.004

Low, W. L., Lee, J., & Teoh, P. (2002). Didafit: Detecting intrusions in databases through fingerprinting transactions. In ICEIS (pp. 121–128). Academic Press.

Majumdar, R., & Sen, K. (2007, May). Hybrid concolic testing. In *29th international conference on software engineering (icse'07)* (p. 416-426). Academic Press. 10.1109/ICSE.2007.41

Mathew, S., Petropoulos, M., Ngo, H. Q., & Upadhyaya, S. (2010). A data-centric approach to insider attack detection in database systems. In *Proceedings of the 13th international conference on recent advances in intrusion detection* (pp. 382–401). Berlin: Springer-Verlag. doi:10.1007/978-3-642-15512-3_20

Mukkamala, S., Janoski, G., & Sung, A. (2002). Intrusion detection using neural networks and support vector machines. In Neural networks, 2002. ijcnn '02. proceedings of the 2002 international joint conference on (Vol. 2, p. 1702-1707). Academic Press. doi:10.1109/IJCNN.2002.1007774

Ning, P., & Jajodia, S. (2004). Intrusion detection techniques. In *The internet encyclopedia*. John Wiley & Sons, Inc.; doi:10.1002/047148296X.tie097

Patzakis, J. (2003). *New incident response best practices: Patch and proceed is no longer acceptable incident response, vormetric (Tech. Rep.).* Guidance Software.

Pieczul, O., & Foley, S. N. (2013, Oct). Discovering emergent norms in security logs. In *2013 IEEE conference on communications and network security (cns)* (p. 438-445). IEEE. doi: 10.1109/CNS.2013.6682758

Pieczul, O., & Foley, S. N. (2016). Runtime detection of zero-day vulnerability exploits in contemporary software systems. In S. Ranise & V. Swarup (Eds.), *Data and applications security and privacy xxx: 30th annual ifip wg 11.3 conference, dbsec 2016, trento, italy, july 18-20, 2016. proceedings* (pp. 347–363). Cham: Springer International Publishing. 10.1007/978-3-319-41483-6_24

Predd, J., Pfleeger, S. L., Hunker, J., & Bulford, C. (2008, July). Insiders behaving badly. *IEEE Security Privacy, 6*(4), 66-70. doi: .2008.8710.1109/MSP

Probst, C. W., Hunker, J., Bishop, M., & Gollmann, D. (2008). *08302 summary - countering insider threats. In Countering insider threats, 20.07. - 25.07.2008.* Retrieved from http://drops.dagstuhl.de/opus/ volltexte/2008/1793/

Report, C. (2007). *27 suspended for Clooney file peek.* Retrieved from http://edition. cnn .com/2007/SHOWBIZ/10/10/clooney.records/index.html?eref=ew

Sallam, A., Bertino, E., Hussain, S. R., Landers, D., Lefler, R. M., & Steiner, D. (2015). Dbsafe:an anomaly detection system to protect databases from exfiltration attempts. *IEEE Systems Journal.* doi:10.1109/JSYST.2015.2487221

Sallam, A., Fadolalkarim, D., Bertino, E., & Xiao, Q. (2016). Data and syntax centric anomaly detection for relational databases. *Wiley Interdisciplinary Reviews: Data Mining and Knowledge Discovery, 6*(6), 231–239. doi: 10.1002/widm.1195

Sen, K. (2007). Concolic testing. In *Proceedings of the twenty-second ieee/acm international conference on automated software engineering* (pp. 571–572). New York, NY: ACM. doi:10.1145/1321631.1321746

Sen, K., Marinov, D., & Agha, G. (2005). Cute: A concolic unit testing engine for c. In *Proceedings of the 10th European software engineering conference held jointly with 13th acm sigsoft international symposium on foundations of software engineering* (pp. 263–272). New York, NY: ACM. doi:10.1145/1081706.1081750

Union, E. (2016). *General data protection regulation.* eur-lex: Eu law. Retrieved from http://eur-lex.europa.eu/legal-content/EN/ ALL/?uri=CELEX:32016R06792

Valeur, F., Mutz, D., & Vigna, G. (2005). A Learning-Based Approach to the Detection of SQL Attacks. Detection of Intrusions and Malware, and Vulnerability Assessment Lecture Notes in Computer Science, 123-140. doi:10.1007/11506881_8

Verizon. (2016). *Data breach investigations report* (Tech. Rep.). Verizon.

Wressnegger, C. (2013). A close look on n-Grams in intrusion detection. *Proceedings of the 2013 ACM Workshop on Artificial intelligence and security - AISec 13.* doi:10.1145/2517312.2517316

Wu, G. Z., Osborn, S. L., & Jin, X. (2009). Database intrusion detection using role profiling with role hierarchy. In W. Jonker & M. Petković (Eds.), *Secure data management: 6th vldb workshop, sdm 2009, lyon, france, august 28, 2009. proceedings* (pp. 33–48). Berlin: Springer Berlin Heidelberg. 10.1007/978-3-642-04219-5_3

Compilation of References

2015. Cost of Cybercrime: Global (Tech. Rep.). (2015). Ponemon Institute.

AbdAllah, E. G., Hassanein, H. S., & Zulkernine, M. (2015). A survey of security attacks in information-centric networking. *IEEE Communications Surveys and Tutorials*, *17*(3), 1441–1454. doi:10.1109/COMST.2015.2392629

Abdullahi, I., Arif, S., & Hassan, S. (2015). Survey on caching approaches in information centric networking. *Journal of Network and Computer Applications*, *56*, 48–59. doi:10.1016/j.jnca.2015.06.011

Abed, A. S., Clancy, T. C., & Levy, D. S. (2015). Applying bag of system calls for anomalous behavior detection of applications in linux containers. In 2015 IEEE Globecom Workshops (p. 1-5). IEEE. doi:10.1109/GLOCOMW.2015.7414047

Accenture. (2017a). *Building Confidence: Facing the Cybersecurity Conundrum in Singapore*. Retrieved November 18, 2017, from https://www.accenture.com/t20170406T010037Z__w__/sg-en/_acnmedia/PDF-38/Accenture-Facing-Cybersecurity-Conundrum-Singapore.pdf

Accenture. (2017b). *Accenture Survey: One in Four Cyberattacks in Singapore Result in a Security Breach, Yet Most Organisations Remain Confident in Their Ability to Protect Themselves*. Retrieved November 18, 2017, from https://www.accenture.com/sg-en/company-newsroom-accenture-survey-one-four-cyberattacks

Action Aid. (2015). *Corruption and Poverty in Nigeria: A Report*. Abuja, Nigeria: Action Aid.

Adepetun, A. (2016, November 9). Is cybercrime proving difficult to tackle? *The Guardian*, p. 36.

Adeyemo, A. B. (2011). E-government Implementation in Nigeria: An Assessment of Nigeria's Global e-governance Ranking. *Journal of Internet and Information System*, *2*(1), 11–19.

Adogame, A. (2007). *The 419 code as business unusual: Youth and the unfolding of the advance fee fraud online discourse*. International Sociology Association. Retrieved from http://www.isa-sociology.org/publ/e-bulletin/E-bulletin7.pdf

Afanasyev, A. (2013). *Addressing Operational Challenges in Named Data Networking Through NDNS Distributed Database* (PhD thesis). University of California, Los Angeles, CA.

Agrawal, R., Imieliński, T., & Swami, A. (1993, June). Mining association rules between sets of items in large databases. *SIGMOD Rec., 22*(2), 207–216. doi: 10.1145/170036.170072

Agrawal, S., Sethi, P., & Mittal, M. (2015). E-Governance: An Analysis of Citizens' Perception. *IUP Journal of Information Technology, 11*(3), 34.

Aides, A., & Di Tella, R. (1999). Rents, Competition, and Corruption. *American Economic Review, 89*(4), 982-993. 10.1257/aer.89.4.982

Aidt, T. S. (2003). Economic Analysis of Corruption: A Survey. *Economics Journal, 113*, 632-652. 10.1046/j.0013-0133.2003.00171.x

Ajanaku, L. (2017, October 31). Why phishing attacks remain effective. *Nation (New York, N.Y.)*, 13.

Ajie, H. A. & Wokekoro, O. E. (2012). The Impact of Corruption on Sustainable Economic Growth and Development in Nigeria. *International Journal of Economic Development Research and Investment, 3*(1), 91-109.

Akdeniz, Y. (2008). *Internet child pornography and the law: National and international responses*. Farnham, UK: Ashgate Publishing Limited.

Akpome, A. (2015). What is Nigeria? unsettling the myth of exceptionalism. *Africa Spectrum, 50*(1), 65–78.

Albesher, A. S., & Stone, R. T. (2016). Current state of m-government research: Identifying future research opportunities. *International Journal of Electronic Governance, 8*(2), 1–10. doi:10.1504/IJEG.2016.078118

Almuraqab, N. A. S., & Jasimuddin, S. J. (2017). Factors that Influence End-Users' Adoption of Smart Government Services in the UAE: A Conceptual Framework. *Electronic Journal of Information Systems Evaluation, 20*(1), 11–23.

Al-Rodhan, N. R. F. (2011). *The Politics of Emerging Strategic Technologies: Implications for Geopolitics, Human Enhancement and Human Destiny*. London: Palgrave Macmillan. doi:10.1057/9780230304949

Al-Thunibat A, Zin N, Sahari N. (2011). Identifying User Requirements of Mobile Government Services in Malaysia Using Focus Group Methodology. *Journal of E-Government Studies and Best Practice*, 1–14.

Andersen, T., & Rand, J. (2006). *Does E-Government Reduce Corruption*. University of Copenhagen, Department of Economics, Working Paper.

Anderson, T. B. (2009). E-government as an Anti-Corruption Strategy. *Information Economics and Policy, 21*(3), 201–210. doi:10.1016/j.infoecopol.2008.11.003

Andreasen, A. (1994). Social marketing: Its definition and domain. *Journal of Public Policy & Marketing, 13*(1), 108–114.

Apvrille, L., & Roudier, Y. (2014). Towards the model-driven engineering of secure yet safe embedded systems. *1st International Workshop on Graphical Models for Security.* 10.4204/EPTCS.148.2

Arena, R., Guazzi, M., & Mianov, L. (2015). Healthy lifestyle interventions to combat non-communicable disease. *European Heart Journal*, 2097–2109. doi:10.1093/eurheartj/ehv207 PMID:26524498

Armando, A., Carbone, R., Compagna, L., Li, K., & Pellegrino, G. (2010). Model-Checking Driven Security Testing of Web-Based Applications. In *Proceedings of the 2010 Third International Conference on Software Testing, Verification, and Validation Workshops, ICSTW'10.* IEEE Computer Society Press. 10.1109/ICSTW.2010.54

Arzapalo, D., Gallon, L., & Aniorte, P. (2013). *MoDELO: a MOdel-Driven sEcurity poLicy approach based on Orbac. In 8ème conférence sur la Sécurité des Architectures Réseaux et des Systèmes d'Information.* Mont de Marsan.

Atun, J., Jaffar, S., Nishtar, S., Knaul, F. M., Barreto, M. L., Nyirenda, M., ... Piot, P. (2013). Improving responsiveness of health systems to non-communicable diseases. *Lancet*, *381*(9867), 690–697. doi:10.1016/S0140-6736(13)60063-X PMID:23410609

Australian Government. F. R. o. L. (2017). *Privacy amendment (notifiable data breaches) act 2017.* Retrieved from https://www.legislation.gov.au/ Details/C2017A00012

Avdic, D., Avdic, A., Spalević, Z., Marovac, U., & Crnisanin, A. (2014). M-government Application Intended to Search Documents Written in Serbian Language. *Journal of Applied Sciences (Faisalabad)*, 902–906.

Awan, O. (2015). Bringing citizens closer to government: Is there a role for m-governance in Pakistan? *Commonwealth Governance Handbook*, *2013*(14), 87–90.

Azeez, K. (2013, August 15). Concerns mount over poor cyber security. *National Mirror*, p. 35.

Bagui, L., Sigwejo, A., & Bytheway, A. (2011). Public participation in government: assessing m-Participation in South Africa and Tanzania. In A. Koch, & P. A. van Brakel (Ed.), *Proceedings of the 13th Annual Conference on World Wide Web Applications* (pp. 5-26). Johannesburg: Cape Peninsula University of Technology.

Banerjee, A., Duflo, E., Imbert, C., Mathew, S., & Pande, R. (2016). *E-governance, Accountability, and Leakage in Public Programs: Experimental Evidence from a Financial Management Reform in India (No. w22803).* National Bureau of Economic Research India. doi:10.3386/w22803

Bari, M., Rahman Chowdhury, S., Ahmed, R., Boutaba, R., & Mathieu, B. (2012). A survey of naming and routing in information-centric networks. *Communications Magazine, IEEE*, *50*(12), 44–53. doi:10.1109/MCOM.2012.6384450

Barry, B. I. A., & Chan, H. A. (2010). Intrusion detection systems. In P. Stavroulakis & M. Stamp (Eds.), Handbook of information and communication security (pp. 193–205). Berlin: Springer. doi:10.1007/978-3-642-04117-4_10

Basu, S. (2004). E-governance and Developing Countries: An Overview. *International Review of Law Computers*, *18*(1).

Bayo-Moriones, A., Billon, M., & Lera-Lopez, F. (2013). Perceived performance effects of ICT in manufacturing SMEs. *Industrial Management & Data Systems*, *113*(1), 117–135. doi:10.1108/02635571311289700

Bayuk, J. L., Healey, J., Rohmeyer, P., Sachs, M. H., Schmidt, J., & Weiss, J. (2012). *Cyber Security Policy Guidebook*. Hoboken, NJ: Wiley. doi:10.1002/9781118241530

Belanger, F., & Jannie, S. H. (2006). A framework for e-government: Privacy implications. *Business Process Management Journal*, *12*(1), 48–60. doi:10.1108/14637150610643751

Bertino, E., Bettini, C., Ferrari, E., & Samarati, P. (1996, February). A temporal access control mechanism for database systems. *IEEE Transactions on Knowledge and Data Engineering*, *8*(1), 67–80. doi:10.1109/69.485637

Bertolino, A., Inverardi, P., & Muccini, H. (2001). An Explorative Journey from Architectural Tests Definition down to Code Tests Execution. In *Software Engineering, 23rd International Conference on Software Engineering (ICSE'01)*. IEEE Computer Society Press.

Bertot, J., Jaeger, P., & Grimes, J. (2010). Using ICT to Create A Culture of Transparency: E-Government and Social Media as Openness and Anti-Corruption Tools for Societies. *Government Information Quarterly*, *27*(3), 264–271. doi:10.1016/j.giq.2010.03.001

Bhargava, V., & Bolongaita, E. (2004). *Challenging Corruption in Asia: Case Studies and A Framework for Action*. The International Bank for Reconstruction and Development/ The World Bank. Working Paper No. 27580.

Bhatnagar, S. (2003). E-government and Access to Information. In R. Hodess, T. Inowlocki, T. Wolfe, & T. International (Eds.), Global Corruption Report 2003, (pp. 24-32). Academic Press.

Bhunia, P. (2017a). *Public-Private Alliance Launched by Singapore Police Cybercrime Command*. Retrieved November 6, 2017, from http://opengovasia.com/articles/7778-public-private-alliance-launched-by-singapore-police-cybercrime-command

Bhunia, P. (2017b). *Singapore Enters into Seventh Bilateral Agreement on Cybersecurity Cooperation*. Retrieved November 13, 2017, from http://opengovasia.com/articles/7785-singapore-enters-into-seventh-bilateral-agreement-on-cybersecurity-cooperation

Bhunia, P. (2017c). *New Steps from Singapore Government to Build Cybersecurity Capabilities in Singapore and ASEAN Region in Collaboration with Industry*. Retrieved November 13, 2017, from http://opengovasia.com/articles/8020-new-steps-from-singapore-government-to-build-cybersecurity-capabilities-in-singapore-and-asean-region-in-collaboration-with-industry

Bian, C., Zhu, Z., Afanasyev, A., Uzun, E., and Zhang, L. (2013). *Deploying key management on ndn testbed*. UCLA, Peking University and PARC, Tech.Rep.

Compilation of References

Bishop, M., & Gates, C. (2008). Defining the insider threat. In *Proceedings of the 4th annual workshop on cyber security and information intelligence research: Developing strategies to meet the cyber security and information intelligence challenges ahead* (pp. 15:1–15:3). New York: ACM. Retrieved from http://doi.acm.org/10.1145/1413140.1413158

Bishop, C. M. (2006). *Pattern recognition and machine learning.* New York: Springer.

BMG Rights Mgmt LLC v. Cox Communications Inc. (4th Cir. 2018)

Boyd, D., & Ellison, B. (2008). Social network sites: Definition, history, and scholarship. *Computer Medicine Communication, 13*(1), 210–230. doi:10.1111/j.1083-6101.2007.00393.x

Brannen, A. (2001). E-governance in California: Providing Services to Citizens through the Internet. *Spectrum (Lexington, Ky.), 74*(2).

Brenner, B. (2017). *Healthcare data breaches 'mostly caused by insiders'.* Retrieved 23-02-2017, from https://nakedsecurity.sophos.com/2017/ 02/23/healthcare-data-breaches-mostly-caused-by-insiders/

Brooks R. (2000). *The basics of social marketing: how to use marketing change behaviours.* University of Washington.

Brown, D. (2005). Electronic government and public administration. *International Review of Administrative Sciences, 71*(2), 241–254. doi:10.1177/0020852305053883

Brun, M., Delatour, J., & Trinquet, Y. (2008). Code Generation from AADL to a Real-Time Operating System: An Experimentation Feedback on the Use of Model Transformation. In *Proceedings of the 13th IEEE International Conference on on Engineering of Complex Computer Systems (ICECCS '08).* IEEE Computer Society.

Bucchiarone, Muccini, & Pelliccione. (2007). Architecting Fault-tolerant Component-based Systems: From requirements to testing. In *Electronic Notes in Theoretical Computer Science.* Elsevier.

Burke, J., Horn, A., & Marianantoni, A. (2012). *Authenticated lighting control using named data networking.* UCLA, NDN Technical Report NDN-0011.

Caba, C., Lopez, A. M., & Rodriguez, M. P. (2005). Citizen's access to on-line governmental financial information: Practices in the European Union Countries. *Government Information Quarterly, 22*(2), 258-276. 10.1016/j.giq.2005.02.002

Capitol Records, LLC, et al. v. Vimeo, LLC (2d Cir. June 16, 2016)

Capurro, D., Cole, K., Echavarria, M., Joe, J., Neogi, T., & Turner, A. M. (2014). The Use of Social Networking Sites for Public Health Practice and Research: A Systematic Review. *Journal of Medical Internet Research, 16*(3), e79. doi:10.2196/jmir.2679 PMID:24642014

Carr, J. (2008). *Breach of Britney spears patient data reported, sc magazine for it security professionals.* Retrieved from https://www.scmagazine.com/ breach-of-britney-spears-patient-data-reported/article/ 554340/

Carroll, J. (2006). 'What's in It for Me?': Taking M-Government to the People. Paper presented at the 19th Bled eConference eValue, Bled, Slovenia.

Cashshield. (2017). *A Pact Against CyberCrime: CashShield and the Singapore Police Force Join Forces to Secure the Digital World.* Retrieved November 6, 2017, from http://www.cashshield.com/a-pact-against-cybercrime-cashshield-and-the-singapore-police-force-join-forces-to-secure-the-digital-world/

Castanet, R., & Rouillard, R. (2002). Generate Certified Test Cases by Combining Theorem Proving and Reachability Analysis. *Proceedings of the IFIP 14th International Conference on Testing Communicating Systems.* 10.1007/978-0-387-35497-2_19

CBC News. (2002, March 26). *Sharpe not guilty of possessing written child pornography.* CBC News.

CERT. (2004). *E-crime watch survey.* Retrieved from https://resources.sei .cmu.edu/asset_files/ WhitePaper/2004_019_001_53391.pdf

CERT. (2014). *Us state of cybercrime survey.* Retrieved from https://resources.sei.cmu.edu/ asset_files/Presentation/ 2014_017_001_298322.pdf

Chang, W. (2013). *Amendments to Singapore's Computer Misuse Act.* Retrieved November 4, 2017, from http://www.cnplaw.com/en/media/files/services/EFPLP.pdf

Channel NewAsia. (2015, May 11). *Cyber Security Agency, IDA Maintain High Level of Vigilance over Govt Networks: Yaacob.* Retrieved October 26, 2017, from http://www.channelnewsasia.com/news/singapore/cyber-security-agency-ida-maintain-high-level-of-vigilance-over--8264556

Channel NewAsia. (2016, April 11). *New Cybersecurity Act to be Tabled in 2017: Yaacob Ibrahim.* Retrieved November 18, 2017, from http://www.channelnewsasia.com/news/singapore/new-cybersecurity-act-to-be-tabled-in-2017-yaacob-ibrahim-8088054

Channel NewsAsia. (2017, May 14). *Tiong Bahru Plaza's Digital Directory Hit by Global Ransomware Attack: Mall Operator.* Retrieved October 30, 2017, from http://www.channelnewsasia.com/news/singapore/tiong-bahru-plaza-s-digital-directory-hit-by-global-ransomware-8846096

Chari, S. N., & Cheng, P.-C. (2003, May). Bluebox: A policy-driven, host-based intrusion detection system. *ACM Transactions on Information and System Security, 6*(2), 173–200. doi:10.1145/762476.762477

Chatfield, A. T. (2009). Public Service Reform through e-Government: A Case Study of e-Tax in Japan. *Electronic Journal of E-Government, 7*(2).

Chawki, M., Darwish, A., Khan, M. A., & Iyagi, S. (2015b). 419 scam: An evaluation of cybercrime and criminal code in Nigeria. In *Cybercrime, Digital Forensics and Jurisdiction. Studies in Computational Intelligence* (Vol. 593). New York: Springer, Cham. doi:10.1007/978-3-319-15150-2_9

Chen, M., Mishra, P., & Kalita, D. (2008). Coverage-driven automatic test generation for uml activity diagrams. In *Proceedings of the 18th ACM Great Lakes symposium on VLSI (GLSVLSI '08)*. ACM 10.1145/1366110.1366145

Chou, W. Y., Hunt, Y. M., Beckjord, E. B., Moser, R. P., & Hesse, B. W. (2009). Social media use in the United States: Implications for health communication. *Journal of Medical Internet Research, 11*(4), e48. doi:10.2196/jmir.1249 PMID:19945947

Christou, G., & Simpson, S. (2009). New Governance: the Internet, and Country Code Top-Level Domains in Europe. *Governance: an International Journal of Policy, Administration and Institutions, 22*(4), 599-624. 10.1111/j.1468-0491.2009.01455.x

Chung, C. J., Khatkar, P., Xing, T., Lee, J., & Huang, D. (2013, July). Nice: Network intrusion detection and countermeasure selection in virtual net-work systems. *IEEE Transactions on Dependable and Secure Computing, 10*(4), 198–211. doi:10.1109/TDSC.2013.8

Chung, C. Y., Gertz, M., & Levitt, K. (2000). Integrity and internal control information systems. Norwell, MA: Kluwer Academic Publishers. Retrieved from http://dl.acm.org/citation.cfm?id=342030.342078

Cichos, O., Lochau, & Schürr. (2011). Model-based coverage-driven test suite generation for software product lines. *Proceedings of the 14th international conference on Model driven engineering languages and systems (MODELS'11)*.

Clark. (2007). Illegal downloads: sharing out online liability: sharing files, sharing risks. *Journal of Intellectual Property Law & Practice, 2*, 402-409.

Clark, J. A., & Tsiaparas, A. (2002). Bandwidth-On-Demand Networks - A Solution to Peer-To-Peer File Sharing. *BT Technology Journal, 20*(1), 53–55. doi:10.1023/A:1014518008964

CNN.com. (2003, November 11). *Singapore Clamps Down on Hackers*. Retrieved November 4, 2017, from http://edition.cnn.com/2003/TECH/internet/11/11/singapore.internet.reut/

Coker, .A., Ugwu, D.U., & Adams, J.A. (2012). Corruption and Direct Foreign Investments in Nigeria: Challenges of Implementing Anti-corruption Programmes under Obasanjo, 1999–2007. *Global Advanced Research Journal of History, Political Science and International Relations, 1*(4), 79-88.

Cookey, P. (2005, February). Corruption Stalls Nigeria's Development -World Bank. *Financial Standard*, 9.

Costante, E., den Hartog, J., Petkovic, M., Etalle, S., & Pechenizkiy, M. (2016). A white-box anomaly-based framework for database leakage detection. *Journal of Information Security and Applications*. Retrieved from http://www.sciencedirect.com/science/article/pii/S2214212616302629

Creech, G., & Hu, J. (2014, April). A semantic approach to host-based intrusion detection systems using contiguous and discontiguous system call patterns. *IEEE Transactions on Computers, 63*(4), 807–819. doi:10.1109/TC.2013.13

Criminal Code of Canada. (2004). Definition of child pornography. Section 163.1. Electronic Frontier.

Cross Domain Solutions. Cyber Crimes. (n.d.). Retrieved from http:www.crossdomatinsolutions.com/cyber-crime/

Crosson-Tower, C. (2005). *Understanding child abuse and neglect*. Boston: Allyn and Bacon.

Cubby Inc. v. CompuServe Inc., 776 F. Supp. 135 (S.D.N.Y. 1991).

Cyanre. SA Cyber Crimes. (n.d.). Retrieved from http://www.cyanre.co.za/tag/Sa-cyber-crime

Cyber Security Agency of Singapore, & Personal Data Protection Commission. (2016). *Cyber Safety Issue 2*. Retrieved November 18, 2017, from https://www.csa.gov.sg/gosafeonline/~/media/gso/images/activity_book/cyber_security_activity_book_2.ashx?la=en

Cyber Security Agency of Singapore. (2016a). *Singapore's Cybersecurity Strategy*. Retrieved November 5, 2017, from https://www.csa.gov.sg/news/publications/singapore-cybersecurity-strategy

Cyber Security Agency of Singapore. (2016b). *Singapore Strengthens Partnership with the United States*. Retrieved November 13, 2017, from https://www.csa.gov.sg/news/press-releases/singapore-us-mou

Cyber Security Agency of Singapore. (2017a). *Singapore Cyber Landscape 2016*. Retrieved October 29, 2017, from https://www.csa.gov.sg/~/media/csa/documents/publications/singaporecyberlandscape2016.ashx?la=en

Cyber Security Agency of Singapore. (2017b). *Our Organisation*. Retrieved November 5, 2017, from https://www.csa.gov.sg/about-us/our-organisation

Cyber Security Agency of Singapore. (2017c). *MCI and CSA Seek Public Feedback on Proposed Cybersecurity Bill*. Retrieved November 4, 2017, from https://www.csa.gov.sg/news/press-releases/mci-and-csa-seek-public-feedback-on-proposed-cybersecurity-bill#sthash.g9mjneAk.dpuf

Cyber Security Agency of Singapore. (2017d). *Cybersecurity Public Awareness Survey 2016 Key Findings*. Retrieved November 15, 2017, from https://www.csa.gov.sg/~/media/csa/documents/key_findings/key%20findings-cybersecurity%20public%20awareness%20survey%202016.ashx?la=en

Daft, R. L., & Lengel, R. H. (1986). Organizational information requirements, media richness and structural design. *Management Science, 32*(5), 554–571. doi:10.1287/mnsc.32.5.554

Dannewitz, C. (2013). *NETINF Network of Information, An Information-Centric Networking Architecture for the Future Internet* (PhD thesis). Faculty of Computer Science, Electrical Engineering and Mathematics, University of Paderborn, Germany.

Dannewitz, C., Golic, J., Ohlman, B., & Ahlgren, B. (2010). Secure naming for a network of information. In *Proceedings of the 29th Conference on Computer Communications Workshops (INFOCOM)* (pp. 1-6). IEEE. 10.1109/INFCOMW.2010.5466661

Dannewitz, C., Kutscher, D., Ohlman, B., Farrell, S., Ahlgren, B., & Karl, H. (2013). Network of information (netinf)-an information-centric networking architecture. *Computer Communications, 36*(7), 721–735. doi:10.1016/j.comcom.2013.01.009

Dash, S. S., Sethi, I. P. S., & Gupta, O. P. (2016,). Measuring performance outcome of e-Governance projects through eTaal. In *Computing for Sustainable Global Development (INDIACom), 2016 3rd International Conference on* (pp. 23-27). Academic Press.

Dawson, J. (2010). *Doctors join patients in going online for health information.* New Media Age.

Deloitte. (2016). *Asia-Pacific Defense Outlook 2016: Defense in Four Domains.* Retrieved July 25, 2017 from https://www2.deloitte.com/content/dam/Deloitte/global/Documents/Public-Sector/gx-ps-ap-defense-outlook-2016-160216.pdf

Denecke, K., & Nejdl, W. (2009). How valuable is medical social media data? Content analysis of the medical web. *Inform Sciences, 179*(12), 1870–1880. doi:10.1016/j.ins.2009.01.025

Denning, D. E. (2000). Cyberterrorism: The Logic Bomb versus the Truck Bomb. *Global Dialogue, 2*(4), 29–37.

Dierks, T. (2008). *The transport layer security (tls) protocol version 1.2.* Rfc 5246, Internet Engineering Task Force.

Digiknow. (2013). *Child porn video game rated PG in Australia.* Author.

Douglas, E. (2009). Childhood Obesity Prevention in South Africa: Media, Social Influences, and Social Marketing Opportunities. *Social Marketing Quarterly, 15,* 22-48.

Doyon-Martin, J. (2015). Cybercrime in West Africa as a result of transboundary e-waste. *Journal of Applied Security Research, 10*(2), 207–220. doi:10.1080/19361610.2015.1004511

ECPAT (2015). *End child pornography.* ECPAT.

E-Government in Support of Sustainable Development United Nations New York. (n.d.). Retrieved from www.publicadministration.un.org

Elahi, G., & Yu, E. (2007). *A goal-oriented approach for modeling and analyzing security trade-offs.* International Conference on Conceptual Modeling, Auckland, New Zealand. 10.1007/978-3-540-75563-0_26

El-Kiki, T., Lawrence, E., & Steele, R. (2005). *A management framework for mobile government services.* CollECTeR. Retrieved from http://spa.hust.edu.cn/ 2008/ uploadfile/2009-4/20090427230800732.pdf

Elliott, K. A. (1997). *Corruption and the Global Economy.* Washington, DC: Institute for International Economics.

Ellis, S. (2016). *This present darkness: A history of Nigerian organized crime.* Oxford, UK: Oxford University Press.

Elmasri, R., & Navathe, S. (2017). *Fundamentals of database systems.* 1272 Seiten: S.n.

Emechele, O. J. (2009). *A Critical Review of the Role of Economic and Financial Crime Commission (EFCC) in Public Sector Accountability* (Unpublished Thesis). Madonna University, Okija.

Emerson, M. F. (2012). Social media marketing from A to Z. *The New York Times.*

Enofe, A. O., Ogbaisi, S. A., & Mboto, O. H. (2015). E-governance and Corruption in Nigeria. *International Journal of Multidisciplinary Research and Development, 2*(8), 640–645.

European Commission. (2003). The Role of e-governance for Europe's Future. Communication from the Commission to the Council, the European Parliament, the European Economic and Social Committee and the Committee of the Regions, Brussels.

Everard, P. (2008). NATO and Cyber Terrorism. In Centre of Excellence Defence Against Terrorism (Ed.), Responses to Cyber Terrorism (pp. 118-126). IOS Press.

Ezigbo, O. (2007, February). Nigerian Image Still not Good, says World Bank. *This Day.*

Fair, O. (2013). *The importance of technology in economic and social development.* Retrieved from https://www.fairobserver.com/regionafrica -technology-economic-and-soical-development/

Fang, Z. (2002). E-governance in Digital Era: Concept, Practice and Development. *International Journal of the Computer, the Internet and Management, 10*(2).

Fench, J., Blair-Stevens, C., Merritt, R., & McVey, D. (2010). *Social Marketing and Public health, theory and practice.* Oxford University Press.

Fidler, D. P. (2016). Cyberspace, Terrorism and International Law. *Journal of Conflict and Security Law, 21*(3), 475–493. doi:10.1093/jcsl/krw013

Find Law. Cyber Crimes. (n.d.). Retrieved from www.criminal.findlaw.com/criminal-charges/cyber-crimes.html

Finkelhor, D. (1994). Current information on the scope and nature of child sexual abuse. *The Future of Children, 4*(2), 31–53. doi:10.2307/1602522 PMID:7804768

Fisher, D. H. (1987). *Knowledge acquisition via incremental conceptual clustering.* Academic Press.

Forbes. (2016). *Cyber Crime Costs Projected To Reach $2 Trillion by 2019*. Retrieved from https://www.forbes.com/sites/stevemorgan/2016/01/17/cyber-crime-costs-projected-to-reach-2-trillion-by-2019/

Forrest, S., Hofmeyr, S., & Somayaji, A. (2008, Dec). The evolution of system-call monitoring. In *2008 annual computer security applications conference (acsac)* (p. 418-430). Academic Press. 10.1109/ACSAC.2008.54

Forrest, S., Hofmeyr, S. A., Somayaji, A., & Longstaff, T. A. (1996, May). A sense of self for unix processes. In *Proceedings 1996 ieee symposium on security and privacy* (p. 120-128). IEEE. 10.1109/SECPRI.1996.502675

Fournier de Saint Maur, A. (1999, January). Sexual abuse of children on the Internet: A new challenge for INTERPOL. In *Expert meeting on sexual abuse of children, child pornography and paedophilia on the Internet: An international challenge*. UNESCO.

Franca, R. B., Bodeveix, J., Filali, M., Rolland, J., Chemouil, D., & Thomas, D. (2007). The AADL behaviour annex -- experiments and roadmap. In *Proceedings of the 12th IEEE international Conference on Engineering Complex Computer Systems*. IEEE Computer Society.

Frankel, S., & Krishnan, S. (2011). *Ip security (ipsec) and internet key exchange (ike) document roadmap*. Rfc 6071, Internet Engineering Task Force.

Freeman, B., & Chapman, S. (2007). Is "YouTube" telling or selling you something? Tobacco content on the YouTube video-sharing website. *Tobacco Control, 16*(3), 207–210. doi:10.1136/tc.2007.020024 PMID:17565142

Gafny, M., Shabtai, A., Rokach, L., & Elovici, Y. (2011). Poster: Applying unsupervised context-based analysis for detecting unauthorized data disclosure. In *Proceedings of the 18th acm conference on computer and communications security* (pp. 765–768). New York, NY: ACM. doi:10.1145/2046707.2093488

GBDe. (2001). *e-Government*. GBDe. Retrieved December 13, 2012, from http://www.gbd-e.org/ig/egov/eGov_Recommendation_Sep01.pdf

Gennari, J. H., Langley, P., & Fisher, D. (1989). *Models of Incremental Concept Formation. Ft. Belvoir*. Defense Technical Information Center.

Ghodsi, A., Koponen, T., Rajahalme, J., Sarolahti, P., & Shenker, S. (2011a). Naming in content-oriented architectures. In *Proceedings of the ACM SIGCOMM workshop on Information-centric networking* (pp. 1-6). ACM.

Ghodsi, A., Shenker, S., Koponen, T., Singla, A., Raghavan, B., & Wilcox, J. (2011b). Information-centric networking: seeing the forest for the trees. In *Proceedings of the 10th ACM Workshop on Hot Topics in Networks* (p. 1). ACM. 10.1145/2070562.2070563

Ghyasi, F., & Kushchu, I. (2004). M-Government: Cases of Developing Countries. *Proceedings from the fourth European conference on e-government*, 887–898.

Google v. Louis Vuitton OJ C134, 22.5.2010.

Gorantla, M. C., Gangishetti, R., & Saxena, A. (2005). A survey on id-based cryptographic primitives. *IACR Cryptology ePrint Archive*, 94.

Górski, J., Rydzak, F., Breistrand, L., Sveen, F., Qian, Y., & Gonzalez, J. (2006). *Exploring Resilience Towards Risks in eOperations in the Oil and Gas Industry.* Computer Safety, Reliability, and Security. LNCS.

GoSafeOnline. (2017). *Cyber Safety Activity Book.* Retrieved November 18, 2017, from https://www.csa.gov.sg/gosafeonline/resources/activity-book

Government of the Netherlands. Cyber Crimes. (n.d.). Retrieved from https://www.government.nl/topics/ cybercrime/forms-of-cybercrime

GovTech. (2017). *Opening GOH Address by Dr. Janil Puthucheary for GovInsider Innovation Labs World Conference 2017.* Retrieved October 25, 2017, from https://www.tech.gov.sg/media-room/speeches/2017/09/opening-goh-address-by-dr-janil-puthucheary-for-govinsider-innovation-labs-world-conference-2017

Gracia-Marco, L., Moreno, L., & Vicente-Rodríguez, G. (2012). Impact of Social Marketing in the Prevention of Childhood Obesity. *An Advanced in nutrition, an International Review Journal*, 6115-6155.

Grand theft data data exfiltration study: Actors, tactics, and detection (Tech.Rep.). (2015). Intel security and McAfee.

Grant, K., Hackney, R., & Edgar, D. (2010). *Strategic Information Systems Management.* Andover: Cengage Learning.

Grier, S., & Bryant, C. (2005). Social marketing in public health. *Annual Review of Public Health*, 26(1), 319–339. doi:10.1146/annurev.publhealth.26.021304.144610 PMID:15760292

Griffiths, J., Maggs, H., & George, E. (2007). *Stakeholder Involvement.* Background paper prepared for the WHO/WEF Joint Event on Preventing Noncommunicable Diseases in the Workplace.

Gross, M. L., Canetti, D., & Vashdi, D. R. (2016). The Psychological Effects of Cyber Terrorism. *Bulletin of the Atomic Scientists*, 72(5), 284–291. doi:10.1080/00963402.2016.1216502 PMID:28366962

Gupta, S., Davoodi, H., & Alonso-Terme, R. (1998). *Does Corruption Affect Income Inequality and Poverty.* International Monetary Fund. Working Paper. Retrieved from http://bit.ly/V8Ojq8

Hadi, F., & Muhaya, F. T. B. (2011). Essentials for the e-government security. In *Information Society (i-Society), 2011 International Conference on* (pp. 237-240). IEEE.

Halder, D., & Jaishankar, K. (2011). *Cybercrime and the victimization of women: Laws, rights, and regulations.* Hershey, PA: IGI Global.

Hamdane, B., Serrhrouchni, A., Fadlallah, A., & Guemara El Fatmi, S. (2012). Named-data security scheme for named data networking. In *Proceedings of the Third International Conference on the Network of the Future (NoF)* (pp. 1-7). IFIP - IEEE. 10.1109/NOF.2012.6464002

Hamdane, B., Boussada, R., Elhdhili, M. E., & El Fatmi, S. G. (2017). Hierarchical identity based cryptography for security and trust in named data networking. In *26th International Conference on Enabling Technologies: Infrastructure for Collaborative En-terprises (WETICE).* IEEE. 10.1109/WETICE.2017.33

Hamdane, B., Guemara El Fatmi, S., & Serrhrouchni, A. (2014). A novel name-based security mechanism for information-centric networking. In *Proceedings of the Wireless Communications and Networking Conference (WCNC)* (pp. 2928-2933). IEEE. 10.1109/WCNC.2014.6952919

Hasina. (2009). Decentralised P2P technology: Can the unruly be ruled? *International Review of Law, Computers & Technology, 23,* 123-124.

Hathawat & Sawage. (2012, March). *Duties of ISPs, Cyber Dialogue.* Available on https://www.belfercenter.org/sites/default/files/legacy/files/cyberdialogue2012_hathaway-savage.pdf

Heeks, R. (1999). *Information and communication technologies, poverty and development.* Development informatics working paper no. 5. IDPM, University of Manchester.

Hessel, L., & Mikucionis, N. Pettersson, & Skou. (2008). Testing real-time systems using UPPAAL. In Lecture Notes In Computer Science: Vol. 4949. Springer-Verlag.

Hioe, W. (2001). *National Infocomm Strategy and Policy: Singapore's Experience.* Retrieved October 18, 2017, from http://www.unapcict.org

Hofmeyr, S. A., Forrest, S., & Somayaji, A. (1998, August). Intrusion detection using sequences of system calls. *J. Comput. Secur., 6*(3), 151–180. Retrieved from http://dl.acm.org/citation.cfm?id=1298081.1298084

Hopper, T., Tsamenyi, M, Uddin, S., & Wickramasinghe, D. (2009). Management accounting in less developed countries: what is known and needs knowing. *Accounting, Auditing and Accountability Journal, 22*(3), 469-514. 10.1108/09513570910945697

Hu, G., Pan, W., Lu, M., & Wang, J. (2009). The Widely Shared Definition of E-Government: An Exploratory Study. *The Electronic Library, 27.*

Hui, C. (2015, Oct 27). *Cyber Security in Businesses Gets a Boost with New Employee Kit.* Retrieved November 18, 2017, from http://www.channelnewsasia.com/news/business/cyber-security-in-businesses-gets-a-boost-with-new-employee-kit-8234376

Hunker, J., & Probst, C. W. (2011). Insiders and insider threats An overview of definitions and mitigation techniques. *Journal of Wireless Mobile Networks, Ubiquitous Computing and Dependable Applications,* 4–27.

Hussain, S. R., Sallam, A. M., & Bertino, E. (2015). Detanom:detecting anoma-lous database transactions by insiders. In Proc. 5th ACM codaspy (p. 25-35). San Antonio, TX: ACM.

Hu, Y., & Sundar, S. (2010). Effects of online health sources on credibility and behavioral Intentions. *Communication Research*, *37*(1), 105–132. doi:10.1177/0093650209351512

Ibrahim, S. (2016). Causes of socioeconomic cybercrime in Nigeria (Parents' Perspectives). In *Proceedings of the 4th International Conference on Cybercrime and computer Forensics*. Canada, Vancouver: IEEE Xplore Publishing.

Indian Law Institute. (2000). *Introduction to cyberlaw*. Available at www.ili.ac.in/e-learnCL.html

Infocomm Development Authority of Singapore. (2000). *Infocomm 21: Singapore Where the Digital Future Is*. Retrieved August 31, 2017, from https://www.imda.gov.sg/about/corporate-publications/past-publications/past-infocomm-plans

Infocomm Development Authority of Singapore. (2003). *Connected Singapore: Unleashing Potential, Realizing Possibilities, through Infocomm*. Retrieved August 31, 2017, from https://www.tech.gov.sg/-/media/GovTech/About-us/Corporate-Publications/Past-infocomm-plans/Connected.pdf?la=en

Infocomm Development Authority of Singapore. (2005). *Three-year Infocomm Security Masterplan Unveiled*. Retrieved November 12, 2017, from https://www.imda.gov.sg/about/newsroom/archived/ida/media-releases/2005/20050712110643

Infocomm Development Authority of Singapore. (2008). *Plan Aims to Bolster National Readiness to Counter Cyber Threats*. Retrieved November 12, 2017, from https://www.tech.gov.sg/media-room/media-releases/2008/04/new-s70m-masterplan-to-boost-singapores-infocomm-s

Infocomm Development Authority of Singapore. (2010). *Realising the iN2015 Vision: Singapore: An Intelligent Nation, A Global City, Powered by Infocomm*. Retrieved August 31, 2017, from https://www.tech.gov.sg/-/media/GovTech/About-us/Corporate-Publications/PDFs/iN2015-Reports/realisingthevisionin2015.pdf

Infocomm Development Authority of Singapore. (2013a). *National Cyber Security Masterplan 2018*. Retrieved November 12, 2017, from https://www.itu.int/en/ITU-D/Cybersecurity/Documents/National_Strategies_Repository/Singapore_2013_AnnexA.pdf

Infocomm Development Authority of Singapore. (2013b). *Enhanced Cyber-Watch Centre to Strengthen Infocomm Security*. Retrieved November 6, 2017, from https://www.tech.gov.sg/-/media/GovTech/Media-Room/Media-Releases/2013/5/AnnexDpdf.pdf

Infodev. (2002). *The e-government handbook for developing countries*. Retrieved May 15, 2006, from the Center for Democracy and Technology Website: http://www.cdt.org/egov/handbook/part1.shtml

Inokoba, P.A. & Ibegu, W.T. (2011). Economic and Financial Crime Commission (EFCC) and Political Corruption Implication for the Consolidation of Democracy in Nigeria. *Anthropologist*, *13*(4).

Insider threat report, insider threat security statistics, vormetric (Tech. Rep.). (2015). Vormetric.

ISACA. (2016). *Isaca survey: 63% of it professionals are against governments having backdoor access to encrypted information systems.* Retrieved from www.isaca.org/About-ISACA/Press-room/ News-Releases/2016/Pages/ISACA-Cybersecurity-Snapshot-Survey.aspx

Jacobson, V., Smetters, D. K., Thornton, J. D., Plass, M. F., Briggs, N. H., & Braynard, R. L. (2009). Networking named content. In *Proceedings of the 5th international conference on Emerging networking experiments and technologies* (pp. 1-12). ACM.

Jain, A. K. (2001). Corruption: a Review. *Journal of Economic Surveys, 15*, 72-121. 10.1111/1467-6419.00133

Jajodia, S., Samarati, P., Sapino, M. L., & Subrahmanian, V. S. (2001, June). Flexible support for multiple access control policies. *ACM Trans. Database Syst., 26*(2), 214–260. Retrieved from http://doi.acm.org/10.1145/383891.383894

Jamrozik, K., von Styp-Rekowsky, P., & Zeller, A. (2016, May). Mining sand-boxes. In *2016 ieee/acm 38th international conference on software engi-neering (icse)* (pp. 37-48). IEEE. doi: 10.1145/2884781.2884782

Jennifer, N. (2007, July). *Internet Service Provider Liability.* Paper presented at ASEAN-USPTO Workshop on Digital Copyright and Copyright Collective Management, Bangkok. Retrieved from http://asean.org/wp content/uploads/images/2012/Economic/sectoral_aem/service/agreement/ASEAN-USPTO%20Workshop%20on%20Digital%20Copyright%20and%20Copyright.pdf

Jin, Z. (2000). *A Software Architecture-based Testing Technique* (PhD thesis). George Mason University.

Jin, Z., & Offutt, J. (2001). Deriving Tests From Software Architectures. In *Proceedings of the 12th International Symposium on Software Reliability Engineering (ISSRE '01).* IEEE Computer Society.

Joseph, R. C. (2017). There's an App for That? Perspectives from the Public Sector. *Proceedings for the Northeast Region Decision Sciences Institute (NEDSI).*

Jurjens, J. (2005). *Secure Systems Development with UML.* Springer-Verlag.

Jurjens, J. (2008). *Model-based Security Testing Using UMLsec. Electronic Notes in Theoretical Computer Science.* Springer.

Kamra, A., Terzi, E., & Bertino, E. (2008, August). Detecting anomalous access patterns in relational databases. *The VLDB Journal, 17*(5), 1063–1077. doi: 10.100700778-007-0051-4

Kaplan, A. M., & Haenlein, M. (2010). Users of the world unite! The challenges and opportunities of social media. *Business Horizons, 53*(1), 59–68. doi:10.1016/j.bushor.2009.09.003

Kauffmann, B., & Peltier, J.-F. (2013). Final netinf architecture. *4WARD EU FP7 Project, Deliverable D.3.3 v1. 1.*

Kaufmann, D., Kraay, A., & Zoida-Lobaton, P. (2000). Governance Matters: from measurement to action. *Finance and Development: World Bank Policy Research, 37*(2). Retrieved from http://bit.ly/XYS9S9

Kaynar, D. K., Lynch, N., Segala, R., & Vaandrager, F. (2003). Timed I/O Automata: A Mathematical Framework for Modeling and Analyzing Real-Time Systems. In *Proceedings of the 24th IEEE International Real-Time Systems Symposium (RTSS '03)*. IEEE Computer Society. 10.1109/REAL.2003.1253264

Kemmerer, R. A., & Vigna, G. (2002, April). Intrusion detection: A brief history and overview. *Computer, 35*(4), 27–30. doi:10.1109/MC.2002.1012428

Khan, M. I., & Foley, S. N. (2016). Detecting anomalous behavior in dbms logs. In International conference on risks and security of internet and systems (crisis2016). Roscoff, France: Academic Press.

Khoong, H. Y. (2001). *Khoong Hock Yun, Assistant Chief Executive, Infocomm Development, IDA Singapore – Speech CIAPR Forum - Singapore Day Symposium, Grand Hyatt Shanghai, China*. Retrieved October 19, 2017, from https://www.imda.gov.sg/about/newsroom/archived/ida/speeches/2001/20061212150610

Kietzmann, J. H., Hermkens, K., McCarthy, I. P., & Silvestre, B. S. (2011). Social media? Get serious! Understanding the functional building blocks of social media. *Business Horizons, 54*(3), 241–251. doi:10.1016/j.bushor.2011.01.005

Kim, C. (2007). A cross-national analysis of global E-government. *Public Organization Review, 7*(10), 317-329. 10.100711115-007-0040-5

Kim, S., Kim, H. J., & Lee, H. (2009). An Institutional Analysis of an E-174 Government System for Anti-Corruption: The Case of Open. *Government Information Quarterly, 26*(1), 42–50. doi:10.1016/j.giq.2008.09.002

Klain, E. J., Heather, J. D., & Molly, A. H. (2001). *Child pornography: The criminal justice system response*. National Centre for Missing and Exploited Children.

Kok, X. H. (2013 November 30). MOM Site Duplicated, Art Museum Site Breached. *Today*. Retrieved October 26, 2017, from http://www.todayonline.com/singapore/mom-site-duplicated-art-museum-site-breached

Koo & Mishra. (2009). Functional test generation using design and property decomposition techniques. *ACM Trans. Embed. Comput. Syst.*

Kor, V. (2017). *Cybersecurity: A Concentric Approach*. Retrieved November 4, 2017, from https://www.tech.gov.sg/TechNews/Opinions/2017/04/07/08/06/Cybersecurity-A-Concentric-Approach

Kotler, P., & Lee, N. (2008). *Social Marketing: Influencing Behaviors for Good*. Sage Publications.

Kotler, P., & Zaltman, G. (1971). Social marketing: An approach to planned social change. *Journal of Marketing, 35*(3), 3–12. doi:10.2307/1249783 PMID:12276120

Kudo, H. (2010). E-Governance As Strategy Of Public Sector Reform: Peculiarity Of Japanese IT Policy And Its Institutional Origin. *Financial Accountability & Management, 26*(1), 65-84. 10.1111/j.1468-0408.2009.00491.x

Kul, G., Luong, D., Xie, T., Coonan, P., Chandola, V., Kennedy, O., & Upadhyaya, S. (2016). Ettu: Analyzing query intents in corporate databases. In *Proceedings of the 25th international conference companion on world wide web* (pp. 463–466). Geneva, Switzerland: International World Wide Web Conferences Steering Committee. 10.1145/2872518.2888608

Kumar, M., & Sinha, O. P. (2007). M-Government – Mobile Technology for eGovernment. In *Towards Next Generation E-government, iceg'07*. Retrieved from http://www.iceg.net/2007/books/2/32_343_2.pdf

Kumar, S., & Spafford, E. H. (1994). A pattern matching model for misuse in-trusion detection. *Proceedings of the 17th national computer security conference*, 11–21.

Kushchu, I. (2007). *Mobile government: An emerging direction in e-government*. Hershey, PA: IGI. doi:10.4018/978-1-59140-884-0

Kushchu, I., & Kuscu, H. (2003). From E-government to M-government: Facing the Inevitable. Paper Presented at the *European Conference on E-Government (ECEG 2003)*, Dublin, Ireland.

Kutscher, D., Eum, S., Pentikousis, K., Psaras, I., Corujo, D., Saucez, D., Schmidt, T., and Waehlisch, M. (2016). *Icn research challenges, draft-irtf-icnrg-challenges-06*. Technical report, ICNRG, Internet-Draft, Expires, September 20.

Kutscher, D., Farrell, S., & Davies, E. (2012). *The netinf protocol-draft-kutscher-icnrg-netinf-proto-01*. Technical report, Internet Draft, IETF, Expires, August 14.

Kvochko, E. (2013). *Five ways technology can help the economy*. Available at https://www.weforum.org/agenda/2013/04/five-ways-technology-can-help-the-economy/

Kwang, K. (2015, August 4). Internet 'Was Not Designed for Safety': Cyber Security Agency Chief. *Channel NewsAsia*. Retrieved November 6, 2017, from http://www.channelnewsasia.com/news/singapore/internet--was-not-designed-for-safety--cyber-security-agency-chi-8237784

Kyem, P. A. (2016). Mobile Phone Expansion and Opportunities for e-Governance in Africa. *The Electronic Journal on Information Systems in Developing Countries*, 75.

L'Oreal v. eBay [2009] EWHC 1094 (Ch).

Lagutin, D. (2010). *Securing the Internet with digital signatures* (PhD thesis). Aalto University, Department of Computer Science and Engineering.

Larkin, J. H., & Simon, H. A. (1987). Why a diagram is (sometimes) worth ten thousand words. *Cognitive Science, 11*(1), 65–100. doi:10.1111/j.1551-6708.1987.tb00863.x

Laszka, A., Abbas, W., Sastry, S. S., Vorobeychik, Y., & Koutsoukos, X. (2016). Optimal thresholds for intrusion detection systems. In *Proceedings of the symposium and bootcamp on the science of security* (pp. 72–81). New York, NY: ACM. Retrieved from http://doi.acm.org/10.1145/2898375.2898399

Lee, C. (2017, May 30). *Cyber Security Resources, Grants Available to SMEs*. Retrieved November 18, 2017, from http://www.todayonline.com/voices/cyber-security-resources-grants-available-smes

Lee, H. L. (1996). *Speech - Launch of the Singapore Government Internet Web Site and Intranet*. Retrieved August 30, 2017, from https://www.imda.gov.sg/about/newsroom/archived/ida/speeches/1996/20050728144718

Lee, T. (2013). *'Anonymous' Hackers Threaten War with Singapore Government*. Retrieved October 26, 2017, from https://www.techinasia.com/youtube-anonymous-hacker-group-threatens-war-singapore-govt-video-removed-viral

Lee, U. (2017 March 1). *Mindef's Internet System Breached in Cyberattack*. Retrieved October 26, 2017, from http://www.businesstimes.com.sg/technology/mindefs-internet-system-breached-in-cyberattack

Lee, N., & Kotler, P. (2011). *Social Marketing, influencing behaviors for good* (4th ed.). Sage Publications, Inc.

Lee, S. Y., Low, W. L., & Wong, P. Y. (2002). Learning fingerprints for a database intrusion detection system. In *Proceedings of the 7th European symposium on research in computer security* (pp. 264–280). London: Springer-Verlag. doi:10.1007/3-540-45853-0_16

Lemon, S. (2009). *Singapore to Form National Cyber-Security Agency*. Retrieved November 5, 2017, from https://www.cio.com/article/2424366/government/singapore-to-form-national-cyber-security-agency.html

Lettnin, W., Braun, G., & Ruf, K., & Rosenstiel. (2007). Coverage Driven Verification applied to Embedded Software. In *Proceedings of the IEEE Computer Society Annual Symposium on VLSI (ISVLSI '07)*. IEEE Computer Society.

Leung, E. (2003). *Speech by the Secretary for Justice at Internet Law Symposium*. Retrieved November 19, 2017, from http://www.doj.gov.hk/eng/archive/pdf/sj260903e.pdf

Levesque, R. J. R. (1999). *Sexual abuse of children: A human rights perspective*. Bloomington, IN: Indian University Press.

Liang, B., & Scammon, D. L. (2011). E-Word-of-Mouth on health social networking sites: An opportunity for tailored health communication. *Journal of Consumer Behaviour, 10*(6), 322–331. doi:10.1002/cb.378

Liao, H.-J., Richard Lin, C.-H., Lin, Y.-C., & Tung, K.-Y. (2013, January). Review: Intrusion detection system: A comprehensive review. *Journal of Network and Computer Applications, 36*(1), 16–24. doi:10.1016/j.jnca.2012.09.004

LICRA et UEJF v. Yahoo! Inc and Yahoo France, 20 November 2000, Tribunal de Grande Instance de Paris, Superior Court of Paris) p14.

Lim, K., Lynch, & Mitra. (2005). Translating timed i/o automata specifications for theorem proving in PVS. *Proceedings of the Third international conference on Formal Modeling and Analysis of Timed Systems (FORMATS'05)*.

Lodderstedt, T., Basin, D., & Doser, J. (2002). SecureUML: A UMLBased Modeling Language for Model-Driven Security. *International Conference Unified Modeling Language, Model Engineering, Languages Concepts and Tools*. 10.1007/3-540-45800-X_33

Loh, P. J. (2010). APEC Trojan Email Attacks. *Home Team Journal, 2*, 43-6. Retrieved October 26, 2017, from https://www.mha.gov.sg/HTA/Documents/Home%20Team%20Journal%20 Issue%202.pdf

Loke, K. F. (2017, February 28). *MINDEF Internet System Breached; Data Stolen from National Servicemen, Employees*. Retrieved October 26, 2017, from http://www.channelnewsasia.com/ news/singapore/mindef-internet-system-breached-data-stolen-from-national-servic-7617146

Low, W. L., Lee, J., & Teoh, P. (2002). Didafit: Detecting intrusions in databases through fingerprinting transactions. In ICEIS (pp. 121–128). Academic Press.

Lupu, D., & Lazar, C. (2015). Influence of E-Government on the Level of Corruption in Some EU and Non-EU States. *Procedia Economics and Finance, 20*, 365–371. doi:10.1016/S2212-5671(15)00085-4

LVMH v. eBay TC Paris, 1ere Ch B, June 30, 2008.

Lynch, N., & Tuttle, M. R. (1989). An Introduction to Input/Output Automata. C. W. I. Quarterly, 2(3).

Maddena, G., Bohlinb, E., Onikic, H., & Tran, T. (2013). Potential Demand for M-government Services in Japan. *Applied Economics Letters, 20*(8), 732–736. doi:10.1080/13504851.2012.736939

MAFTIA Consortium. (2003). Conceptual Model and Architecture of MAFTIA (Malicious- and Accidental-Fault Tolerance for Internet Applications), Public Deliverable, EU MAFTIA Project. Retrieved from http://spiderman-2.laas.fr/TSF/cabernet/maftia/deliverables/D21.pdf

Maitanmi, O., Ogunlere, S., Ayinde, S., & Adekunle, Y. (2013). Impact of cybercrimes on Nigerian economy. *International Journal of Engineering Science, 2*(4), 45–51.

Majumdar, R., & Sen, K. (2007, May). Hybrid concolic testing. In *29th international conference on software engineering (icse'07)* (p. 416-426). Academic Press. 10.1109/ICSE.2007.41

Manner, Siniketo, & Polland. (2009). *The Pirate Bay Ruling—When The Fun and Games End*. Retrieved from file:///C:/Users/DLL/Desktop/the-pirate-bay-ruling.pdf

Maor, M. (2004). Feeling the Heat? Anticorruption Mechanisms in Comparative Perspective. *Governance: An International Journal of Policy, Administration and Institutions, 17*(11), 1-28. 10.1111/j.09521895.2004.00235.x

MappingS. (n.d.). Retrieved from http://www.stakeholdermapping.com/smm-maturity-maturity-model/

Mario, S. (2009). E-governance in Transition Economies. *World Academy of Science, Engineering and Technology*.

Marquis, S., Dean, T. R., & Knight, S. (2005). SCL: a language for security testing of network applications. *Proceedings of the 2005 conference of the Centre for Advanced Studies on Collaborative research (CASCON '05)*.

Marshman, S. D. (2011). Giving a country of Pirates a chance: Using the three step test to accommodate the shifting of national attitudes on Copyright Protection. *The George Washington International Law Review, 43*(4), 707.

Martins Library. (n.d.). Retrieved from https://martins.library.blogspot.com/2013/08/

Mathew, S., Petropoulos, M., Ngo, H. Q., & Upadhyaya, S. (2010). A data-centric approach to insider attack detection in database systems. In *Proceedings of the 13th international conference on recent advances in intrusion detection* (pp. 382–401). Berlin: Springer-Verlag. doi:10.1007/978-3-642-15512-3_20

Mauro, P. (1997). Corruption and Growth. *The Quarterly Journal of Economics, 110*(3), 681–712. doi:10.2307/2946696

Medianet. (n.d.). *Social Media in Africa: Key Statistical Indicators*. Retrieved from http://blog.medianet.com.tn/blog/chiffres-cles-sur-les-reseaux-sociaux-en-afrique-facebook-linkedin-instagram-presentes-lafrican

Meijer, A. (2015). E-governance innovation: Barriers and strategies. *Government Information Quarterly, 32*(2), 198–206. doi:10.1016/j.giq.2015.01.001

Mengistu, Zo, & Rho. (2009). *M-government: Opportunities and Challenges to Deliver Mobile Government Services in Developing Countries*. Academic Press.

Milner, C., & O'Donnel, I. (2007). *Child pornography: Crime, computers and society*. Milton Park: Willan Publishing Limited.

Ministry of Finance, & Infocomm Development Authority of Singapore. (2003). *Singapore E-government*. Retrieved August 31, 2017, from https://www.tech.gov.sg/-/media/GovTech/About-us/Corporate-Publications/eGov/eGap-II.pdf?la=en

Ministry of Finance, & Infocomm Development Authority of Singapore. (2006). *iGov2010: From Integrating Service to Integrating Government*. Retrieved August 31, 2017, from https://www.tech.gov.sg/-/media/GovTech/About-us/Corporate-Publications/eGov/iGov.pdf?la=en

Ministry of Finance, Ministry of Information, Communications and the Arts, & Infocomm Development Authority of Singapore. (2011). *E-government Masterplan 2011-2015: Collaborative Government*. Retrieved August 31, 2017, from https://www.tech.gov.sg/-/media/GovTech/About-us/Corporate-Publications/eGov/eGovBOOK1115.pdf?la=en

Ministry of Home Affairs. (2014). *2014 National Security Conference at Suntec Singapore Convention & Exhibition Centre - Opening Address by Mr S Iswaran, Minister, Prime Minister's office, Second Minister for Home Affairs and Trade & Industry*. Retrieved November 12, 2017, from https://www.mha.gov.sg/Newsroom/speeches/Pages/2014-National-Security-Conference-at-Suntec-Singapore-Convention---Exhibition-Centre---Opening-Address-by-Mr-S-Iswaran,-Min.aspx

Ministry of Home Affairs. (2016). *National Cybercrime Action Plan*. Retrieved November 12, 2017, from https://www.mha.gov.sg/Newsroom/press-releases/PublishingImages/Pages/Launch-of-the-National-Cybercrime-Action-Plan-at-RSA-Conference-Asia-Pacific-Japan/NCAP%20Document.pdf

Ministry of Home Affairs. (2017a). *Official Launch of Interpol World 2017 – Speech by Mr Desmond Lee, Second Minister for Home Affairs and Second Minister for National Development*. Retrieved November 6, 2017, from https://www.mha.gov.sg/newsroom/speeches/Pages/Official-Launch-of-Interpol-World-2017-%E2%80%93-Speech-by-Mr-Desmond-Lee.aspx

Ministry of Home Affairs. (2017b). *Computer Misuse and Cybersecurity (Amendment) Bill*. Retrieved November 4, 2017, from https://www.mha.gov.sg/Newsroom/press-releases/Pages/Computer-Misuse-and-Cybersecurity-(Amendment)-Bill-.aspx

Ministry of Information and the Arts. (1995). *Speech by BG (NS) George Yeo, Minister for Information & the Arts and Minister of Health, at the Launch of SINGAPORE INFOMAP on Wednesday, 8 March 1995 at 10.00 am*. Retrieved October 19, 2017, from http://www.nas.gov.sg/archivesonline/data/pdfdoc/yybg19950308s.pdf

Model Legislation and Global Review. (2008). *Child pornography*. Available at https://www.issuelab.org/resource/child-pornography-model-legislation-global-review.html

Moen, A., Smørdal, O., & Sem, I. (2009). Web-based resources for peer support - opportunities and challenges. *Studies Health Technology Information*, 302–306.

Moon, M. J. (2002). The Evolution of E-governance Among Municipalities: Rhetoric or Reality? *Public Administration Review*, *62*(4), 424–433. doi:10.1111/0033-3352.00196

Moore, R. (2005). *Cybercrime: Investigating high technology computer crime*. Cleveland, MI: Anderson Publishing.

Morgan, S. (2016). *Cybercrime costs projected to reach $2 trillion by 2019*. Retrieved from https://www.forbes.com/sites/stevemorgan/ 2016/01/17/cybercrime-costs-porjected-to-reach-2-trillion-by-2019/

Mouelhi, T., Fleurey, F., Baudry, B., & Traon, Y. (2008). A Model-Based Framework for Security Policy Specification, Deployment and Testing. *Proceedings of the 11th international conference on Model Driven Engineering Languages and Systems (MoDELS '08)*. 10.1007/978-3-540-87875-9_38

Mouratidis & Giorgini. (2007). *Security Attack Testing (SAT)-testing the security of information systems at design time. Information Systems Journal.*

Mozas-Moral, A., Bernal-Jurado, E., Medina-Viruel, M. J., & Fernández-Uclés, D. (2016). Factors for success in online social networks: An fsQCA approach. *Journal of Business Research, 69*(11), 5261–5264. doi:10.1016/j.jbusres.2016.04.122

Muccini, H. (2002). *Software Architecture for Testing, Coordination and Views Model Checking* (PhD Thesis). University La Sapienza, Rome, Italy.

Mukkamala, S., Janoski, G., & Sung, A. (2002). Intrusion detection using neural networks and support vector machines. In Neural networks, 2002. ijcnn '02. proceedings of the 2002 international joint conference on (Vol. 2, p. 1702-1707). Academic Press. doi:10.1109/IJCNN.2002.1007774

Mullin, G., & Lake, E. (2017, August 4). What Is Wannacry Ransomware? Malware Used to Cripple NHS in 2017 Cyber Attack. *The Sun*. Retrieved October 30, 2017, from https://www.thesun.co.uk/tech/3562470/wannacry-ransomware-nhs-cyber-attack-hackers-virus/

National Center for Missing and Exploited Children. (2015). *Child pornography*. Available at www.missingkids.com/dam/documents

National Computer Board. (1997). *National Computer Board Annual Report 1996/1997*. Retrieved August 30, 2017, from https://www.imda.gov.sg/about/newsroom/archived/ida/speeches/1997/20050728143225

National Institutes of Health. (2007). *Understanding Emerging and Re-emerging Infectious Diseases*. Author.

Ndou, V. (2004). *E-Government for developing countries: Opportunities and challenges.* Retrieved from http://unpan1.un.org/intradoc/groups/public/documents/UNTC/UNPAN018634.pdf

Networks Asia. (2015). *Singapore Business Federation unveils Employee Cyber Security Kit for SMBs*. Retrieved November 18, 2017, from https://www.networksasia.net/article/singapore-business-federation-unveils-employee-cyber-security-kit-smbs.1446085033

Networks Asia. (2016). *Singapore Launches National Cybercrime Action Plan*. Retrieved November 6, 2017, from https://www.networksasia.net/article/singapore-launches-national-cybercrime-action-plan.1469025526?source=transform-security&qt-breaking_news_most_read=0

Newton-Ward, Andreasen, & Hastings. (2004). Positioning Social Marketing. *Social Marketing Quarterly, 10*(3), 17-22.

Ng, J. (2014). *Staying Ahead of Digital Criminals through Robust Cyber Security Training.* Retrieved November 11, 2017, from https://www.hometeam.sg/article.aspx?news_ sid=20141113RNtrYzE8rlqH

Ng, J. (2015). *New Cyber Security Agency Set to Lead the way in Combating Emerging Cyber Threats.* Retrieved November 5, 2017, from https://www.hometeam.sg/article.aspx?news_ sid=201501282Uakllrzrg7S

Ng, J. Y. (2014 June 5). 1,560 SingPass User Accounts Breached. *Today.* Retrieved October 29, 2017, from http://www.todayonline.com/singapore/1560-singpass-user-accounts-breached

Ng, K. (2015 January 23). Hacker 'Messiah' Pleads Guilty to 39 Computer Misuse Charges. *Today.* Retrieved October 26, 2017, from http://www.todayonline.com/singapore/hacker-messiah-pleads-guilty-cyberattacks

Ngugi, M. (2005). *Law on cybercrime overdue.* Available at www.crimeresearch.org

Ning, P., & Jajodia, S. (2004). Intrusion detection techniques. In *The internet encyclopedia.* John Wiley & Sons, Inc.; doi:10.1002/047148296X.tie097

Nordqvist, C., Hanberger, L., Timpka, T., & Nordfeldt, S. (2009). Health professionals' attitudes towards using a Web 2.0 portal for child and adolescent diabetes care: Qualitative study. *Journal of Medical Internet Research, 11*(2). PMID:19403464

Norris, P. (2003). *Deepening democracy via e-governance.* Report for the UN World Public Sector Report. Retrieved May 15, 2006: http://ksghome.harvard.edu/~pnorris/ACROBAT/e-governance.pdf

Ntaliani, M., Costopoulou, C., & Karetsos, S. (2008). Mobile government: A challenge for agriculture. *Government Information Quarterly, 25*(4), 699–716. doi:10.1016/j.giq.2007.04.010

Nwabuzor, A. (2005). Corruption and Development: New Initiatives in Economic Openness and Strengthened Rule of Law. *Ethics, 59*(1), 121–138.

Odo, L. U. (2015). The Impact and Consequences of Corruption on the Nigerian Society and economy. *International Journal of Arts and Humanities, 4*(1), 177–190.

OECD. (2010). *The OECD Innovation Strategy. Getting a head start on Tomorrow.* OECD Publishing.

OECD. (2011). *Communiqué on Principles for Internet Policy Making.* Delivered at an OECD High-Level Meeting, The Internet Economy: Generating Innovation and Growth, Paris, France.

Ojedokun, U.A., & Eraye, M.C. (2012). Socioeconomic lifestyles of the yahoo-boys: A case study of perceptions of university students in Nigeria. *International Journal of Cyber Criminology, 6*(2), 1001-1013.

Okeshola, F.B., & Adeta, A.K. (2013). The nature, causes and consequences of cybercrime in tertiary institutions in Zaria, Kaduna State, Nigeria. *American International Journal of Contemporary Research, 3*(9).

Olaleye, O. (2017, November 1). Cybercrime: Experts proffer solutions as IoT grows. *Daily Sun*, p. 33.

Ong, J. (2017 May 12). *NUS, NTU Networks Hit by 'Sophisticated' Cyber Attacks*. Retrieved October 29, 2017, from http://www.channelnewsasia.com/news/singapore/nus-ntu-networks-hit-by-sophisticated-cyber-attacks-8840596

Organization for Economic Co-Operation and Development (OECD). (2005). *e-Government for Better Government*. Retrieved from http://www.oecd.org/gov/digital-government/egovernmentforbettergovernment.htm#HTO

Orion, W. LLC (2017). *Amendments to the Computer Misuse and Cybersecurity Act*. Retrieved November 4, 2017, from http://www.orionw.com/blog/news/security/amendments-to-the-computer-misuse-and-cybersecurity-act

Otalor, J. I., & Eiya, O. (2013). Combating Corruption in Nigeria: The Role of the Public Sector Auditor. *Research Journal of Finance and Accounting, 4*(4), 123-124. Retrieved from www.iiste.org

Oye, N. D. (2013). Reducing Corruption in African Developing Countries: The Relevance of E-Governance. *Greener Journal of Social Sciences, 3*(1), 6–13. doi:10.15580/GJSS.2013.1.103112183

Pan, J., Paul, S., & Jain, R. (2011). A survey of the research on future internet architectures. *Communications Magazine, IEEE, 49*(7), 26–36. doi:10.1109/MCOM.2011.5936152

Park, O. C., & Hopkins, R. (1992). Instructional conditions for using dynamic visual displays: A review. *Instructional Science, 21*(6), 427–449. doi:10.1007/BF00118557

Patzakis, J. (2003). *New incident response best practices: Patch and proceed is no longer acceptable incident response, vormetric (Tech. Rep.)*. Guidance Software.

Peltier, W. Y., & Simon, G. (2012). *Information-centric networking: current research activities and challenges. In Media Networks: Architectures* (p. 141). Applications, and Standards.

PermNewsletter. (2012, April). *Understanding the importance of stakeholder engagement*. Retrieved from https://www.cansr.msu.du/uploads/files

Petrenko, Y., & Huo. (2003). Testing transition systems with input and output testers. In *Proceedings of the 15th IFIP international conference on Testing of communicating systems (TestCom'03)*. Springer-Verlag.

Phneah, E. (2013). *Singapore to Open Cyber Security Lab to Train Law Enforcers*. Retrieved November 6, 2017, from http://www.zdnet.com/article/singapore-to-open-cyber-security-lab-to-train-law-enforcers/

Pieczul, O., & Foley, S. N. (2013, Oct). Discovering emergent norms in security logs. In *2013 IEEE conference on communications and network security (cns)* (p. 438-445). IEEE. doi: 10.1109/CNS.2013.6682758

Pieczul, O., & Foley, S. N. (2016). Runtime detection of zero-day vulnerability exploits in contemporary software systems. In S. Ranise & V. Swarup (Eds.), *Data and applications security and privacy xxx: 30th annual ifip wg 11.3 conference, dbsec 2016, trento, italy, july 18-20, 2016. proceedings* (pp. 347–363). Cham: Springer International Publishing. 10.1007/978-3-319-41483-6_24

Piro, G., Cianci, I., Grieco, L. A., Boggia, G., & Camarda, P. (2014). Information centric services in smart cities. *Journal of Systems and Software, 88,* 169–188. doi:10.1016/j.jss.2013.10.029

Playboy Enterprises v. Frena 839 F. Supp. 1552 (M.D. Fla. 1993)

Precious Communications. (2013). *McAfee Survey Reveals Average Internet User in Singapore Has S$57,500 Of Under-Protected 'Digital Assets'.* Retrieved November 16, 2017, from http://www.mynewsdesk.com/sg/preciouscommunications/pressreleases/mcafee-survey-reveals-average-internet-user-in-singapore-has-s-57-500-of-under-protected-digital-assets-871659

Predd, J., Pfleeger, S. L., Hunker, J., & Bulford, C. (2008, July). Insiders behaving badly. *IEEE Security Privacy, 6*(4), 66-70. doi: .2008.8710.1109/MSP

Pretschner, A., Holling, D., Eschbach, R., & Gemmar, M. (2013). A Generic Fault Model for Quality Assurance. In A. Moreira, B. Schätz, J. Gray, A. Vallecillo, & P. Clarke (Eds.), Lecture Notes in Computer Science: Vol. 8107. *Model-Driven Engineering Languages and Systems. MODELS 2013.* Berlin: Springer. doi:10.1007/978-3-642-41533-3_6

Pretschner, A., Mouelhi, T., & Le Traon, Y. (2008), Model-Based Tests for Access Control Policies. In *Proceedings of the 2008 International Conference on Software Testing, Verification, and Validation (ICST '08).* IEEE Computer Society Press 10.1109/ICST.2008.44

Priyambodo, T. K., & Suprihanto, D. (2016). *Information security on egovernment as information-centric networks.* Academic Press.

Priyambodo, T. K., Venant, U., Irawan, T., & Waas, D. V. (2017). A comprehensive review of e-government security. *Asian Journal of Information Technology, 16*(2-5), 282–286.

Probst, C. W., Hunker, J., Bishop, M., & Gollmann, D. (2008). *08302 summary - countering insider threats. In Countering insider threats, 20.07. - 25.07.2008.* Retrieved from http://drops.dagstuhl.de/opus/ volltexte/2008/1793/

Pyhnen, P., & Stranberg, O. (2011). *The network of information: Architecture and applications.* 4WARD EU FP7 Project, DeliverableD.B.1 v1. 0.

Quarshie, H.O., & Martin-Odoom, A. (2012). Fighting cybercrime in Africa. *Computer Science and Engineering, 2*(6), 98-100. Doi:105923/j.computer.20120206.03

Raihan & Uddin. (2009). Towards Model-Based Automatic Testing of Attack Scenarios. *Proceedings of the 28th International Conference on Computer Safety, Reliability, and Security (SAFECOMP '09).*

Rannu, R., Saksing, S., & Mahlakõiv, M. (2010). *MobileGovernment: 2010 and beyond.* Mobil Solutions Ltd. Retrieved Dec. 17, from: http://www.mobisolutions.com

Religious Technology Center v. Netcom Online Communication Services, Inc., 907 F.Supp. 1361 (N.D. Cal. 1995).

Ren, J. (2006). *A Connector-Centric Approach to Architectural Access Control* (PhD thesis). University of California, Irvine, CA.

Report, C. (2007). *27 suspended for Clooney file peek.* Retrieved from http://edition.cnn.com/2007/SHOWBIZ/10/10/clooney.records/index.html?eref=ew

Ribadu, N. (2003). *Economic Crime and Corruption in Nigeria: The Causes, Effects, and Efforts aimed at combating these vices in Nigeria.* Paper presented at the Monaco World Summit 5th International Summit on Transnational Crime Monte Carlo.

Ribadu, N. (2007). Corruption Drains Africa of $140bn Annually. *Punch Nigeria.* Retrieved from http://www.efccnigeria.org/index.php?option=comcontent=view&id-1347&Itemid=2

Richardson, D. J., & Wolf, A. L. (1996). Software testing at the architectural level. *Joint proceedings of the second international software architecture workshop (ISAW-2) and international workshop on multiple perspectives in software development (Viewpoints '96) on SIGSOFT '96 workshops (ISAW '96).* 10.1145/243327.243605

Ries, B. (2009). *SESAME - A Model-driven Process for the Test Selection of Small-size Safety-related Embedded Software* (PhD thesis). Laboratory for Advanced Software Systems, University of Luxembourg.

Robson. (2004). *TIOA and UPPAAL* (Master's thesis). MIT. Retrieved from http://dspace.mit.edu/bitstream/handle/1721.1/17979/57188153.pdf?sequence=1

Rodriguez-Dominguez, L., Sanchez, I. M. G., & Alvarez, I. G. (2011). From Emerging to Connected E-Government: The Effects of Socioeconomics and Internal Administration Characteristics. *The International Journal of Digital Accounting Research, 11*(1), 85–109. Retrieved from http://bit.ly/TTJjzE

Rose-Ackerman, S. (1999). *Corruption and Government: Causes, Consequences and Reform.* Cambridge, UK: Cambridge University Press. doi:10.1017/CBO9781139175098

Saidane & Guelfi. (2011). Towards improving security testability of AADL architecture models. In *Proceedings of the International Conference on Network and System Security.* IEEE.

Saidane & Guelfi. (2012). SETER: towards architecture model-based security engineering. International Journal of Secure Software Engineering.

Saidane & Guelfi. (2013). Towards test-driven and architecture model-based security and resilience engineering. In Designing, Engineering, and Analyzing Reliable and Efficient Software. IGI Global.

Sallam, A., Fadolalkarim, D., Bertino, E., & Xiao, Q. (2016). Data and syntax centric anomaly detection for relational databases. *Wiley Interdisciplinary Reviews: Data Mining and Knowledge Discovery, 6*(6), 231–239. doi: 10.1002/widm.1195

Sallam, A., Bertino, E., Hussain, S. R., Landers, D., Lefler, R. M., & Steiner, D. (2015). Dbsafe:an anomaly detection system to protect databases from exfiltration attempts. *IEEE Systems Journal.* doi:10.1109/JSYST.2015.2487221

Sanford, A. A. (2010). "I Can Air My Feelings Instead of Eating Them": Blogging as Social Support for the Morbidly Obese. *Communication Studies, 61*(5), 567–584. doi:10.1080/10510 974.2010.514676

Scarlet v. Sabam (2011) C-70/10 para. 54.

Schulz, S., Honkola, J., & Huima, A. (2007). Towards Model-Based Testing with Architecture Models. *Proceedings of the 14th Annual IEEE International Conference and Workshops on the Engineering of Computer-Based Systems (ECBS '07).* 10.1109/ECBS.2007.73

Seck, M. (2014). *Tackling the challenges of cybersecurity in Africa. Policy Brief.* United Nations Economic Commission for Africa.

Sedereviciute, K., & Valentini, C. (2011). Towards a more holistic stakeholder analysis approach. Mapping known and undiscovered stakeholders from social media. *International Journal of Strategic Communication, 5*(4), 221–239. doi:10.1080/1553118X.2011.592170

Sen, K. (2007). Concolic testing. In *Proceedings of the twenty-second ieee/acm international conference on automated software engineering* (pp. 571–572). New York, NY: ACM. doi:10.1145/1321631.1321746

Sen, K., Marinov, D., & Agha, G. (2005). Cute: A concolic unit testing engine for c. In *Proceedings of the 10th European software engineering conference held jointly with 13th acm sigsoft international symposium on foundations of software engineering* (pp. 263–272). New York, NY: ACM. doi:10.1145/1081706.1081750

Sheldon, K., & Howitt, D. (2007). *Sex offenders and the Internet.* John Wiley and Sons.

Shim, D. C., & Eom, T. H. (2008). E-Government and Anti-Corruption: Empirical Analysis of International Data. *International Journal of Public Administration, 31*(3), 298–331. doi:10.1080/01900690701590553

Shim, D. C., & Eom, T. H. (2009). Anti-Corruption Effects of Information Communication Technology (ICT) and Social Capital. *International Review of Administrative Sciences, 75*(1), 99–116. doi:10.1177/0020852308099508

Siau, K., & Long, Y. (2006). Using Social Development Lenses to Understand E-Government Development. *Journal of Global Information Management, 14*(1), 47-62. 10.4018/jgim.2006010103

Singapore Police Force. (2011). *Annual Crime Brief 2011*. Retrieved November 1, 2017, from https://www.police.gov.sg/news-and-publications/statistics?page=2

Singapore Police Force. (2015). *Annual Crime Brief 2014*. Retrieved November 1, 2017, from https://www.police.gov.sg/news-and-publications/statistics?page=1

Singapore Police Force. (2016). *Annual Crime Brief 2015*. Retrieved November 1, 2017, from https://www.police.gov.sg/news-and-publications/statistics?page=1

Singapore Police Force. (2017a). *Annual Crime Brief 2016*. Retrieved November 1, 2017, from https://www.police.gov.sg/news-and-publications/statistics?page=1

Singapore Police Force. (2017b). *Mid-year Crime Statistics for January to June 2017*. Retrieved November 1, 2017, from https://www.police.gov.sg/news-and-publications/statistics?page=1

Singapore Statutes Online. (1993). *Computer Misuse Act 1993*. Retrieved November 4, 2017, from http://160.96.185.113/aol/search/display/view.w3p;page=0;query=DocId%3A%228a3534 de-991c-4e0e-88c5-4ffa712e72af%22%20Status%3Apublished%20Depth%3A0%20%20Transa ctionTime%3A%2216%2F02%2F2017%22;rec=0;whole=yes

Singapore Statutes Online. (1998). *Computer Misuse (Amendment) Act 1998*. Retrieved November 4, 2017, from http://statutes.agc.gov.sg/

Singh, G., Pathak, R., Naz, R., & Belwal, R. (2010). E-Governance for Improved Public Sector Service Delivery in India, Ethiopia and Fiji. *International Journal of Public Sector Management, 23*(3), 254-275. 10.1108/09513551011032473

Smart Nation Singapore. (2017). *Enablers*. Retrieved October 25, 2017, from https://www.smartnation.sg/about-smart-nation/enablers

Smetters, D. K., & Jacobson, V. (2009). *Securing network content*. PARC Tech Report TR-2009-1, Xerox Palo Alto Research Center-PARC.

Smith, D. J. (2008). *A culture of corruption: Everyday deception and popular discontent in Nigeria*. Princeton, NJ: Princeton University Press.

Sony v. Universal Studios; 464 U.S. 417 (1984)

Sreedharan, S. (2013, December 7). 647 StanChart Clients' Bank Statements Stolen. *Today*. Retrieved October 26, 2017, from http://www.todayonline.com/singapore/647-stanchart-clients-bank-statements-stolen?page=1

Stapenhurst, R., Johnston, N., & Pelizzo, R. (2006). *The Role of Parliament in Curbing Corruption*. World Bank Institute of Development Studies. doi:10.1596/978-0-8213-6723-0

State of Texas E-government Task Force. (2003). Retrieved from www.dir.state.tx.us/taskforce/Surveys/State_Survey/app_b.htm

Stead, M., Gordon, R., Angus, K., & McDermott, L. (2007). A systematic review of social marketing effectiveness. *Health Education, 107*(2), 126–191. doi:10.1108/09654280710731548

Stratton Oakmont Inc. v. Prodigy Services Co., 1995 WL 323710 (N.Y. Sup. Ct. 1995).

Strowel, A. (2009). *Peer-to-peer File Sharing and Secondary Liability in Copyright Law*. Cheltenham, UK: Edward Elgar Publishing. doi:10.4337/9781848449442

Subramaniam, M., Xiao, L., Guo, B., & Pap, Z. (2009). An Approach for Test Selection for EFSMs Using a Theorem Prover. *Proceedings of the 21st IFIP WG 6.1 International Conference on Testing of Software and Communication Systems and 9th International FATES Workshop (TESTCOM '09/FATES '09)*. 10.1007/978-3-642-05031-2_10

Sulaiman, H. A., Othman, M. A., Othman, M. F. I., Rahim, Y. A., & Pee, N. C. (2015). Advanced Computer and Communication Engineering Technology. In *Proceedings of ICOCOE 2015* (vol. 362). Springer.

Sun, D. (2017, August 29). *More Falling for Online Love Scams*. Retrieved November 1, 2017, from http://www.tnp.sg/news/singapore/more-falling-online-love-scams

Sunde, L. (2013). *Netinf node for bluetooth enabled android devices* (Master's thesis). Uppsala Universitet, Department of Information Technology, Uppsala, Sweden.

Supportz. The Five Most Common Types of Cyber Crime. (n.d.). Retrieved from http://supportz. com/the-five-most-common-types-ofcyber-crime/

Svensson, J. (2005). Eight Questions about Corruption. *Journal of Economic Perspectives, 19*(3), 19-42. Retrieved from, 10.1257/089533005774357860

Syemantic. Newsroom. (n.d.). Retrieved from https://www.symantec.com/about/newsroom / press-releases/2009/symantec09/1001

Tade, O., & Aliyu, I. (2011). Social organization of Internet fraud among university undergraduates in Nigeria. *International Journal of Cyber Criminology, 5*(2), 860–875.

Tan, C. Y. (2004). *Taking the Lead on Regional Infocomm Security*. Retrieved November 5, 2017, from https://www.tech.gov.sg/media-room/speeches/2004/10/taking-the-lead-on-regional-infocomm-security

Tan, T. M. (2017, July 5). Private Sector, Police Tie up to Fight Cyber Criminals. *Straits Times*. Retrieved November 6, 2017, from http://www.straitstimes.com/singapore/courts-crime/private-sector-police-tie-up-to-fight-cyber-criminals

Tan, W. (2015, January 28). New National Agency to Tackle Cyber Threats. *Today*. Retrieved November 5, 2017, from http://www.todayonline.com/singapore/new-national-agency-tackle-cyber-threats

Tan, W. (2017, September 19). *S'pore Gives S$1.5m to Boost ASEAN Cyber Security*. Retrieved November 13, 2017, from http://www.todayonline.com/business/spore-gives-s15m-boost-asean-cyber-security

Tan, B., Ling, P. S., & Cha, V. (2013). The Evolution of Singapore's Infocomm Plans: Singapore's E-government Journey from 1980 to 2007. In G. Pan (Ed.), *Dynamics of Governing IT Innovation in Singapore: A Case Book* (pp. 1–39). World Scientific. doi:10.1142/9789814417839_0001

Tanzi, V. (1998). *Corruption around the World: Causes, Consequences, Scope and Cures.* International Monetary Fund. Working Paper 98/63. Retrieved from http://bit.ly/5BIhBw

Tanzi, V., & Davoodi, H. (1997). *Corruption, Public Investment and Growth.* International Monetary Fund. Working Paper 97/139.

Technology Times. Cyber Crime in Nigeria. (n.d.). Retrieved from http://www.technologytimes.ng/cyber-crime-in-nigeria-increasing-at-alarming-rate/

Technopedia. Dictionary. (n.d.). Retrieved from https://www.techopedia.com/dictonary/

Tehrani, P. M. (2017). *Cyberterrorism: The Legal and Enforcement Issues.* World Scientific Publishing Europe Ltd. doi:10.1142/q0063

Thackeray, R., Neiger, B. L., Hanson, C. L., & McKenzie, J. F. (2008). Enhancing promotional strategies within social marketing programs: Use of Web 2.0 social media. *Health Promotion Practice*, *9*(4), 338–343. doi:10.1177/1524839908325335 PMID:18936268

Tham, I. (2017, May 25). New Govt Centre to Detect Cyber Threats. *Straits Times*. Retrieved November 6, 2017, from http://www.straitstimes.com/tech/new-govt-centre-to-detect-cyber-threats

The Electronic Delivery of Services Bill (EDS). (2011). *Bill 2011 Draft 16th November 2011.* Retrieved from http://meity.gov.in/sites/upload_files/dit/files/Electronic_Delivery_of_Services_Bill_2011_16thNov_Legal_17112011.pdf

The Ministry of Communications, & Information and the Cyber Security Agency of Singapore. (2017). *Public Consultation Paper on the Draft Cybersecurity Bill.* Retrieved November 5, 2017, from https://www.csa.gov.sg/~/media/csa/cybersecurity_bill/consult_document.ashx?la=en

The Nation. (2016). *Cost of cyber crime to hit $6 trillion annually – Report.* Retrieved from www.thenationonlineng.net/cost-cyber-crime-hit-6-trillion-annually-report/

The Singapore Computer Emergency Response Team. (2015). *Frequently Asked Questions.* Retrieved November 5, 2017, from https://www.csa.gov.sg/singcert/about-us/faqs

The Statistics Portal. Most Famous Social Networking Sites as of January 2018. (n.d.). Retrieved from https://www.statista.com/statistics/272014/global-social-networks-ranked-by-number-of-users/

The World Bank Group. (2011). *Definition of E-Government.* World Bank. Retrieved December 13, 2012, from http://go.worldbank.org/M1JHE0Z280

Theohary, C. A., & Rollins, J. W. (2015). *Cyberwarfare and Cyberterrorism: In Brief.* Retrieved October 25, 2017, from https://fas.org/sgp/crs/natsec/R43955.pdf

Compilation of References

Thompson, E. (2017). *Building a HIPAA-Compliant Cybersecurity Program: Using NIST 800-30 and CSF to Secure Protected Health Information.* Apress. doi:10.1007/978-1-4842-3060-2

ThornW. A.PornographyC.StatsA. (n.d.). Retrieved from https://www.wearethorn.org/child-pornography-and-abuse-statistics/ http://www.missingkids.com/en_us/documents/CP_Legislation_Report.pdf

TODAY. (2015, March 10). *Curtin Singapore's Website Defaced by Hackers Claiming to Represent ISIS.* Retrieved October 29, 2017, from http://www.todayonline.com/singapore/curtin-singapores-website-defaced-hackers-claiming-represent-isis

TODAY. (2017, May 12). *NUS-NTU Hack: Other Recent Cyber Breaches in Singapore.* Retrieved October 26, 2017, from http://www.todayonline.com/singapore/recent-cyber-security-attacks

Toh, E. M. (2017 May 13). Global Cyber Attack: Don't Pay the Ransom, Says S'pore's Cyber Security Agency. *Today.* Retrieved October 30, 2017, from http://www.todayonline.com/singapore/singapores-govt-agencies-and-critical-infrastructure-not-affected-global-cyber-attack-csa

Torres, L., Pina, V., & Acerate, B. (2006). E-Governance Developments in European Union Cities: Reshaping Government's Relationship with Citizens. *Governance: An International Journal of Policy, Administration, and Institutions, 19*(2), 277-302. 10.1111/j.1468-0491.2006.00315.x

Trimi, S., & Shen, H. (2008). Emerging Trends in M-Government. *Communications of the ACM, 51*(5), 53–58. doi:10.1145/1342327.1342338

Union, E. (2016). *General data protection regulation.* eur-lex: Eu law. Retrieved from http://eur-lex.europa.eu/legal-content/EN/ ALL/?uri=CELEX:32016R06792

United Nations Development Programme (UNDP). (2012). *Mobile Technologies and Empowerment: Enhancing human development through participation and innovation.* Democratic Governance Division, United Nations Development Programme.

United Nations Division for Public Economics and Public Administration, & American Society for Public Administration. (2002). *Benchmarking E-government: A Global Perspective.* Retrieved October 23, 2017, from https://publicadministration.un.org/egovkb/Portals/egovkb/Documents/un/English.pdf

United Nations E-Government Survey. (2016b). *E-Government in Support of Sustainable Development.* United Nations. Retrieved from http://www.un.org/desa https://publicadministration.un.org

United Nations. (2001). *Benchmarking E-government: A Global Perspective Assessing the UN Member States Assessing the Progress of the UN Member States United Nations Division for Public Economics and Public Administration.* American Society for Public Administration.

United Nations. (2003). *UN Global E-government Survey 2003.* Retrieved October 23, 2017, from https://publicadministration.un.org/egovkb/Portals/egovkb/Documents/un/2003-Survey/Complete-Survey.pdf

United Nations. (2004). *UN Global E-Government Readiness Report 2004: Towards Access for Opportunity.* Department of Economic and Social Affairs Division for Public Administration and Development Management United Nations.

United Nations. (2004). *United Nations Global E-government Readiness Report 2004: Towards Access for Opportunity.* Retrieved October 23, 2017, from https://publicadministration.un.org/egovkb/Portals/egovkb/Documents/un/2004-Survey/Complete-Survey.pdf

United Nations. (2005). *UN Global E-government Readiness Report 2005 From E-government to E-inclusion. Department of Economic and Social Affairs Division for Public Administration and Development Management.* United Nations.

United Nations. (2005). *United Nations Global E-government Readiness Report 2005: From E-government to E-inclusion.* Retrieved October 23, 2017, from https://publicadministration.un.org/egovkb/Portals/egovkb/Documents/un/2005-Survey/Complete-survey.pdf

United Nations. (2008). *From e-Government to Connected Governance e-Government Survey 2008. Department of Economic and Social Affairs Division for Public Administration and Development Management.* United Nations.

United Nations. (2008). *UN E-government Survey 2008: From E-government to Connected Governance.* Retrieved October 23, 2017, from https://publicadministration.un.org/egovkb/Portals/egovkb/Documents/un/2008-Survey/Complete-survey.pdf

United Nations. (2008). *United Nations e-governance Survey 2008 – From e-governance to Connected Governance.* New York: Department of Economic and Social Affairs, Division for Public Administration and Development Management.

United Nations. (2010). *United Nations E-Government Survey 2010 Leveraging e-government at a time of financial and economic crisis UN Publishing Section.* Author.

United Nations. (2010). *United Nations E-government Survey 2010: Leveraging E-government at a Time of Financial and Economic Crisis.* Retrieved October 23, 2017, from https://publicadministration.un.org/egovkb/Portals/egovkb/Documents/un/2010-Survey/Complete-survey.pdf

United Nations. (2012). *United Nations E-Government Survey 2012 United Nations E-Government Survey 2012 E-Government for the People.* Department of Economic and Social Affairs United Nations.

United Nations. (2012). *United Nations E-government Survey 2012: E-government for the People.* Retrieved October 23, 2017, from https://publicadministration.un.org/egovkb/Portals/egovkb/Documents/un/2012-Survey/Complete-Survey.pdf

United Nations. (2014). *United Nations E-government Survey 2014: E-government for the Future We Want.* Retrieved October 23, 2017, from https://publicadministration.un.org/egovkb/Portals/egovkb/Documents/un/2014-Survey/E-Gov_Complete_Survey-2014.pdf

United Nations. (2014). *United Nations E-Government Survey: E-Government For The Future We Want*. Department of Economic and Social Affairs.

United Nations. (2016). *United Nations E-government Survey 2016: E-government in Support of Sustainable Development*. Retrieved October 23, 2017, from http://workspace.unpan.org/sites/Internet/Documents/UNPAN97453.pdf

United Nations. (2016a). *E-Government Survey Department of Economic and Social Affairs*. Author.

Ursala, S. (2010). *Importance of the role of ICT for development*. Retrieved from https://www.adb.org/news/speeches/importance-role-ict-development

Usman, S. H. (2013). A Review of Responsibilities of Internet Service Providers Toward Their Customers' Network Security. *Journal of Theoretical and Applied Information Technolog, 49*(1), 70–78.

Valeur, F., Mutz, D., & Vigna, G. (2005). A Learning-Based Approach to the Detection of SQL Attacks. Detection of Intrusions and Malware, and Vulnerability Assessment Lecture Notes in Computer Science, 123-140. doi:10.1007/11506881_8

Van Dijck, P., & Verbruggen, H. (1987). The Case of Singapore. In H. Linnemann (Ed.), *Export-oriented Industrialization in Developing Countries* (pp. 381–415). Singapore: Singapore University Press.

Vasilakos, A. V., Li, Z., Simon, G., & You, W. (2015). Information centric network: Research challenges and opportunities. *Journal of Network and Computer Applications, 52*, 1–10. doi:10.1016/j.jnca.2015.02.001

Verizon. (2016). *Data breach investigations report* (Tech. Rep.). Verizon.

Verizon. (2017). *Data breach investigation report paints a bleak picture of the current state of cybersecurity*. Retrieved from www.silicon.co.uk/security/verizon-cyber-attacks-210499

Viacom Inc v. YouTube Inc No.1:07-cv-02103 (S.D.N. *Y.*), (2008)

Vijayakumar, S., Sabarish, K., & Krishnan, G. (2010). *Innovation and M-Governance: The Kerala Mobile Governance Experience and Road-Map for a Comprehensive M-Governance Strategy*. Retrieved from: http://www.ipeglobal.com/newsletter/May_2011/Kerala%20Mgovernance%20Strategy.pdf

Vittal, N. (2003). *Corruption in India*. New Delhi, India: Academic Foundation.

Vlachvei, A., & Notta, O. (2015). Greek Food Manufacturing Firms' Social Media Efforts: Evidence from Facebook. *Procedia: Social and Behavioral Sciences, 175*(1), 308–313.

von Oheimb & Lotz. (2002). Formal Security Analysis with Interacting State Machines. In *Proceedings of the 7th European Symposium on Research in Computer Security (ESORICS '02)*. Springer-Verlag.

Wakefiled, M., Loken, B., & Hornik, R. (2014). *Use of mass media campaigns to change health behaviour.* HHS Author manuscripts.

Wang, L., Hoque, A., Yi, C., Alyyan, A., & Zhang, B. (2012). *Ospfn: An ospf based routing protocol for named data networking.* University of Memphis and University of Arizona, Tech. Rep.

Wang, W., & Ji. (2009). An Automatic Generation Method of Executable Test Case Using Model-Driven Architecture. In *Proceedings of the 2009 Fourth International Conference on Innovative Computing, Information and Control (ICICIC '09).* IEEE Computer Society.

Warren, G., & Jay, G. H. (2002). *Computer forensics: Incident response essentials.* Boston: Addison-Wesley.

Waseda University, & International Academy of CIO. (2014). *WASEDA – IAC 10th International E-Government Ranking 2014.* Retrieved October 23, 2017, from http://www.e-gov.waseda.ac.jp/pdf/2014_e-gov_press_release.pdf

Waseda University, & International Academy of CIO. (2015). *2015 WASEDA – IAC International E-Government Ranking Survey.* Retrieved October 23, 2017, from http://www.e-gov.waseda.ac.jp/pdf/2015_Waseda_IAC_E-Government_Press_Release.pdf

Waseda University, & International Academy of CIO. (2016). *The 12th Waseda - IAC International e-Government Rankings Survey 2016 Report.* Retrieved October 23, 2017, from http://www.e-gov.waseda.ac.jp/pdf/2016_E-Gov_Press_Release.pdf

Waseda University, & International Academy of CIO. (2017). *THE 13TH WASEDA – IAC International Digital Government Rankings 2017 Report.* Retrieved October 23, 2017, from http://www.e-gov.waseda.ac.jp/pdf/2017_Digital-Government_Ranking_Press_Release.pdf

Weiler, S., & Blacka, D. (2013). *Clarifications and implementation notes for dns security (dnssec).* Rfc 6840, Internet Engineering Task Force.

Wells, M., Finkelhor, D., Wolak, J., & Mitchell, K. (2007). Defining child pornography: Law enforcement dilemmas in investigations of Internet child pornography possession. *Police Practice and Research, 8*(3), 269–282. doi:10.1080/15614260701450765

West, D. (2004). E-Government and the Transformation of Service Delivery and Citizen Attitudes. *Public Administration Review, 64*(1), 15-27. 10.1111/j.1540-6210.2004.00343.x

Wikipedia. (n.d.). *Cyercrime.* Retrieved from https:/en.m.wikipedia.org/wiki/cybercrime

Wikipedia. Internet of Things. (n.d.). Retrieved from https://en.m.wikipedia.org/wiki/Internetofthings

Wikipedia. Stakeholder Engagement. (n.d.). Retrieved from https://en.m.wikipedia.org/wiki/stakeholder-engagement

Williams, B.K., & Sawyer, S.C. (n.d.). *Using information technology* (11th ed.). New York: McGraw Hill.

Williams, R., & Edge, D. (1996). The social shaping of technology. *Research Policy, 25*.

Wimmer, M., & Traunmuller, R. (2001). Trends in Electronic Government: Managing Distributed Knowledge. In *Proceedings of the 11th International Workshop on Database Expert Systems Applications*, Springer.

Wong, Y. Y. J., Gerber, R., & Toh, K. A. (2003). A Comparative Study of Diffusion of Web-based Education (WBE) in Singapore and Australia. In A. Aggarwal (Ed.), *Web-Based Education: Learning from Experience* (pp. 347–370). Hershey, PA: IGI Global. doi:10.4018/978-1-59140-102-5.ch021

World Bank. (1992). *Governance and Development*. Washington, DC: World Bank.

World Bank. (2015). *e-Government*. Retrieved from http://www.worldbank.org/en/topic/ict/brief/e-government Assessed on 28/6/2017

World Congress Against CSEC. (2002). *Child pornography*. Author.

World economic forum and Harvard school of public health. (2011). *The global economic burden of Non communicable diseases*. Author.

World Health Organization. (2005a). *Preventable hospital infections are a major cause of death and disability for patients*. WHO.

World Health Organization. (2010). *Global statue report on non communicable disease*. WHO.

World Health Organization. (2015). *Health profile*. Tunisia: WHO.

World Health Organization. (2017). *Non-communicable disease Progress Monitor*. WHO.

World Stage Group. (n.d.). Retrieved from www.worldstagegroup.com/worldstagenew/Index.php? active=news&newscid=256138&catid=2

Wortley, R., & Smallbone, S. (n.d.). Child pornography on the Internet. *Problem Oriented Guides for Police, 41*, 14-16.

Wressnegger, C. (2013). A close look on n-Grams in intrusion detection. *Proceedings of the 2013 ACM Workshop on Artificial intelligence and security - AISec 13*. doi:10.1145/2517312.2517316

Wu, G. Z., Osborn, S. L., & Jin, X. (2009). Database intrusion detection using role profiling with role hierarchy. In W. Jonker & M. Petković (Eds.), *Secure data management: 6th vldb workshop, sdm 2009, lyon, france, august 28, 2009. proceedings* (pp. 33–48). Berlin: Springer Berlin Heidelberg. 10.1007/978-3-642-04219-5_3

Wu, H., Ozok, A. A., Gurses, A. P., & Wei, J. (2009). User aspects of electronic and mobile government: Results from a review of current research. *Electronic Government: An International Journal, 6*(3), 233–251. doi:10.1504/EG.2009.024942

Xiong, P., Stepien, B., & Peyton, L. (2009). *Model-Based Penetration Test Framework for Web Applications Using TTCN-3. E-Technologies: Innovation in an Open World*. Springer.

Xylomenos, G., Ververidis, C. N., Siris, V. A., Fotiou, N., Tsilopoulos, C., Vasilakos, X., ... Polyzos, G. C. (2014). A survey of information-centric networking research. *IEEE Communications Surveys and Tutorials*, *16*(2), 1024–1049. doi:10.1109/SURV.2013.070813.00063

Yang, J., Wang, & Xia. (2009). A Task-Deployment Model for the Simulation of Computer Network Attack and Defense Exercises. In *Proceedings of the 2009 First IEEE International Conference on Information Science and Engineering (ICISE '09)*. IEEE Computer Society.

Yan, M. (2012). The law surrounding the facilitation of online copyright infringement. *European Intellectual Property Review*, *34*(2), 122–126.

Yaqub, M. A., Ahmed, S. H., Bouk, S. H., & Kim, D. (2016). Information-centric networks (icn). In *Content-Centric Networks* (pp. 19–33). Springer. doi:10.1007/978-981-10-0066-9_2

Yildiz, M. (2004). E-governance Research: Reviewing the Literature, Limitations, and Ways Forward. *Government Information Quarterly*, 24.

Yu, E. (2006). *S'pore: New Center to Monitor Govt Systems*. Retrieved November 6, 2017, from http://www.zdnet.com/article/spore-new-center-to-monitor-govt-systems-2039419454/

Yusuf, O. (2006). *Solutions for E-Government Development in Nigeria*. Accenture EIU Government Research.

Yu, Y., Afanasyev, A., Zhu, Z., & Zhang, L. (2014). *Ndn technical memo: Naming conventions. Technical report*. UCLA.

Zejnullahu, F., & Baholli, I. (2017). Overview of researches on the influential factors of m-government's adoption. *European Journal of Management and Marketing Studies*, *2*(2), 1-19. Available at: https://oapub.org/soc/index.php/EJMMS/article/view/166/488

Zhang, L., Afanasyev, A., Burke, J., Jacobson, V., Crowley, P., & Papadopoulos, C. (2014). Named data networking. *Computer Communication Review*, *44*(3), 66–73. doi:10.1145/2656877.2656887

Zhou, J. (2011). Singapore Law on Information Technology. *IT Connect*, 20. Retrieved November 4, 2017, from http://enewsletter.ntu.edu.sg/itconnect/2011-08/Pages/SingaporeLawOnIT.aspx

Zhou, C., & Kumar, R. (2009). Modeling Simulink Diagrams Using Input/Output Extended Finite Automata. In *Proceedings of the 2009 33rd Annual IEEE International Computer Software and Applications Conference* (vol. 2). IEEE. 10.1109/COMPSAC.2009.176

Zmijewska, A., Elaine, L., & Seele, R. (2004). Towards understanding of factors influencing user acceptance of mobile payment systems. *Proceedings of IADIS International Conference*.

Related References

To continue our tradition of advancing information science and technology research, we have compiled a list of recommended IGI Global readings. These references will provide additional information and guidance to further enrich your knowledge and assist you with your own research and future publications.

Abdel-Hameid, S. O., & Wilson, E. (2018). Gender, Organization, and Change in Sudan. In N. Mahtab, T. Haque, I. Khan, M. Islam, & I. Wahid (Eds.), *Handbook of Research on Women's Issues and Rights in the Developing World* (pp. 107–120). Hershey, PA: IGI Global. doi:10.4018/978-1-5225-3018-3.ch007

Abdulazeez, N. J. (2016). Reconciliation of Identity Groups in Iraq: Conflict Analysis and Political Means of Ethnic Accommodation. In F. Cante & H. Quehl (Eds.), *Handbook of Research on Transitional Justice and Peace Building in Turbulent Regions* (pp. 278–297). Hershey, PA: IGI Global. doi:10.4018/978-1-4666-9675-4. ch014

Abdullahi, R. B. (2018). Volunteerism in Urban Development the Case of Non-Cash, Non-Digital Crowdfunding Growth in Nigeria. In U. Benna & A. Benna (Eds.), *Crowdfunding and Sustainable Urban Development in Emerging Economies* (pp. 188–210). Hershey, PA: IGI Global. doi:10.4018/978-1-5225-3952-0.ch010

Abioye, T. O., Oyesomi, K., Ajiboye, E., Omidiora, S., & Oyero, O. (2017). Education, Gender, and Child-Rights: Salient Issues in SDGS Years in ADO-ODO/ OTA Local Government Area of Ogun State, Nigeria. In O. Nelson, B. Ojebuyi, & A. Salawu (Eds.), *Impacts of the Media on African Socio-Economic Development* (pp. 141–154). Hershey, PA: IGI Global. doi:10.4018/978-1-5225-1859-4.ch009

Acuña, Y. G. (2016). From the Studies of Violences to Memories: The Construction of Victims and its Articulations with the State. In F. Cante & H. Quehl (Eds.), *Handbook of Research on Transitional Justice and Peace Building in Turbulent Regions* (pp. 332–355). Hershey, PA: IGI Global. doi:10.4018/978-1-4666-9675-4.ch017

Adhikary, M., & Khatun, M. (2016). Issues of Convergence: Some Evidences of SAARC Countries. In R. Das (Ed.), *Handbook of Research on Global Indicators of Economic and Political Convergence* (pp. 119–143). Hershey, PA: IGI Global. doi:10.4018/978-1-5225-0215-9.ch006

Adisa, W. B. (2018). Land Use Policy and Urban Sprawl in Nigeria: Land Use and the Emergence of Urban Sprawl. In A. Eneanya (Ed.), *Handbook of Research on Environmental Policies for Emergency Management and Public Safety* (pp. 256–274). Hershey, PA: IGI Global. doi:10.4018/978-1-5225-3194-4.ch014

Afolabi, O. S., Amao-Kolawole, T. G., Shittu, A. K., & Oguntokun, O. O. (2018). Rule of Law, Governance, and Sustainable Development: The Nigerian Perspective. In K. Teshager Alemu & M. Abebe Alebachew (Eds.), *Handbook of Research on Sustainable Development and Governance Strategies for Economic Growth in Africa* (pp. 273–290). Hershey, PA: IGI Global. doi:10.4018/978-1-5225-3247-7.ch015

Agyei-Mensah, B. K. (2016). Impact of Adopting IFRS in Ghana: Empirical Evidence. In E. Uchenna, M. Nnadi, S. Tanna, & F. Iyoha (Eds.), *Economics and Political Implications of International Financial Reporting Standards* (pp. 191–230). Hershey, PA: IGI Global. doi:10.4018/978-1-4666-9876-5.ch010

Agyemang, O. S. (2018). Institutional Structures and the Prevalence of Foreign Ownership of Firms: Empirical Evidence From Africa. In K. Teshager Alemu & M. Abebe Alebachew (Eds.), *Handbook of Research on Sustainable Development and Governance Strategies for Economic Growth in Africa* (pp. 455–479). Hershey, PA: IGI Global. doi:10.4018/978-1-5225-3247-7.ch024

Aham-Anyanwu, N. M., & Li, H. (2017). E-State: Realistic or Utopian? *International Journal of Public Administration in the Digital Age, 4*(2), 56–76. doi:10.4018/IJPADA.2017040105

Ahmad, M. B., Pride, C., & Corsy, A. K. (2016). Free Speech, Press Freedom, and Democracy in Ghana: A Conceptual and Historical Overview. In L. Mukhongo & J. Macharia (Eds.), *Political Influence of the Media in Developing Countries* (pp. 59–73). Hershey, PA: IGI Global. doi:10.4018/978-1-4666-9613-6.ch005

Al-Jamal, M., & Abu-Shanab, E. (2018). Open Government: The Line between Privacy and Transparency. *International Journal of Public Administration in the Digital Age*, 5(2), 64–75. doi:10.4018/IJPADA.2018040106

Alsaç, U. (2017). EKAP: Turkey's Centralized E-Procurement System. In R. Shakya (Ed.), *Digital Governance and E-Government Principles Applied to Public Procurement* (pp. 126–150). Hershey, PA: IGI Global. doi:10.4018/978-1-5225-2203-4.ch006

Amadi, L. A., & Igwe, P. (2018). Open Government and Bureaucratic Secrecy in the Developing Democracies: Africa in Perspective. In A. Kok (Ed.), *Proliferation of Open Government Initiatives and Systems* (pp. 1–28). Hershey, PA: IGI Global. doi:10.4018/978-1-5225-4987-1.ch001

Anthopoulos, L., Janssen, M., & Weerakkody, V. (2016). A Unified Smart City Model (USCM) for Smart City Conceptualization and Benchmarking. *International Journal of Electronic Government Research*, 12(2), 77–93. doi:10.4018/IJEGR.2016040105

Ayeni, A. O. (2018). Environmental Policies for Emergency Management and Public Safety: Implementing Green Policy and Community Participation. In A. Eneanya (Ed.), *Handbook of Research on Environmental Policies for Emergency Management and Public Safety* (pp. 40–59). Hershey, PA: IGI Global. doi:10.4018/978-1-5225-3194-4.ch003

Ayodele, J. O. (2017). The Influence of Migration and Crime on Development in Lagos, Nigeria. In G. Afolayan & A. Akinwale (Eds.), *Global Perspectives on Development Administration and Cultural Change* (pp. 192–230). Hershey, PA: IGI Global. doi:10.4018/978-1-5225-0629-4.ch009

Baarda, R. (2017). Digital Democracy in Authoritarian Russia: Opportunity for Participation, or Site of Kremlin Control? In R. Luppicini & R. Baarda (Eds.), *Digital Media Integration for Participatory Democracy* (pp. 87–100). Hershey, PA: IGI Global. doi:10.4018/978-1-5225-2463-2.ch005

Bagwell, T. C., & Jackson, S. L. (2016). The Mode of Information – Due Process of Law and Student Loans: Bills of Attainder Enter the Digital Age. In R. Cropf & T. Bagwell (Eds.), *Ethical Issues and Citizen Rights in the Era of Digital Government Surveillance* (pp. 16–34). Hershey, PA: IGI Global. doi:10.4018/978-1-4666-9905-2.ch002

Balakrishnan, K. (2017). The Rationale for Offsets in Defence Acquisition from a Theoretical Perspective. In K. Burgess & P. Antill (Eds.), *Emerging Strategies in Defense Acquisitions and Military Procurement* (pp. 263–276). Hershey, PA: IGI Global. doi:10.4018/978-1-5225-0599-0.ch015

Banerjee, S. (2017). Globalization and Human Rights: How Globalization Can Be a Tool to Protect the Human Rights. In C. Akrivopoulou (Ed.), *Defending Human Rights and Democracy in the Era of Globalization* (pp. 1–16). Hershey, PA: IGI Global. doi:10.4018/978-1-5225-0723-9.ch001

Batırel, Ö. F. (2016). The Distributional Effects of Tax Policy: Tax Expenditures in Turkey. In M. Erdoğdu & B. Christiansen (Eds.), *Handbook of Research on Public Finance in Europe and the MENA Region* (pp. 391–428). Hershey, PA: IGI Global. doi:10.4018/978-1-5225-0053-7.ch018

Batrancea, L., Nichita, A., Batrancea, I., & Kirchler, E. (2016). Tax Compliance Behavior: An Upshot of Trust in and Power of Authorities across Europe and MENA. In M. Erdoğdu & B. Christiansen (Eds.), *Handbook of Research on Public Finance in Europe and the MENA Region* (pp. 248–267). Hershey, PA: IGI Global. doi:10.4018/978-1-5225-0053-7.ch012

Bessant, J. (2017). Digital Humour, Gag Laws, and the Liberal Security State. In R. Luppicini & R. Baarda (Eds.), *Digital Media Integration for Participatory Democracy* (pp. 204–221). Hershey, PA: IGI Global. doi:10.4018/978-1-5225-2463-2.ch010

Boachie, C. (2016). The Effect of International Financial Reporting Standards Adoption on Foreign Direct Investment and the Economy. In E. Uchenna, M. Nnadi, S. Tanna, & F. Iyoha (Eds.), *Economics and Political Implications of International Financial Reporting Standards* (pp. 342–361). Hershey, PA: IGI Global. doi:10.4018/978-1-4666-9876-5.ch017

Boachie, C. (2017). Public Financial Management and Systems of Accountability in Sub-National Governance in Developing Economies. In E. Schoburgh & R. Ryan (Eds.), *Handbook of Research on Sub-National Governance and Development* (pp. 193–217). Hershey, PA: IGI Global. doi:10.4018/978-1-5225-1645-3.ch009

Boachie, C., & Adu-Darko, E. (2018). Socio-Economic Impact of Foreign Direct Investment in Developing Countries. In V. Malepati & C. Gowri (Eds.), *Foreign Direct Investments (FDIs) and Opportunities for Developing Economies in the World Market* (pp. 66–81). Hershey, PA: IGI Global. doi:10.4018/978-1-5225-3026-8.ch004

Bolgherini, S., & Lippi, A. (2016). Italy: Remapping Local Government from Re-Allocation and Re-Shaping to Re-Scaling. In U. Sadioglu & K. Dede (Eds.), *Theoretical Foundations and Discussions on the Reformation Process in Local Governments* (pp. 265–287). Hershey, PA: IGI Global. doi:10.4018/978-1-5225-0317-0.ch011

Borràs, S. (2017). Rights of Nature to Protect Human Rights in Times of Environmental Crisis. In C. Akrivopoulou (Ed.), *Defending Human Rights and Democracy in the Era of Globalization* (pp. 225–261). Hershey, PA: IGI Global. doi:10.4018/978-1-5225-0723-9.ch010

Brusca, I., Olmo, J., & Labrador, M. (2018). Characterizing the Risk Factors for Financial Sustainability in Spanish Local Governments. In M. Rodríguez Bolívar & M. López Subires (Eds.), *Financial Sustainability and Intergenerational Equity in Local Governments* (pp. 206–223). Hershey, PA: IGI Global. doi:10.4018/978-1-5225-3713-7.ch009

Caccioppoli, L. (2016). Bridging the Gaps with Nonprofits: The Intersection of Institutions, Interests, and the Health Policy Process. In R. Gholipour & K. Rouzbehani (Eds.), *Social, Economic, and Political Perspectives on Public Health Policy-Making* (pp. 233–256). Hershey, PA: IGI Global. doi:10.4018/978-1-4666-9944-1.ch011

Callanan, M. (2016). Institutionalizing the Politics-Administration Dichotomy in Local Government: Reforming the Council-Manager System in Ireland. In U. Sadioglu & K. Dede (Eds.), *Theoretical Foundations and Discussions on the Reformation Process in Local Governments* (pp. 153–178). Hershey, PA: IGI Global. doi:10.4018/978-1-5225-0317-0.ch007

Campbell, A. (2016). "Imperialism" and "Federalism": The Ambiguity of State and City in Russia. In U. Sadioglu & K. Dede (Eds.), *Theoretical Foundations and Discussions on the Reformation Process in Local Governments* (pp. 353–372). Hershey, PA: IGI Global. doi:10.4018/978-1-5225-0317-0.ch015

Carini, C., & Teodori, C. (2016). Potential Uses and Usefulness of Italian Local Government Consolidated Financial Reporting: The Case of the Town Council of Brescia. In A. Ferreira, G. Azevedo, J. Oliveira, & R. Marques (Eds.), *Global Perspectives on Risk Management and Accounting in the Public Sector* (pp. 68–89). Hershey, PA: IGI Global. doi:10.4018/978-1-4666-9803-1.ch004

Carter, S. D. (2016). Increased Workforce Diversity by Race, Gender, and Age and Equal Employment Opportunity Laws: Implications for Human Resource Development. In J. Prescott (Ed.), *Handbook of Research on Race, Gender, and the Fight for Equality* (pp. 398–423). Hershey, PA: IGI Global. doi:10.4018/978-1-5225-0047-6.ch018

Cebeci, K., & Zülfüoğlu, Ö. (2016). Financial Market Regulations in a Globalized World: Some Remarks for the MENA Region. In M. Erdoğdu & B. Christiansen (Eds.), *Comparative Political and Economic Perspectives on the MENA Region* (pp. 180–198). Hershey, PA: IGI Global. doi:10.4018/978-1-4666-9601-3.ch008

Chen, M., & Su, F. (2017). Global Civic Engagement as an Empowering Device for Cross-Ethnic and Cross-Cultural Understanding in Taiwan. In R. Shin (Ed.), *Convergence of Contemporary Art, Visual Culture, and Global Civic Engagement* (pp. 24–45). Hershey, PA: IGI Global. doi:10.4018/978-1-5225-1665-1.ch002

Cheng, J. Y. (2016). Local Governments in China. In U. Sadioglu & K. Dede (Eds.), *Comparative Studies and Regionally-Focused Cases Examining Local Governments* (pp. 207–227). Hershey, PA: IGI Global. doi:10.4018/978-1-5225-0320-0.ch010

Cheong, D. D. (2016). Countering Online Violent Extremism: State Action as Strategic Communication. In M. Khader, L. Neo, G. Ong, E. Mingyi, & J. Chin (Eds.), *Combating Violent Extremism and Radicalization in the Digital Era* (pp. 283–306). Hershey, PA: IGI Global. doi:10.4018/978-1-5225-0156-5.ch014

Chigwata, T. C. (2017). Fiscal Decentralization: Constraints to Revenue-Raising by Local Government in Zimbabwe. In E. Schoburgh & R. Ryan (Eds.), *Handbook of Research on Sub-National Governance and Development* (pp. 218–240). Hershey, PA: IGI Global. doi:10.4018/978-1-5225-1645-3.ch010

Chowdhury, M. A. (2017). The Nexus Between Institutional Quality and Foreign Direct Investments (FDI) in South Asia: Dynamic Heterogeneous Panel Approach. In T. Dorożyński & A. Kuna-Marszałek (Eds.), *Outward Foreign Direct Investment (FDI) in Emerging Market Economies* (pp. 293–310). Hershey, PA: IGI Global. doi:10.4018/978-1-5225-2345-1.ch015

Christopher, M. E., & Tsushima, V. G. (2017). Police Interactions with Persons-in-Crisis: Emergency Psychological Services and Jail Diversion. In C. Mitchell & E. Dorian (Eds.), *Police Psychology and Its Growing Impact on Modern Law Enforcement* (pp. 274–294). Hershey, PA: IGI Global. doi:10.4018/978-1-5225-0813-7.ch014

Citro, F., Lucianelli, G., & Santis, S. (2018). Financial Conditions, Financial Sustainability, and Intergenerational Equity in Local Governments: A Literature Review. In M. Rodríguez Bolívar & M. López Subires (Eds.), *Financial Sustainability and Intergenerational Equity in Local Governments* (pp. 101–124). Hershey, PA: IGI Global. doi:10.4018/978-1-5225-3713-7.ch005

Covell, C. E. (2018). Theoretical Application of Public Sector Planning and Budgeting. In M. Rodríguez Bolívar & M. López Subires (Eds.), *Financial Sustainability and Intergenerational Equity in Local Governments* (pp. 248–279). Hershey, PA: IGI Global. doi:10.4018/978-1-5225-3713-7.ch011

Cuadrado-Ballesteros, B., García-Sánchez, I. M., & Martínez-Ferrero, J. (2016). Commercialization of Local Public Services. In A. Ferreira, G. Azevedo, J. Oliveira, & R. Marques (Eds.), *Global Perspectives on Risk Management and Accounting in the Public Sector* (pp. 132–150). Hershey, PA: IGI Global. doi:10.4018/978-1-4666-9803-1.ch007

Cunha, A., Ferreira, A. D., & Fernandes, M. J. (2016). The Influence of Accounting Information in the Re-Election of the Mayors in Portugal. In A. Ferreira, G. Azevedo, J. Oliveira, & R. Marques (Eds.), *Global Perspectives on Risk Management and Accounting in the Public Sector* (pp. 108–131). Hershey, PA: IGI Global. doi:10.4018/978-1-4666-9803-1.ch006

Cunha, A. M., Ferreira, A. D., & Fernandes, M. J. (2018). The Impact of Accounting Information and Socioeconomic Factors in the Re-Election of Portuguese Mayors. In G. Azevedo, J. da Silva Oliveira, R. Marques, & A. Ferreira (Eds.), *Handbook of Research on Modernization and Accountability in Public Sector Management* (pp. 406–432). Hershey, PA: IGI Global. doi:10.4018/978-1-5225-3731-1.ch019

da Rosa, I., & de Almeida, J. (2017). Digital Transformation in the Public Sector: Electronic Procurement in Portugal. In R. Shakya (Ed.), *Digital Governance and E-Government Principles Applied to Public Procurement* (pp. 99–125). Hershey, PA: IGI Global. doi:10.4018/978-1-5225-2203-4.ch005

Daramola, O. (2018). Revisiting the Legal Framework of Urban Planning in the Global South: An Explanatory Example of Nigeria. In K. Teshager Alemu & M. Abebe Alebachew (Eds.), *Handbook of Research on Sustainable Development and Governance Strategies for Economic Growth in Africa* (pp. 258–271). Hershey, PA: IGI Global. doi:10.4018/978-1-5225-3247-7.ch014

Dau, L. A., Moore, E. M., Soto, M. A., & LeBlanc, C. R. (2017). How Globalization Sparked Entrepreneurship in the Developing World: The Impact of Formal Economic and Political Linkages. In B. Christiansen & F. Kasarcı (Eds.), *Corporate Espionage, Geopolitics, and Diplomacy Issues in International Business* (pp. 72–91). Hershey, PA: IGI Global. doi:10.4018/978-1-5225-1031-4.ch005

Dean, G. (2016). Framing the Challenges of Online Violent Extremism: "Policing-Public-Policies-Politics" Framework. In M. Khader, L. Neo, G. Ong, E. Mingyi, & J. Chin (Eds.), *Combating Violent Extremism and Radicalization in the Digital Era* (pp. 226–259). Hershey, PA: IGI Global. doi:10.4018/978-1-5225-0156-5.ch012

Drenner, K. (2017). Introduction to Faith in State Legislatures: Land of the Brave and the Home of the Free – The Star-Spangled Banner. In *Impacts of Faith-Based Decision Making on the Individual-Level Legislative Process: Emerging Research and Opportunities* (pp. 1–25). Hershey, PA: IGI Global. doi:10.4018/978-1-5225-2388-8.ch001

Drenner, K. (2017). The Holy Wars of Marriage. In *Impacts of Faith-Based Decision Making on the Individual-Level Legislative Process: Emerging Research and Opportunities* (pp. 92–116). Hershey, PA: IGI Global. doi:10.4018/978-1-5225-2388-8.ch004

Drenner, K. (2017). The Implications of Religious Liberty. In *Impacts of Faith-Based Decision Making on the Individual-Level Legislative Process: Emerging Research and Opportunities* (pp. 143–162). Hershey, PA: IGI Global. doi:10.4018/978-1-5225-2388-8.ch006

Edwards, S. B. III. (2016). The Right to Privacy Is Dying: Technology Is Killing It and We Are Letting It Happen. In R. Cropf & T. Bagwell (Eds.), *Ethical Issues and Citizen Rights in the Era of Digital Government Surveillance* (pp. 103–126). Hershey, PA: IGI Global. doi:10.4018/978-1-4666-9905-2.ch006

Elena, S., & van Schalkwyk, F. (2017). Open Data for Open Justice in Seven Latin American Countries. In C. Jiménez-Gómez & M. Gascó-Hernández (Eds.), *Achieving Open Justice through Citizen Participation and Transparency* (pp. 210–231). Hershey, PA: IGI Global. doi:10.4018/978-1-5225-0717-8.ch011

Eneanya, A. N. (2016). Health Policy Implementation and Its Barriers: The Case Study of US Health System. In R. Gholipour & K. Rouzbehani (Eds.), *Social, Economic, and Political Perspectives on Public Health Policy-Making* (pp. 42–63). Hershey, PA: IGI Global. doi:10.4018/978-1-4666-9944-1.ch003

Eneanya, A. N. (2018). Integrating Ecosystem Management and Environmental Media for Public Policy on Public Health and Safety. In A. Eneanya (Ed.), *Handbook of Research on Environmental Policies for Emergency Management and Public Safety* (pp. 321–338). Hershey, PA: IGI Global. doi:10.4018/978-1-5225-3194-4.ch017

Erdoğdu, M. M., Yılmaz, B. E., Aydın, M., & User, İ. (2016). Political Economy of Tax Evasion and Tax Loss in the Real Estate Sector: A Property Tax Reform Proposal for Turkey. In M. Erdoğdu & B. Christiansen (Eds.), *Handbook of Research on Public Finance in Europe and the MENA Region* (pp. 268–298). Hershey, PA: IGI Global. doi:10.4018/978-1-5225-0053-7.ch013

Essien, E. D. (2018). Strengthening Performance of Civil Society Through Dialogue and Critical Thinking in Nigeria: Its Ethical Implications. In S. Chhabra (Ed.), *Handbook of Research on Civic Engagement and Social Change in Contemporary Society* (pp. 82–102). Hershey, PA: IGI Global. doi:10.4018/978-1-5225-4197-4.ch005

Fanaian, T. (2017). The Theocratic Deception Trap: Khomeini's Persuasion Techniques and Communication Patterns in His Books, Guardianship of the Jurist 1979 and Testament 1989. In E. Lewin, E. Bick, & D. Naor (Eds.), *Comparative Perspectives on Civil Religion, Nationalism, and Political Influence* (pp. 62–105). Hershey, PA: IGI Global. doi:10.4018/978-1-5225-0516-7.ch003

Farrag, N. A., & Ezzat, A. M. (2016). The Impact of Corruption on Economic Growth: A Comparative Analysis between Europe and MENA Countries. In M. Erdoğdu & B. Christiansen (Eds.), *Handbook of Research on Comparative Economic Development Perspectives on Europe and the MENA Region* (pp. 74–97). Hershey, PA: IGI Global. doi:10.4018/978-1-4666-9548-1.ch005

Farzanegan, M. R. (2016). Demographic Transition, Oil, and Institutions: Lessons from the Global Experience for Iran. In M. Erdoğdu & B. Christiansen (Eds.), *Comparative Political and Economic Perspectives on the MENA Region* (pp. 261–291). Hershey, PA: IGI Global. doi:10.4018/978-1-4666-9601-3.ch012

Feickert, H. (2016). Enforcing Central Authority: Nuri al-Maliki and the Tradition of Iraq's Authoritarian State. In F. Cante & H. Quehl (Eds.), *Handbook of Research on Transitional Justice and Peace Building in Turbulent Regions* (pp. 233–252). Hershey, PA: IGI Global. doi:10.4018/978-1-4666-9675-4.ch012

Fidanoski, F., Sergi, B. S., Simeonovski, K., Naumovski, V., & Sazdovski, I. (2018). Effects of Foreign Capital Entry on the Macedonian Banking Industry: Two-Edged Sword. In B. Sergi, F. Fidanoski, M. Ziolo, & V. Naumovski (Eds.), *Regaining Global Stability After the Financial Crisis* (pp. 308–338). Hershey, PA: IGI Global. doi:10.4018/978-1-5225-4026-7.ch015

Fiske, R. R. (2016). The Borders of Corruption: Living in the State of Exception. In R. Cropf & T. Bagwell (Eds.), *Ethical Issues and Citizen Rights in the Era of Digital Government Surveillance* (pp. 1–15). Hershey, PA: IGI Global. doi:10.4018/978-1-4666-9905-2.ch001

Franconi, A. I. (2018). Economic Variations and Their Impact on Labor Legislation Throughout History in Argentina. In S. Amine (Ed.), *Employment Protection Legislation in Emerging Economies* (pp. 77–98). Hershey, PA: IGI Global. doi:10.4018/978-1-5225-4134-9.ch004

Franzke, J. (2016). Structure of the Local Tiers in Germany: Trends and Challenges in Local Governance and Autonomy. In U. Sadioglu & K. Dede (Eds.), *Comparative Studies and Regionally-Focused Cases Examining Local Governments* (pp. 51–70). Hershey, PA: IGI Global. doi:10.4018/978-1-5225-0320-0.ch003

Friedrich, P., & Chebotareva, M. (2017). Options for Applying Functional Overlapping Competing Jurisdictions (FOCJs) for Municipal Cooperation in Russia. In M. Lewandowski & B. Kożuch (Eds.), *Public Sector Entrepreneurship and the Integration of Innovative Business Models* (pp. 73–107). Hershey, PA: IGI Global. doi:10.4018/978-1-5225-2215-7.ch004

Gałuszka, J. (2016). Decentralization and Sub-National Government in Poland: Territorial Governance, Competencies, Fiscal Autonomy of Local Governments. In U. Sadioglu & K. Dede (Eds.), *Comparative Studies and Regionally-Focused Cases Examining Local Governments* (pp. 91–112). Hershey, PA: IGI Global. doi:10.4018/978-1-5225-0320-0.ch005

Game, C. (2016). Decentralisation and Devolution in the United Kingdom. In U. Sadioglu & K. Dede (Eds.), *Comparative Studies and Regionally-Focused Cases Examining Local Governments* (pp. 1–34). Hershey, PA: IGI Global. doi:10.4018/978-1-5225-0320-0.ch001

García, M. J., & Sancino, A. (2016). Directly Elected Mayors vs. Council Appointed Mayors – Which Effects on Local Government Systems?: A Comparison between Italy and Spain. In U. Sadioglu & K. Dede (Eds.), *Theoretical Foundations and Discussions on the Reformation Process in Local Governments* (pp. 288–303). Hershey, PA: IGI Global. doi:10.4018/978-1-5225-0317-0.ch012

Garita, M. (2018). The Negotiation and Effects of Fiscal Privileges in Guatemala. In M. Garita & C. Bregni (Eds.), *Economic Growth in Latin America and the Impact of the Global Financial Crisis* (pp. 119–137). Hershey, PA: IGI Global. doi:10.4018/978-1-5225-4981-9.ch008

Gascó-Hernández, M. (2017). Digitalizing Police Requirements: Opening up Justice through Collaborative Initiatives. In C. Jiménez-Gómez & M. Gascó-Hernández (Eds.), *Achieving Open Justice through Citizen Participation and Transparency* (pp. 157–172). Hershey, PA: IGI Global. doi:10.4018/978-1-5225-0717-8.ch008

Gáspár-Szilágyi, S. (2017). Human Rights Conditionality in the EU's Newly Concluded Association Agreements with the Eastern Partners. In C. Akrivopoulou (Ed.), *Defending Human Rights and Democracy in the Era of Globalization* (pp. 50–79). Hershey, PA: IGI Global. doi:10.4018/978-1-5225-0723-9.ch003

Gavrielides, T. (2017). Reconciling Restorative Justice with the Law for Violence Against Women in Europe: A Scheme of Structured and Unstructured Models. In D. Halder & K. Jaishankar (Eds.), *Therapeutic Jurisprudence and Overcoming Violence Against Women* (pp. 106–120). Hershey, PA: IGI Global. doi:10.4018/978-1-5225-2472-4.ch007

Gechlik, M., Dai, D., & Beck, J. C. (2017). Open Judiciary in a Closed Society: A Paradox in China? In C. Jiménez-Gómez & M. Gascó-Hernández (Eds.), *Achieving Open Justice through Citizen Participation and Transparency* (pp. 56–92). Hershey, PA: IGI Global. doi:10.4018/978-1-5225-0717-8.ch004

Gerst, M., & Gao, X. (2016). IP and Electric Vehicles Standards: Local Policies vs. Global Standards? Standardization Management in a Multi-Stakeholder Environment in China. In K. Jakobs (Ed.), *Effective Standardization Management in Corporate Settings* (pp. 236–264). Hershey, PA: IGI Global. doi:10.4018/978-1-4666-9737-9.ch011

Gessler, H. A. (2016). Reformulating Government-Citizen Relations in a Digitally Connected World: The Twitter Ban Phenomenon in Turkey. In T. Deželan & I. Vobič (Eds.), *R)evolutionizing Political Communication through Social Media* (pp. 75–93). Hershey, PA: IGI Global. doi:10.4018/978-1-4666-9879-6.ch005

Gholipour, R. (2016). Policy Making: A New Method to Manage Public Issues. In R. Gholipour & K. Rouzbehani (Eds.), *Social, Economic, and Political Perspectives on Public Health Policy-Making* (pp. 1–19). Hershey, PA: IGI Global. doi:10.4018/978-1-4666-9944-1.ch001

Gillath, N. (2017). Avoiding Conscription in Israel: Were Women Pawns in the Political Game? In E. Lewin, E. Bick, & D. Naor (Eds.), *Comparative Perspectives on Civil Religion, Nationalism, and Political Influence* (pp. 226–256). Hershey, PA: IGI Global. doi:10.4018/978-1-5225-0516-7.ch009

Giousmpasoglou, C., Marinakou, E., & Paliktzoglou, V. (2016). Economic Crisis and Higher Education in Greece. In P. Ordóñez de Pablos & R. Tennyson (Eds.), *Impact of Economic Crisis on Education and the Next-Generation Workforce* (pp. 120–148). Hershey, PA: IGI Global. doi:10.4018/978-1-4666-9455-2.ch006

Gomes, P., Camões, S. M., & Carvalho, J. (2016). Determinants of the Design and Use of PMS in Portuguese Government Agencies: A Complementary Theoretical Approach. In A. Ferreira, G. Azevedo, J. Oliveira, & R. Marques (Eds.), *Global Perspectives on Risk Management and Accounting in the Public Sector* (pp. 320–345). Hershey, PA: IGI Global. doi:10.4018/978-1-4666-9803-1.ch016

Gonçalves, T. A., & Rosendo, D. (2016). New Communication Technologies: Women's Rights Violations, Limits on Freedom of Expression, and Alternative ways to Promote Human Rights. In J. Wilson & N. Gapsiso (Eds.), *Overcoming Gender Inequalities through Technology Integration* (pp. 144–162). Hershey, PA: IGI Global. doi:10.4018/978-1-4666-9773-7.ch007

Grant, B., Woods, R., & Tan, S. F. (2017). Subnational Finance in Australia and China: The Case for Municipal Bond Banks. In E. Schoburgh & R. Ryan (Eds.), *Handbook of Research on Sub-National Governance and Development* (pp. 150–166). Hershey, PA: IGI Global. doi:10.4018/978-1-5225-1645-3.ch007

Grecco, M. C., & Geron, C. M. (2016). The Brazilian Case of IFRS Adoption: The Impacts and the New Perspectives. In E. Uchenna, M. Nnadi, S. Tanna, & F. Iyoha (Eds.), *Economics and Political Implications of International Financial Reporting Standards* (pp. 303–318). Hershey, PA: IGI Global. doi:10.4018/978-1-4666-9876-5.ch015

Gül, H., Kamalak, İ., & Kiriş, H. M. (2016). Local and Urban Administrations, Politics, and Elections in Turkey. In U. Sadioglu & K. Dede (Eds.), *Comparative Studies and Regionally-Focused Cases Examining Local Governments* (pp. 182–206). Hershey, PA: IGI Global. doi:10.4018/978-1-5225-0320-0.ch009

Guner, A., & Keles, R. (2016). A Comparative Study of Local Governments in the Constitutions of Selected EU Countries and Turkey. In U. Sadioglu & K. Dede (Eds.), *Comparative Studies and Regionally-Focused Cases Examining Local Governments* (pp. 349–363). Hershey, PA: IGI Global. doi:10.4018/978-1-5225-0320-0.ch016

Gür, B. (2016). Economic and Political Factors Affecting Foreign Direct Investment in the MENA Region. In M. Erdoğdu & B. Christiansen (Eds.), *Comparative Political and Economic Perspectives on the MENA Region* (pp. 221–245). Hershey, PA: IGI Global. doi:10.4018/978-1-4666-9601-3.ch010

Gurpinar, B. (2018). Supporter, Activist, Rebel, Terrorist: Children in Syria. In C. Akrivopoulou (Ed.), *Global Perspectives on Human Migration, Asylum, and Security* (pp. 97–114). Hershey, PA: IGI Global. doi:10.4018/978-1-5225-2817-3.ch005

Gussen, B. F. (2018). The United States. In *Ranking Economic Performance and Efficiency in the Global Market: Emerging Research and Opportunities* (pp. 109–136). Hershey, PA: IGI Global. doi:10.4018/978-1-5225-2756-5.ch005

Hadji-Janev, M. (2016). International Legal Aspects of Protecting Civilians and Their Property in the Future Cyber Conflict. In M. Hadji-Janev & M. Bogdanoski (Eds.), *Handbook of Research on Civil Society and National Security in the Era of Cyber Warfare* (pp. 423–449). Hershey, PA: IGI Global. doi:10.4018/978-1-4666-8793-6.ch019

Hankel, G. (2016). Gacaca Courts in Rwanda: Experience and Perspectives. In F. Cante & H. Quehl (Eds.), *Handbook of Research on Transitional Justice and Peace Building in Turbulent Regions* (pp. 218–231). Hershey, PA: IGI Global. doi:10.4018/978-1-4666-9675-4.ch011

Haque, T. (2018). Women-Friendly Working Environment in Bangladesh: Critical Analysis. In N. Mahtab, T. Haque, I. Khan, M. Islam, & I. Wahid (Eds.), *Handbook of Research on Women's Issues and Rights in the Developing World* (pp. 52–68). Hershey, PA: IGI Global. doi:10.4018/978-1-5225-3018-3.ch004

Hartzel, K. S., & Gerde, V. W. (2016). Using Duality Theory to Reframe E-Government Challenges. In R. Cropf & T. Bagwell (Eds.), *Ethical Issues and Citizen Rights in the Era of Digital Government Surveillance* (pp. 35–56). Hershey, PA: IGI Global. doi:10.4018/978-1-4666-9905-2.ch003

Heilmann, D. (2016). Post-Conflict Justice in Cambodia: The Legacy of the Khmer Rouge Tribunal. In F. Cante & H. Quehl (Eds.), *Handbook of Research on Transitional Justice and Peace Building in Turbulent Regions* (pp. 201–217). Hershey, PA: IGI Global. doi:10.4018/978-1-4666-9675-4.ch010

Heuva, W. E. (2017). Deferring Citizens' "Right to Know" in an Information Age: The Information Deficit in Namibia. In N. Mhiripiri & T. Chari (Eds.), *Media Law, Ethics, and Policy in the Digital Age* (pp. 245–267). Hershey, PA: IGI Global. doi:10.4018/978-1-5225-2095-5.ch014

Idris, S. (2016). Challenge of Democracy and Local Governance in Pakistan. In U. Sadioglu & K. Dede (Eds.), *Comparative Studies and Regionally-Focused Cases Examining Local Governments* (pp. 259–279). Hershey, PA: IGI Global. doi:10.4018/978-1-5225-0320-0.ch012

Islam, M. R. (2018). Abuse Among Child Domestic Workers in Bangladesh. In I. Tshabangu (Ed.), *Global Ideologies Surrounding Children's Rights and Social Justice* (pp. 1–21). Hershey, PA: IGI Global. doi:10.4018/978-1-5225-2578-3.ch001

Jankovic-Milic, V., & Džunić, M. (2017). Measuring Governance: The Application of Grey Relational Analysis on World Governance Indicators. In J. Stanković, P. Delias, S. Marinković, & S. Rochhia (Eds.), *Tools and Techniques for Economic Decision Analysis* (pp. 104–128). Hershey, PA: IGI Global. doi:10.4018/978-1-5225-0959-2.ch005

Jenne, C. (2016). Increase of Transportation Efficiencies and Emission Reduction within a City. In G. Hua (Ed.), *Smart Cities as a Solution for Reducing Urban Waste and Pollution* (pp. 91–125). Hershey, PA: IGI Global. doi:10.4018/978-1-5225-0302-6.ch004

Jiménez-Gómez, C. E. (2017). Open Judiciary Worldwide: Best Practices and Lessons Learnt. In C. Jiménez-Gómez & M. Gascó-Hernández (Eds.), *Achieving Open Justice through Citizen Participation and Transparency* (pp. 1–15). Hershey, PA: IGI Global. doi:10.4018/978-1-5225-0717-8.ch001

Kabullah, M. I., & Wahab, S. (2016). The Curbing of Corruption by Formal and Informal Accountability at the Indonesian Local Governments: Learning from Yogyakarta City. In U. Sadioglu & K. Dede (Eds.), *Theoretical Foundations and Discussions on the Reformation Process in Local Governments* (pp. 441–461). Hershey, PA: IGI Global. doi:10.4018/978-1-5225-0317-0.ch018

Karatzimas, S., & Miquela, C. G. (2018). Two Approaches on Local Governments' Financial Sustainability: Law vs. Practice in Catalan Municipalities. In M. Rodríguez Bolívar & M. López Subires (Eds.), *Financial Sustainability and Intergenerational Equity in Local Governments* (pp. 58–81). Hershey, PA: IGI Global. doi:10.4018/978-1-5225-3713-7.ch003

Kerasidou, X., Buscher, M., Liegl, M., & Oliphant, R. (2016). Emergency Ethics, Law, Policy & IT Innovation in Crises. *International Journal of Information Systems for Crisis Response and Management*, 8(1), 1–24. doi:10.4018/IJISCRAM.2016010101

Khanh, N. T., Danh, M. T., & Gim, G. (2016). E-Government in Vietnam: Situation, Prospects, Trends, and Challenges. In I. Sodhi (Ed.), *Trends, Prospects, and Challenges in Asian E-Governance* (pp. 256–280). Hershey, PA: IGI Global. doi:10.4018/978-1-4666-9536-8.ch013

Kiran, M. (2016). Legal Issues Surrounding Connected Government Services: A Closer Look at G-Clouds. In Z. Mahmood (Ed.), *Cloud Computing Technologies for Connected Government* (pp. 322–344). Hershey, PA: IGI Global. doi:10.4018/978-1-4666-8629-8.ch013

Kita, Y. (2017). An Analysis of a Lay Adjudication System and Open Judiciary: The New Japanese Lay Adjudication System. In C. Jiménez-Gómez & M. Gascó-Hernández (Eds.), *Achieving Open Justice through Citizen Participation and Transparency* (pp. 93–109). Hershey, PA: IGI Global. doi:10.4018/978-1-5225-0717-8.ch005

Klimczuk, A., & Klimczuk-Kochańska, M. (2016). Changes in the Local Government System and Regional Policy in Poland: The Impact of Membership in the European Union. In U. Sadioglu & K. Dede (Eds.), *Theoretical Foundations and Discussions on the Reformation Process in Local Governments* (pp. 328–352). Hershey, PA: IGI Global. doi:10.4018/978-1-5225-0317-0.ch014

Klimovský, D. (2016). Experience with Managerial and Political Reform Measures at the Local Level in Slovakia: Intended and Unintended Outcomes. In U. Sadioglu & K. Dede (Eds.), *Comparative Studies and Regionally-Focused Cases Examining Local Governments* (pp. 135–160). Hershey, PA: IGI Global. doi:10.4018/978-1-5225-0320-0.ch007

Küçükali, U. F. (2016). Ecological Influences on the Evolving Planning System in Turkey. In U. Benna & S. Garba (Eds.), *Population Growth and Rapid Urbanization in the Developing World* (pp. 298–312). Hershey, PA: IGI Global. doi:10.4018/978-1-5225-0187-9.ch015

Kumari, S., Patil, Y., & Rao, P. (2017). An Approach to Sustainable Watershed Management: Case Studies on Enhancing Sustainability with Challenges of Water in Western Maharashtra. In P. Rao & Y. Patil (Eds.), *Reconsidering the Impact of Climate Change on Global Water Supply, Use, and Management* (pp. 252–271). Hershey, PA: IGI Global. doi:10.4018/978-1-5225-1046-8.ch014

Kumburu, N. P., & Pande, V. S. (2018). Decentralization and Local Governance in Tanzania: Theories and Practice on Sustainable Development. In K. Teshager Alemu & M. Abebe Alebachew (Eds.), *Handbook of Research on Sustainable Development and Governance Strategies for Economic Growth in Africa* (pp. 131–148). Hershey, PA: IGI Global. doi:10.4018/978-1-5225-3247-7.ch007

Kunock, A. I. (2017). Boko Haram Insurgency in Cameroon: Role of Mass Media in Conflict Management. In N. Mhiripiri & T. Chari (Eds.), *Media Law, Ethics, and Policy in the Digital Age* (pp. 226–244). Hershey, PA: IGI Global. doi:10.4018/978-1-5225-2095-5.ch013

Laha, A. (2016). Association between Governance and Human Development in South Asia: A Cross Country Analysis. In R. Das (Ed.), *Handbook of Research on Global Indicators of Economic and Political Convergence* (pp. 254–273). Hershey, PA: IGI Global. doi:10.4018/978-1-5225-0215-9.ch012

Lawrie, A. (2017). The Subnational Region: A Utopia? The Challenge of Governing Through Soft Power. In E. Schoburgh & R. Ryan (Eds.), *Handbook of Research on Sub-National Governance and Development* (pp. 96–115). Hershey, PA: IGI Global. doi:10.4018/978-1-5225-1645-3.ch005

Lewin, E., & Bick, E. (2017). Introduction: Civil Religion and Nationalism on a Godly-Civil Continuum. In E. Lewin, E. Bick, & D. Naor (Eds.), *Comparative Perspectives on Civil Religion, Nationalism, and Political Influence* (pp. 1–31). Hershey, PA: IGI Global. doi:10.4018/978-1-5225-0516-7.ch001

Lisney, T., & Kiefer, A. (2016). Cooperation between Local Authorities in Europe as a Force for Strengthening Local Democracy. In U. Sadioglu & K. Dede (Eds.), *Theoretical Foundations and Discussions on the Reformation Process in Local Governments* (pp. 85–109). Hershey, PA: IGI Global. doi:10.4018/978-1-5225-0317-0.ch004

Lobina, M., & Bottone, M. (2016). Building Trust in Politics: Causes of Widespread Disillusionment in Latin American Countries. In M. Garita & J. Godinez (Eds.), *Business Development Opportunities and Market Entry Challenges in Latin America* (pp. 127–157). Hershey, PA: IGI Global. doi:10.4018/978-1-4666-8820-9.ch007

Lourenço, R. P. (2016). Evidence of an Open Government Data Portal Impact on the Public Sphere. *International Journal of Electronic Government Research*, *12*(3), 21–36. doi:10.4018/IJEGR.2016070102

Luyombya, D. (2018). Management of Records and Archives in Uganda's Public Sector. In P. Ngulube (Ed.), *Handbook of Research on Heritage Management and Preservation* (pp. 275–297). Hershey, PA: IGI Global. doi:10.4018/978-1-5225-3137-1.ch014

Mabe, M., & Ashley, E. A. (2017). The Local Command Structure and How the Library Fits. In *In The Developing Role of Public Libraries in Emergency Management: Emerging Research and Opportunities* (pp. 44–60). Hershey, PA: IGI Global. doi:10.4018/978-1-5225-2196-9.ch004

Magalhães, F. R., & Santos, C. (2016). Online Financial Transparency: Local Governments of the MERCOSUR Member Countries. In A. Ferreira, G. Azevedo, J. Oliveira, & R. Marques (Eds.), *Global Perspectives on Risk Management and Accounting in the Public Sector* (pp. 252–273). Hershey, PA: IGI Global. doi:10.4018/978-1-4666-9803-1.ch013

Maher, C. (2016). Public Policies Impact on Third Sector Social Enterprises in UK Regions. In L. Carvalho (Ed.), *Handbook of Research on Entrepreneurial Success and its Impact on Regional Development* (pp. 246–266). Hershey, PA: IGI Global. doi:10.4018/978-1-4666-9567-2.ch012

Maher, C. (2018). Legal Framework, Funding, and Procurement Polices to Accelerate the Growth of the Social Enterprise Ecosystem. In *Influence of Public Policy on Small Social Enterprises: Emerging Research and Opportunities* (pp. 52–83). Hershey, PA: IGI Global. doi:10.4018/978-1-5225-2770-1.ch003

Malik, I., Putera, V. S., & Putra, I. E. (2018). Traditional Leaders in the Reconciliation of Muslim-Christian Conflicts in Moluccas. In A. Campbell (Ed.), *Global Leadership Initiatives for Conflict Resolution and Peacebuilding* (pp. 235–248). Hershey, PA: IGI Global. doi:10.4018/978-1-5225-4993-2.ch011

Manzoor, A. (2016). Cloud Computing Applications in the Public Sector. In Z. Mahmood (Ed.), *Cloud Computing Technologies for Connected Government* (pp. 215–246). Hershey, PA: IGI Global. doi:10.4018/978-1-4666-8629-8.ch009

Marinescu, V. (2016). The Crisis of Public Health as a Media Event: Between Media Frames and Public Assessments. In A. Fox (Ed.), *Global Perspectives on Media Events in Contemporary Society* (pp. 78–89). Hershey, PA: IGI Global. doi:10.4018/978-1-4666-9967-0.ch006

Martin, S. M. (2017). Transnational Crime and the American Policing System. In M. Dawson, D. Kisku, P. Gupta, J. Sing, & W. Li (Eds.), Developing Next-Generation Countermeasures for Homeland Security Threat Prevention (pp. 72-92). Hershey, PA: IGI Global. doi:10.4018/978-1-5225-0703-1.ch004

Marwah, G. S., & Ladhani, V. (2016). Financial Sector in Afghanistan: Regulatory Challenges in Financial Sector of Afghanistan. In A. Kashyap & A. Tomar (Eds.), *Financial Market Regulations and Legal Challenges in South Asia* (pp. 224–262). Hershey, PA: IGI Global. doi:10.4018/978-1-5225-0004-9.ch011

Masrom, M. (2016). E-Government, E-Surveillance, and Ethical Issues from Malaysian Perspective. In R. Cropf & T. Bagwell (Eds.), *Ethical Issues and Citizen Rights in the Era of Digital Government Surveillance* (pp. 249–263). Hershey, PA: IGI Global. doi:10.4018/978-1-4666-9905-2.ch013

McNeal, R. S., Schmeida, M., & Holmes, J. (2016). The E-Government Surveillance in the United States: Public Opinion on Government Wiretapping Powers. In R. Cropf & T. Bagwell (Eds.), *Ethical Issues and Citizen Rights in the Era of Digital Government Surveillance* (pp. 208–230). Hershey, PA: IGI Global. doi:10.4018/978-1-4666-9905-2.ch011

Mhiripiri, N. A., & Chikakano, J. (2017). Criminal Defamation, the Criminalisation of Expression, Media and Information Dissemination in the Digital Age: A Legal and Ethical Perspective. In N. Mhiripiri & T. Chari (Eds.), *Media Law, Ethics, and Policy in the Digital Age* (pp. 1–24). Hershey, PA: IGI Global. doi:10.4018/978-1-5225-2095-5.ch001

Mishaal, D. A., & Abu-Shanab, E. A. (2017). Utilizing Facebook by the Arab World Governments: The Communication Success Factor. *International Journal of Public Administration in the Digital Age*, 4(3), 53–78. doi:10.4018/IJPADA.2017070105

Morim, A. C., Inácio, H., & Vieira, E. (2018). Internal Control in a Public Hospital: The Case of Financial Services Expenditure Department. In G. Azevedo, J. da Silva Oliveira, R. Marques, & A. Ferreira (Eds.), *Handbook of Research on Modernization and Accountability in Public Sector Management* (pp. 77–102). Hershey, PA: IGI Global. doi:10.4018/978-1-5225-3731-1.ch005

Mupepi, M. G. (2017). Developing Democratic Paradigms to Effectively Manage Business, Government, and Civil Society: The African Spring. In E. Schoburgh & R. Ryan (Eds.), *Handbook of Research on Sub-National Governance and Development* (pp. 432–462). Hershey, PA: IGI Global. doi:10.4018/978-1-5225-1645-3.ch020

Nam, T. (2016). Citizen Attitudes about Open Government and Government 2.0: A Path Analysis. *International Journal of Electronic Government Research, 12*(4), 46–66. doi:10.4018/IJEGR.2016100104

Navaratnam, R., & Lee, I. Y. (2017). Globalization as a New Framework for Human Rights Protection. In C. Akrivopoulou (Ed.), *Defending Human Rights and Democracy in the Era of Globalization* (pp. 17–49). Hershey, PA: IGI Global. doi:10.4018/978-1-5225-0723-9.ch002

Naz, R. (2016). Challenges En-Route towards E-Governance in Small Developing Island Nations of the South Pacific: The Case of Papua New Guinea. In I. Sodhi (Ed.), *Trends, Prospects, and Challenges in Asian E-Governance* (pp. 1–34). Hershey, PA: IGI Global. doi:10.4018/978-1-4666-9536-8.ch001

Nemec, J., Meričková, B. M., Svidroňová, M. M., & Klimovský, D. (2017). Co-Creation as a Social Innovation in Delivery of Public Services at Local Government Level: The Slovak Experience. In E. Schoburgh & R. Ryan (Eds.), *Handbook of Research on Sub-National Governance and Development* (pp. 281–303). Hershey, PA: IGI Global. doi:10.4018/978-1-5225-1645-3.ch013

Nemec, J., Soukopova, J., & Merickova, B. M. (2016). Local Public Service Delivery Arrangements in the Czech Republic and Slovakia. In U. Sadioglu & K. Dede (Eds.), *Comparative Studies and Regionally-Focused Cases Examining Local Governments* (pp. 405–423). Hershey, PA: IGI Global. doi:10.4018/978-1-5225-0320-0.ch019

Neupane, A., Soar, J., Vaidya, K., & Aryal, S. (2017). Application of E-Government Principles in Anti-Corruption Framework. In R. Shakya (Ed.), *Digital Governance and E-Government Principles Applied to Public Procurement* (pp. 56–74). Hershey, PA: IGI Global. doi:10.4018/978-1-5225-2203-4.ch003

Nurdin, N., Stockdale, R., & Scheepers, H. (2016). Influence of Organizational Factors in the Sustainability of E-Government: A Case Study of Local E-Government in Indonesia. In I. Sodhi (Ed.), *Trends, Prospects, and Challenges in Asian E-Governance* (pp. 281–323). Hershey, PA: IGI Global. doi:10.4018/978-1-4666-9536-8.ch014

Ogunde, O. (2017). Democracy and Child Rights Protection: The Problem of the Nigerian Constitution. In C. Akrivopoulou (Ed.), *Defending Human Rights and Democracy in the Era of Globalization* (pp. 123–144). Hershey, PA: IGI Global. doi:10.4018/978-1-5225-0723-9.ch006

Ohsugi, S. (2016). Changing Local Government System in Japan: "Unfinished" Decentralization Reform and Local Revitalization. In U. Sadioglu & K. Dede (Eds.), *Theoretical Foundations and Discussions on the Reformation Process in Local Governments* (pp. 373–399). Hershey, PA: IGI Global. doi:10.4018/978-1-5225-0317-0.ch016

Ojedokun, U. A. (2017). Crime Witnesses' Non-Cooperation in Police Investigations: Causes and Consequences in Nigeria. In S. Egharevba (Ed.), *Police Brutality, Racial Profiling, and Discrimination in the Criminal Justice System* (pp. 89–99). Hershey, PA: IGI Global. doi:10.4018/978-1-5225-1088-8.ch005

Okeke, G. S. (2018). The Politics of Environmental Pollution in Nigeria: Emerging Trends, Issues, and Challenges. In A. Eneanya (Ed.), *Handbook of Research on Environmental Policies for Emergency Management and Public Safety* (pp. 300–320). Hershey, PA: IGI Global. doi:10.4018/978-1-5225-3194-4.ch016

Ökten, S., Akman, E., & Akman, Ç. (2018). Modernization and Accountability in Public-Sector Administration: Turkey Example. In G. Azevedo, J. da Silva Oliveira, R. Marques, & A. Ferreira (Eds.), *Handbook of Research on Modernization and Accountability in Public Sector Management* (pp. 18–39). Hershey, PA: IGI Global. doi:10.4018/978-1-5225-3731-1.ch002

Oladapo, O. A., & Ojebuyi, B. R. (2017). Nature and Outcome of Nigeria's #NoToSocialMediaBill Twitter Protest against the Frivolous Petitions Bill 2015. In O. Nelson, B. Ojebuyi, & A. Salawu (Eds.), *Impacts of the Media on African Socio-Economic Development* (pp. 106–124). Hershey, PA: IGI Global. doi:10.4018/978-1-5225-1859-4.ch007

Olukolu, Y. R. (2017). Harmful Traditional Practices, Laws, and Reproductive Rights of Women in Nigeria: A Therapeutic Jurisprudence Approach. In D. Halder & K. Jaishankar (Eds.), *Therapeutic Jurisprudence and Overcoming Violence Against Women* (pp. 1–14). Hershey, PA: IGI Global. doi:10.4018/978-1-5225-2472-4.ch001

Omwoha, J. (2016). The Political Significance and Influence of Talk Radio Debates in Kenya. In L. Mukhongo & J. Macharia (Eds.), *Political Influence of the Media in Developing Countries* (pp. 75–96). Hershey, PA: IGI Global. doi:10.4018/978-1-4666-9613-6.ch006

Onyebadi, U., & Mbunyuza-Memani, L. (2017). Women and South Africa's Anti-Apartheid Struggle: Evaluating the Political Messages in the Music of Miriam Makeba. In U. Onyebadi (Ed.), *Music as a Platform for Political Communication* (pp. 31–51). Hershey, PA: IGI Global. doi:10.4018/978-1-5225-1986-7.ch002

Osmani, A. R. (2017). Tipaimukh Multipurpose Hydroelectric Project: A Policy Perspective – Indo-Bangla Priorities, Indigenous Peoples' Rights, and Environmental Concerns. In P. Rao & Y. Patil (Eds.), *Reconsidering the Impact of Climate Change on Global Water Supply, Use, and Management* (pp. 227–251). Hershey, PA: IGI Global. doi:10.4018/978-1-5225-1046-8.ch013

Owolabi, T. O. (2018). Free Media and Bank Reforms in West Africa: Implications for Sustainable Development. In A. Salawu & T. Owolabi (Eds.), *Exploring Journalism Practice and Perception in Developing Countries* (pp. 18–39). Hershey, PA: IGI Global. doi:10.4018/978-1-5225-3376-4.ch002

Oz, S. (2016). Diffusion of Technology via FDI and Convergence of Per Capita Incomes: Comparative Analysis on Europe and the MENA Region. In M. Erdoğdu & B. Christiansen (Eds.), *Handbook of Research on Comparative Economic Development Perspectives on Europe and the MENA Region* (pp. 236–264). Hershey, PA: IGI Global. doi:10.4018/978-1-4666-9548-1.ch012

Paez, G. R. (2016). Retaliation in Transitional Justice Scenarios: The Experiences of Argentina and Colombia. In F. Cante & H. Quehl (Eds.), *Handbook of Research on Transitional Justice and Peace Building in Turbulent Regions* (pp. 315–331). Hershey, PA: IGI Global. doi:10.4018/978-1-4666-9675-4.ch016

Panara, C. (2016). Concept and Role of Local Self-Government in the Contemporary State. In U. Sadioglu & K. Dede (Eds.), *Theoretical Foundations and Discussions on the Reformation Process in Local Governments* (pp. 42–84). Hershey, PA: IGI Global. doi:10.4018/978-1-5225-0317-0.ch003

Panda, P., & Sahu, G. P. (2017). Public Procurement Framework in India: An Overview. In R. Shakya (Ed.), *Digital Governance and E-Government Principles Applied to Public Procurement* (pp. 229–248). Hershey, PA: IGI Global. doi:10.4018/978-1-5225-2203-4.ch010

Pande, V. S., & Kumburu, N. P. (2018). An Overview of Population Growth and Sustainable Development in Sub-Saharan Africa. In K. Teshager Alemu & M. Abebe Alebachew (Eds.), *Handbook of Research on Sustainable Development and Governance Strategies for Economic Growth in Africa* (pp. 480–499). Hershey, PA: IGI Global. doi:10.4018/978-1-5225-3247-7.ch025

Paulin, A. A. (2017). Informating Public Governance: Towards a Basis for a Digital Ecosystem. *International Journal of Public Administration in the Digital Age*, *4*(2), 14–32. doi:10.4018/IJPADA.2017040102

Pečarič, M. (2016). The Awareness of Mentality in Public Administration as the Key for the Management of Its Complexity. In A. Ferreira, G. Azevedo, J. Oliveira, & R. Marques (Eds.), *Global Perspectives on Risk Management and Accounting in the Public Sector* (pp. 1–24). Hershey, PA: IGI Global. doi:10.4018/978-1-4666-9803-1.ch001

Perelló-Sobrepere, M. (2017). Building a New State from Outrage: The Case of Catalonia. In M. Adria & Y. Mao (Eds.), *Handbook of Research on Citizen Engagement and Public Participation in the Era of New Media* (pp. 344–359). Hershey, PA: IGI Global. doi:10.4018/978-1-5225-1081-9.ch019

Pohl, G. M. (2017). The Role of Social Media in Enforcing Environmental Justice around the World. In K. Demirhan & D. Çakır-Demirhan (Eds.), *Political Scandal, Corruption, and Legitimacy in the Age of Social Media* (pp. 123–156). Hershey, PA: IGI Global. doi:10.4018/978-1-5225-2019-1.ch006

Popoola, I. S. (2016). The Press and the Emergent Political Class in Nigeria: Media, Elections, and Democracy. In L. Mukhongo & J. Macharia (Eds.), *Political Influence of the Media in Developing Countries* (pp. 45–58). Hershey, PA: IGI Global. doi:10.4018/978-1-4666-9613-6.ch004

Popoola, T. (2017). Ethical and Legal Challenges of Election Reporting in Nigeria: A Study of Four General Elections, 1999-2011. In N. Mhiripiri & T. Chari (Eds.), *Media Law, Ethics, and Policy in the Digital Age* (pp. 78–100). Hershey, PA: IGI Global. doi:10.4018/978-1-5225-2095-5.ch005

Porras-Sanchez, F. J. (2016). Local Government and Governance in Mexico. In U. Sadioglu & K. Dede (Eds.), *Comparative Studies and Regionally-Focused Cases Examining Local Governments* (pp. 323–348). Hershey, PA: IGI Global. doi:10.4018/978-1-5225-0320-0.ch015

Rahman, K. F. (2016). Human Rights Education for Peace and Conflict Resolution. In K. Pandey & P. Upadhyay (Eds.), *Promoting Global Peace and Civic Engagement through Education* (pp. 89–105). Hershey, PA: IGI Global. doi:10.4018/978-1-5225-0078-0.ch006

Rahman, M. S. (2017). Politics-Administration Relations and the Effect on Local Governance and Development: The Case of Bangladesh. In E. Schoburgh & R. Ryan (Eds.), *Handbook of Research on Sub-National Governance and Development* (pp. 256–279). Hershey, PA: IGI Global. doi:10.4018/978-1-5225-1645-3.ch012

Reddy, P. S. (2017). Political-Administrative Interface at the Local Sphere of Government with Particular Reference to South Africa. In E. Schoburgh & R. Ryan (Eds.), *Handbook of Research on Sub-National Governance and Development* (pp. 242–255). Hershey, PA: IGI Global. doi:10.4018/978-1-5225-1645-3.ch011

Reid, M. (2016). Contemporary Local Government Reform in New Zealand: Efficiency or Democracy. In U. Sadioglu & K. Dede (Eds.), *Theoretical Foundations and Discussions on the Reformation Process in Local Governments* (pp. 205–236). Hershey, PA: IGI Global. doi:10.4018/978-1-5225-0317-0.ch009

Rombo, D. O., & Lutomia, A. N. (2018). Tracing the Rights of Domestic and International Kenyan House Helps: Profiles, Policy, and Consequences. In N. Mahtab, T. Haque, I. Khan, M. Islam, & I. Wahid (Eds.), *Handbook of Research on Women's Issues and Rights in the Developing World* (pp. 1–18). Hershey, PA: IGI Global. doi:10.4018/978-1-5225-3018-3.ch001

Rouzbehani, K. (2017). Health Policy Implementation: Moving Beyond Its Barriers in United States. In N. Wickramasinghe (Ed.), *Handbook of Research on Healthcare Administration and Management* (pp. 541–552). Hershey, PA: IGI Global. doi:10.4018/978-1-5225-0920-2.ch032

Ruano, J. M., & Álvarez, J. M. (2016). Local Structure and Municipal Associations in Spain: Facts, Trends and Problems. In U. Sadioglu & K. Dede (Eds.), *Comparative Studies and Regionally-Focused Cases Examining Local Governments* (pp. 71–90). Hershey, PA: IGI Global. doi:10.4018/978-1-5225-0320-0.ch004

Ruffin, F., & Martins, W. K. (2016). Legal Empowerment as Social Entrepreneurship: The KwaZulu-Natal Cases of Bulwer and New Hanover. In Z. Fields (Ed.), *Incorporating Business Models and Strategies into Social Entrepreneurship* (pp. 267–291). Hershey, PA: IGI Global. doi:10.4018/978-1-4666-8748-6.ch015

Ryan, R., & Woods, R. (2017). Decentralization and Subnational Governance: Theory and Praxis. In E. Schoburgh & R. Ryan (Eds.), *Handbook of Research on Sub-National Governance and Development* (pp. 1–33). Hershey, PA: IGI Global. doi:10.4018/978-1-5225-1645-3.ch001

Sabao, C., & Chingwaramusee, V. R. (2017). Citizen Journalism on Facebook and the Challenges of Media Regulation in Zimbabwe: Baba Jukwa. In N. Mhiripiri & T. Chari (Eds.), *Media Law, Ethics, and Policy in the Digital Age* (pp. 193–206). Hershey, PA: IGI Global. doi:10.4018/978-1-5225-2095-5.ch011

Sadioglu, U., & Dede, K. (2016). Current Discussions on the Question: Remarks of Local Government's Reform through Comparative Perspective. In U. Sadioglu & K. Dede (Eds.), *Theoretical Foundations and Discussions on the Reformation Process in Local Governments* (pp. 1–23). Hershey, PA: IGI Global. doi:10.4018/978-1-5225-0317-0.ch001

Sadioglu, U., Dede, K., & Yüceyılmaz, A. A. (2016). The Significance of The 2014 Local Elections in Turkey for Decentralisation and Local Autonomy. In U. Sadioglu & K. Dede (Eds.), *Comparative Studies and Regionally-Focused Cases Examining Local Governments* (pp. 364–389). Hershey, PA: IGI Global. doi:10.4018/978-1-5225-0320-0.ch017

Sanchez-Barrios, L. J., Gomez-Araujo, E., Gomez-Nuñez, L., & Rodriguez, S. (2016). Opportunities and Challenges for Entrepreneurial Activity and Non-Entrepreneurial Engagement in Colombia. In M. Garita & J. Godinez (Eds.), *Business Development Opportunities and Market Entry Challenges in Latin America* (pp. 170–198). Hershey, PA: IGI Global. doi:10.4018/978-1-4666-8820-9.ch009

Santoro, L., & Capasso, S. (2016). Public Spending and Governance Performance: Evidence from Europe and the MENA Region. In M. Erdoğdu & B. Christiansen (Eds.), *Handbook of Research on Public Finance in Europe and the MENA Region* (pp. 136–155). Hershey, PA: IGI Global. doi:10.4018/978-1-5225-0053-7.ch007

Scherr, K. M. (2016). Of Justice, Accountability, and Reconciliation: Preliminary Stocktaking on Transitional Justice Efforts in South Sudan. In F. Cante & H. Quehl (Eds.), *Handbook of Research on Transitional Justice and Peace Building in Turbulent Regions* (pp. 181–200). Hershey, PA: IGI Global. doi:10.4018/978-1-4666-9675-4.ch009

Schmeida, M., & McNeal, R. S. (2016). U.S. Public Support to Climate Change Initiatives?: Setting Stricter Carbon Dioxide Emission Limits on Power Plants. In M. Erdoğdu, T. Arun, & I. Ahmad (Eds.), *Handbook of Research on Green Economic Development Initiatives and Strategies* (pp. 605–624). Hershey, PA: IGI Global. doi:10.4018/978-1-5225-0440-5.ch026

Shahsavandi, E., Mayah, G., & Rahbari, H. (2016). Impact of E-Government on Transparency and Corruption in Iran. In I. Sodhi (Ed.), *Trends, Prospects, and Challenges in Asian E-Governance* (pp. 75–94). Hershey, PA: IGI Global. doi:10.4018/978-1-4666-9536-8.ch004

Shakya, R. K., & Schapper, P. R. (2017). Digital Governance and E-Government Principles: E-Procurement as Transformative. In R. Shakya (Ed.), *Digital Governance and E-Government Principles Applied to Public Procurement* (pp. 1–28). Hershey, PA: IGI Global. doi:10.4018/978-1-5225-2203-4.ch001

Siphambe, H., Kolobe, M., & Oageng, I. P. (2018). Employment Protection Legislation and Unemployment in Botswana. In S. Amine (Ed.), *Employment Protection Legislation in Emerging Economies* (pp. 157–191). Hershey, PA: IGI Global. doi:10.4018/978-1-5225-4134-9.ch008

Slaveski, S., & Popovska, B. (2016). Access to Information in the Republic of Macedonia: Between Transparency and Secrecy. In M. Hadji-Janev & M. Bogdanoski (Eds.), *Handbook of Research on Civil Society and National Security in the Era of Cyber Warfare* (pp. 162–179). Hershey, PA: IGI Global. doi:10.4018/978-1-4666-8793-6.ch008

Snauwaert, D. T. (2016). Securing a Human Right to Peace: A Peace Education Imperative. In K. Pandey & P. Upadhyay (Eds.), *Promoting Global Peace and Civic Engagement through Education* (pp. 19–35). Hershey, PA: IGI Global. doi:10.4018/978-1-5225-0078-0.ch002

Sodhi, I. S. (2016). E-Government in China: Status, Challenges, and Progress. In I. Sodhi (Ed.), *Trends, Prospects, and Challenges in Asian E-Governance* (pp. 36–54). Hershey, PA: IGI Global. doi:10.4018/978-1-4666-9536-8.ch002

Song, M. Y., & Abelson, J. (2017). Public Engagement and Policy Entrepreneurship on Social Media in the Time of Anti-Vaccination Movements. In M. Adria & Y. Mao (Eds.), *Handbook of Research on Citizen Engagement and Public Participation in the Era of New Media* (pp. 38–56). Hershey, PA: IGI Global. doi:10.4018/978-1-5225-1081-9.ch003

Sonmez, Y. (2016). Latest Developments on the Way to EU Accession: Turkish Case. In V. Erokhin (Ed.), *Global Perspectives on Trade Integration and Economies in Transition* (pp. 166–184). Hershey, PA: IGI Global. doi:10.4018/978-1-5225-0451-1.ch009

Stacey, E. (2018). Networked Protests: A Review of Social Movement Literature and the Hong Kong Umbrella Movement (2017). In S. Chhabra (Ed.), *Handbook of Research on Civic Engagement and Social Change in Contemporary Society* (pp. 347–363). Hershey, PA: IGI Global. doi:10.4018/978-1-5225-4197-4.ch020

Stamatakis, N. (2017). Authority and Legitimacy: A Quantitative Study of Youth's Perceptions on the Brazilian Police. In S. Egharevba (Ed.), *Police Brutality, Racial Profiling, and Discrimination in the Criminal Justice System* (pp. 151–213). Hershey, PA: IGI Global. doi:10.4018/978-1-5225-1088-8.ch009

Sugars, J. M. (2017). Refoulement and Refugees. In C. Akrivopoulou (Ed.), *Defending Human Rights and Democracy in the Era of Globalization* (pp. 181–197). Hershey, PA: IGI Global. doi:10.4018/978-1-5225-0723-9.ch008

Tabansky, L. (2016). Israel's Cyber Security Policy: Local Response to the Global Cybersecurity Risk. In M. Hadji-Janev & M. Bogdanoski (Eds.), *Handbook of Research on Civil Society and National Security in the Era of Cyber Warfare* (pp. 475–494). Hershey, PA: IGI Global. doi:10.4018/978-1-4666-8793-6.ch021

Tan, S. F. (2017). Local Representation in Australia: Preliminary Findings of a National Survey. In E. Schoburgh & R. Ryan (Eds.), *Handbook of Research on Sub-National Governance and Development* (pp. 368–384). Hershey, PA: IGI Global. doi:10.4018/978-1-5225-1645-3.ch017

Tavares, M. D., & Rodrigues, L. L. (2018). Strategic Responses of Public Sector Entities to GRI Sustainability Reports. In G. Azevedo, J. da Silva Oliveira, R. Marques, & A. Ferreira (Eds.), *Handbook of Research on Modernization and Accountability in Public Sector Management* (pp. 159–188). Hershey, PA: IGI Global. doi:10.4018/978-1-5225-3731-1.ch008

Thakre, A. G. (2017). Sexual Harassment of Women in Workplace in India: An Assessment of Implementation of Preventive Laws and Practicing of Therapeutic Jurisprudence in New Delhi. In D. Halder & K. Jaishankar (Eds.), *Therapeutic Jurisprudence and Overcoming Violence Against Women* (pp. 135–146). Hershey, PA: IGI Global. doi:10.4018/978-1-5225-2472-4.ch009

Tiwary, A. (2017). Key Elements of CEAF. In *Driving Efficiency in Local Government Using a Collaborative Enterprise Architecture Framework: Emerging Research and Opportunities* (pp. 25–61). Hershey, PA: IGI Global. doi:10.4018/978-1-5225-2407-6.ch002

Toscano, J. P. (2017). Social Media and Public Participation: Opportunities, Barriers, and a New Framework. In M. Adria & Y. Mao (Eds.), *Handbook of Research on Citizen Engagement and Public Participation in the Era of New Media* (pp. 73–89). Hershey, PA: IGI Global. doi:10.4018/978-1-5225-1081-9.ch005

Tosun, M. S., Uz, D., & Yılmaz, S. (2016). Fiscal Decentralization and Local Borrowing in Turkish Provinces. In M. Erdoğdu & B. Christiansen (Eds.), *Handbook of Research on Public Finance in Europe and the MENA Region* (pp. 505–519). Hershey, PA: IGI Global. doi:10.4018/978-1-5225-0053-7.ch022

Treiber, M. (2016). Informality and Informalization among Eritrean Refugees: Why Migration Does Not Provide a Lesson in Democracy. In F. Cante & H. Quehl (Eds.), *Handbook of Research on Transitional Justice and Peace Building in Turbulent Regions* (pp. 158–180). Hershey, PA: IGI Global. doi:10.4018/978-1-4666-9675-4. ch008

Tshishonga, N. (2017). Operation Sukuma-Sakhe: A New Social Contract for Decentralized Service Delivery and Responsive Governance in KwaZulu-Natal. In E. Schoburgh & R. Ryan (Eds.), *Handbook of Research on Sub-National Governance and Development* (pp. 304–323). Hershey, PA: IGI Global. doi:10.4018/978-1-5225-1645-3.ch014

Tsygankov, S., & Gasanova, E. (2017). Electronification of the Public Procurement System: A Comparative Analysis of the Experience of the Russian Federation and Ukraine. In R. Shakya (Ed.), *Digital Governance and E-Government Principles Applied to Public Procurement* (pp. 267–277). Hershey, PA: IGI Global. doi:10.4018/978-1-5225-2203-4.ch013

Tüzünkan, D. (2018). The International Migration Movements and Immigrant Policies From the Ottoman Empire 1299 to Republican Turkey 2016. In Ş. Erçetin (Ed.), *Social Considerations of Migration Movements and Immigration Policies* (pp. 13–45). Hershey, PA: IGI Global. doi:10.4018/978-1-5225-3322-1.ch002

Uchenna, E., & Iyoha, F. (2016). IFRS, Foreign Investment, and Prevailing Institutional Structure in Africa. In E. Uchenna, M. Nnadi, S. Tanna, & F. Iyoha (Eds.), *Economics and Political Implications of International Financial Reporting Standards* (pp. 83–104). Hershey, PA: IGI Global. doi:10.4018/978-1-4666-9876-5.ch005

Ugangu, W. (2016). Kenya's Difficult Political Transitions Ethnicity and the Role of Media. In L. Mukhongo & J. Macharia (Eds.), *Political Influence of the Media in Developing Countries* (pp. 12–24). Hershey, PA: IGI Global. doi:10.4018/978-1-4666-9613-6.ch002

Vaillancourt, F., & Bird, R. M. (2016). Decentralization in European and MENA Countries: Glue or Solvent? In M. Erdoğdu & B. Christiansen (Eds.), *Comparative Political and Economic Perspectives on the MENA Region* (pp. 1–27). Hershey, PA: IGI Global. doi:10.4018/978-1-4666-9601-3.ch001

Vakkala, H., & Leinonen, J. (2016). Current Features and Developments of Local Governance in Finland: The Changing Roles of Citizens and Municipalities. In U. Sadioglu & K. Dede (Eds.), *Theoretical Foundations and Discussions on the Reformation Process in Local Governments* (pp. 304–327). Hershey, PA: IGI Global. doi:10.4018/978-1-5225-0317-0.ch013

Valenzuela, R., & Ochoa, A. (2018). Open Mexico Network in the Implementation of National Open Data Policy. In A. Kok (Ed.), *Proliferation of Open Government Initiatives and Systems* (pp. 50–67). Hershey, PA: IGI Global. doi:10.4018/978-1-5225-4987-1.ch003

Vaquero, M. G., & Saiz-Alvarez, J. M. (2016). Smart Cities in Spain – Policy, Sustainability, and the National Plan: New Political Measures, Agents, and Sustainability. In A. Goswami & A. Mishra (Eds.), *Economic Modeling, Analysis, and Policy for Sustainability* (pp. 266–283). Hershey, PA: IGI Global. doi:10.4018/978-1-5225-0094-0.ch014

Waller, P. (2017). Co-Production and Co-Creation in Public Services: Resolving Confusion and Contradictions. *International Journal of Electronic Government Research*, *13*(2), 1–17. doi:10.4018/IJEGR.2017040101

Washington, A. L. (2016). The Interoperability of US Federal Government Information: Interoperability. In A. Aggarwal (Ed.), *Managing Big Data Integration in the Public Sector* (pp. 1–19). Hershey, PA: IGI Global. doi:10.4018/978-1-4666-9649-5.ch001

Whyte, D. (2016). The Neo-Colonial State of Exception in Occupied Iraq. In F. Cante & H. Quehl (Eds.), *Handbook of Research on Transitional Justice and Peace Building in Turbulent Regions* (pp. 298–313). Hershey, PA: IGI Global. doi:10.4018/978-1-4666-9675-4.ch015

Williams, K. Y. (2016). The Need for a National Data Breach Notification Law. In E. de Silva (Ed.), *National Security and Counterintelligence in the Era of Cyber Espionage* (pp. 190–202). Hershey, PA: IGI Global. doi:10.4018/978-1-4666-9661-7.ch011

Wodecka-Hyjek, A. (2017). Co-Operation between the Public Administration and Non-Profit Organisations as a Condition of the Development of Public Entrepreneurship: On the Example of the Selected World Solutions. In V. Potocan, M. Üngan, & Z. Nedelko (Eds.), *Handbook of Research on Managerial Solutions in Non-Profit Organizations* (pp. 253–275). Hershey, PA: IGI Global. doi:10.4018/978-1-5225-0731-4.ch012

Yang, J. G. (2016). The Principle of Nexus in E-Commerce Tax. In I. Lee (Ed.), *Encyclopedia of E-Commerce Development, Implementation, and Management* (pp. 329–341). Hershey, PA: IGI Global. doi:10.4018/978-1-4666-9787-4.ch025

Yang, J. G. (2016). What Is New York's Amazon Tax on Internet Commerce? In I. Lee (Ed.), *Encyclopedia of E-Commerce Development, Implementation, and Management* (pp. 397–409). Hershey, PA: IGI Global. doi:10.4018/978-1-4666-9787-4.ch029

Yang, J. G., Lohrey, P. L., & Lauricella, L. J. (2016). Current Developing Trend of Sales Tax on E-Business. In I. Lee (Ed.), *Encyclopedia of E-Commerce Development, Implementation, and Management* (pp. 1045–1057). Hershey, PA: IGI Global. doi:10.4018/978-1-4666-9787-4.ch074

Yang, K. C., & Kang, Y. (2017). Social Media, Political Mobilization, and Citizen Engagement: A Case Study of the March 18, 2014, Sunflower Student Movement in Taiwan. In M. Adria & Y. Mao (Eds.), *Handbook of Research on Citizen Engagement and Public Participation in the Era of New Media* (pp. 360–388). Hershey, PA: IGI Global. doi:10.4018/978-1-5225-1081-9.ch020

Yeo, S., Birch, A. S., & Bengtsson, H. I. (2016). The Role of State Actors in Cybersecurity: Can State Actors Find Their Role in Cyberspace? In E. de Silva (Ed.), *National Security and Counterintelligence in the Era of Cyber Espionage* (pp. 217–246). Hershey, PA: IGI Global. doi:10.4018/978-1-4666-9661-7.ch013

Zhao, B. (2018). A Privacy Perspective of Open Government: Sex, Wealth, and Transparency in China. In A. Kok (Ed.), *Proliferation of Open Government Initiatives and Systems* (pp. 29–48). Hershey, PA: IGI Global. doi:10.4018/978-1-5225-4987-1.ch002

Zhi-Wei, T., Fei, D., & Ping, J. (2016). An Empirical Study on Temporal Evolution Rule of Network Clustering Behavior. *International Journal of Information Systems for Crisis Response and Management*, 8(4), 56–70. doi:10.4018/IJISCRAM.2016100104

About the Contributors

Ryma Abassi received her engineering degree in Networks & Telecommunications in 2004, and her MSc and PhD degrees from the Higher Communication School, Sup'Com in 2006 and 2010, respectively. Currently, she is an Assistant Professor and the Associate Director at ISET'Com and member of the "Digital Security" unit at SUP'Com. Dr Ryma Abassi was a Fulbright scholar at Tufts University, MA, USA where she worked on formal methods for security protocols validation. Moreover, she obtained the SSHN grant two times in 2014 and 2017 and is a visiting professor at University of Limoges. Her current researches are focusing on MANET/VANET security, trust management, security protocols validation, IoT security etc. She has more than 30 publications in impacted journals and classified conferences and is co-supervising four PhD students.

* * *

Saleh Al-Sharieh (LLB; MA in Law; LLM in Law & Technology; LLD) is a Senior Researcher at the European Technology Law and Human Rights Division of the Department of European and Economic Law at the University of Groningen Faculty of Law. He is a member of STeP, the 'Security, Technology and e-Privacy Research Group.' His research focuses on technology law, intellectual property law, and human rights law. Prior to joining STeP, he taught law at the University of Ottawa and Carleton University in Ottawa, Canada.

Opeyemi Aluko is a proficient scholar in the field of Political Science. His areas of research are Judicial Studies, Security Studies, Comparative politics and Research Methodology. He is currently a doctoral candidate in the Political Science Department Kwara State University Malete Kwara State Nigeria.

Benjamin Enahoro Assay teaches mass communication at Delta State Polytechnic, Ogwashi-Uku, Nigeria. He holds BA and MA degrees in mass communication from Delta State University, Abraka and University of Nigeria, Nsukka respectively. Assay is on the verge of being awarded a doctorate degree in mass communication by the Benue State University, Makurdi, Nigeria. He has published articles in scholarly journals and contributed chapters in several books locally and internationally. His research interests cover areas such as information and communication technology and national development; international communication and comparative media studies, media, democracy and good governance, population and health communication, and public relations and advertising. He is a member of several professional bodies, including African Council for Communication Education (ACCE) Nigeria chapter, Advertising Practitioners Council of Nigeria (APCON), Association of Communication Scholars and Professionals of Nigeria (ACSPN), Nigeria Institute of Public Relations (NIPR), Association for Promoting Nigerian Languages and Culture (APNILAC), National Association for Research Development (NARD), among others.

Nisha Dewani is a research Scholar in Jamia Millia Islamia University (India). Her Graduation and Post Graduation in law is also from Jamia University. She has worked on many themes on IPR like Major Issues involved in IPR and Competition Law, Traditional Knowledge and IPR with IGI Global Publication. Her research areas are IPR, International Trade Law, International Commercial Law and Information Technology.

Simon Foley is a Research Director at IMT Atlantique where he leads the research in the IMT Chair of cyber security for critical infrastructures. His primary research interests are security modelling, trust, threat management, secure cyber-physical systems and user-experience. Prior to joining IMT, he was a member of the Computer Science faculty at University College Cork. He serves on the editorial board of the Journal of Computer Security, and past PC chair of the European Symposium on Research in Computer Security, Computer Security Foundations and New Security Paradigms workshops.

Balkis Hamdane has obtained a PhD degree in ICT from the Higher School of Communication of Tunis (Sup'Com) in November 2016. She obtained a master and an engineer diploma in Telecommunications from Sup'Com in 2009, and 2010 respectively. In September 2010, Dr Hamdane joined the Higher Institute of Computer Science of El Manar (ISI) to teach several courses in the field of networking. Since October 2014, she is an assistant in the National Engineering School of Tunis

(ENIT). Dr Hamdane's actual research interests include network security, information centric networking, trust management, etc. She has published several papers in international conferences.

Thokozani Ian Nzimakwe teaches in the Faculty of Law & Management at the University of KwaZulu Natal (SA). His research focuses on public governance, service quality and local government and public policy.He has published in journals and books. He does both post grad and undergraduate teaching at UKZN.

Muhammad Imran Khan is a PhD student at Insight Centre for Data Analytics, University College Cork, Ireland. Before joining Insight Centre, He completed his Masters Degree in Computer Science from University of Kaiserslautern, Germany. He holds another Masters degree in Electrical and Electronic Engineering. His Bachelor degree is in Computer Engineering. He has several scientific publications.

Sabrina Ching Yuen Luk is Assistant Professor in Public Policy and Global Affairs, Nanyang Technological University, Singapore. She was awarded her PhD from the Department of Political Science and International Studies, University of Birmingham, the United Kingdom, and her MPhil and Bachelor of Social Science (First Class Honours) from the Department of Government and Public Administration, the Chinese University of Hong Kong. Her publications include Health Insurance Reforms in Asia (2014, Abingdon, Oxon; New York, NY: Routledge), The Logic of Chinese Politics: Cores, Peripheries and Peaceful Rising (with Peter Preston) (2016, UK: Edward Elgar Publishing Ltd) and Financing Health Care in China: Towards Universal Health Insurance. (2017, Abingdon, Oxon; New York, NY: Routledge).

Ines Mezghani is an Assistant Professor of Management in Higher Institute of Technological Studies in Communications, Technopark, El Ghazala, Tunis, Tunisia. Head department of ICT Management.

Vannie Naidoo is a full-time staff member at the University of KwaZulu-Natal, South Africa, in the Faculty of Management and Law. Her field of teaching is in management, corporate strategy, project management and entrepreneurship. The research areas pursued by Dr Naidoo are in the areas of management, marketing, service marketing, entrepreneurship and social media and e-learning or learning with new technologies. She has presented papers at international conferences throughout the world and has written on various issues in management and marketing in journal articles and books.

Barry O'Sullivan holds the Chair of Constraint Programming at the Department of Computer Science at University College Cork, Ireland. He is the founding director of the Insight Centre for Data Analytics at UCC which, nationally, involves more than 420 researchers and staff. He is a past president of the Association for Constraint Programming and currently serves as deputy president of the European Artificial Intelligence Association. His research interests include artificial intelligence, constraint programming, operations research, and ethics. He received his PhD in computer science from University College Cork and his undergraduate degree from the University of Limerick. He is a Member of the Royal Irish Academy.

Ayda Saidane is Senior information security advisor at the information security governance unit of Revenu Quebec. She has an extensive academic research experience covering a wide range of aspects in dependability and security engineering.

Index

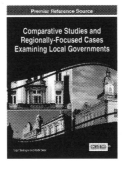
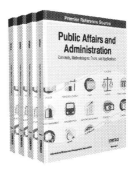

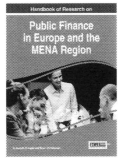

Stay Current on the Latest Emerging Research Developments

Become an IGI Global Reviewer for Authored Book Projects

The overall success of an authored book project is dependent on quality and timely reviews.

In this competitive age of scholarly publishing, constructive and timely feedback significantly decreases the turnaround time of manuscripts from submission to acceptance, allowing the publication and discovery of progressive research at a much more expeditious rate. Several IGI Global authored book projects are currently seeking highly qualified experts in the field to fill vacancies on their respective editorial review boards:

Applications may be sent to:
development@igi-global.com

Applicants must have a doctorate (or an equivalent degree) as well as publishing and reviewing experience. Reviewers are asked to write reviews in a timely, collegial, and constructive manner. All reviewers will begin their role on an ad-hoc basis for a period of one year, and upon successful completion of this term can be considered for full editorial review board status, with the potential for a subsequent promotion to Associate Editor.

If you have a colleague that may be interested in this opportunity, we encourage you to share this information with them.

InfoSci®-OnDemand

Comprehensive Service

- Over 81,600+ journal articles, book chapters, and case studies.
- All content is downloadable in PDF format and can be stored locally for future use.

No Subscription Fees

- One time fee of $37.50 per PDF download.

Instant Access

- Receive a download link immediately after order completion!

Database Platform Features:

- Comprehensive Pay-Per-View Service
- Written by Prominent International Experts/Scholars
- Precise Search and Retrieval
- Updated With New Material on a Weekly Basis
- Immediate Access to Full-Text PDFs
- No Subscription Needed
- Purchased Research Can Be Stored Locally for Future Use